THE SMALL BUSINESS COMPUTER GUIDE

THE SMALL BUSINESS COMPUTER GUIDE

by

Joseph S. Beckman

Digital Press
Boston • Oxford • Melbourne • Singapore • Toronto • Munich • New Delhi • Tokyo

Digital Press™ is an imprint of Butterworth–Heinemann.

Library of Congress Cataloging-in-Publication Data

Beckman, Joseph S.
The small business computer guide / by Joseph S. Beckman
p. cm.
Includes index.
ISBN 1-55558-136-6
1. Small business—Data processing. 2. Microcomputers—Purchasing.
3. Small business—Automation. I. Title.
HF5548.2.B3613 1995
004—dc20 94-46815
CIP

British Library Cataloguing-in-Publication Data
A catalogue record for this book is available from the British Library.

The publisher offers discounts on bulk orders of this book.
For information, please write:

Manager of Special Sales, Digital Press
Butterworth–Heinemann
313 Washington Street
Newton, MA 02158–1626

Order number: EY–S795E–DP

10 9 8 7 6 5 4 3 2 1

Printed in the United States of America

To my wife, Karen, and my daughters, Alyssa and Michelle, for all their love and support. . .

and in memory of my brother, Michael Paul Beckman, whose charm, wit and love live on in all that knew him

TABLE OF CONTENTS

SECTION I

SECTION II

SECTION III

SECTION IV

SECTION V

SECTION VI

SECTION VII

SECTION VIII

SECTION I

Chapter 1

Energizing Your Business

Every business must be productive to be profitable. How profitable depends upon its efficiency. To visualize this let's imagine two businesses marketing the same product. In an ideal market, each could get the same price; no more and no less. The business that creates and markets the product most efficiently, however, will make the greater profit.

So it is with any business. Take the following example from the practice of law.

Two firms are involved in a bankruptcy action involving a large chain of stores. Each firm has to file a pleading and forward copies of that pleading to each creditor. To do this, as they do each time they take a bankruptcy case, the first firm sets aside a paralegal and an afternoon to type the names and addresses into its computer. From that list the firm can prepare mailing labels or envelopes for mailing. Not a bad process overall. Each time the firm has to send out another pleading, no time is wasted preparing the list again. The firm sends out a bill for the pleading.

The second firm however, is unable to spare a paralegal for an afternoon each time it takes on such a case. Perhaps the firm does not have the additional support staff or just cannot profit from employing additional staff for instances such as this. But the second firm has a solution. With the use of a scanner or even the ubiquitous fax machine, the paralegal can scan the list into the computer. With a few keystrokes, the paralegal has a database to prepare labels or envelopes. It takes perhaps thirty minutes. The client is happy and the paralegal can work on other, more productive matters. The second firm sends out the same bill.

Which business would you rather be?

Although the above example may be simplistic, it does illustrate the principles of efficiency and productivity as the precursors to a profitable business. Perhaps two hours were saved by scanning the information into the computer. Not much...but multiply that figure by fifty cases a year and you have saved one hundred hours. Two and one-half weeks of full time help. Assuming the scanner costs your business approximately $1,500.00, you will quickly recoup your capital investment in the scanner and you would certainly capitalize or amortize its cost, thereby further reducing your investment and increasing your productivity and profitability.

Now apply these principles to each person in the office. With the efficient use of computers, you can:

- review entire client files without interruption;
- review current billings and accounts receivables for clients;
- review forms on file in the business database;
- update and catalogue research materials for cross-reference and access
- review and revise the work product of associates, supervised help or subordinates;
- transmit draft copies of contracts and proposals that are likely to transverse numerous draft and proposal stages before completion.

With a greater investment of money (and a little time), you can also:

- conduct research and access information bases;
- access financial information relating to potential or current clients or adversaries;
- access court records; and
- access state governmental records;

Why would you want to access files or all the above information through a computer rather than relying on tried and true methods. Let's say you are involved in a service-related business. You can be an accountant, architect, financial adviser or even an attorney. You have interviewed a prospective client needing your services. You have set aside the time to speak with the client and are necessarily taking notes. Names, dates, times, places, and writings are all information needed to properly assess the situation. You have noted this information and have discussed the appropriate fee arrangement with the client. If your business operates anything like my own, you have a client information sheet which is placed in your central database and likewise placed with accounting and administration. Of course, you will have your secretary stop whatever she is doing to decipher your notes and transfer the appropriate information to these forms, take the forms to the copy room, await her turn to use the copier and then run copies to administration where they must stop what they are doing, at some time, to properly file the information. Meanwhile, your secretary has opened a physical client file and placed the sheets in there as well.

Even if it took 10 minutes, it was 10 minutes too long. You already had to take the information and so it should have been placed in the computer. While interviewing the client, this information should be placed in a client database from which it can be accessed, for any purpose, at any time. Once it is placed there, administration has their copy and you have yours. For that matter, every person in your firm has a copy available, assuming you want the information freely accessible. The information is immediately available for cross-reference purposes or just to review an associate's progress. While you have gone on to more interesting matters in the interview, the computer can be cross-checking the client for conflicts of interest.

Carried to its logical extreme, the few minutes saved here and there in the normal day will contribute greatly to the firm's overall productivity. But don't take my word for it. Consult almost any guide to better business productivity. Most productivity gurus will suggest methods and pointers which, at best, will better focus your efforts on one area of business over another. Other suggestions will save perhaps a few minutes here or a few minutes there.

One of the most often suggested tips for greater productivity is to set aside a block of time to concentrate on a list of work to be accomplished. These gurus will vary on the amount of time but most suggest anywhere from one half hour to as much as three or four hours. By setting aside this time, apart from interrupting phone calls, secretaries or associates, your productivity, they say, will improve dramatically. Your ability to concentrate on the task at hand will be measurably improved and the results will speak profits for your business.

Applying this methodology to any business makes sense. I know this is the case in the practice of law. Trial attorneys must formulate trial strategies not unlike playing chess. Most any attorney drafting a contract, estate plan or legal memorandum needs to concentrate on the details of his work to exact a concise and authoritative treatise in his respective field. Attempting to formulate, organize and draft extensive or in-depth trial memorandums or reports requires absolute quiet and a substantial block of time in which to concentrate: not only on the current details but on what remains to be accomplished. Without this uninterrupted time, what is drafted ten or twenty pages ago, and why it was important may be lost after answering two or three calls, accessing the files to respond to those calls and answering your secretary's questions regarding the file she may be working on.

It is exactly for this reason that the proper use of the computer in your business can increase your productivity. All those little interruptions, necessary interruptions to be sure, are curtailed or eliminated entirely. Think about it. How many little, insignificant blocks of time do you lose each day. Perhaps you received a telephone call from a client or customer wanting an update. Rather than accessing the answer on the computer, you must take time to call in, locate or otherwise "pin down" your co-worker or assistant on the matter to discuss the results of the work that may be delegated to others. Or maybe you have to interrupt both yourself and your secretary to locate and pull the file to discuss recent developments. Sometimes the file isn't easily found or perhaps the documents were not labeled or tabbed for easy retrieval. No one likes to wait on hold while you track down the information. Whether they understand and are patient about it may depend on whether you are billing them for the time to retrieve the information. In either event, it comes out of someone's pocket. If it ends up coming out of yours, you can see where the time saved during the day pays for itself over a period of weeks or months.

Other mundane interruptions will eat up little but significant chunks of your time and money. At my old firm, I was taught the advantages of keeping research folders containing caselaw for issues concerning current files. In addition, to the caselaw, these folders would sometimes contain motions, pleadings or memoranda covering numerous issues. When another case was opened for which previous research or a prior pleading would prove helpful, the litigation partner would send me or his secretary in search of the appropriate file. Sometimes all he would remember would be the old case name. Sometimes the pleading or research would be under an obscure heading which made sense at the time but eluded our best efforts nonetheless. When the file was finally located, no one could remember when it was last updated or cite-checked. And, finally, even though other attorneys in the firm would litigate and could possibly have benefited from these files, they were "safely" tucked away in his office and at his secretary's station: an increasingly crowded station.

Now let's assume he wanted to increase productivity. Let's assume that he didn't want me or his secretary searching for ten or fifteen minutes for the particular pleading or case he would find helpful. Let's also assume he wanted to incorporate the pleading with minimal changes into a current document and that he wanted it to reflect new caselaw not contained in the original. If the pleading or memorandum were contained on the computer, filed and tagged with the assistant of a PIM (Personal Information Manager), it could be found, sitting at his desk by searching the disk by keyword or phrase. If he were looking for information on the state venue law, he could find it in that memorandum dealing with venue and fraud, even though the memo was filed under fraud as the principal issue. By reviewing the file's date code, he could know the last time the file was updated and, with the assistance of on-line research services, he could cite check the document and incorporate updated caselaw directly into the file. Finally, the real estate attorney in the office that very rarely litigates but finds himself with an old client needing such services, has access to that same file, searching by keyword, and finding the file, even though he never knew it was there. He didn't waste time "cornering" the litigation partner or an associate to dig up the information because it was available and there was a methodology in place to access the information.

Certainly, increased productivity does not rely solely upon the equipment you purchase. In addition to wisely investing in equipment, you and your co-workers must be capable of utilizing the equipment to its fullest potential. This one fact is lost on many small businesses. By way of example...most office still rely upon trial and error methods of scheduling appointments between co-workers. Assuming one person is the coordinating project manager, that person should use scheduling software to access the schedules of the project team, overlay those schedules to pinpoint mutually available time, and schedule a project meeting accordingly. The co-workers should account for their time during office hours on that schedule and the scheduling software should notify those co-workers that their schedule has been updated. The equipment may be available but the team must use the equipment properly to realize its benefits. In chapter 22, I offer a few tips for using equipment to a fuller potential than that realized in the average business.

Now let's review the array of computer equipment available.

SECTION II

Chapter 2

Making Practical Choices

Every business owner realizes that a vast array of computer equipment is available in today's market. As this is written, standards are and will continue to change, prices will likely drop for the same equipment over time and manufacturers will update their product lines. Because of the quick rate of change in the computer market, any discussions regarding particular manufacturers or models are for your reference only. I will try to emphasize trends in the business and educate you to shop for equipment that meets your needs...now and in the future.

There are three thing you must know before you shop for equipment:

1. Your budget:
2. Your working needs: and
3. Your adaptability to new working environments.

The problem may be your budget...

I mention budget first and foremost because, if your budget is extremely tight, it would do little good for me to suggest an investment of $5,000.00 if you can spend only $2,500.00. Still, keep your budget flexible because you may find that money can be better spared in other budgeted concerns than your initial capital investment in computer equipment. If your business requires the utmost graphics and presentation capability, then you should properly invest in a computer that can process the information and run the sophisticated software packages available for desktop publishing today. You should further invest in larger, more capable monitors than the average business user and perhaps, a color printer. While a 14" color monitor can be purchased for $250-$300 today and may meet the minimum needs of another business, desktop publishing and marketing businesses are better served with the crop of 17"-20" monitors available today for $900-$2500.00. If your business demands publishing precision, then you may not be able to apply a $2500.00 budget to essential business tools requiring a minimum investment of $5000.00.

...the solution is to pick your equipment wisely.

In the above instance, I would recommend investing in the larger monitor, an item not likely to see such huge technological gains as the computer and printer components (and so less likely to be obsolete during its useful life) and to subcontract for the color printing that may be necessary to your business. While color printer technology is still maturing, product lines are changing and prices continue to drop. When your better able to invest in the color printer, you will purchase a better printer at a lower cost than today's products. In that time, your larger monitor will not be supplemented by considerably superior products and, in the meantime, the larger face of the monitor will allow you to work more productively and produce a better product for your business. Although you may be tempted to invest your money in a snazzy color printer, the above example provides a budget tradeoff better suited to improving your business productivity. This raises the second element listed above.

What is software?

Your working needs are your primary concern. Unless computers are your hobby, your investment is to further your business needs, not your personal needs. To meet your business needs the computer must be capable of manipulating data to produce your intended product. Computers use software to process data and produce output that is useful to their human operators. Software packages are commonly referred to as applications because the package allows the use to apply data in a particular manner to produce a particular product. Examples of commonly used software products include word processing software, accounting and spreadsheet software, time and billing software, graphics and presentation software and communication software. Each of these products allows the user to format, output or communicate information in a different manner. Other software applications allow the user to better manage the computer, its physical components, the software applications and data. These applications are commonly known as system applications or utilities. At a later point we will discuss these applications and utilities in more detail but, for now, it is imperative that you understand your business needs will be met by the software applications and utilities. In other words, first determine what software you will need to operate your business and then you may intelligently purchase the computer hardware necessary to operate that software.

What else will you need? How about a mouse and modem?

You must also consider the additional equipment you may need in your business in addition to the computer, monitor and printer. At a minimum, most businesses will require the ability to use a mouse for graphical environments (see Chapter 4) and a modem or fax/modem for communications (This is a *strong* recommendation. For the reasons why, see Section V). In addition to these virtual necessities, I would also recommend a tape backup system to protect your investment in time (see Chapter 14). As the technology matures, I will probably recommend you later consider the ability to add sound capability to your computer. While many now consider sound an entertainment luxury, current developments in voice recognition will enable future computer systems to accept voice input rather than keyboard input or mouse input. While I will recommend this at a later time, I must also caution you that the processing and storage requirements that enable computers to now accept voice input are tremendous and, as the capability grows, these demands will become greater. Therefore, this recommendation is tempered by your system's ability to utilize this technology. For now, its relegated solely to upper end systems. Nevertheless, even those upper end systems will find their way to the bottom of the price ladder at some point *and then....*

What about portable computers?

At some point you will consider the plethora of portable computers available today. Again, consider your true needs now and in the future. Portables (also called laptops, notebooks or sub-notebooks) have their advantages. They also have their disadvantages. Some of their advantages include enabling you to work outside the office, work while traveling, work at home, provide greater data security through the use of removable hard disks, and allocate computer use to part-time computer users more efficiently. Some lesser heralded advantages include automatic battery backup capability and the ability to be placed in sleep mode without the necessity of re-starting the machine to resume work.

This is a greater capability than you may imagine in terms of work productivity and efficiency. I use a portable at my office desk. If I am working within a program when another matter requires my attention, sleep mode enables me to stop work while keeping my place. When I am ready to resume work, I am back in place within seconds. As any writer or analyst will tell you, creativity and thought do not wait a minute for your computer to start up. If it takes longer than 5 seconds to resume work, you are losing potential productivity and creativity. This advantage is discussed in more detail in Chapter 15.

Some of their disadvantages include allowing you to work at home, providing greater risk of theft, providing greater risk of damage, and providing less storage and expansion capabilities than desktop systems while costing more for the same features found on desktop systems. Again, consider your true needs now and in the future. If you do travel extensively, if you do work extensively outside the office, including at home, if your work entails using or accessing large amounts of data or providing services to clients at their place of business, the portables advantages probably outweigh its disadvantages. If you almost always will do your work at a single location, you require massive storage capabilities or use specialized computer equipment on a regular basis, then the portability is not a virtue you need to pay for at this time. If you require extensive expansion capabilities and have a limited budget, then a truly capable portable may be beyond your capabilities. Consider how you will work with the computer before deciding on a desktop system versus a portable. Portables are discussed in greater detail in Chapter 15.

The third element in our triad of purchase considerations is your adaptability to new working environments. Earlier, I said that increased productivity through the efficient use of computers required that people be willing to learn and make the best use of what they have. I implied that, even if you are not intending to invest in new equipment, you can increase your productivity. This increase can only arise through your willingness to adapt to a new working environment.

What is an operating system and what about Windows and OS/2?

New operating systems and operating environments now provide greater capabilities for increased productivity. When I speak of working environments or operating systems, I am speaking of the software that interprets commands from your software applications and communicates those commands to the computer hardware. MS-DOS is an operating system. So are Microsoft Windows and IBM's OS/2. These last two are graphical operating systems while the various permutations of DOS are character-based operating systems. Even before picking up this book, I'm fairly certain you must have heard of DOS, Microsoft Windows, Windows NT or OS/2.

Windows and OS/2 seem to bring out the religious fervor of computerphiles and each system has its supporters and detractors. In all fairness, each has its strengths and weaknesses.

To disclose any prejudice you may feel I have, let me just say that I use Microsoft Windows, almost exclusively, and I will continue to do so. Let me also tell you it isn't perfect or close to it. I rely on a number of third-party utilities to make my Windows environment as productive as possible and, as history bears out, even when Microsoft improves Windows (or MS-DOS) with subsequent releases, other vendors will manage to provide improvements worth having (for a discussion of utilities, see Chapter 14).

Windows is now marketed as both a personal computer operating system, a small network operating system and as a large network operating system suitable for large corporate and government needs. The first two marketing niches are met by Windows 3.1 and Windows for Workgroups (a network add-on for Windows 3.1) or version 3.1's successor, Windows 4.0 (called "Chicago" during its development). The third niche, large corporate and government networking needs, is met by Windows NT. These are definitely two different animals...Microsoft sees it that way and you should too.

Windows 3.1 is a decent yet flawed multi-tasking environment.

Windows 3.1 (4.0) is an operating system designed for single processor 386, 486 and Pentium computers or small network systems. It should meet the needs of 95% or more of the people that read this book. While Windows 3.1 is a 16 bit operating system which takes some advantage of the capabilities built into the 386 and 486 processor chips, it still relies upon the increasingly antiquated DOS operating system to access and manage critical computer components including the memory and hard disk drive. If you have Windows 3.1 on your system, you also have MS-DOS (or its equivalent) on your system. Without getting too technical, its reliance on DOS is a major contributing factor for reports of system lockups and crashes in Windows. These lockups and crashes are caused by memory conflicts when a Windows program requests memory that is already taken by another program. In theory, the operating system should be able to intercept these improper requests but, since Windows 3.1 relies upon an installed copy of DOS to manage memory, it doesn't intercept the requests and the system "crashes". Windows applications that are developed with these problems in mind should, and usually do, avoid improper requests and the use of mainstream Windows applications results in a very stable working environment. Windows 3.1 is also hampered by DOS's file allocation and storage standards. Its these old standards which require filenames to be no more than 11 characters in length. Finally, Windows 3.1 has its own limitations. Windows reserves memory solely for the purpose of storing information regarding applications in use during the Windows session. As applications are opened and closed, this memory is eventually exhausted. Unlike the computer's RAM memory, which is emptied each time an application is closed, this special memory, called "system resources" is not emptied. Eventually, this special memory is reduced to the point that Windows cannot store more information and it "gives up". The result is an unstable environment. The computer must be restarted. Windows 3.1 also uses a form of multi-tasking called cooperative multi-tasking. When two or more applications must share the processing power of the computer in Windows 3.1, the applications and not the operating system (3.1) decide when to switch processor control from one to the other application. This is their "cooperation". If one application is not well designed (some call it "misbehaved") however, it can refuse to "cooperate" and let the other application use the processor. The result is an unstable or unusable system. It must be restarted.

Taking all these drawbacks into consideration, Windows 3.1 still manages to operate, in most instances, as it was designed to operate. It provides a working environment where all applications (ideally) operate and function in a similar manner. Applications can exchange information across formats and multiple applications can share processing power to cooperatively multitask. In theory, Windows 3.1 allows the user to perform spreadsheet recalculations in their spreadsheet application while simultaneously drafting a letter in their word processing application. I regularly use it to download or upload files through my modem application, all in the background, while still working in my word processing application. In practice, multi-tasking results depend upon the memory, processing power and behavior of the applications being used. Finally, Windows 3.1 provides common display and printing controls for all applications with support for new display standards and printers at the hardware level instead of by software manufacturers. The result is greater consistency and cooperation between software applications (tools) to help you accomplish your computer goals.

Windows 4.0 is a true 32 bit multi-tasking environment for your 486 or Pentium computer and network.

Windows 4.0 is an evolutionary step in personal computer operating systems. It improves upon Windows 3.1 by eliminating the constraints of the underlying DOS system and incorporating all the memory and hardware management functions in a 32 bit Windows operating system. As a result, the 32 bit capabilities of 486 computers may now actually be utilized to speed up system responsiveness through reduced file and memory access times. Data can now be managed by the system software as quickly as the system hardware is providing it. Gone are memory conflicts caused by improper memory access, gone is the 11 character file allocation and storage system and gone is the control Windows 3.1 previously ceded to other Windows applications. Windows 4.0 is a true operating system in control of its environment. It uses preemptive multitasking which places control over the processor in the hands of the operating system and not the applications. As a result, the operating system can remove processor control from what would otherwise be a "misbehaved" application to supply processing power to other applications on the system. Control is with the parent and not the child. The end result is a more responsive system (speed), better cooperation and integration between software applications (multi-tasking and information exchange) and easier access and productivity (longer filenames and direct object/file manipulation).

Windows 4.0 has built-in networking and better application/file manipulation.

Owing to the wide increase in network use even among very small businesses, Windows 4.0 also integrates Microsoft's Workgroup capabilities into the system rather than marketing the separate product and further improves its desktop (screen) to integrate file and application management and improve access. This redesign of the desktop screen is another instance of Microsoft taking the best features of other vendor's products and incorporating them into Microsoft's new product. Having relied upon many of the features found in Windows 4.0 by using Norton Desktop for Windows as part of my Windows 3.1 screen, I can attest that these are true productivity enhancements.

Windows 4.0 also provides some very important productivity improvements above and beyond its improved file and memory management and desktop design. Windows 4.0 integrates Plug and Play support for easy accessory configuration (see chapter 3), support for OLE 2 (seamless exchange of multiple application objects within a single document) and device-independent color matching capability (for matching screen colors to your color printer output).

You'll have to upgrade your existing 16 bit Windows 3.1 software to get the true benefits of Windows 4.0.

Now for the bad news. Most of the improvements that make Windows 4.0 a superior operating system to Windows 3.1 require 32 bit software applications. Windows 3.1 software applications are 16 bit applications and, while they will work as well in Windows 4.0 as they did in Windows 3.1, they will not benefit from the foundational improvements to Windows which improve file access, memory access or multi-tasking operations. The end result is that most of the improvements in file and memory access will not be enjoyed until you have either purchased new software or upgraded your existing software. While this shouldn't dissuade you from Windows 4.0 (particularly if you are presently using Windows 3.1) being aware of these temporary performance limitations will ensure that you don't make an investment based on misconceptions regarding the product.

Windows NT is overkill for small system networks but great for cross-platform integration.

Windows NT is Microsoft's powerhouse. It's an enormous operating system more at home on a network file server than on a LAN or single user personal computer. Windows NT is a cross-platform network operating system which means that Microsoft designed the system to work on Intel-based computers as well as systems using other types of processors such as the Alpha processor chip or the PowerPC chip. This is in line with the intended market of Windows NT which may include corporations or government facilities using a combination of IBM personal computers, Apple PowerPC computers and RISC workstations. Its cross-platform portability is a plus for Microsoft's pocketbook since many other 32 bit operating systems lack the ability to run different architectures with reasonable performance. Its also a plus to the corporation that wants to integrate different departments and computer architectures with a single interface and operating system.

> I can even foresee a small business taking advantage of Windows NT to integrate its business systems. Its entirely possible that a small graphics or publishing service may wish to use both PowerPC and IBM compatible computer systems to meet customer needs. Windows NT, although requiring substantial hardware resources, could do this. Similarly, a small CAD business may need to integrate its IBM PC's with its RISC workstations.

Windows NT also supports multiple processors within a single machine, dividing the processing workload accordingly (called symmetric multiprocessing-SMP), and strong networking capabilities by including support for many network communication protocols even across platforms (chip designs). Finally, NT's security is second to none (for the price anyway) and meets governmental security standards. The price for this power is 75 MB of hard disk space for files and temporary hard disk memory and a minimum of 16 MB of RAM memory (double this for decent performance). Obviously, if you don't have the need to run multiple processors, operate across different computer platforms and maintain a large, complex network, the enormous disk space and RAM requirements of NT should keep it off your wish list. As if running a business weren't difficult enough, trying to tame a Fortune 500 level network operating system without a knowledgeable network administrator just may convince you to give up the ship.

OS/2 is a 32 bit multi-tasking system with much of the power of Windows NT but with Windows 4.0's economy of scale.

IBM's OS/2 is a strong contender for either of the Windows' markets. Its system requirements of 8 MB RAM memory and 40 MB of hard disk storage place it squarely between Windows 3.1 (4.0) and Windows NT. Being a 32 bit operating system with multi-processor support and the ability to exchange information across platforms (through numerous network and communication protocol packages), OS/2 is a capable competitor to Windows NT. Out of the box, it also supports DOS and Windows applications, as does Windows NT, and provides the 32 bit file and disk management capabilities of both Windows 4.0 and Windows NT. Having a lower price than Windows NT, as well as lower hardware requirements, while still offering multiple processor support and excellent cross-platform connectivity, OS/2 is the logical choice for a company utilizing multiple platforms across a small network system.

Make sure your business software is designed for your chosen operating system.

The prior discussion of operating systems has hopefully helped you focus upon your business needs for a particular operating system by differentiating the best markets for each product. The focus of this chapter has been to impress upon you that software applications should be your primary concern in fixing your needs. Towards this end, you should consider that these 32 bit operating systems are still relatively new. If you decide to upgrade to a new operating system or are shopping for an operating system to help your business today, look carefully at the software applications you intend to run on that system. You may find that your intended application is available solely in a Windows 3.1 version and is not due for an immediate 32 bit upgrade. Also consider that some systems, most notably OS/2, have not garnered the immediate and widespread support of software developers that mainstream MS-DOS and Windows systems have received and support for that system has been slow (albeit steady).

These considerations are important because your commitment to a new working environment should be rewarded with continual development and support for the software that operates in that environment. However, since you want to run your business today, you do not have the luxury of waiting for software support to arrive next year or the year after. While many of these systems are technologically wonderful, you may not be able to purchase your choice of updated software that takes advantage of their environments. Furthermore, since many of these products are new and continuously being developed, new standards may bring these products in non-compatible directions leaving you following a yellow brick road to nowhere. This your business does not need. Even if products are now available for your chosen operating system, you may not have the diversity of products that mainstream systems offer and, accordingly, do not have the intense competition that drives prices for this software lower and lower. The trend towards competitive software upgrades is focused more in the Windows environment than anywhere else. For years to come, this competition will keep software that would otherwise costs hundred of dollars selling for $99.00 to $129.00. Finally, Windows will not be abandoned by Microsoft in favor of non-compatible platforms. Even as Microsoft has developed its 32 bit Windows NT and Windows 4.0, it has maintained backward compatibility to protect its installed base of customers. For these reasons, most of my discussions will center on IBM compatible products using mainstream MS-DOS and Windows environments. Both products have a great track record and have garnered undiminished support from a vast array of software vendors and developers. In most instances, if you need a product, it will probably be available in these environments. Now that I have hopefully qualified my purchasing recommendations, let's review the computer components one by one.

Chapter 3

The Computer Components

PROCESSOR CHIPS

A Brief History.

Computers come in a variety of configurations. Lets start at the beginning. Back in 1981, IBM first released its PC with the 8088. It operated at speeds ranging from 5 MHz to 10 MHz. The 808x number refers to the central processing chip of the computer. This "brain" is the main processor into which information is fed and results are output to the display and printer. As the processor numbers have advanced in the following years from 8088 to 80286 to 80386 to 80486 to Intel's Pentium, the ability of this brain to process data has exponentially increased.

What is the difference between 25 MHz and 66 MHz?

The xxMHz speed rating refers to the internal "clock" of the chip that, much like a metronome, dictates the rate at which information flows in and out of the chip. On a very simple level, as the chip numbers have increased, a two to four-fold increase in performance has been noted. A one-step increase in available clock speeds on the same chip(such as from 20 MHz 486 to a 25 MHz 486 or 25 MHz to 33 MHz) has generally resulted in a 20%-25% increase in processing speed. Mixing these numbers produces varying degrees of performance increases.

Who is Intel and what about AMD and Cyrix?

The matter of chip selections has also grown increasingly confusing in recent years with the introduction of chip manufacturers competing with once-omnipotent Intel

Corporation. Intel, a trademark symbol found on some advertised computer brands and models, is a manufacturer of processor chips. Its monopoly in the market has been supplanted by Cyrix Corporation, AMD Corporation, IBM Corporation and a very few others, all producing competitive processor chips. Almost all these companies market their processor chips using number designations very close to Intel's. That is, a 386 chip or a 486 chip may be Intel manufactured or AMD manufactured. The question is, why should you care?

So you want a 486...be careful, not all 486's are created equal !

Although two processor chips, each manufactured by a different company, may be advertised as 486 chips, that is mere marketing hype. Of greater importance to you is how that processor chip operates internally and so compares with similarly priced competition. While a chip may be advertised as a 486, certain 486 chips use Intel's 32 bit information path (analogous to a 32 lane highway) and others use a 16 bit information path. Obviously, the 32 bit path sends more information in and out of the processor than the 16 bit path. Moreover, some 486 chips also contain math co-processor capabilities while others do not include such capabilities on their chips.

The co-processor chip provides processing capabilities useful for calculating large spreadsheets or calculating engineering studies. A math co-processor does not provide greater processing capability for managing large databases, word-processing documents or in producing complicated graphics (with the exception of engineered graphics producing by some engineering programs). Even in accounting programs, the processor may be utilized to varying degrees and, in some instances, may not be used at all. For this reason, manufacturers offer processor chips with and without the math co-processor. If you don't need it, spend your money elsewhere.

Again, Intel initially offered the co-processor on its 486 chips while later offering a version without the co-processor. Finally, 486 chips marketed by Intel have an 8K on-board cache while other chips have caches of varying sizes (from 1K to 16K) depending upon the manufacturer. The cache allows the processor to keep information it is likely to need close at hand rather than ask your computer to re-send the information down its 16 bit or 32 bit highway. Obviously, the more information it can keep close at hand, the faster it may process the information when needed. This is a factor in the cost of the computer.

Other types of "caches" also exist and a computer being advertised as having a cache should not necessarily be mistaken for one having a processor with an on-board cache. While all caches operate on the same principle, the computer may utilize caches for holding information in its memory, on its hard disk, within video components or printer components.

What's the difference between a 486SX and 486DX...and what about the 486DX2 and DX4?

In addition to being educated about the differences in chip manufacturers, you must also be aware of the great number of chip configurations such as DX, SX, SL, SLX, SLC, SLC/e, DLC, DX2, DRX2. Let's run through these by manufacturer. First, Intel manufactures the DX, SX, SL, DX2 and DX4 chips and initially released them in that order. Until the SX chip was released the DX designation was not needed. On Intel's 486 chips, SX signifies the absence of a math co-processor on the processor chip(discussed above) and so DX now designates the presence of a math co-processor. This is the sole substantial difference between Intel 486 DX chips and Intel 486 SX chips. In Intel's 386 chips however, the SX moniker means an entirely different thing. An Intel 386SX operates internally at 32 bits (meaning the simultaneous process of 32 bits of information) but communicates with the computer's memory and other components through the 16 bit pathway. The Intel 386DX communicates with memory and components through a 32 bit pathway, resulting in quicker performance. Intel introduced the SL line of chips in 1991 as a highly integrated processing unit for portable computers requiring less power consumption per processing unit than Intel's conventional chips. The integration allowed Intel to build power consumption monitoring into functions which controlled components of the computer other than the processor. In this way, the disk drives, hard drive, video and ports could be controlled through integrated power management. Power consumption was estimated at 20%-25% less than Intel's conventional chips.

What's an "Overdrive" chip?

Intel's DX2 and DX4 line of chips are also known as Overdrive chips. These chips, depending upon the design of the computer, either directly replace the processor chip in the computer or are placed in a sister slot on the computer board, thereby supplanting the slower processor chip. These chips increase performance in the computer by increasing the processor chip's internal clock speed. The DX2 chips double the chip's speed resulting in a 66 MHz speed rating from a 33 MHz processor chip. The DX4 chips, despite the moniker, triple, not quadruple, the chip's speed. Consequently, a 75 MHz 486 DX4 is based on a 25 MHz chip and a 100 MHz 486 DX4 is based on a 33 MHz processor chip. By altering the processor to operate at 100 MHz instead of 33 MHz, the processor computes instructions three times as fast. The gain in performance, however is not double or triple (depending upon the DX2 or DX4 moniker). The old adage about the weakest link in the chain still holds true. Even though the processor can calculate twice or three times as fast internally, it can receive information from memory no faster and can output its results to memory no faster. The gain is generally a 60%-80% (DX2) to 100% (DX4) jump in performance for processor intensive applications. Still, the $500.00 cost of upgrading your computer for a 60% gain in performance substantially offsets the alternative of investing $3000.00 for a new system giving a 100% boost in performance.

Intel has further blurred the chip definitions by marketing "SL Enhanced" versions of its mainstream 486SX and 486DX chips. Now commonly found in portable computers, these chips are not SL chips but are the less-integrated desktop chips incorporating the static memory features of the SL chip (static memory enables the chip to reduce its clock speed to 0 MHz and still retain the contents of RAM memory). Consequently, these chips allow easier implementation of power management features such as rest and resume without requiring the higher cost of the SL chip which also includes numerous other functions within its highly integrated design.

What's the "Pentium" and should I get it ?

Finally, Intel released the Pentium. Operating at twice the performance level of the same speed 486, Pentium utilizes a 64 bit pathway compared to the 486's 32 bit pathway. It incorporates a combination of chip architectures to maintain backward compatibility with all current PC software while incorporating advanced decoding and operation techniques generally found in RISC chips. Its closest competition is from specialized manufacturers of work-stations utilized for high end CAD, modeling or graphics-intensive work and from the newer PowerPC chip co-developed and marketed by IBM, Motorola and Apple Computer. One caveat if you are considering the Pentium. Some of its design features which account for its increased performance require software engineered to take advantage of the Pentium design.

The Pentium utilizes superscalar, branch prediction and pipelining technology, which is generally considered RISC chip technology, to increase the speed at which software instructions are executed. "Superscalar" means that the chip decodes more than one software instruction per clock cycle. While the 386 chip performs an instruction every two clock cycles and the 486 chip performs one instruction every clock cycle, the Pentium performs two instructions every clock cycle. "Branch prediction" seeks to speed up decoding by "predicting" which instructions depend upon the results of other instructions. If one instruction does not depend upon another, such as if instruction B does not depend upon instruction A, then the processor can begin decoding the second instruction even as the first is still being decoded. This leads us to "pipelining" which further speeds the decoding process by allowing instructions and data to simultaneously "flow" through data pathways. If branch prediction says that instructions A and B are not dependent upon each other, then instruction A does not need to complete before instruction B can be started. Consequently, both instructions can proceed down the pipeline simultaneously. Both branch prediction and pipelining, however are features which are best implemented by software optimized for these features by including instructions for the processor so that it knows which instructions aren't dependent upon others and so can be simultaneously executed. Finally, the Pentium includes, not one, but two caches. While the Intel 486 chip uses an 8K cache to store data and instructions for repeated use, the Pentium provides 16K of cache space and divides this on-chip memory into space for stored data (instruction results) and stored software code (instructions). By providing more cache and dividing it by category, the system has more information "at hand" and knows where to find it quicker than using a common cache.

Until this software is widely available, mainstream businesses will not initially recoup the investment in their Pentium machines. Ultimately, over time, the software will become widely available and the Pentium will not command a hefty price premium. Unless you are intending to keep a new purchase for more than a few years and will make the investment in upgraded software when its available, seriously consider your present need for the higher-priced Pentium in lieu of a 486/66 or DX4. Having said that, I will say that there is a reasonably low price difference between high-end 486 computers and low-end Pentium systems to justify the Pentium computer for graphics work and other processor-intensive applications like scanning or OCR conversion. If I were to buy today, I would spend the few extra dollars for the Pentium machine. And, if you do shop for a Pentium, be aware that earlier Pentium chips (60 MHz and 66 MHz) are based on a 5 volt, 18 watt design which runs considerably hotter than the newer 3.3 volt , 4 watt designs (90 MHz and faster). The result is less processing power with more energy and heat. The lower heat and energy consumption is accomplished by using advanced manufacturing techniques which result in finer electronic pathways being encoded on the chip (0.6 micron rather than 0.8 micron pathways). If you do purchase a Pentium, don't settle for less than the 3.3 volt design. Heat is the enemy of every electronic device (computers included) and, despite the innovative methods employed to keep heat under control in the 5 volt (60-66 MHz) Pentium machines (extra-large cooling fins, chip fans and extra cooling fans), the production of low heat chips is the best solution of all.

AMD Corporation currently produces chips with SX, DX, and DX2 designations. AMD's 386 and 486 chips contain features comparable to those of Intel's chips.

Performance of these chips is on par with Intel chips of the same clock speed and no software compatibility problems have been noted.

Cyrix Corporation chips ?

Cyrix Corporation currently produces chips with SLC/e, DLC, S, S2, and M7 designations. The Cyrix chips may be advertised as 486 chips but their comparison to the Intel 486 chip stops there. As with Intel's 386SX processor, the Cyrix SLC/e chips use a 32 bit information path within the chip itself but input and output information along a 16 bit information path. The Cyrix chips do, however, include a 1K internal cache. The Cyrix DLC series uses a 32 bit path both internally and externally and so is comparable to the Intel 386DX series of processor chips. The Cyrix M7 series utilizes an internal math co-processor and 8K cache and is a direct competitor to the Intel 486 chip series. Be aware that Cyrix SLC and DLC processor chips may be advertised or available under the Texas Instrument banner as well as the Cyrix logo.

Finally, Cyrix (and AMD) has its own "Pentium" design to keep pace with Intel. One of the differences between the Intel Pentium and Cyrix's design is that Cyrix is optimizing its chip so that software designed for the 386 and 486 Intel processor chips receives the benefits of the superscalar design. Another is the aggressive approach Cyrix has built into the chip for branch prediction. In branch prediction, the chip, which is trying to execution more than one instruction at the same time will attempt to predict which instructions do not depend on other instruction results before it can itself be executed. Intel has designed the Pentium to receive an answer to this question before proceeding with the second instruction while Cyrix has told the chip to assume the answer is "yes". Consequently, when the answer is "yes", as it is most times, the Cyrix chip will have already begun secondary instruction execution.

What about IBM computers?

IBM also markets its own processor chips, also known by the SLC (without the /e)moniker. The IBM processor chips are a licensed offshoot of Intel's own chips and are a curious hybrid of 386 and 486 features. The IBM chips are similar to Intel's 386SX by using a 32 bit internal, but 16 bit external information path, but contain a 16K cache in comparison to Intel's 486 8K cache. In one respect, IBM may have topped Intel. IBM's newer chips are designed to accept, and IBM is reportedly close to releasing, clock-tripling upgrades. These upgrades would incur the same limitations as Intel's clock-doubling technology, as discussed above, but processor-intensive applications would still see a substantial increase in performance. In performance comparisons, IBM's chip compares favorably with Intel's offerings of the same or similar clock speeds.

What is the PowerPC and is it better than a Pentium?

When IBM, Motorola and Apple first released the PowerPC chip, Intel cringed. The PowerPC is a RISC based chip in comparison to Intel's line of x86 CISC chips. All this means is that the chip uses different computer code to identify and process application commands. Generally speaking, however, RISC chips process information faster than CISC chips. Consequently, RISC chip development for desktop applications, at prices competitive with Intel's CISC x86 chip line makes for a very competitive computer market. Currently, the PowerPC is comparable to the Pentium in power, but at a lower cost and with less constraints on its expansion possibilities (expansion of its superscalar capabilities, for instance, to execute 4 or more instructions per clock cycle).

> Its superiority to the Pentium is only apparent in floating point operations, the high ground of RISC chips, and useful primarily in analysis or high-end graphics computations. Since the bulk of business software does not rely upon floating point operations, however, this advantage amounts to very little if any performance edge. The average business, relying primarily upon their word processing or data-processing applications, needs fast integer operation, found in both the Pentium and PowerPC.

To improve on the Intel processing chips however, the PowerPC employs design features which make it incompatible with IBM based software. If you decide to replace your current IBM-based PC with the PowerPC, this means that you will have to either replace all your software applications with PowerPC compatible software (called native applications) or use an emulation program. Emulation programs convert the software's instructions into the equivalent PowerPC instructions so the chip can understand and process the instructions. As you might expect, converting instructions takes time and processing power and emulation programs have varied success. The end result is usually a slower PowerPC computer than an equivalent priced Pentium.

The PowerPC is a direct competitor to the Intel-based PC just as the Apple Macintosh computer is a direct competitor. Each is a different platform with its own forms of software support and hardware integration. While Macintosh software won't run on an IBM compatible PC (using Intel chips), neither will IBM compatible software operate on the PowerPC. Software developers will likely "port" their applications to the PowerPC (meaning market separate software applications written for the PowerPC chip) precluding the need to use software emulators however, with the exception of WordPerfect, I know of no company that provides for cross-platform upgrades. Consequently, if you have a large stake in your IBM based software applications, you may find it economically unfeasible to switch loyalties.

What does all this mean for you? The two roads diverge...and you have to make a choice. Just as people had to choose between IBM compatible PC's and Apple computers in the eighties, people will now have to choose between Intel based computers and PowerPC computers in the nineties. I'm a big believer in the law of inertia which says that most businesses, having seen the successful advance of Intel based machines and developed a comfort level with those machines, will be hard pressed to justify a change of course. The PowerPC crowd, on the other hand, will likely be the same people that first "jumped" to IBM's OS/2 operating system or Windows NT, Macintosh owners (having little choice since Apple has bet its future on the PowerPC chip) and other adventurous souls. Eventually, the PowerPC will likely have it own markets just like the Macintosh developed its own markets in relation to the IBM PC.

My recommendation is Intel processors and here's why.

Of all these alternative designs, I am prejudiced in favor of Intel's chips. Intel's chips do not provide any additional power savings over other comparable designs. Other designs also provide clock speeds not offered by Intel which increase the measured performance of that chip compared to its closest Intel competition. Nevertheless, Intel has shown a propensity to develop and engineer features into its processor chips which show great promise and provide the impetus for other manufacturers and developers to develop complementary products. When Intel developed its SL chips it co-pioneered the advent of the Enhanced Parallel Port (EPP). The practical result of incorporating EPP capability into its SL line of chips was an increase in printer performance resulting in decreased print time. For those using portable computers, the increased communication rates available through an enhanced parallel port also mean that, with support from a manufacturer, a parallel port device such as external tape backups, CD-ROM units, external hard drives or other equipment could communicate with the computer at rates approaching those of internally connected components.

One of the drawbacks of portable computers is the lack of expansion capabilities. Although docking units are available for some portable models (and discussed elsewhere in this book), such units tend to be limited and expensive. With the explosion of portable computer sales, portable peripherals have come of age and, in most instances, are connected through the portable's parallel port. Speed is the issue here. A tape backup installed in a desktop system with a proprietary board generally will transfer data at a faster rate than any parallel port tape backup. With manufacturer support however, the EPP increases this data rate and narrows the gap considerably.

Intel's SL line also integrated more control on the chip thereby reducing the potential size of the computer's processing unit and the potential size of the computer itself. Intel's DX2 line was the first to incorporate clock-doubling technology to extend the potential useful life of a computer. Although other companies have followed suit with similar innovations, Intel, being the largest, and having the greatest reserves available for research, development, marketing and development cooperation with manufacturers, appears to be first with many products. That said, most of the chips placed in mainstream products, regardless of chip manufacturer, have, to date, been fully software compatible with Intel's designs. The PowerPC, being the exception, will rely on software designed for its internal processing methods or will rely on emulation software to decode Intel-based software for it. Ultimately, the chip is but one consideration in your purchase decision.

Plug and Play makes it easy to add components to your computer and get them working on the first try.

While you are comparing computers, you will probably run across the term "Plug and Play". "Plug and Play" is a concept co-pioneered by a number of hardware and software vendors that attempts to remove the trial and error of installing computer boards and devices into or attached to computers. These boards and devices may be sound cards, video cards, modems, scanner boards, tape backup boards or other such devices. Computers use hardware interrupt requests to channel attention to and from these devices when they are under use within the computer. Effectively, this is each device's way of telling the computer, "pay attention to me, I am trying to work and I need your processing power for a second". Until "Plug and Play" was developed, the interrupt requests were defined either by default or by configuring each device using either software or a series of little switches on the device or board (called dip switches). If there were very few devices attached to the computer, the default interrupt requests were usually sufficient. Otherwise, interrupt conflicts arose between devices that simultaneously vied for the computer's attention at the same time. The result was a locked (frozen) computer that needed to be re-booted. A common example of this is the use of more than two serial devices on a computer. Serial ports on a computer are designated COM 1, COM 2 and so on, usually up to COM 4. COM 1 and COM 3 share the same interrupt request definition (it's actually called an "address") and COM 2 and COM 4 also share the same address. The result is that using more than two serial devices is likely to cause a frozen computer at some point (or malfunctioning devices) when the two devices sharing the same address both try to operate at the same time.

"Plug and Play" removes the guesswork associated with installing boards and devices in a computer by providing automatic sensing and configuration of installed devices. The computer does this by reading instructions on configuration that are coded into its ROM memory by the computer's BIOS. The BIOS is computer code (not unlike a mini-software program) that provides configuration data to the computer when it is started that allow the computer to sense and recognize its components and devices. The BIOS code can be updated by the computer manufacturer and installed into computers to upgrade their ability to recognize new devices and take advantage of new functions such as power management and PCMCIA support. When shopping for a computer, consider "Plug and Play" to be a vital capability if you intend to add components to the system during its life.

Flash BIOS is a very convenient feature to maintain your computer's upgradability.

If so, also be certain that the computer uses "Flash BIOS", which means that the BIOS can be upgraded by inserting a disk in the computer and running a BIOS upgrade utility. In the "old days", BIOS code was contained on a chip that couldn't be updated. If the BIOS code was upgraded as new devices reached the market, the owner had to return the computer to a repair facility so that the old chip could be removed and a new BIOS chip installed. What a pain ! With FLASH BIOS, the BIOS code can be downloaded from a company BBS and installed by the owner without leaving their desk.

Why bother to upgrade the BIOS? If you have an old computer, it's possible it may not recognize the high density drives that are used today, if one were installed in the computer. That's because the computer's BIOS was not coded for such devices because they didn't exist at the time. This is one common example of why the BIOS is necessarily upgraded.

COMPUTER BOARD ARCHITECTURE

The computer board architecture, also referred to as BUS Architecture, is as important to the efficient flow of computing power, as a well-designed and well-maintained road system is to the flow of city traffic. Bottlenecks caused by lane reductions, speed reductions or lack of coordination between traffic control signals can bring traffic to a halt. The same goes for inefficient BUS Architectures.

What is bus architecture and what are "ISA", "EISA", "VL-BUS" and "PCI"?

As processor chips have gained the ability to process more information in a given period of time and graphic-based operating systems have required more data be relayed between the processor and screen, computer systems have struggled to transfer this information back and forth between the computer's processor and its peripheral systems. The problem has been computer architecture. Until recently, most computer architecture operated on 8 bit or 16 bit pathways while processors were inputting and outputting information on 32 bit and now 64 bit pathways. The architecture was a performance bottleneck as sure as any attempt to squeeze a highway full of cars onto one exit ramp. Added to this was the speed bottleneck. Despite processor speeds of 66 Mhz or greater in many of today's computer processors, the BUS speed was a miserly 8 MHz. Try going 10 m.p.h. on your way to work tomorrow and you'll get the idea.

ISA is a standard but slow architecture unacceptable for faster systems.

A standard, but slow, BUS architecture still in use is Industry Standard Architecture (ISA). Found in low to moderately priced systems, this architecture should not be found in any DX4 or Pentium based system. Utilizing a 16 bit pathway and 8 MHz speed, it's totally unsuitable for moving the large amounts of information being handled by high-end processors and graphic subsystems. On anything but bargain-basement systems, this architecture should be combined with a VL-Bus local video architecture and video board to reduce the system's video performance bottleneck (for more on this see Video Boards and Processors, below).

EISA increases ISA performance but still provides a speed bottleneck.

The next step above ISA is, of course, Extended Industry Standard Architecture (EISA). Using a 32 bit pathway, this architecture still cripples the data flow at a measly 8 MHz. EISA is to be preferred over ISA and its support for a large variety of hardware devices, due to its longevity, places it as the best base architecture for most middle-road business systems. Any decent EISA architecture should be supplemented however, with either of the two newer local bus architectures, (Vesa Local Bus) VL-Bus and Peripheral Component Interconnect (PCI).

VL-BUS comes in two "flavors" and eliminates the speed bottleneck of EISA.

The first release of VL-Bus in 1993 sped data down a 32 bit pathway at 33 MHz for a fourfold increase in EISA throughput and a fifteen times increase in ISA throughput. Since then VL-Bus, Version 2.0 has increased to meet the demands of the 64 bit Pentium and 100 MHz clock speeds by incorporating a 64 bit pathway and 50 MHz transfer rates. If the specifications state "VL-Bus" check to see which version you are receiving. For a Pentium system, Version 2.0 is obviously preferred since the processor and its peripherals can all communicate across a 64 bit pathway.

PCI is the 64 bit bus architecture of the immediate future.

Intel's PCI bus was the first to communicate along a 64 bit pathway and operates at speeds of 33 MHz (with greater speed in the works). Regarded as the high-end bus architecture, PCI is designed to work with newer 3.3 volt systems and incorporates Plug and Play support. It's processor independent which means that, unlike the VL-Bus design, it may be used in RISC workstations and the Apple PowerPC. What this means to the end-user is a probable shift by manufacturers towards implementing PCI architecture and improving PCI performance due to its wider market potential. Since you can't insert a VL-Bus video graphics card (or any other type of expansion card) in a PCI expansion slot, your choice of bus architecture will dictate your future upgrade purchases. If it were my money, I'd bet on PCI over VL-Bus.

VIDEO BOARDS AND PROCESSORS

Your video card is an important part of your system's performance.

On systems using Windows or a similar graphics operating system, the video subsystem follows a close second behind the processing chip on the perceived or actual performance of your computer. In a graphical environment, each pixel (dot) on your monitor must be continually updated by the computer to reflect changes in the screen display. If you use a VGA color display then you are updating (640 x 480) pixels each refresh period.

The refresh period is measured as a vertical and horizontal scan or refresh rate. This figure is quoted in Hertz (Hz) and is a measure of how many times the screen display is "re-drawn" by the computer every second. If this figure is too slow, a flicker or flash would be annoyingly noticeable. In many instances, the flicker can be intentionally noticed on the screen by turning your head slightly from the monitor and focusing on another part of the room. The monitor face will give the impressions of flickering as if its content was being changed.

If you ever watch computer shows on television or see a computer screen on a television show, you may wonder why the computer monitors are constantly flickering as if their vertical hold were out of whack. Those aren't cheap monitors...the television transmission does a good job, however, of showing you the refresh flicker you wouldn't notice if you were in the same room as the monitor. More on this later.

If the main processor chip must handle this chore it cannot focus upon the job of processing your data. The system slows down. Furthermore, if the processor must split its time between processing video signals and applications then the video picture appears to refresh slowly. Hence the perceived and actual performance degradation. If you view your work in SVGA mode, the performance hit is even greater since the computer now has (786 x 1028) pixels to update. Most new systems today, utilize local bus technology with either video co-processors or bitmap processors to speed video performance. What this means is that a video board installed in the computer independently handles the processing of video signals and channels the information between the board and the monitor without requiring attention from the computer's main processor. The main processor can then process your work without diverting its attention to system overhead.

What about video colors? Do I need 16 million colors?

System performance is also affected by the color depth your video board outputs to the monitor. Depending upon the video card you install in your system, the monitor will be capable of displaying a range of colors from 16 different colors to 16,777,216 different colors. The range of colors is increased by increasing the color depth which is measured in bits and now ranges from 4 bits to 24 bits.

Color depth is increased by increasing the number of bits communicated to each pixel. Much as a painter will acquire shades and hues on his palette by mixing different paints of solid colors, the computer uses this same method to approximate the shades and hues of a graphic image. If the computer can mix only 4 bits in a single pixel, then its range of shades and hues is limited (2^4=16 colors). If that same computer is allowed to mix 24 bits (2^{24}= 16777216.0000 colors)of information in a single pixel, it can more closely approach picture quality images.

The greater these figures, the closer you approach actual picture quality. A flower's onscreen image using a range of 16 colors at 4 bit color depth will attempt to blend the 16 colors to produce a close rendering of the shades and color definitions found in a picture of that flower. The use of 16 million colors (24 bit depth) will come closest to approximating a true color rendering of the flower.

As the resolution increases and the number of available colors increases, the video subsystem requires more memory to store the information necessary to "paint" your monitor. For this reason, higher-end systems will include video boards with more memory installed than lower end systems. Of course, unless you work in graphics-intensive applications requiring substantial color definition or resolution (such as desktop publishing or color picture renditions) you can reduce the system overhead by working in VGA resolution. Remember, only pay for what you can productively use.

One final point that bears mentioning, if you value your eyes, you won't try to eke every last resolution capability out of your monitor (particularly when working with text). I personally don't care that some people consider 600 x 800 resolution to be a good resolution for a 14" or 15" monitor nor do I care that they may think they are being more productive using the higher resolution. Years from now, when they are looking through glasses and I still have 20/20 vision, I'll have the last laugh. I use my 14" monitor in VGA (480 x 640) resolution and, when I move up to a 17" monitor, then I'll "up" my resolution to 600 x 800 (or *occasionally* higher as circumstances require).

The resolution used by the computer must be capable of being handled by the computer monitor. This is usually not a problem since even low-end color monitors today will handle SVGA resolution. Nevertheless, just because you have a SVGA monitor capable of displaying 64,000 colors, you do not necessarily need to display your work in this mode. Most word processing work and business applications are better served by using standard VGA 16 color resolution on 14" monitors with SVGA resolution being reserved for 17" or larger monitors.

HARD DISK STORAGE

What is a hard disk and how much do I need?

After processor considerations have been addressed, data storage is another consideration. The software computers use and the data you input are stored on the computer's hard disk (also known as the computer's fixed disk to differentiate it from the computer's removable disks, the floppy disks.). The information is retrieved from the hard disk and placed in memory for use by the processor chip.

Although different types of disk technology are currently available, most all disks within a given size operate with similar efficiency. Consequently, don't worry about the type of disk (IDE, ISA, SCSI, etc.). Base your purchase more on the disk capacity and price between comparably equipped computers. With the advent of graphical environments (and the new 32 bit operating systems), no computer should have less than 200 MB (Megabytes) of hard disk capacity (and I suggest considerably more capacity).

Do not mistake megabyte (MB) capacities figures quoted for hard disks and for RAM (Random Access Memory). RAM is the memory into which the information stored on the hard disk is placed for use by the processor. chip. Similarly do not confuse figures quoted for disk caches and for hard disk storage. While information is temporarily retained by your RAM memory or cache memories while the computer is operating, the information is lost when power is lost. The information contained on the hard disk is retained on the hard disk until it is over-written or deleted by the user. It is not lost when power is lost.

At the risk of being elitist, that figure is quoted for those people intending on purchasing portable computers as their primary computers. For desktop systems, a storage capacity of 350 MB to 500 MB is my perceived minimum for present and future needs.

Here's why 80 MB hard drives are no bargain.

By way of example, I have a Zenith 386SL portable computer with an 83 MB hard disk and 8 MB of RAM. I operate almost exclusively in Windows using Windows applications and a few DOS programs. I purchased the computer at the beginning of 1992 as a replacement for a 286 computer with a 40 MB hard disk. Almost immediately, I filled the hard disk almost to capacity. The following table shows how:

DOS	3.2 MB
WINDOWS 3.X	14 MB
NORTON DESKTOP	15 MB
WORD PROCESSING PROGRAM	15 MB
SPREADSHEET PROGRAM	11 MB
PRESENTATION PROGRAM	9.5 MB
COMMUNICATION PROGRAM	2 MB
FAX PROGRAM	3 MB
ACCOUNTING PROGRAM	2.5 MB

DATA FILES	14 MB
TOTAL	**89.2 MB**

Add to this number assorted utilities that I find indispensable (I'll discuss them later), assorted business-specific programs or files, and that disk is more than full (I use compression software to fill the disk beyond its rated capacity. For an explanation of compression software, see Chapter 14, Utilities). My compression software has more than doubled the disk to an effective 170 MB capacity. The result is I have now added more sophisticated communication and fax software, optical character recognition software and other assorted utilities to the disk. I receive a very real productivity advantage from using these additional programs however my disk is now holding approximately 140 MB of data. This is why I cannot condone investing in a 120 MB capacity portable or desktop computer. I stand by my minimum recommended capacities.

RAM MEMORY

RAM Memory is also measured in megabytes (MB). How much do you need?

The hard disk isn't the only component whose capacity is critical to the computer's performance. Graphical environments also require considerable RAM memory. This is the memory, also measured in megabytes (MB), that holds applications and data ready for the processor. Without sufficient RAM, your computer will not run certain programs, may run programs very slowly or may operate only certain portions of programs. Before Windows, computers could effectively utilize only 640 K of memory. With the advent of Windows, computers are now capable of utilizing all the available memory that can be installed in the system to operate larger, more sophisticated applications and hold more than one application in memory at a time. Since the computer can hold more of an application in memory, it does not need to request that information from the hard disk (a relatively slow process) and the processor is not left idle while the information is retrieved.

If you are using Windows, 4 MB RAM is a practical MINIMUM !

Most Windows programs will require a minimum of 4 MB of RAM memory while others may command 6 MB or more to operate efficiently. Be careful when shopping however. The RAM capacity of a computer is not the same as the installed RAM. While the computer may hold 16 MB of RAM or 32 MB of RAM or more, it may come installed with only 2 MB or 4 MB. The cost of upgrading and installing more RAM to the point that you can use the software your business needs should be considered in the final cost of the system.

Also be wary of the upgrade path. The memory chips the computer will accept is dependent upon the motherboard design. The motherboard is the main circuit board containing the main processor chip, slots for RAM memory chips and varying degrees of controller circuitry and expansion slots.

RAM upgrade can be costly.

Some computers may accept 4 MB chips while others may require 8 MB or 16 MB RAM memory chips to increase the installed memory. If you purchase a computer with 4 MB of RAM and intend to upgrade to 8 MB of RAM, be sure the motherboard will accept memory chips less than 8 MB. On portable computers this issue is even more important. While many of today's portables initially ship with 4 MB of RAM and sport capacities of 20 MB or more, their upgrade paths leave much to be desired. Toshiba portables require the purchase of memory cards (IC cards) in either 4MB, 8MB or 16MB capacities. These memory cards are then placed in a single available memory expansion slot on the portable to increase installed RAM. If the purchaser can only afford the 4MB card and purchases the card to upgrade his computer and increase its performance he cannot thereafter recoup his investment in that 4 MB card if he later needs to increase RAM capacity to 12 MB or 20 MB. In fact, extensive use of Windows will almost dictate that the user upgrade the base 4MB of RAM but very few users will have the budget to purchase an 8MB card for an additional $600.00 or a 16 MB card for $1,000.00.

Toshiba isn't alone however. Even those companies that don't use cards still may require the purchaser to decide how much total memory to install and base their purchase accordingly. Many portables I have reviewed in recent months have come with 4 MB RAM installed with a 20 MB total capacity. That capacity is met by a choice of purchasing either an 8 MB memory module or a 16 MB memory module, both at considerable expense. Better designs, in my opinion, would provide numerous memory slots for the memory modules. My portable, upgradable to a total capacity of 8 MB, allowed the installation of 2 MB memory modules, each priced less than $150.00. Over time, and without a substantial outlay of cash at any one time, I was able to upgrade my memory to its capacity with minimal pain to my checkbook. This is how it should be.

Now that systems come with the capability to increase RAM memory to 32 MB or beyond, how much do you really need? Beyond 8 MB of installed RAM, the performance increase in using multiple Windows applications is marginal. Generally speaking, computer efficiency will double with an increase from 4MB RAM to 8MB

RAM. Thereafter, an increase in RAM from 8MB to 16 MB results in performance gains, on average, of less than 10%.

New 32 bit operating systems will require even more RAM !

If you intend to invest in the 32 bit operating systems now available on market, however, increases beyond 8 MB of RAM will likely show greater performance gains. This is due, in large part, to the much larger size of the operating system software and the expected increase in size of its compatible 32 bit software applications. Again, the idea is to hold enough of the application in RAM memory for the processor's immediate and near future needs. Even if you intend to invest in 32 bit software in the future, most 486 and Pentium computer systems built today will provide ample RAM capacity for your needs.

> Most of these high-end systems produced today provide RAM capacities of 32 MB, 64 MB or even 128 MB. At this point, it is unlikely that any medium size business will have a need for even 64 MB of RAM. Don't pay for what you won't use during the useful life of the product.

FLOPPY DISK DRIVES

Always get a 3.5" 1.44MB floppy drive.

Next for consideration is the number and type of floppy drives (known as removable media drives) your system needs. Floppy drives come in two sizes, 5 ¼" and 3 ½". The size refers to the diameter of the disk that is inserted in the drive. Very simply, if you have just one drive, it should be a 3 ½" drive. For a nominal cost, most systems may include two drives. The two drives may even be manufactured as one unit and contained within one drive bay. TEAC produces such a unit. This would be advantageous if expansion capabilities of the computer were limited. Computer cases come in a variety of sizes ranging from towers to slim-line designs. Towers cost more but offer greater internal storage and expansion capabilities. The drive bays available on a computer will hold the hard drive and floppy drive units. Such bays may also hold tape backup units and CD-ROM players. If a slim-line case offers only two available drive bays, the ability to place a dual drive floppy in one bay rather than two offers the possibility of installing a tape drive or CD-ROM drive at a later date.

While 5 ¼" floppy units were initially offered with 360K storage capacity per disk, newer units now use floppy disks holding 1.2 MB of data. 3 ½" disks, initially offered in 720K capacity now hold a standard 1.44 MB capacity. Certain manufacturers also produce 3 ½" drives which utilize 3 ½" disks holding more than the standard 1.44 MB. One company markets a floppy drive using disks holding 2.88 MB and another company, using Floptical technology, uses similar appearing disks holding a whopping 21 MB! The disks and drives are substantially more expensive and require an investment that is better left to other components. Their utility is further limited by their non-standard format which renders disks written on them useless to systems that do not contain the proper non-standard drives.

The older capacities are obsolete and you should not expect to see a computer system advertised with a 360K or 720K floppy drive. The newer drives will also read older disks and are advertised as 1.2 MB or 1.44 MB floppy drives. Between the two, assuming you are given a choice of one on a packaged system, I recommend the 3 ½" 1.44 MB floppy drive. The disks hold more data, are substantially more durable and are more compact for storage or transport.

EXPANSION SLOT CAPABILITIES

Expansion Bay and Expansion Slots...chances are you will use them.

The next consideration is available expansion capabilities of the computer. (For a discussion of what type of expansion slots you want, see *Computer Board Architecture* earlier in this chapter) Most computers are advertised with a certain number of total expansion slots and a certain number of available expansion slots. As with RAM, don't confuse these terms. As I stated earlier, the hard disk drive and the floppy disk drive will each fill a bay leaving a certain number available for additions. Similarly, the system video card and a parallel port, serial port card will take up a few slots leaving the remainder available for accessories. The expansion capabilities of computer systems is one area where manufacturers cut costs to offer attractively priced systems to the consumer. While upper end systems will generally have five bays and eight slots with a fair number available for accessories, the lower end or value-priced systems will generally have only three bays and four or five slots total. After the addition of the drives and standard expansion cards, this leaves just one available bay and two or three available slots. While such a system may meet your needs today, also consider your longer-term needs.

Also be aware that expansion card slots can be 8 bit, 16 bit, 32 bit or even 64 bit slots depending upon the bus architecture support. As with the processor, the difference is in the amount of information that can be moved along the information pathway in a given period of time. New systems should not contain any 8 bit slots and when possible, lean towards the higher-end 32 and 64 bit slots in anticipation of future upgrades. Finally, and this may seem ridiculous, be certain that you can actually install a card in an available slot. Poor internal case design in some instances results in available expansion slots being effectively removed from service by components or wiring that displaces the card. While this is generally not found in most mainstream systems, be aware that it is possible and guard against the possibility if you are counting on using every available slot in your computer.

PORTS, PORTS AND MORE PORTS

Serial ports and parallel ports...what's the difference?

Most any system likely to be marketed today comes standard with a 25 pin parallel port and a 9 pin serial port. The parallel port communicates, as the name implies, by transmitting information in parallel, eight bits at a time. The serial port (also described as a RS-232C port) transmits information sequentially. The difference is the difference between sending eight cars down an eight lane highway or sending the same eight cars down a one lane highway. Obviously, the parallel port has the greater potential to transmit information more efficiently. For this reason, all modern printers come standard with parallel port connections. This is also the reason external devices such as tape backup units or CD-ROM players will use a parallel port connection if the device is intended for portable computers. Be aware however that not all external devices are intended for portable computers and so not all use a parallel port connection. Many such devices are intended for desktop systems and use an included expansion board intended to be installed in the desktop system (see expansion slots.)

Serial ports are also available in a 25 pin configuration found exclusively on desktop systems. At a minimum you want one serial port connection. Two are better. The serial ports are standard connections for many brands of mice (Microsoft Mouse, Logitech Mouse and others), for modem and fax/modem communication devices and are also used for linking two computers together temporarily via cables for the transfer of data between the two computers.

> This feature is often referred to as linking or lap-linking after the popular software program Lap-Link.

If you regularly have a mouse or other input device connected to your computer via one serial port it is very convenient to have the second serial port available for computer linking cables or an external communication device. Since the cost for the second port is minimal, I highly recommend it.

The 16550 UART is a "must" for any modern serial port.

If you will be using the serial port for a modem or fax/modem, you should insist (stamp your feet, if necessary) on a 16550 UART (Universal Asynchronous Receiver Transmitter) chip for that serial port. Without belaboring the technicalities of it, the 16550 UART provides a 16 byte buffer instead of the 1 byte buffer provided by the 8250 or 16450 UART chips. This means that a high-speed modem will not "overload" your computer by sending or receiving information faster than the computer can provide it.

If you are shopping computers and want an easy way to check for this feature, among others, go to any computer with MS-DOS installed and type "c:\dos\msd" at the C prompt (or have the salesman do this for you). "MSD" stands for Microsoft Diagnostics and is included with MS-DOS. The resulting screen with have information on the computer components. Go to the button marked "COM Ports" and open it (via keyboard or mouse). At the bottom of the screen, the UART chips for each installed serial port will be identified. If you don't see 16550, it isn't there and you should insist on a new serial board if the salesman wants to sell you that computer.

What's a PS/2 port?

One other port is worth mentioning at this time. The IBM PS/2 connector, initially found only on IBM brand computers can now be found on virtually all portable computers and even some desktop systems. The PS/2 connector is a round 6 pin connector (not to be confused with the standard 5 pin keyboard connector) commonly used to connect a Microsoft-compatible mouse. If your intended purchase has such a connector and you are able to relegate your mouse to this port, you can forego the second serial port. Other ports can be found on computers, both portable and desktop. Keyboard connectors, keypad connectors, video connectors, external floppy drive connectors, docking station connectors and even scanning port connectors can be found. Except for the keyboard connector, all the others are generally found, in some combination, on portable computers. These will be discussed in greater detail in Chapter 15 on portable computers.

KEYBOARDS

So... you have an awesome computer but you can't stand the keyboard.

Keyboards are a standard item in any computer purchase. Just because they are included as standard however, they are not to be given short shrift. One of the most important considerations in my recommendations on a portable computer is the keyboard. This is because the keyboard is built into the computer and cannot be exchanged at a later time.

In this chapter I will primarily focus on desktop keyboard recommendations. For my recommendations and concerns regarding portable keyboard layouts, see chapter 15, Portable Computers

---

On desktop systems the keyboard can be detached and exchanged for another model. Keyboard layout, key feel and key feedback are very personal preferences and, given the reasonable cost of replacement keyboards, there is no reason to suffer with a clunky keyboard.

Most desktop keyboards today conform to the IBM standard 101 key layout with 12 function keys laid out on the top of the keyboard and a number pad with cursor keys (arrow keys) set on the right hand side of the keyboard. If you purchase a packaged system today, this is the likely configuration you will receive with the package. The older keyboard layouts used on the original IBM XT set the function keys in two rows along the left side of the keyboard. If this design appeals to you (for instance, you are left-handed as I am), then consider investing in a replacement keyboard. At this time, Northgate Industries produces such a keyboard. Some keyboards go beyond mere rearrangement of layout and add built-in trackballs of varying sizes to the keyboard, obviating the need for a separate mouse. Some manufacturers go beyond the basic layout and offer customizable keyboards with removable or replaceable keys. Maxi Switch, a manufacturer of keyboards, produces one of the most customizable keyboards available today. Each key can be reprogrammed to produce a different letter or symbol and key combinations can be configured to operate commands.

Test-driving a keyboard.

If you are unhappy with your current keyboard, don't suffer. One alternative is to take a trip to your nearest computer superstore and test the wide availability of reasonably priced alternatives. Be aware however, that even most superstores won't have some of the more exotic offerings available today.

What about "healthy" keyboards?

If you are concerned that extensive time at the keyboard makes you or your employees a good candidate for carpal tunnel syndrome, then consider the more recent, exotic offerings marketed with ergonomic comfort and health concerns in mind. Most of these alternatives bend the keyboard in unusual shapes designed to conform to your hands or split the keyboard into two or more sections to relieve unnatural wrist movement or positioning. These keyboards are not cheap, but neither is health care. Some are priced in the vicinity of $600-$700 and you won't find them advertised by many mail-order businesses or carried by many stores. If you are interested give, Applied Learning Corporation (215-688-6866), Health Care Keyboard (414-253-4131)or Kinesis Corporation (206-455-9220) a call.

Chapter 4

Of Mice And Trackballs

Why get a mouse?

With the advent of graphical environments in DOS, Windows, OS/2 and many other operating systems, mice or similar input devices are ubiquitous. Let me say this...if you are not using a mouse or similar item, you are probably taking more time to perform functions on the computer than you need to. New windows compatible software and even some DOS programs provide "drag and drop" editing for word processors, spreadsheets and other programs where data may be reorganized as a normal part of the editing process. This can only be done with a mouse and it is far faster and more efficient than blocking the text or material going to the menu to cut it and then placing the cursor on the new location and going to the menu to paste the block of text in place. A mouse is also necessary to efficiently navigate multiple windows and to move information from one window to another. It can be done with the keyboard but you don't want to. It's slow and awkward.

If you haven't tried a mouse before now or you have just upgraded to a graphical program (whether DOS or Windows) you may find the mouse to be awkward. There are a number of mice or mouse alternatives available today and, like the keyboard, their is no reason to suffer with one that doesn't fit your hand or doesn't operate smoothly. Again, as with keyboards, shop the superstores for a mouse or alternative that fits your hand and has the correct connections for your computer (remember serial or PS/2 alternatives). Mice are hardware and there is no reason you should not be able to "test-drive" the mouse for a reasonable period under the store's return policy and return it or exchange it if it doesn't meet your needs. I have returned mice that skipped their roller ball on the table producing an erratic mouse pointer on the monitor screen, mice that were not compatible with my existing mouse software, or mice whose button locations were not to my liking. The mouse, like the keyboard, is a very personal preference.

What about mouse alternatives? Trackballs and pens...

In addition to the traditional mouse there are a number of alternatives available today. The dramatic increase in portable sales and graphical software has prompted an explosion of mouse developments and alternatives. One very appealing alternative to the mouse is the trackball. While a mouse operates by moving the entire mouse body on a table or pad and thereby moving the roller ball situated on the mouse bottom, a trackball works like an upside down mouse. The trackball body remains stationary and the user moves the roller ball projecting out the top of the body with their thumb or finger. Although such devices have been touted as the savior of portable computers, I use one every day while sitting at my desk. My personal favorite is the Microsoft Ballpoint Mouse trackball however, there are a great number of other trackball manufacturers. Logitech Corporation markets a trackball similar to the Microsoft product and furthermore markets trackballs designed solely for desktop use. These latter trackballs have larger bases, roller balls and buttons than the portable units and so may provide easier control over the pointer. Each product has a different shape, is designed for control and movement in a different manner and has different button placement. I find the Microsoft product to be ergonomically pleasing. I can leave it flat on the desktop and roll the trackball or cup it in my hand. The two buttons are conveniently placed by my index finger. Logitech's offering, on the other hand, is slightly larger than the Microsoft product and is designed to sit on the desktop at a right angle rather than flat. Its first button is convenient to the index finger but its second button is placed away from the fingers requiring unnecessary movement in my opinion. The desktop units are generally designed to have the roller ball moved with the palm of the hand and the buttons triggered with the fingertips. Again, test-drive the different models to find the one that best suits you.

In addition to the traditional mouse and the newer trackball, various other devices are available. Some products are marketed as combination mouse/trackball units. Such products can be moved like a mouse or flipped over and handled like a trackball. In my experience, these do-everything products tend to exhibit many of the shortcomings of both such products and are not the bargain they may appear. Also available are mouse "pens" or styli. Shaped like a pen with a roller ball at the bottom, these products may provide better drawing control than a trackball or mouse. In practice, however, the ones marketed to date have not exhibited great precision. Try it first. Other companies have marketed mouse "joysticks" and a mouse built into a keyboard key (known as the "J" mouse for its location on the "J" key of portable keyboards). In the end, it's all a matter of personal preference.

What about mouse software? What's the difference?

Mice, trackballs and their alternatives use software to communicate with the computer and its software applications. Virtually every mouse marketed today will be Microsoft Mouse compatible, Logitech Mouse compatible or Mouse Systems compatible. Many others will provide their own software and mouse utilities to enhance the mouse's capabilities. If you are using Windows or expect to be, don't worry about mouse compatibility. Windows provides mouse software (called a mouse driver) for all major brands and compatibles. The only issue where software may be concerned is if two or more mice may be used in one computer

> Why more than one mouse? If you use a portable computer, it is very possible that you may keep a trackball or portable mouse in the computer's travel bag while keeping a larger trackball or traditional mouse on your desktop ready for use. In that case, you do not want to have to re-configure the computer by unloading one mouse driver and loading another.

What do all those specifications mean? Which ones are really important?

In that case, my recommendation would be to purchase a Microsoft Mouse for the excellent software that is included with the mouse and keep your purchases to mice that are Microsoft compatible. While you are now probably assuming that I own stock in Microsoft Corporation. I don't...although its probably a good investment. I will recommend what works regardless of manufacturer and Microsoft has many excellent products. In addition, my philosophy has always been to purchase products from a company with the capability and incentive to provide excellent support for its current products and future upgrades. Microsoft regularly provides maintenance releases of its products, provides additional written materials and macros to enhance its products for professional use and upgrades its products to remain competitive with similar offerings, regularly receiving Editor's Choice Awards for its software.

Mice have performance figures like everything else in the computer industry. Advertised on the package will be resolution capabilities, acceleration capabilities, ballistic sensitivity ratings and perhaps a few other touted features. The hardware resolution of mice is the amount of movement necessary on your desktop to move the on-screen mouse pointer across the screen. Microsoft and Logitech use 400-cpi (counts per inch) as a standard. Budget-priced mice may provide hardware resolution of 200-300 cpi. In either event, the software that operates the mouse will allow adjustments in this figure well beyond any reasonable range.

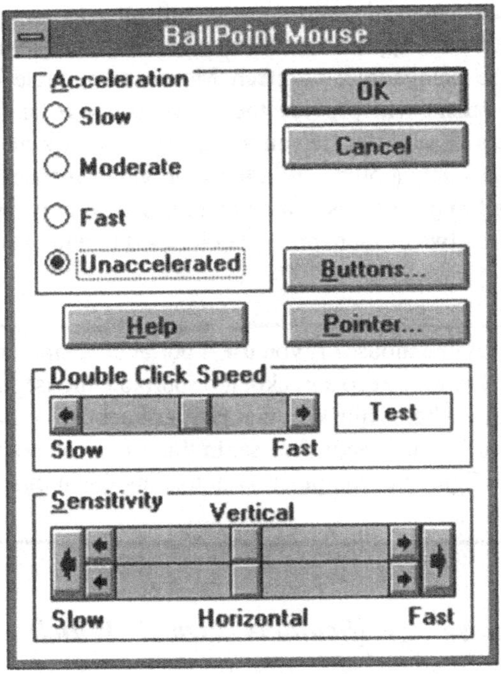

Figure 4-1 Microsoft Mouse software lets you customize mouse "responsiveness".

With software adjustments, the mouse can be tailored to move its pointer over the screen with minimum movement and optimal precision. These adjustments are usually accomplished through a configuration screen such as that shown in Figure 4-1. In my experience with my trackball, I find the best adjustment being that which allows me to move the pointer across the screen in either direction without removing my thumb from the roller ball. Similarly, with a traditional mouse, it can be adjusted so that, with your wrist firmly planted on the desk or a wrist pad, the pointer can be moved across the screen. Acceleration resolution or ballistic sensitivity enables the user to move the mouse pointer across greater distances just by moving the mouse ball or trackball quicker. The software can gauge the speed at which the mouse is moved and increase the pointer movement accordingly. With this feature, even if your hardware resolution is adjusted to require substantial movement of the mouse, just by moving the mouse quicker you can move the pointer across the screen with less hand movement. Of course, there is a trade-off in precision of movement which some people may find unsettling. Finally, most software will allow the user to set the orientation of the mouse, to pick the first and second buttons and to invoke other features of the particular software.

The mouse software, in addition to moving the cursor or mouse arrow, will also provide a number of options. Microsoft mouse software includes the ability to select a variety of different mouse sizes and colors. See Figure 4-2. The growth function makes the mouse arrow grow when the mouse is moved. This allows a less obtrusive arrow when the mouse is not used but a larger arrow to make it easier to follow the mouse movement on your display. For laptop displays, the mouse trails feature enables a trail of mouse shadows to more easily follow the mouse on a LCD display.

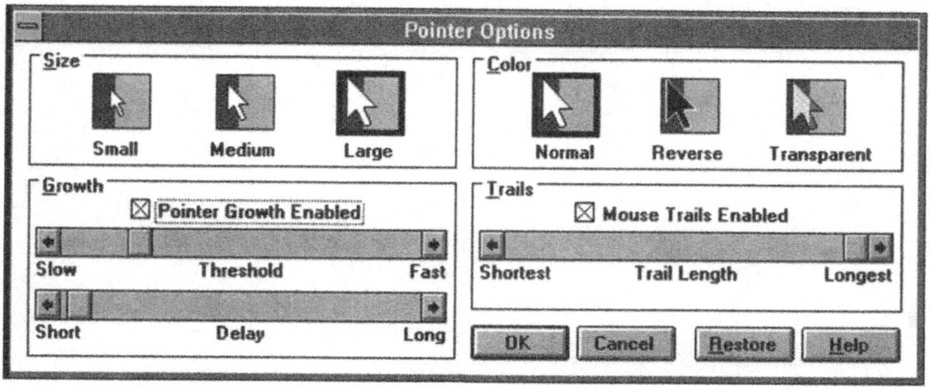

Figure 4-2 Mouse visibility on the computer screen is a big concern. The options on this menu will let you choose between "baby" mice, "monster" mice or anything in between.

Microsoft Mouse 2.0 software allows the user to move the pointer to the opposite side of the screen by moving it beyond the boundary of the screen. For example, to move a mouse pointer located on the screen's far left the user would move the pointer off the left side and it would reappear on the screen's far right. Another feature, called SnapTo, will automatically move the mouse pointer to the default choice in prompt boxes that appear on the screen. This feature, however, has received mixed reviews. The final caveat for this chapter is that computer mice and their software, are very personal to the user and what's good for me may not be good for you. Shop around and experiment.

Chapter 5

Video Monitors

It's included with the system...so why worry about it?

Just as a good stereo salesman will advise you that a stereo system's sound reproduction is no better than its speakers, a good computer salesperson will emphasize the need for a quality monitor. While the mere replacement of your monitor cannot guarantee increased productivity, a low quality monitor will certainly impede your ability to perform. While minor performance differences in hard disk speed or processor speeds can and will go undetected, poor picture quality will manifest itself in eye strain and fatigue. This hampers productivity. First let us review the video standards available today, then focus upon the proper size of the monitor. Finally, we will discuss the performance figures quoted for displays and what they mean to you.

VGA, SVGA and EVGA...what do they mean and which one do I want?

I won't even waste time discussing monochrome (including Hercules compatible monochrome) displays. Its sufficient to say that such displays should be relegated to bottom-end servers not regularly used for input by a human user. In today's market, there is no reason why anyone should consider anything less than a color monitor. The standards available today include VGA, SVGA, EVGA and Tiga. VGA stands for Video Graphics Array and provides 640 pixels (dots) horizontally and 480 pixels (dots) vertically. SVGA (Super Video Graphics Array) and EVGA (Extended Video Graphics Array) provide respective resolutions of 800 x 600 (SVGA), 1,024 x 768 (EVGA), 1,280 x 1,024 (EVGA) and even 1,600 x 1,200. This last resolution is generally found on higher-end monitors typically costing in excess of $1,000.00 and is not a likely choice for most business needs.

While increasing resolution may appear an attractive option (after all, isn't more always better), in practical use these finer resolutions require monitors larger than the 14" and 15" monitors included in most base systems. If you attempted to display a document in a 14" monitor at 1,024 x 768 resolution, you would probably fit the entire page of the document on the screen. Good luck reading it though. The same holds true for a large spreadsheet. Surely you want to display the entire spreadsheet so that you can see the figures in context. But try to stretch the ability of your 14" (or 15") monitor beyond your ability to easily view the contents and you are asking for trouble. Your productivity won't increase...it will decrease. Of course, your most important consideration should be your eyesight. Again, stretching that 14" monitor beyond its capabilities won't help your eyesight (See what I have to say in chapter 3 in the Video Board section). The same holds true for 800 x 600 resolution. Generally speaking, 640 x 480 resolution is an optimal fit for a 14" or 15" monitor. 800 x 600 will display more information, *at approximately the same size*, on a 17" monitor and 1024 x 768 resolution will require a 21" monitor to display even more information on-screen while keeping the characters reasonably legible. By way of example, I currently use a 14" monitor capable of 1024 x 768 resolution. I use the monitor, however, in standard 640 x 480 resolution.

Most monitors are capable of displaying in a variety of resolutions ranging from 640 x 480 to 1024 x 768. The resolution that the monitor actually displays depends on the capabilities of the video card in the computer and the configuration of the video driver. The system is configured by using a video driver, a software file that tells the computer what resolution should be output to the monitor. Windows and most other mainstream software programs include a variety of video drivers, each one compatible with one or more video cards and providing a one or more resolution choices. Remember, just because the monitor may be advertised as capable of higher resolutions, that doesn't mean that you will benefit from it.

There is another reason you may want to favor a standard 640 x 480 resolution instead of the higher resolutions. The amount of information that must be processed by the computer and pasted on the monitor screen grows tremendously at higher resolutions. Standard VGA resolution (640 x 480) produces 307,200 total pixels while EVGA resolution (1,024 x 768) produces 786,432 pixels. If the computer must process information for more than twice as many pixels, its going to take longer to display the image and perceived computer performance is reduced. If the main processor chip must do this processing then actual computer performance is reduced. This is why newer video subsystems incorporate some processing capabilities into the video board (see chapter 3, Video Boards). The result is this. If you have a larger monitor and can utilize the higher resolutions or require the higher resolutions for your business (usually graphics based or desktop publishing businesses will require this performance), then use the higher resolutions. If you will be using a 14" or 15" monitor and generally produce text based documents, don't use the higher resolutions.

This doesn't mean that you can't plan for the future, however. Even though you may be using a 14" or 15" monitor today, if you are in the process of shopping for a video board or entire computer system and realistically anticipate that you will upgrade the monitor at a later date, consider purchasing a board that will provide the processing power, memory and resolutions necessary for your anticipated purchase. This is more likely if your business could benefit from the larger monitor but you cannot afford the current $1000-$2000 prices. This scenario is not likely if your business does not need the larger monitor but you anticipate upgrading to a new system in a few years just to get the newer technology. In that case, don't bother spending the extra dollars for the upgraded video board.

What is the dot pitch?

Displays, like everything else, have their own performance figures and specifications. Such specifications include the monitor's dot pitch, refresh or scan rates, bandwidth, electromagnetic emissions (EM rates) and interlacing capabilities. Dot pitch is the distance between pixels on the monitor. The greater the dot pitch the grainier the image may appear. As the dot pitch decreases, the cost of monitors increases, even if only incrementally. You will pay more for a .28 dot pitch monitor than a .52 dot pitch monitor. The optimal dot pitch specification for your intended monitor will depend upon the intended resolution (VGA, SVGA, etc.) and the size of the monitor. Using my prior recommended matched resolutions and monitor sizes, the following guidelines can be used. A 14" monitor using standard VGA (640 x 480) resolution should advertise a dot pitch of .35 or less. A 17" monitor using SVGA (800 x 600) resolution should advertise a dot pitch of .34 or less and a 20" monitor using EVGA (1,024 x 768) resolution should advertise a dot pitch of .31 or less. Practically speaking, these figures are easily matched and exceeded by most manufactures and, if you are in the market for a 15" or 17" monitor, it's likely you will see dot pitch specifications of .25 or .26.

What is the refresh rate or scan rate and why do I care?

The monitor's refresh or scan rate measures the number of times the screen is re-drawn by the computer every second. This specification is measured both vertically and horizontally and is variably known and advertised as the frame rate, refresh rate or scanning frequency. Separate specifications are quoted for both vertical measurements and horizontal measurements. Each of these specifications should meet minimum standards to produce an acceptable image. If these minimum standards are not met, the monitor screen may appear to flicker or flash

Although the monitor must be advertised as capable of meeting these specifications so as to be capable of performing, it is the video board that provides the signal or output necessary to utilize these capabilities. A monitor capable of meeting these specifications will not produce an acceptable result if coupled with a video board incapable of outputting at these minimum rates.

What is an "interlaced" monitor?

The minimum acceptable standard will vary based on the intended resolution of the monitor. The Video Electronics Standards Association (VESA) recommends a vertical refresh rate of 72 Hz for VGA (640 x 480) and SVGA (800 x 600) resolution, and 70 Hz for EVGA (1,024 x 768) resolution. You must be careful when shopping however. The refresh rate is generally advertised as falling within a certain range of numbers. The minimum acceptable rate may only be met at a lower resolution than you intended. For example, a monitor that advertises its vertical scanning frequency (refresh rate) at between 52 Hz and 96 Hz may only provide the acceptable 72 Hz refresh rate at a resolution of 640 x 480. If you were to operate the monitor at 800 x 600 resolution, the refresh rate could drop below 72 Hz and produce flicker. Similarly, if the monitor operates as an interlaced monitor rather than a non-interlaced monitor, the refresh rate is effectively halved. This is because interlaced monitors operate by re-drawing every other line on the monitor screen during a single pass and then re-draw the remaining lines on its second pass. At an advertised refresh rate of 90 Hz, the effective refresh rate is only 45 Hz, well below minimum standards. When shopping, be aware that interlacing may be found even on monitors advertised as non-interlaced. The monitor, while capable of non-interlaced operation at 640 x 480 and 800 x 600 resolution may resort to interlacing if operated at 1,024 x 768 resolution. If you intend to operate the monitor solely at the lower resolutions (as discussed above) then this is a moot issue for you as it was for me. Again, don't dish out money for a feature you won't use.

Horizontal refresh rates (scan rates or scanning frequencies) must also meet certain minimum standards. Generally, 640 x 480 resolution will require a monitor capable of a horizontal scanning frequency exceeding 38 kHz, 800 x 600 resolution will require 47.5 kHz and 1,024 x 768 will require 59 kHz.

What is bandwidth?

The bandwidth of a monitor measures the rate at which the picture beam in the monitor "pulses". If the bandwidth is not sufficient, the pixels can be blurred (there are other reasons why pixels may appear blurred) and picture quality suffers. Again, as a general guideline, 640 x 480 resolution will require a monitor producing a bandwidth of 27.6 MHz, 800 x 600 resolution will require 51.8 MHz and 1,024 x 768 will require 97 MHz. This figure, although not generally advertised is important and affects the final picture quality. The monitor's documentation will probably contain such information and the salesperson you deal with should be willing to let you review a copy of the product's manual before your purchase.

I've heard a lot about monitor emission...what are they and what can I do about them?

Monitor emissions have been the focus of greater attention in the past year and may be a consideration in your purchase. ELF (extremely low frequency) and VLF (very low frequency) emissions have been credited with increased miscarriages and birth related problems in pregnant women. These same emissions have also been suspected of contributing to other work related health risks however, at this time, no definitive proof has been offered and there is wide disagreement within the community on the actual effects of such emissions. Standards have been established by the Swedish National Board for Measurements and Testing (MPR). The Board initially released its first standard dealing solely with VLF limits and called MRP I. MRP II sets defined acceptable limits on both VLF and ELF emissions. When shopping, be aware that such specifications may not be advertised by the manufacturer. If the issue is important to you, for instance, you are a woman that is concerned with pregnancy issues or you are a supervisor concerned with the potential work-related health risks posed by non-MRP monitors, then make a point to call the manufacturer of your proposed purchase for more information.

What else do I need to know about my monitor?

Monitors today contain the usual control knobs and buttons such as power, centering, size, brightness and contrast. These controls should be located at the front of a well designed monitor for easy access and adjustment. For better control, the newer buttons, offering digital control, are preferred over the older, analog knobs. When it comes to control however, some monitor's go beyond the basics. Many 17" or larger monitors will provide controls for repositioning an entire screen, presetting screen adjustments for different environments (such as DOS vs. Windows), and even matching the on-screen colors to the results output by a color printer. This last feature, of course, is generally of benefit only to those businesses outputting their product to color printers and it is a feature that the user will pay for in the price of the monitor. Finally, in deference to the rising sentiment of energy conservation that has swept the computer industry, many monitors also incorporate power-down features reducing the wattage utilized by the monitor after a defined period of non-use. This feature may be advertised by the manufacturer as an adherence to the Environmental Protection Agency's Energy Star program. Such monitor's are said to be Energy Star compliant.

In addition to the traditional CRT (Cathode Ray Tube) monitors that have graced corporate desks for the past decade, new offerings may appear in the next few years. Again, the explosion of portable computer sales has generated tremendous industry research in the areas of LCD (Liquid Crystal Displays) and TFT (Thin Film Transistor) displays. CRT displays operate on the same principle as your television set by using a picture tube which is "painted" by an electron gun projecting a beam on the rear of the tube. LCD displays operate by activating individual pockets of crystals laid out in a flat grid pattern. TFT technology, utilized in the high-end color portables available today, uses a flat grid of transistors which are switched on and off by control circuitry to produce the display picture. In addition to involving more complex display circuitry and controller circuitry, the initial low yields of acceptable circuit boards for this product have kept the price at a premium. Both LCD and TFT technology however, use a flat grid of elements (whether crystals or circuits) rather than a large, heavy tube. For this reason, these technologies are generally accepted as likely to replace CRT technology. Since the display can be increased in size without adding substantial weight or depth to the monitor, such technology has been the subject of projection-size monitor research. At this point, IBM has released a 10.4" TFT desktop monitor using the same circuit-laden screen as found on its high-end portables. Despite the advances, however, the cost of such technology will not allow its mainstream acceptance in the near future. CRT displays will continue to be the more viable offerings for the near future and should be your primary purchasing concern at this time.

Chapter 6

Printers

While everything we've discussed to this point is important to the user for processing information and obtaining output, it is the printer that communicates this information to your customers, clients and contacts. In most instances, these people don't care if you have a 486 computer or a 386 computer. What they know and perceive about your business is affected by the materials they hold in their hands or view through an overhead projector. While the information your computer holds may be phenomenal, you must communicate it to your clients through the printer. If that printer is unable to produce a professional result or is physically incapable of meeting your business needs either in terms of its versatility or reliability, everything you've done on the computer will have been for naught. This discussion will focus first on the available technologies, then features, accessories and finally shopping for the right printer combination.

Dot-matrix printers are a viable choice for special needs or limited budgets.

There are currently three major technologies used in today's printers: (1) Dot matrix technology,(2) laser technology, and (3) ink-jet technology. Dot matrix printers are the oldest and least expensive of today's choices. Dot matrix printers operate by using pins to strike a ribbon to the paper. Multiple strikes of the ribbon produces dots which, combined, approximate letters and symbols. While older 9 pin dot matrix printers produced less than professional documents, the 24 pin printers generally offered today produce acceptable results for text produced by character based software programs.

By way of example, a document produced by a DOS program such as WordPerfect 5.1 or WordPerfect 6.0 could be printed with acceptable results on a 24 pin dot matrix printer. Graphical programs, however, such as those in Windows, format a page of text as a picture and print the page as if printing a picture. The results are generally poor and not acceptable for commercial ventures.

Since higher end printers, such as laser printers, have dropped in price in recent years, dot matrix manufacturers have necessarily reduced the price of dot matrix printers to keep the product competitive. Today, a high-quality 24 pin dot matrix printer can be purchased for less than $200.00. These printers may also feature desirable options such as scaleable fonts, color printing (through the use of a special

---

A "font" is a particular typeface. This sentence is printed in Times New Roman typeface. This sentence is printed in Arial typeface. `And this sentence is printed in a Courier typeface.`

Scaleable fonts are fonts that may be reduced or increased in size. This feature is discussed in greater detail in chapter 9 on Windows word processors.

---

ribbon) and quiet operation. This last feature has been incorporated into more dot matrix printers in deference to the complaints regarding the annoying whine or noise level of traditional dot matrix printers.

What's a wide carriage printer?

More expensive dot matrix printers are available and, in some instances, out-price even laser printers. Such dot matrix printers include wide-carriage printers capable of printing 132 columns across the page instead of the standard 80 columns. Wide carriage printers may be advantageous for a business that needs to output substantial financial data for in-house use. Dot matrix printers are also available in high-speed configurations for heavy data processing use in medium to large corporate settings. Such printers may approach or exceed $10,000.00 in price and are generally not of interest to the mainstream business user.

Do you print labels or multi-part forms on a regular basis?

Finally, dot matrix printers remain the only reasonable solution for businesses that rely on multipart forms. They also remain one of the most convenient and cost-effective solution to printing mailing labels. Businesses that require these services on a regular basis should consider the addition of a dot matrix printer for these needs

As I will discuss later, your printing needs should dictate your purchase decisions. If one department requires such specialized services, the purchase of a low cost dot matrix printer, permanently set up to produce labels or print on multi-part forms may be more productive than incurring the downtime to produce these same results through the use of typewriters or central office printer.

Dot matrix printers, although nudged out of the mainstream by the more capable laser and ink-jet printers are still a viable option for meeting these special needs at a reasonable cost.

Laser Printers...how do they work?

Laser printers operate similarly to that of the copy machine. A laser beam is rapidly pulsed off a rotating mirror into the toner cartridge. The toner cartridge contains a drum coated with light sensitive material. The laser beam generates a static charge to each area it contacts the drum. As the drum rotates, the statically charged material retains toner which, in turn, is passed to the paper fed through the printer. The paper, which also contains a static charge, retains the toner as the drum rotates past it. The drum is then cleaned and the remaining static charge dissipated by a discharge wire in its path. The paper now contains printing, via the toner transmitted onto it by the drum. It is then passed through fusing rollers which use heat and pressure to fuse the toner to the paper. If you ever experienced a printer jam and removed the paper before it had completed its cycle, you may have noticed the printing smeared very easily if handled. This is the result of toner placed but not fused to the paper.

Ink-jet printers...are these as good as laser printers?

Ink-jet printers operate much like the dot-matrix printer, substituting multiple ink nozzles for the pins found on the dot matrix printer. The technology has improved in recent years and early problems with clogged ink jet nozzles (print heads), messy refills and easily smudged pages have been reduced or eliminated altogether. Ink jet printers provide a cost effective alternative to the initially higher purchase price of laser printers. Ink-jet resolution is on par with that of most current laser printers (300 dpi) however laser output is marginally superior. This margin is due to ink's propensity to be absorbed into the paper material and spread out, producing jagged borders on characters. Manufacturers have countered this propensity by continuously endeavoring to market ever-quicker drying inks for their printers. Another problem is that today's inks, whether water-based or oil-based can be smudged if the page is handled prematurely. Still, these issues are much less of a problem with current printers and technologies. For heavy business use, comparably priced ink-jets will not print with the speed of a laser printer and, while the initial cost of an ink-jet printer may be less than a laser printer, consumables such as print heads, ink and paper can range from 4 cents to 10 cents per page.

Color...what if I need color?

Ink-jets do have advantages to lasers however. The great advantage of ink-jet printers is affordable color. While color laser technology is still priced in the multiple thousands of dollars ($2,500.00 or more), both Hewlett-Packard and Canon market high quality color ink-jet printers for approximately $550.00, about the price of a low-end laser printer. If your business needs to regularly generate color presentations (or even if it really doesn't but color would possibly give you an edge on your competition), ink-jets make it possible. The color quality is good. The cost of color cartridges and specially coated paper will drive the price per sheet higher than average output (50 cents to 75 cents per page) however, such printers can also use a black (monochrome) cartridge and regular paper for everyday use. The initial cost difference, quiet operation, near-laser quality and affordable color printing have made ink-jet printers enthusiastic alternatives to laser printers.

How fast a printer do I need and can I trust the manufacturer's advertising?

The features and specifications that abound in today's printer market are enormous. For this reason, I will attempt to focus on the features and specifications that should be of greatest concern to a small or medium business. First, the speed of a printer will define its general use and price. The speed of dot matrix printers is measured in characters per second (cps) and is further separated into rated speeds for draft printing and high-quality (or letter-quality) printing. Laser printers are rated by the page per minute. The manufacturer's advertised rating can be misleading however. If you are going to use the printer for graphical work as opposed to text-based work, you should ascertain the printer's graphic printing speed, generally a fraction of its text printing speed

> This is another instance when the type of work will dictate your purchase decisions. There can be wide variations in the graphics printing speed of similarly rated laser printers. In some instances, this difference may be due to special software or hardware the manufacturer of one printer may include to optimize the printer for such use.

I report these low-end performance figures because, in most instances, a business should only purchase a dot matrix printer if it meets special needs or if it costs less than available laser or ink-jet printers. Although the Mannesmann Tally dot matrix printer can produce 2.5 graphics pages per minute, it costs approximately $900.00.

Ink-jet printers are also measured both in terms of text print speed and graphics print speed. Text speed is measured as with dot matrix printers (cps) in both draft and quality mode, and graphics speed is measured in pages per minute (ppm) as with laser printers. Dot matrix printers will print, between 50 cps and 100 cps in text quality mode and will print between 0.5 ppm and 2.5 ppm for graphics. Within the price range of low end dot matrix printers ($300.00 or less), the speeds generally average 60 cps and 1 ppm respectively.

Laser printers will produce text speeds from 4 ppm to 10 ppm for personal use or light to medium shared use and 12 ppm to 20 ppm (and up) for the network-compatible, heavy-duty printers Some laser printers are available that exceed these figures however the cost and intended use is usually not compatible with small to medium business needs.

Graphics printing speeds of both the personal use printers and the network printers varies from 1 ppm to 3 ppm. Ink-jet printers range in text speed from 40 cps to 75 cps with the mainstream Hewlett Packard Deskjets leading the pack. Graphics speeds range from less than 0.5 ppm to approximately 2 ppm for the Deskjet. Obviously, for most business tasks the laser printers, with their faster text-based output, are the animal of choice. The choice of speed will be dictated by budget and the projected output of the printer.

What resolution do I want and what's the difference to me?

Resolution and resolution enhancement specifications will also affect the final price of your chosen product. Dot matrix printers come in a variety of resolutions, as discussed above. Its sufficient to say that 9 pin models will not produce the professional output or speed that you desire. The 24 pin models are acceptable for text based printing but do not offer sufficient resolution for proper graphics printing. Ink-jet printers as, said before, offer 300 dpi resolution with some models bumping that figure to 360 dpi. The resolution or clarity of the image is affected by the idiosyncrasies of ink. Laser printers have been a hotbed of resolution enhancement in the past years. While 300 dpi resolution had been the de facto standard, a few companies upped the ante by releasing 600 dpi printers at mainstream prices. By reducing the area per dot and effectively placing four times as many dots on the page, the clarity of the image is considerably enhanced.

When shopping for one of these 600 dpi printers, however, it is important to carefully confirm that the printer is physically capable of 600 dpi resolution and is not merely enhanced to give 600 dpi-like resolution. Likewise, the shopper should be aware that resolution is measured both horizontally and vertically and that true 600 dpi printers provide this resolution in both instances (600 x 600) rather than in one instance (600 x 300). **Finally, and perhaps most important, some printers can output 600 dpi only in Postscript mode and not in Hewlett-Packard's popular PCL language. Since PCL output is generally faster than Postscript (and requires much less memory) the competitive ability of a printer to output 600 dpi in PCL as opposed to Postscript is a BIG advantage**. The HP LaserJet 4 provides 600 dpi output in both PCL and Postscript languages.

Prior to the release of 600 dpi printers (and still used in 300 dpi and 600 dpi printers) manufacturers each advertised their own version of resolution enhancement. Hewlett Packard calls this technology RET (Resolution Enhancement Technology) and IBM's is called PQET (Print Quality Enhancement Technology).While the names differ, each such enhancer operates by modulating the laser beam within the printer and utilizing various size dots to produce finer lines and borders. Newer technology also seeks to enhance the perceived clarity of the image by enhancing the half-tones of the image. Half-tones images (also known as gray scale images) consist of an image which emulates the shadings and color differentiation found in true color by blending different proportions of black and white dots on the page to produce shading. Half-tone enhancers increase the resolution by increasing the number of gray scales that can be produced by the printer. In most instances, 300 dpi printers with enhancement technology will produce text images on par with 600 dpi printers. The 600 dpi printers hold a competitive edge in only two respects. First, graphics may benefit from the higher resolution since graphics reproduction has a greater dependence upon the use of gray scaling. Second, a 600 dpi printer is physically capable of printing resolution equal to that of a 300 dpi printer with resolution enhancement. By applying resolution enhancement to the 600 dpi printer, perceived enhancement is elevated to new standards. At this higher, perceived resolution (perhaps 1200 x 1200) even text images may reveal quality differences. The result is, given the budget and perceived need (i.e. business graphics use) the 600 dpi printer is a viable option but by no means the only acceptable solution.

What does HP-compatible mean and what are PCL and Postscript?

Printers communicate with the computer and its software through the use of language. More specifically, the printer is told how to format and print a page based on the software printer driver used by the software application in use. For example, if you are working in WordPerfect to create and print a text document, when you are ready to print the document, WordPerfect must know what type of printer you are using. It must know this so that it can pick from a variety of printer drivers (usually included in the application software), each designed to communicate to a different printer in its own language.

If you did not install the application program, you may not need to make this choice. Many programs, when first installed, ask for the printer you will use and thereafter accept that choice by default. In Microsoft Windows, the applications will generally not include printer driver software. In Windows, printer drivers are centrally located in the Windows program directory and are shared by all Windows compatible applications.

Various languages have evolved in the years with a few becoming de facto standards. Printers may be advertised as using these languages, being compatible with or capable of emulating printers using a standard language. An HP compatible printer is a printer that can use a software driver for the HP printer. An Epson or Panasonic compatible printer is a printer that can use the software printer driver for these printers. This is generally of greater importance in non-Windows (DOS) applications since a software program that must include its own software printer drivers may not include a driver for an unpopular printer. If the printer is compatible or can emulate other more popular printers however, the result is generally the same as if the software was printing to the more popular printer.

Dot matrix printers will generally provide Epson, IBM and Panasonic emulation or compatibility. Ink-jet printers generally use software drivers particular to the model in use. In part this is due to the particular manner in which ink-jet mechanisms vary and, in part, it is due to the need for specialized software to allow the use of multi-color cartridges for color printing. If you intend to purchase an ink-jet printer for use with DOS applications, check with the manufacturer or software vendor for the availability of a printer driver compatible with the application and printer. Again, laser printers have been the subject of upgraded languages in recent years. Perhaps the two most popular languages for these printers are PCL and Postscript. PCL stands for Printer Control Language and is the language used by Hewlett Packard's popular LaserJet printers. When another printer is advertised as HP Compatible, that means it can communicate using the PCL language. At present, PCL is available in two flavors. PCL4 is the language of Hewlett-Packard's LaserJet II series of printers. PCL5 is its newer language included in the LaserJet III family and LaserJet 4 printers. The material difference between PCL4 and PCL5 is PCL5's ability to accept 600 dpi printing instructions. Previously, such instructions required use of the Postscript language. Postscript is a printer language standard set by Adobe Corporation (a marketer of fonts and typefaces) and is also known as Adobe Postscript. It is also available in two versions, Postscript and Postscript Level 2, with Postscript 2 being the faster of the two versions. Generally speaking, Postscript capability adds to a printer's purchase cost but provides a cross-platform printing language that increases the ability to transport documents and graphics between different machines without altering the printed output. Postscript requires more printer memory and print time. For text-based printing and most graphics printing, either of the PCL languages and emulations are sufficient, although you will want PCL5 included if you pay the price for a 600 dpi printer. Any printer that is HP Compatible, LaserJet Compatible or capable of emulating the LaserJet family will meet moderate business needs.

> While shopping, however, be aware that HP or LaserJet compatibility could mean LaserJet II compatibility (PCL4) and not LaserJet III or IV compatibility (PCL5). Also be aware that some manufacturers will advertise PCL5 compatibility but such compatibility will require the purchase of an upgrade (usually a card installed in a slot on the printer). Take this into consideration when comparing the final costs of printers.

What other features can I expect to see?

Other features have been incorporated in the newer line of printers with varying results. Bi-directional port capabilities, faster port transfer rates, duplex printing, dual-page processing, automatic emulation switching, automatic port switching and other features run the gamut of newer developments. Bi-directional port capabilities have been best implemented by the Hewlett Packard LaserJet 4 printers through the release of software that allows the computer and its user to communicate directions to the printer and, for the first time, receive feedback from the printer. For instance, the printer may send an image to your monitor screen showing that it is low on paper or toner or is experiencing a feed failure. This feature is most advantageous, of course, if the printer is located outside your work area.

Most vendors will incorporate some capabilities along these lines in the next year. Developments in faster transfer rates and the use of dual-page processing, the process of formulating each succeeding page of a document in the printer's memory even as the printer is printing out the prior page, can increase the speed at which the printed page is output. Automatic emulation and port switching is generally preferred in network environments where a central office printer may necessarily receive information through more than one port and may need to use more than one printer language to meet the diverse needs of the office personnel. Of all these features, I expect the bi-directional ports and faster port transfer rates to become standards in any reputable printer. The other features are on an as-needed basis and the lack of any one of these features, unless needed, should not dissuade you from a printer otherwise meeting your needs.

Some practical considerations when shopping...

While shopping, you must consider your output requirements and shop accordingly. As we've discussed, many manufacturers produce a printer line consisting of printers utilizing similar technologies but designed for light, medium or heavy use. Furthermore, each printer in the line may offer upgrades or accessories not offered by others in the same line. Your business requirements may dictate two or more light or medium duty printers rather than one printer designed for heavy use. Your budget may also dictate a price range limiting your current choice of printers but your future needs may exceed the present choices. This is where smart shopping will pay off. By carefully choosing a printer, you can secure a reasonably priced printer capable of expansion to meet your later needs.

Here's how I decided what printer to purchase...

As an example of tailoring your purchase to your present and future needs, consider the following example. When first shopping for a laser printer in the summer of 1992, I expected that a light duty printer would meet my present needs and budget. This, of course, enabled me to consider the number of laser printers priced between $600 and $1,000.00. All of these printers were capable of 300 x 300 dpi resolution, accepted letter size paper, included various fonts, printed at advertised rates of 4 pages to 6 pages per minute and included memory varying from 512 KB (½ MB) to 1MB. Each would have met my present needs and budget.

I just couldn't bring myself to purchase one of these printers, however. I wanted the printer to be a long term investment. I already expected that I would add an envelope feeder and perhaps a second paper tray. I also knew that newer printer standards were being developed and that future software purchases would or could require Postscript or these updated standards to operate efficiently. Finally, there was the possibility that faster printer engines would obsolete my printer in just a few years or that I could require a faster printer for an increased workload. The Hewlett Packard LaserJet IIIP was a very attractive option at that time but it would not accept additional trays or an envelope feeder. I continued to shop. Finally, I settled upon an IBM Laserprinter 6, Model 4029.

> The 10 page version of this printer received an Editor's Choice Award in a computer publication's annual printer review. In that review, many of the considerations I discuss here were touted as innovative and practical reasons to consider this printer.

The IBM 4029 printer is a 6 page per minute laser printer. It holds 200 sheets in the included paper tray and its output tray holds 100 sheets. Both of these figures exceed the HP printer's specifications. The IBM printer also uses a very compact footprint (it takes up little space) and holds all its paper completely under the printer. The expandability of the printer is excellent. It can accept additional paper trays, hold a variety of paper sizes and the additional trays are also placed completely under the printer. The additional paper trays can hold 500 sheets and may be linked to the first tray to produce a total capacity of 700 sheets before requiring attention.

It also accepts an envelope feeder holding 75 envelopes of varying sizes. The printer included 1 MB of memory (sufficient memory to hold an average size document) while providing memory expansion to a whopping (at the time it seemed large) 9 MB. IBM also provided slots for upgrades or the use of Postscript languages. Finally, the 4029 model could be upgraded to a faster 10 page per minute printer for approximately $700.00 by purchasing an upgrade board. By purchasing this board, the printer would also be capable of increasing its resolution from the standard 300 x 300 resolution to the newer 600 x 600 resolution.

To date, I have added the envelope feeder which has increased my productivity tremendously. Instead of feeding envelopes one at a time, I can now instruct the printer to print envelopes for entire mailing lists of clients or other contacts while I move on to other matters. As 600 x 600 resolution becomes the standard for newer laser printers, I can update the printer to this standard while increasing the print speed almost 70% for one-half the price of a new printer. As you can see, by carefully considering the features you will need both today and tomorrow, you can purchase a printer that will not be obsoleted by your growing business.

What if I get 2 smaller printers rather than 1 large network printer?

Another consideration when shopping for your business needs is balancing the higher price of heavy duty printers with the lower cost of light or medium duty printers. Heavy duty laser printers are generally rated at 50,000 copies per month in contrast to the 10,000 duty cycle of a personal use printer. If you anticipate your business will generate the larger output, you must decide between purchasing a single high-end printer for your business network or multiple light/medium duty printers, each for use by one or more employees. There is a tradeoff involved for each choice and, in the final analysis, the decision may depend upon the particular needs of your business. In addition to their higher output rating, the network-ready printers will generally output at a faster rate and will be capable of holding more paper and accepting more accessories. In addition, if you average only 35,000 copies per month, the network printer will not approach its rating limitations. While this may be perceived as an inefficient use of the product, remember that approaching any mechanical device's limitations generally means reducing its total life span

Finally, the purchase of a single heavy duty printer capable of outputting 12 ppm to 17 ppm is a less expensive alternative to the purchase of multiple personal use printers.

Remember this point if you decide to invest in light/medium duty printers as well. If you are indeed approaching 35,000 copies monthly, the purchase of three light duty printers will require each to be used to its limit. In that instance, you've increased the possibility that the three overworked printers would probably keel over and die long before the heavy duty printer. In that respect, you will have consumed your investment at a premature rate compared to a similar investment in a heavy duty printer.

Alternatively, the use of multiple light duty printers reduces the risk that printer malfunctions or breakdowns halt all printing pending the unit's service and repair. Moreover, the personal use printers can be placed strategically throughout the business to service groups of people with complementary needs. By doing this, you reduce lost productivity from the constant travel of workers to and from the one office printer and the special printing needs of one group can be met by tailoring their printer to those needs.

This is not a minor consideration. If the office is quite large or split between floors, the time necessary to collect documents from the office printer can add up quickly. Add to this time the lost time encountered by employees traveling to the printer only to find it needs paper, hasn't finished printing their document, has printed the document on the wrong paper or any one of a number of additional problems that workers face in the real world. The second issue is also worthy of consideration. If one group of workers regularly uses a special paper, regularly prints large documents or generally requires the printer to be configured in a non-standard manner, acquiring a printer specifically for that use may greatly benefit your productivity. After all, why should your sales staff be brought to a grinding halt so that administration can print that new 50 page office manual.

Finally, the reduced speed of the personal printer may be offset in practical use by the reduced demands being placed on the printer. If ten employees attempt to use even a 17 page per minute network printer, the last few employees to send their print requests are going to have a long wait. A personal printer operating at half the speed but serving only three employees would probably output those print requests much sooner. The point is this...depending upon your business printing needs, the volume of output, your office layout and your budget, the best alternative is that which allows your business to operate without the bottlenecks that can occur when printing needs are not met.

One final point about printing...if your printer is too slow, don't be too quick to blame the printer. Just as graphics operating systems have overloaded yesterday's video cards and processors, so it is with printers. Instead of being told to print an "a" or a "b", the printer is being told to print about 1000 dots and place them here, there and everywhere. The result...so much information and too little time. The solution...well, if video cards can use graphics accelerators why can't printers use print accelerators. They can. For a very reasonable cost (about $50.00) you can speed up your print jobs tremendously with a little utility called PrintCache. See Figures 6-1 and 6-2. PrintCache (LaserTools Corp. 800-767-8004), which is both

Figure 6-1 Usually only an icon, the PrintCache screen gives you immediate feedback on your printer status.

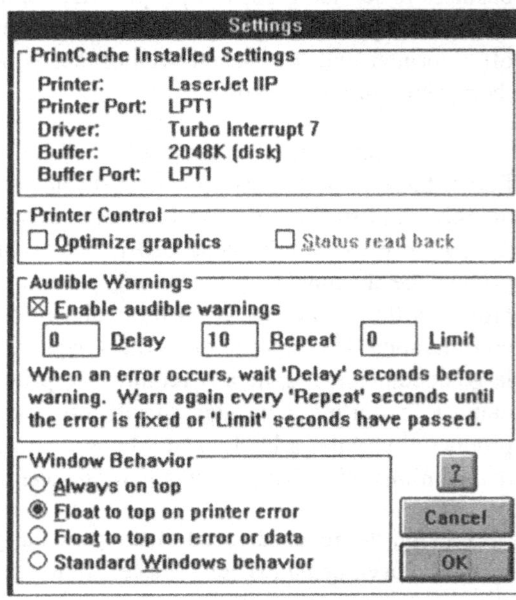

Figure 6-2 PrintCache can be set to be unobtrusive except when you want it to get your attention.

DOS and Windows compatible, caches print data in your memory or on your disk and feeds it to the printer much faster than your standard print drivers. If you use Windows, you know that the Windows Print Manager is notoriously slow. While you give up some flexibility in terms of reordering or canceling individual print jobs, PrintCache makes up for that by returning computer control incredibly quicker and even providing information feedback when printing to printers supporting bi-directional communication (like the Hewlett-Packard LaserJet 4).

Chapter 7

Networks For The Small Business

When computing was accomplished primarily from dumb terminals connected to mainframe computers, everyone couldn't wait for the era of desktop computing to arrive so that they would have their own personal computers at their beck and call. Well, the personal desktop computer has arrived, its more powerful than those mainframes of yesteryear and now the buzzword is...connection. Whether you call it networking or linking or conferencing, group computing is the "in" thing. You've come a long way baby.

This is an introduction to small networking system choices-all that you will likely need.

You may notice that this isn't the longest chapter in this book and yet computer networking isn't simple. There are entire books available to merely introduce you to the concept of networking your computerized office. I'm going to assume, though, that you don't want to know all about networking nor do you want to be inundated with ten or twenty choices for networking topologies (a fancy way of referring to a network layout), networking software and the associated hardware to make it all work. Instead, you want to know how to connect anywhere from two to twenty computers in your office and gain a productivity boost from shared file and printer access (among other things). For this reason, I'm going to skip over entire mountains of networking information and try to distill it all into a few very clear, proven choices for small to medium networking needs. You will also want to review the chapters on software and effective computing for service and home-based businesses for discussions on how networking is implemented and supported by today's collection of software applications.

What's "client-server" networking?

There are at least two major types of networking available today with numerous subsets of each further dividing these two markets. Client-Server networks are one type of network configuration. These systems rely upon a work-horse computer designated as the server. This one server (although there can be more than one) provides the processing power necessary to operate the network's applications and transmit the data to each workstation (client). By retaining the application files and data files at the server and transmitting only the information required of the client, less information is transmitted along the network resulting in quicker response time for each client. The server communicates with the clients through network software and network cards that are installed at each end of the system. Client-server network systems are generally installed for network needs exceeding 10-20 nodes (computer stations) although such a system could be installed with as few as two computers. The reason for this practical minimum is cost...both installation cost and upkeep. While client-server networks provide advantages over the peer-to-peer network system (now you know what's next) in terms of centralizing backup of data and application files, centralized administration and security of system files and powerful reporting features to track file access and usage, they exact a toll in initial setup costs and the incurred cost of dedicating, not only a computer, but a real, live person to maintain and administer the network.

What's "peer-to-peer" networking?

Peer-to-peer networks are the second tier of network systems and are the practical solution for small to medium sized businesses. Zero slot peer network systems rely, not on network cards, but solely upon cable devices between systems, usually via serial or parallel port connectors, to move files or share printer resources. For the very small office, perhaps three or less computers, concerned more with sharing a single printer and some data files, this would probably work. Its greatest attribute is that you have little to lose in time since you don't even have to open the computer case to install it. For simple print-sharing devices, you can try the SmartPrint print sharer by Dresselhaus Computer (909)945-5600 or the Multishare Transmitter/Receivers from Linksys for connecting multiple computer stations to one printer. SoftWorx's PC-Interlink for Windows (800-327-5013) and Coactive's Connector allow printer and file sharing. In their base configurations SmartPrint will connect two computer stations to one printer and PC-Interlink will connect up to four computer stations. The others are sold on a per-node (computer) basis.

Still, with the necessary but reasonable investment in inexpensive network cards and software, the second tier of peer networks offers so much more flexibility and opportunity for growth. This second level uses Ethernet or Token-Ring network cards, cabling and a network operating system (software) to allow all computers on the network equal access to network resources: files, applications, modems, CD-ROM's and printers.

> When shopping by price, be aware that networking systems can be purchased dirt cheap in some instances. Most likely, however, these will be proprietary network systems, with adapter cards and software that will only be supported by that vendor.

You get a lot of flexibility with peer-to-peer networking and give up very little.

With a peer-to-peer network, your business gains most of the advantages of a dedicated server-client network such as e-mail capabilities, group scheduling, the ability to share data and application files between computer stations and the ability to share modem, CD-ROM and printer resources. In some instances, such as in printer resource management and control, peer-to-peer systems exceed the capabilities of the dedicated server-client system. What does the peer-to-peer system give up? Centralized backup of files for one thing. Since application and data files are spread across the network computer system, the backup utility must separately backup each computer station's drive. What else don't you get? The ability to secure files is hampered by the local nature of peer networks as opposed to centralized nature of server networks. While most peer networks offer password security on a directory by directory basis, server-based networking software provides a wide array of security functions including the assignment of users to groups with predefined access rights and passwords, encrypted password functions and sophisticated tracking and reporting tools to gauge usage by file, application, workstation and user. Although peer network systems are slowly incorporating better security and tracking features into their software, they still lag behind the server-based systems.

Even with a peer-to-peer network system you may want to consider setting aside one computer as a "server".

Even though pee-to-peer networks don't anticipate the need for a dedicated server computer as in the server-client networks, once you have your peer-to-peer up and running, you just may decide you want a dedicated server anyway. While interviewing businesses that use peer-to-peer networks, I found that, in some instances, dedicated servers could boost efficiency. If you've purchased a network printer, attached it to someone's computer station and now everyone in the office is sending print jobs to that printer, you may find that person a little frustrated at the response time of their computer. This is because all the office information is being routed through the computer to the printer. Although most network software provides caching capabilities, at some point the transmission load is still likely to degrade computer response. The same situation is also likely if you've placed commonly accessed files and applications on one computer and then have ten or twenty other stations drawing from that one source. With a little planning, the load in both cases can be equalized or, alternatively, a dedicated server can be instituted. In practice, dedicated servers, even on peer-to-peer networks may be a practical choice for heavy information loads at one computer site.

Networking used to be a tedious, expensive and time-consuming proposition...but no longer. In fact, for most small businesses, networking is getting easier and cheaper every day. Just like the wars being fought on the various software fronts and operating system fronts (Windows v. OS/2), vendors are also vying for your networking dollar.

An introduction to networking software and Microsoft's solution.

As with almost any "war" waged in the field of computers, Microsoft managed to get in a few licks. Microsoft released Windows for Workgroups as an adjunct to its Windows 3.1 operating system for integrated peer-to-peer networking capabilities. While the first release had a few shortcomings when compared to products like LANtastic, Microsoft quickly resolved these deficiencies and has brought to market a very reasonably priced peer networking system with lots of room for network growth. While other NOS's will run Windows, Windows for Workgroups is a networking system with Windows built into it. Included in the package is Microsoft Mail for networked e-mail services and Schedule+ for group scheduling using the Mail database. Also included is shared fax capability although full use of the fax features built into WFW will require the use of a Microsoft At Work-compatible fax. WFW supports a number of cross-platform system capabilities including the ability to network with other network systems including Novell, LANtastic, VINES and even TCP/IP for those interested in the Internet protocol. Perhaps its best selling point is that WFW's default protocol, NetBEUI, is also Windows NT's protocol. For those interested in establishing a network system with an eye towards the future, the ability to gravitate towards NT as system loads and needs increase is a powerful inducement to consider WFW. Through WFW, each computer station has full access to print status and shared print manager and file manager resources. Linking through networked DDE commands is another bright point in favor of WFW which implements this feature better than most other peer network systems. Security is perhaps WFW's weak point and is still limited to password protection and printing through the Print Manager is not as quick as the HyperPrinting feature of LANtastic.

Even with these few shortcomings, if Windows is your environment of choice for now and the foreseeable future, then WFW is probably your best bet for good peer-to-peer networking capabilities at a reasonable cost.

LANtastic is a solid networking system with a great track record.

LANtastic is another of the most capable and popular peer networking systems offered today. Actually, users are offered two flavors of LANtastic, the regular and the "lite" version, called Simply LANtastic. Available in single node and packaged versions, LANtastic provides e-mail capabilities (with some limitations on flexibility), shared resource capabilities (printers and modems)and offers remote access (at additional cost). Its printer support through HyperPrinting, a printer spooler, is excellent and its network management options are full-featured for a peer-based network. In addition to individual and group access limits and password assignment, LANtastic provides considerable leeway in the specialized access afforded each user, limiting file access by read, write, modify, or time-specific durations. Protection is available for directories and files and LANtastic further includes some traditional administration tools for account tracking and resource auditing.

Simply LANtastic, the "lite" version, provides the same solid foundation as the full-featured version but tosses aside some configuration and security flexibility. With simple full, no or read-only access and shared resource capabilities, Simply LANtastic won't meet the needs of medium-sized networks needing greater flexibility and security but for the three to five person office, it's a great solution.

An introduction to network adapter cards.

Once you are comfortable with your choice of network operating system, the next step is purchasing the hardware to run it. Very simply, this hardware will include network adapter cards in each computer and cabling to connect the computers. For peer-to-peer networks, the choice is simple. Ethernet cards are reasonably priced, widely available, well supported and provide high through-put (meaning they're fast). So what else do you need to know? For starters, dig out your computer manual and find out the following:

* what type of bus you have (not school bus...is it an ISA, PCI or an EISA based computer system?);
* do you have a full-size expansion slot or only a half-size expansion slot; and
* is it a 16 bit slot (it should be)?

With this information in hand, you want an Ethernet adapter card that:

* auto-configures and has the capability to use interrupts above IRQ 7 (better would be an adapter card that supports the Plug and Play specifications);

* provides support for NetWare, LANtastic and Windows for Workgroups (the more likely and popular choices);

* support for NDIS and ODI drivers;

* provides at least a 16K buffer; and

* support for thin coaxial and twisted pair cabling.

Other nice features would be LED status displays to help troubleshoot networking glitches, diagnostic utilities for the same purpose and an upgradable PROM (like a computer's BIOS).

Network cabling choices for the small to medium network are thin coaxial and twisted pair.

So far as cabling choices are concerned, small networks need only be concerned with thin coaxial and twisted pair cabling. Fiber optic, though oh so cool, is also oh so very expensive and requires specialized installation. While not so "exotic" as fiber optic, thick coaxial cable is overkill, providing multi-channel capabilities and maintaining strong signals over long distances, two qualities unlikely to be exploited in a small office environment. In addition, thick coaxial cable also requires extra hardware to install the cabling, a deficit not shared by thin coaxial or twisted pair cabling. Thin coaxial, on the other hand, is easily and inexpensively installed but limits the distances and number of computer stations the network can comfortably handle. Twisted pair cabling is offered in shielded and unshielded varieties. As you might expect, shielded cable costs more but is better protected from electromagnetic interference, enabling transmission over longer distances than its unshielded sibling. Unshielded twisted pair cable uses RJ-25 modular telephone plugs and is easily installed and maintained. In real local network situation (like in the same room), unshielded twisted pair cable is more than adequate.

Wireless networks are an option with their own tradeoffs.

If you don't like the idea of stringing cables through partitions, walls or ceilings, you're probably a candidate for wireless networking. In the world of wireless networks there are two choices, radio and infrared, each with its own ups and downs.

While long-term maintenance may be reduced, expect higher start-up costs for the wireless transmitter/receivers. Also be aware that transmission speeds, although constantly improving, will likely always lag behind wired networks (which vendors also strive to constantly improve). If you're really concerned about the system slow-down generally associated with the overhead of networking, then maybe you should forego wireless.

Wireless infrared network systems boast high speed and low cost but require careful consideration of physical office layout.

Infrared transmission is gaining popularity for very close proximity data exchanges such as those typically encountered when transferring files between a portable and desktop computer. It's low cost and high speed make it ideal for these situations. It may be less ideal for networking, however. Despite its low cost and high transmission speed, many infrared networks require a "line of sight" between units. With "line of sight", walls and even office objects can interfere with the network connections. Due to these limitations, range is severely limited in "line of sight" wireless network systems. Another type of infrared networking system, less prone to object interference though not immune, is diffuse infrared. With diffuse infrared, the signals can be bounced off but cannot penetrate walls and ceilings. Accordingly, while the range and flexibility of diffuse infrared networking is considerably greater than "line of sight" infrared, it is still limited in its scope and, certainly, to no more than one floor of a building. Another drawback is that infrared technology is also susceptible to interference from other light sources. When transferring files between a portable and desktop, these limitations can be tolerated but repeated interference with the stream of continuous transmissions encountered along a network may begin to fray at your nerves. Consequently, infrared transmission is the more likely choice as an adjunct to a wired network system (for connecting portable computers, for instance) or for close proximity networking within a department (contained within one room).

Radio frequency wireless networks can communicate through walls and floors.

Perhaps the better wireless alternative is radio frequency (also called "spread spectrum") transmission. Radio networks don't require "line of sight" and can be effective even through ceilings and walls. There are currently two types of radio frequency systems, with more on the way. Direct sequence radio technology uses a specific bandwidth for the radio transmission while frequency hopping regularly travels up and down the radio frequency bandwidth in a set pattern. The advantage to the latter technology is increased security and interference prevention due to the constant change of radio frequencies. When shopping for a wireless radio network, keep in mind that the environment will play a large part in how effective the system operates. While infrared has problems with objects and certain light sources, radio networks have to share the airwaves with a tremendous number of other competing devices. The bandwidths designated by the Federal Communications Commission for wireless communications are shared with microwaves, wireless and cellular telephones and car alarms. While much of this traffic is contained within the 902 to 928 MHz frequencies, future crowding of frequencies currently popular with wireless networking are inevitable. Due to the power limits placed on wireless transmissions by the government (such as those placed on cellular phones), interference from stronger radio transmissions is possible. To overcome this power limitation, you can expect "cellular" radio networks to make inroads over the next few years. By placing "cells" or nodes throughout the office, transmissions can travel farther and with less power than traditional radio frequency networks. Additional drawbacks to radio networks are the reduced transmission speed and higher setup costs than infrared. Again, this type of wireless network may be best as an adjunct to a wired network or for systems with low transmission needs.

Making good use of a network system includes using routing and shared faxing capabilities.

Now that we've covered the basics (very basic) of networking for small offices, what's next. Well, you want to take good advantage of your networking investment. One way to take advantage of your network system is to set it up for shared faxing and routing capabilities. Even with the abilities of most businesses to transmit information between computers, most businesses still rely upon the ubiquitous fax machine. In a medium-sized office, the amount of information faxed back and forth can be quite inconvenient. Added to the overhead of lost time is the need for someone to route incoming faxes to the correct people. Not only is this inefficient but it lacks security and privacy as well. If your office is large enough to warrant networking, maybe you should give fax administration over to the network. Alcom LanFax is a product that can "read" incoming faxes by various methods and route the fax to the correct person. It may "read" the fax header for a name, allow routing by DTMF and extension dialing as is used with electronic mailboxes or search for an identification string from the incoming fax. If this feature is a virtual necessity for you you may want to look into Direct Inward Dial trunking (DIDT), which may be an available option through your local telephone carrier. In DIDT, the phone company assigns a separate fax number to each person (or department) in your company (for an extra monthly fee, of course), all contained within one trunk line. Of course, when a call is received, its a simple matter for the system to note which number was called and route the fax accordingly. From an administrative perspective, DIDT is an easier and more reliable methods to automatically route incoming faxes.

Workgroup features abound in today's software applications—and they're put there just for your network.

If you've networked your office to share resources and files, don't forget to enhance productivity further by taking advantage of the workgroup features included in many software applications today. Elsewhere in this book I've discussed using the network to maintain and access a common time-keeping and billing program for service-oriented businesses and I've also discussed the ease with which group scheduling can block free time for an entire group of people with minimal effort. But workgroup productivity goes well beyond these simple productivity tips. Most software manufacturers have incorporated routing features and version managers into their software (Lotus 1-2-3 for Windows being a prime example). With these features, a group of people can simultaneously work with a worksheet. Each person can input projections and alter the underlying data and the software will track changes and comments...*all within the same worksheet.* Routing workfiles should do more for office productivity than e-mail since, in theory, the e-mail was about the work files in the first place (not always a safe assumption, I know).

SECTION III

Chapter 8

Your Software Needs

Maybe you need a software upgrade...not a hardware upgrade.

There have been great strides in computer technology in the past few years. These advances in technology have prompted great advances in software capabilities. Or perhaps the reverse is true. Great software demands great technology. In either event, much of the software available today, while certainly working more smoothly on faster machines commanding greater storage and processing capabilities, will also work on many computers bought within the past five years. While much of the marketing hype may be directed to the Pentium or 486 processor , any 386 processor machine is capable of operating the vast array of recent software offering. In fact, the Pentium and 486 processors are direct descendants of that 386 processor that may be sitting in the machine on your desk right now. While the 486 can process and transfer data at a faster rate, it won't produce better output than your 386. The documents will look the same, the spreadsheets will still arrive at the same numbers, and your graphics will print the same (on the same printer, of course).

It is the weakest link in the computer, software, accessories triad that dictates your business limitations (in so far as computers are concerned.) As you can see from the above example, your business may be better off with a 386 machine operating the same software as the 486 machine but outputting its results to a laser printer instead of a dot matrix printer. While the 386 may process the information slower, it is entirely possible for the combination of the 386 machine with a laser printer to produce quicker, more professional output than the 486 machine with a lower-priced printer.

Unless their is a compelling reason to invest in the newer machine, money may be better invested in software applications that will allow more efficient use of the equipment you already own.

In Section II, I said that your equipment should be purchased to meet your software needs. Software applications differ in capabilities and design. Two publishing applications may each be capable of producing brochures however each may provide different options with one application being better suited to designing your intended brochure. The other application may be better suited to designing newsletters or posters. Obviously, your business could make use of the second application but would sacrifice productivity or results in doing so. This is why knowing the focus and capabilities of the application is important to your business.

What's available in software?

When fixing your software needs, be aware that applications are available for (1)word-processing (document preparation), (2)spreadsheets (data analysis and projections), (3)modem and fax communications, (4)desktop publishing (advanced publishing layouts and special project layouts such as advertising copy, brochures, newsletters and artwork), (5)databases (relational or data-specific cross-references to customer, inventory or financial data lists), (6)accounting (financial book-keeping and analysis), (7)business presentations (overhead and projector slide presentations), (8)drawing and graphics (interior layouts, drafting and three dimensional engineering projections) and (9)scheduling (customer contact, calendaring and group scheduling). Some of these applications have overlapping capabilities to some extent however, each application fulfills a particular need.

> In some instances, applications can work together to produce an integrated report containing a combination of text, numbers and graphics. The user can utilize each application's strengths in manipulating its native data (whether text, numbers or graphics) while working within a primary application to produce the final product. This is sometime referred to as "object-oriented" computing.

In addition, as in the above example, some applications within a group will be better suited to your business than others. Although I cannot review all such available applications, in the following chapters I will review some of the applications I have found most helpful in my business.

Why write about "Shareware"?

An alternative to mainstream software applications is shareware software. While you can get virtually anything and everything in software at computer superstores, if you don't like it or it doesn't work on your system or it doesn't have the features you expected, you are usually stuck with it. Moreover, in the back of your mind you may be wondering why the developer can't cut costs on the product by omitting the written manual, fancy packaging and slick advertisements that add to the money taken out of your pocket every time you shop. This feeling is excaberated every time I see a suggested retail price of $295.00 or $395.00 for a word processor, contact manager, database or other application. So I am a big fan of shareware. In other chapters throughout this book I touch upon the concept of shareware when discussing various applications, so let me give you an introduction to the shareware concept.

What is "Shareware" and how does it work?

Shareware software is a software sales and distribution concept. It differs from freeware (also called "public domain" software) in that shareware is temporarily licensed for a trial period while freeware is provided free of charge to the public.

> While freeware may be provided free of charge, the software rights usually remain with the software developer while the public is granted a free license to use the software. Such licenses may be conditioned upon personal use rather than commercial use and usually provide that the software is not to be altered in any manner as a condition of the free license. Some companies offer products as freeware while marketing the same product with added features and conveniences, as a commercial product.

Shareware software is licensed to a person for a temporary period (usually 20-30 days) for testing and compatibility. Most such software is completely functional and is not handicapped in any way however, registration reminders will appear at times to remind the person to register the software if the software continues to be used after the trial period. If the person finds the software useful, a registration fee is paid to the software developer by check or credit card and a "key" or code is provided to disable the registration screens (also known as "nag" screens for their propensity to nag the person into registering the software). Registration of the software may also provide the registrant with a written instruction manual, disks with updated versions of the software and update notices from the developer. The registrant is usually entitled to upgrades of the product at reduced cost as the upgrades are released. Such shareware is generally very inexpensive and offers substantial savings over comparable commercial products.

In fact, shareware is so good in many instances, that it develops a strong following and may even be offered through retail channels at some point.

The great advantage to this product is the ability to review the software's features and interface. When possible, I highly recommend reviewing shareware products before investing money in retail products. Of course, this advice must be tempered with the type of application being reviewed. At this time, I know of no shareware word processor, spreadsheet or other mainstream application that compares to the retail offerings. Generally, I look to shareware for utilities and secondary application needs such as PIMs, time and billing software and drafting or graphics applications. In this chapter, I will discuss some of the better shareware products I have had the pleasure to review. Be aware however that shareware offerings are always being upgraded and new products are reaching the market every day. If I fail to mention a product, that should not be construed as a slight to the product or its author. Throughout these chapters I will discuss some shareware software that you may find helpful as supporting software for your business.

When I talk of avoiding acquisition costs I do not mean avoiding registration fees for the continued use of the software. These registration fees are more than reasonable in my opinion and serve as an incentive for additional development. Unlike large companies such as Microsoft or Lotus, if you like a shareware product but feel it should include additional features or operate in a different manner, you can contact the software's actual developer/author and communicate your critiques. Most such developers will collect the bulk of such requests and incorporate the features into the next version. Very nice.

Shareware applications also include creative and non-business applications.

In addition to a wide variety of shareware products that compete with the store-bought software for your dollar there are also shareware products for those needing more specialized needs. Particularized financial calculations and investment trackers, specialized database programs for cataloguing or tracking any number of products, group scheduling, charting, drawing, forms generation, mailing lists and zip code tables. Shareware is a fantastic way of building a collection of print fonts or clip-art images if you use these in your business. Shareware is also available for mainstream applications such as word processing, spreadsheets, databases, accounting and graphics presentation tools. In some instances, these applications may meet your individual or small business needs at a reasonable cost compared to the retail offerings from software giants like Lotus and Microsoft. The question is... how do you find this stuff?

How do I get "shareware" software? Try mail-order or your modem.

There are three methods of acquiring the shareware applications for testing. Mail-order catalogs or local shareware displays are one method. Perhaps the most convenient way to compare offerings and be assured of receiving the most recent version is to review shareware catalogs by mail. The companies that sell shareware in this manner make their money by charging the consumer a fixed price per disk for distribution and overhead costs. If the consumer likes the shareware, registration fees are paid directly to the developer with no discount for the initial acquisition costs.

What does mail order "shareware" cost, what does it buy and why would I want to use mail order if I can download the files for free?

Most companies will charge an average of $4.00-$5.00 per disk with 3.5" disks sometimes requiring a premium of $.50 for their higher cost. The catalogs are chock full of shareware selections and most companies will provide "value packs" of related utilities, games or fonts on a single disk. Besides the convenience of catalog shopping, one advantage to mail-order is the support most such companies provide to consumers. Although the company will not tell you how to use the software, it will be available to help with installation, a big plus for people new to shareware. A newer service offered by some office supply houses, bookstores, computer stores and chain stores such as Sears and KMart is shareware display racks. While the selection is not as great as mail-order, the shareware is immediately available for use. One capable mail-order company is Reasonable Solutions. It offers a full-line color catalog and regularly updates the catalog with new and upgraded offerings. Reasonable Solutions can be reached at (800) 876-3475.

Bulletin Board Services (BBS) are a great source of shareware.

A second method of acquiring shareware is through an on-line service, also known as electronic bulletin boards or BBS. These services are accessed by using a modem and transferring the shareware files to your computer over the telephone line.

This is called "downloading" files. When you send a file to the other computer over the telephone line, it is called "uploading" files.

Why pay the access fees for a BBS rather than use a mail-order catalog? Great selection and immediate delivery, that's why.

The shareware that can be transferred from these services is the same shareware you may purchase through catalogs or display racks. There is no difference in the actual software. Most such services however, require membership to access and transfer files and all these services charge the consumer for connect time, the time the consumer spends searching for and transferring the files. While a high speed modem will reduce the connect time, all such services compensate for this by charging higher hourly rates for faster transfer speeds. Unless the consumer is careful, connect charges, usually charged to a credit card, can be surprising when the bill finally arrives. Why use such service then? If you have the time and inclination, such services provide more software applications and utilities than one person could ever use in a lifetime. The selection is without comparison to even a computer superstore and all the software is available on a trial basis. Games, pictures, hobby software, video clips, and everything else from personal to business needs can be found on these bulletin board systems. The services provide separate libraries for sorted searches and further provide the ability to search for software by name or description. Additionally, some services provide members with quarterly newsletters containing updates on new or promising software products available for immediate transfer. Presently, most regions have such subscriber services in addition to the few major national services. CompuServe (800-848-8199) is presently one of the largest nationally available computer services offering a vast selection of shareware in addition to full information and news services. America On-line is another such service (800-827-6363). Prodigy, another national computer network provides shareware access through Ziffnet (800-848-8199), a subservice of CompuServe operated by Ziff-Davis Publishing Company, publishers of PC Magazine and PC Computing among other computer publications. If perusing electronic bulletin board services for shareware appeals to you, consider my third alternative for acquiring shareware.

Private and local Bulletin Boards are a great source of shareware without hourly access charges.

Throughout the United States, there are thousands of available local area bulletin board services. These services are provided by people whose hobby is computers and telecommunications. These people set up computer systems and anywhere from one to ten phone lines or more (usually averaging about 2 or 3 lines) and operate local electronic bulletin boards directly from their homes. These boards are available to all people at various membership or guest rates and provide fantastic services at very reasonable rates. They are to the commercial BBS's what shareware is to retail software.

How do I sign up on a local BBS and what's the charge?

When a person first calls one of these boards, a short questionnaire will register the person and a chosen password for future access. At that point, the person has no obligation to remain with the board and is not charged for their time on the board. Most such boards provide guest privileges to new callers so the caller can peruse the board and determine if it meets their expectations. Guest privileges are usually limited to public lines (versus private lines, more on this later), a time limit of 20 minutes to 1 hour and a limit on the size of files that can be transferred (downloaded). These guest privileges will usually be offered to all persons for an unlimited period of time although some boards may limit such memberships to 30 days. If a person desires to join a board, a small membership fee (usually ranging from $10.00 to $50.00 per year) is paid to the board operator. The advantages of joining a board as a paying member include access to private lines (phone numbers reserved for paying members only), unlimited connect time per session and sometimes no limit to the number of files and size of files that can be transferred. Some boards will limit the number of files subject to their "download/upload ratio" but such limits will be more generous than those limits placed upon board guests. What is a "download/upload ratio", you say? A "download/upload ratio" is the manner in which each board encourages contribution of shareware or freeware software from the guests and members for the privilege of having access to the board's other shareware and freeware products. A download/upload ratio of 10:1 means that the guest or member can download 10 shareware files to his computer for evaluation for every 1 shareware file he transfers to the board's computer. In this way, each board has a constant influx of new and updated software to encourage participation and membership by more people.

> Without this encouragement, it is possible that people would download shareware products and never contribute to the board's offerings. Consequently, the board's selection would become stale and some people would have no incentive to join or participate in board events.

If you are wondering how you can contribute shareware without first buying it through mail order or commercial means, don't worry. Most areas have more than one local BBS operator and each board will probably have files not available on the other. In my experience, it is a simple and natural occurrence to acquire shareware from one local BBS that one or more other bulletin boards do not carry.

The upload must meet certain standards. First, no uploads of commercial or retail software are allowed. Second, the uploaded file (shareware) must be a new offering to the board. Third, files are checked for computer viruses before being accessible to other bulletin members and the uploaded file must not contain a virus.

Local BBS's cost considerably less than retail BBS services...so you can afford to join more than one.

Joining such boards has some great advantages over the larger commercial services or even mail-order catalogs. Very few such boards charge connect time or hourly charges and the annual membership fees are nominal for the services that are provided. Additionally, most such boards will allow a person with a slight but not overwhelming interest or time commitment to remain as a guest of the board with limited time and file access. Some such boards also provide a selection of shareware or freeware as great as the commercial services or mail-order catalogs but without the transfer charges or delayed receipt for mail order products. These boards also offer opportunities to engage in on-line discussions in a wide range of subject matters and to participate in on-line games and activities, just like the larger commercial boards, but again without charge time.

If your area has a great selection of local BBS's, how do you decide which one or two to join. First, this is the purpose of guest privileges. Second, be aware that each board will have unique characteristics and emphasize certain types of activities. Some boards have a poor selection of shareware files but have great on-line communications and chat lines. Other boards will have a great shareware selection in one or more areas but not in others. If you want Windows shareware, one board may be better suited to your needs. If your needs tend towards graphics shareware, OS/2 shareware or even X-rated shareware, then other boards may be more suitable.

Finally, since most regions have a number of these boards, the selection of activities and shareware is potentially greater than relying on a single source of information. The regional nature of the boards also means that subject matters, advertisements or on-line person-to-person contacts can cover local interests and lead to in-person contacts. If you have the time and interest in pursuing this means of on-line communication or product evaluation, the next question is...where do you find these boards?

How do I find out about BBS's in my area? Try your local computer store.

Most board operators in an area will know of each other and it is not unusual for an area computer club to have been initiated or populated by a portion of the area's BBS operators. Some local computer stores will sponsor such clubs or employees will be members. Finding your first local bulletin board is as simple as calling these stores for such information. An alternative is to pick up a copy of the *Computer Shopper*. *Computer Shopper* is an over-sized, softbound computer publication sold at some, although not all, bookstores and computer superstores. It mainly caters to mail order shoppers and is 80-90% advertisements. The remaining 10-20% consists of computer and software reviews and a news section devoted to on-line services and bulletin boards. Over the course of two months, *Computer Shopper* publishes a list of bulletin boards categorized by state. The first month is devoted to states from A to M and the second month finishes the list. On the third month, the A-M list is updated and republished. This list is, by no means, a complete list but it is a beginning. Once you have found one board, it is likely that information on additional boards will be available on-line. Most local board operators provide a listing of other local boards and their numbers when a caller is terminating their connection. This courtesy is all part of the community cooperation between local BBS operators. Find one and you will probably find all of them.

Of the three methods to acquire shareware listed above, I obviously favor the local BBS. This method isn't for everyone, however. If you don't have a modem or don't feel comfortable using a modem, then mail-order catalogs are for you. Additionally, acquiring shareware by using on-line services, local or commercial, requires a commitment of time to search the board(s) for the shareware selections you want.

> Although the process of calling a BBS, searching through its files for a particular shareware product by name or description, downloading the file and terminating the connection can be automated, this process is beyond the scope of this book.

You must be willing to commit a telephone line to your computer for the time it is on-line with a BBS, including the time it takes to transfer files. The cost of this time and resource commitment may be beyond the reasonable cost and convenience of acquiring such products by catalog. Finally, if you do choose to search the BBS circuit for your shareware selections, be aware this process can be both frustrating and addictive. Its frustrating to find busy telephone lines or being unable to find a shareware product praised in a computer magazine or publication on a local BBS. Similarly, once you see the tremendous selection of shareware available on some boards, you may become addicted to collecting and trading shareware. Enjoy your searches but consider these caveats.

Chapter 9

Word-Processing Software

Word processors can do more than print text.

Today's word-processing applications do more than replace your typewriter. Such applications have grown in complexity to the extent that many include the functions of spreadsheets to manipulate numbers in tabular format, desktop publishing applications to produce columnized text and graphics and fax applications to fax documents directly from the computer. Most modern word processors also provide graphing and drawing capabilities. In this manner, charts of numbers can be graphically displayed for financial and sales reports or graphics can be manipulated to produce special effects for use in company-produced newsletters and brochures.

Why a Windows word processor?

The primary purpose of word-processing applications, however, is to communicate using text-based output and most such applications admirably perform this task. Windows-based word processors have received the most attention and development in the past year and for good reason. Despite the increased complexity and wealth of features found in newer word-processing applications, the Windows interface allows users to take advantage of these features with minimal effort and inconvenience. The consistency of the menus and commands offered by the Windows interface is imported into these word-processing applications to provide a familiar working environment. The icon or button bars also provide ready access to many often-used functions precluding the need to pick the command from the menu. Finally, many of these applications include sophisticated macros and macro languages which provide ready access to automated functions.

A macro is a series of instructions contained within a single application command. When the macro is run, the instructions are executed in sequence. Macros are useful to reformat text, produce envelopes or labels from a mailing list or perform any other function that can be programmed using the macro commands available in the application's macro language.

WordPerfect is a popular word processor.

The three "heavy-hitters" for word-processing software are WordPerfect Corporation, Microsoft Corporation and Lotus Corporation. WordPerfect markets WordPerfect for DOS and WordPerfect for Windows. In many businesses, WordPerfect is a word-processing mainstay of the business having graduated from earlier, capable versions of the product. WordPerfect 5.1, the predecessor to WordPerfect 6.0, remained the most popular DOS word processor for many years, regularly selling in the top 10 of all software packages up to the release of Version 6.0. WordPerfect for Windows incorporates the working environment of the DOS version while providing the advantages of a Windows graphical environment for advanced text formatting, graphics capabilities, the ability to utilize Windows multi-tasking and the ability to link with other Windows programs to take advantage of capabilities offered only in dedicated spreadsheet applications or graphics applications.. A chief advantage of the Windows product when upgrading from WordPerfect for DOS is WordPerfect for Window's ability to import and export documents between the DOS and Windows versions without losing text formatting. While other Windows word processors can import WordPerfect files, formatting and text attributes (bold, italic, etc.) are not always imported with 100% accuracy. For a corporation or business with a large stake in a WordPerfect collection of documents and forms, this is a big plus.

Is WordPerfect 6.0 for DOS really that much better than WordPerfect 5.1...and does that mean I don't need a Windows word processor?

WordPerfect for DOS 6.0 was released in the summer of 1993 to replace WordPerfect 5.1 as the pre-eminent DOS word processor. WordPerfect 6.0 however, goes beyond any other DOS word processor by providing integrated functions and a graphical environment usually found only in Windows. See Figure 9-1. While the screen can be set in a "text-page" mode to appear similar to WordPerfect 5.1's DOS screen, WordPerfect 6.0 also can be set in a "graphics-page" mode to appear like a

Windows word processor, complete with customizable button bars and drop-down boxes for text attributes such as fonts and point size.

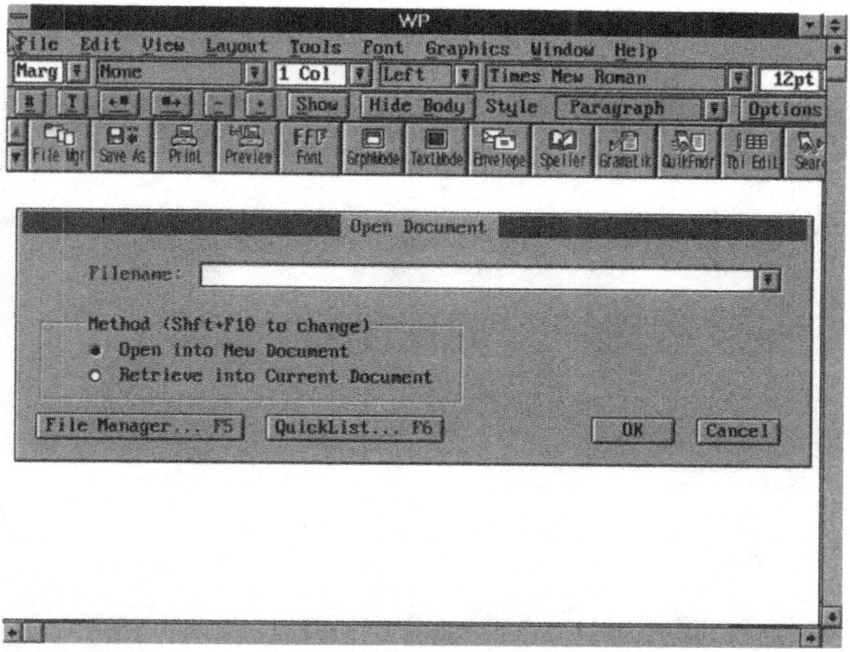

Figure 9-1 Looking a lot like a Windows application, WordPerfect 6.0 for DOS has the features but not the speed to replace WordPerfect 5.1 on your old 286.

Wow!... WordPerfect 6.0 can do all that?

Some of WordPerfect 6.0's newer enhancements include multiple document windows (a la Windows), scaleable fonts (ditto), an integrated file manager, interactive help, envelope customizing, faxing capabilities (with an available fax/modem), e-mail communication (on a network) and spreadsheet capabilities. The spreadsheet capabilities of WordPerfect 6.0 are considered to be one of the most complete built-in offerings of any word processor. The spreadsheet allows not only simple tables and budgets but sophisticated equations for projections and financial scenarios. Although the package does not provide the functionality of a separate spreadsheet program such as Lotus 1-2-3 or Quattro Pro, its capabilities should meet most small business needs.

WordPerfect's File Manager function (Figure 9-2) has received kudos from many industry reviewers for its flexible disk and file management and file search functions. With the File Manager, files can be viewed, sorted and moved from one directory to another without leaving the word processing program. While Microsoft provides some of these capabilities in its FileFind function, WordPerfect's file indexing is much quicker and integrated as part of the normal file access process.

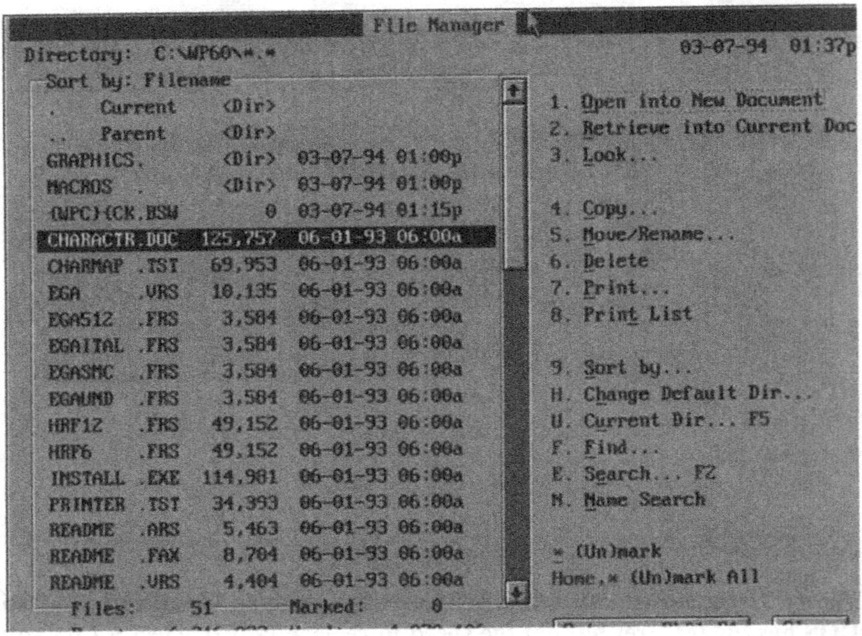

Figure 9-2 WordPerfect's File Manager screen provides so many file management functions that are crucial to effective word processing. WordPerfect led the field in bringing this sort of functionality into the word processing application where it belongs.

WordPerfect 6.0 is a great way to get Windows enhancements on computers that can't operate Windows

The greatest advantage to WordPerfect 6.0 is that millions of 8088 and 286 machines are capable of operating DOS but not capable of operating Windows. With WordPerfect 6.0, millions of people can take advantage of some or all of WordPerfect 6.0's new graphical features to produce documents on par with Windows products. The WYSIWYG preview, scaleable fonts and drag-and-drop editing are productive advantages in outputting a professional report or document. There is one caveat however. Like Windows word processors, WordPerfect 6.0 requires a tremendous amount of hard disk storage (15 MB for a complete installation) and will operate very slowly in its graphical mode on these slower machines. On my 12 MHz 286 machine, WordPerfect 6.0 operates very capably in text mode but slows to a crawl in graphics mode. Still, the machine can run the software and its newer functions provide greater flexibility than earlier versions. I can foresee many users generally typing in "text-mode" and then switching to "graphics-mode" to format their text and produce a final product for printing. In actuality, if they have a 286 computer, they won't have much of a choice. The few times I experimented with WordPerfect 6.0 on 286 and 386 computers, I came away frustrated at its slow speed.

Why should I get WordPerfect for Windows instead of WordPerfect 6.0?

WordPerfect for Windows provides the functionality and appearance of WordPerfect 6.0 with the advantages of a true Windows interface. The button bar and menu items are very similar to the DOS product however the Windows product provides the opportunity for multi-tasking, shared fonts, integration with other Windows programs and the use of embedded data. See Figure 9-3. What do these features mean and why does it matter to you?

Multi-tasking is different from Task-switching

Multi-tasking allows the user to open more than one application and have the processor automatically allocate its time between the two applications. In DOS, rather than keep two applications open at once, most "multi-tasking" shells will temporarily store the non-active program and its data on the hard disk while the user is focusing attention on the second application. When the user switches to the stored application, the second application is inactivated and is placed in temporary storage. In Windows, not only can both applications remain in RAM memory but the application that doesn't have the user's attention can still be doing its job.

This means that one Windows application can be recalculating a spreadsheet, performing a database sort or communicating through the modem, all while the user continues to work in the word processor. Additionally, if the applications are complementary, that is each performs part of one complete job, the programs can be integrated to work together. I often operate my optical scanning application from my word processor to import scanned text directly to the word processor. I can then use the word processor's grammar and spell-checkers to check the document for errors. I also use my fax/modem to fax documents in my word processor directly from my desk. Since both the word processor and fax software are Windows applications, I can fax the document directly from the word processor and then continue to work on a new project...even while the fax software is continuing to send the fax in the background. This would be difficult if not impossible in most DOS programs.

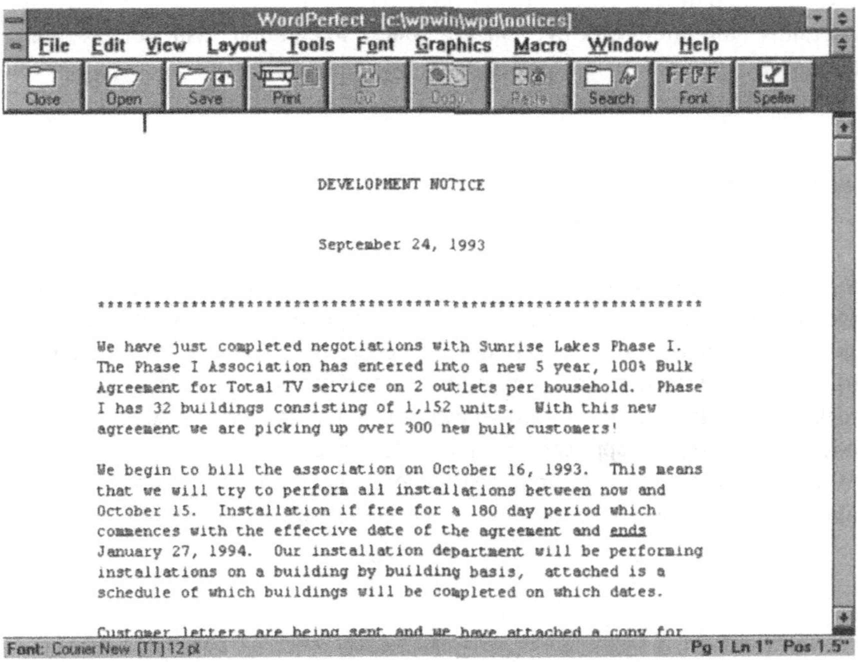

Figure 9-3 WordPerfect for Windows takes advantage of the Windows environment while providing file compatibility with your installed base of WordPerfect files and applications.

While WordPerfect 6.0 provides a fax feature, it requires additional software to be loaded in memory. Keeping this additional software loaded in memory reduces the available memory for all other applications. Furthermore, the document is not off-loaded to the fax program while control is returned to the word processor and user to pursue other tasks. If the document is a long document or is to be sent to many sites, then the user will be on a coffee break while the computer finishes the fax transmission.

Truetype fonts...what's the big deal?

When Microsoft released Windows 3.1, it included a new type of font, Truetype fonts. This was a "big deal" and it still is, for a few reasons. First, prior to Truetype, Adobe type fonts were the industry leader. These fonts were relatively expensive and, due to the expense, most small businesses did not heavily invest in a wide variety of fonts. In effect, Adobe had almost a monopoly on the font market and this monopoly dissuaded the wide distribution of fonts. Second, most font types required that each different typeface characteristic (normal, bold, and italic are three different characteristics) and typeface size (measured in points such as 12 pt. or 18 pt.) be stored separately on the computer. For even a few different typefaces, storing four different typeface characteristics such as normal, bold, italic, and bold italic in sizes from 6 points to 30 points required tremendous storage space. It was impractical for any but dedicated users (such as publishing houses) to collect or otherwise distribute a large selection of fonts. Finally, not all software applications were compatible with all font types and the ability of a printer to print the font type depended upon the software driver supplied by the printer manufacturer.

Scaleable fonts require less hard disk space...a real advantage to small businesses.

Microsoft changed all that. Truetype fonts are scaleable fonts. This means that a single file on the computer contains the information to construct a character 6 points in size or 60 points in size. This reduces the storage needs of the computer and brings most users the ability to store a wide variety of fonts on their computer, even with limited disk space. Microsoft also broke Adobe's monopoly by supplying a good variety of Truetype fonts with Windows 3.1 and other Windows applications. Since then, many manufacturers have marketed Truetype font collections at bargain prices, further reducing the impedance to a wide font collection. Some programs provide fonts not found in Windows 3.1 and so add to the user's collection of available fonts...and this is the "big deal". Truetype fonts are guaranteed to work with and be available in all Windows compatible applications that use text. This means that an investment in fonts for use in your word processor will make those same fonts available to your graphics program or presentation program. Furthermore, since Windows programs all use Windows-compatible print drivers to communicate with the printer, the fonts will be recognized by the printer. While Truetype fonts for DOS are provided by WordPerfect 6.0 and other manufacturers, Truetype fonts are a Windows invention which standardizes the collection of typefaces over all applications and not just the word processor. This is another advantage of the Windows word processor over the DOS version.

Object Linking and Embedding can save you time and effort.

While I've discussed the ability of a Windows word processor to integrate with other applications or work cooperatively with other applications, Windows applications are also capable of progressing beyond mere surface integration. Windows programs can share data and update data between two or more applications. This feature, found in most mainstream Windows programs, and in all the Windows word processors discussed here, is called Object Linking and Embedding or OLE. In fact, OLE is two separate but similar integration processes. Consider, for the moment, your need to produce monthly reports to the supervisor on sales, profit and overhead for each of five different regions. You will use your word processor to prepare the report but it will contain information from spreadsheets and possibly a chart or graph. Object Embedding would allow you to copy that information from the accounting department's spreadsheet and graft the information into your report. This is more than just a simple cut and paste however. The information is "embedded" into the document. This means that, so far as the word processor application is concerned, the information is like an uneditable picture that has been pasted within its borders. The information, however, is editable. If the user desires to edit the information, selecting the information launches the information's native application (the application that first created the information) and allows the user to edit the information. If the changes are saved, the changes are applied to the information contained in the document. This feature allows the user to produce a report using the advanced features of their word processor while "embedding" financial information using the advanced features of their spreadsheet application (or presentation application). In this manner, spreadsheet capabilities and graphing or charting capabilities not available in the word processor are available from within the word processor application while you are working on a document.

While embedding is nice, "Object Linking" goes even further. In Object Linking, if the financial information that has been embedded in your monthly report is changed on the spreadsheet, the information in the report would be automatically updated to reflect these changes. What this means is that monthly reports can be automatically generated by updating the spreadsheet file containing current monthly sales and overhead projections. Each time the report document is loaded in the word processor application, it would be updated to reflect the changes before printing. With some forethought, these capabilities can be used to link or embed video files, sound files, or any other type of information that would be useful in otherwise plain business reports or presentations. Such capabilities also allow one department to make occasional use of high-end applications primarily in use by other departments without necessarily requiring both departments to physically work together. While the presentation department may know how the information should be presented and format the document to embed or link the data in the appropriate manner, the accounting department can prepare the data, charts or graphs for linking. If the information needs to be updated at the last minute, the changes are incorporated in the final product before printing. This type of integration is productive.

OLE has been developed and improved so that very little computer dexterity is necessary to make use of OLE functions. OLE 2 allows objects to actually be dragged from one application to another. This way, you can produce a chart within your spreadsheet and drag the chart into your word processor document. The availability of this "drag and drop embedding" requires that both software applications support OLE 2. Both applications must also support OLE 2 to take advantage of another development, in-document editing. In the first version of OLE, editing an embedded object from another application into your document meant that object editing would require opening the server application's window and editing the object in its native application. OLE 2 fixed this perceptively poor methodology by allowing the server application to replace the menus and icons in the client application with its own tools so that editing could be accomplished "in-place". This serves to preserve the document layout on the display while changes are instituted and is another step in the "object-oriented" development approach sought by the software manufacturers.

Lotus Ami Pro is a powerful Windows word processor.

Lotus Corporation markets Ami Pro for Windows. This Windows word processor incorporates all the advantages of the Windows environment discussed above and goes even further. While the Windows environment provides some standardization between programs such as similar menus, icons, button bars, fonts and integration, some applications implement these features better than other applications. Ami Pro is one of the better applications. In addition to providing sophisticated word processing features, Ami Pro provides a customizable front that makes these features easy to use. Its button bar and icons can be edited or new icons can be created from scratch. The program provides a choice of button bars based upon the type of work being performed and these buttons can be placed in a floating cube rather than affixed to the top of the screen.

Ami Pro is a Windows word processor that takes integration to the edge.

Ami Pro was the first to expand on Microsoft's concept of object linking and embedding by providing "in-document" editing. While Microsoft's OLE originally called up another application to edit embedded data Lotus provided the editing tools as part of the Ami Pro screen. For instance, if you were to embed a drawing in a document you could edit the drawing by selecting it and launching its native application. In some applications this would launch a program such as CorelDraw or Microsoft Draw (or a similar graphics application). Ami Pro however, does not float another application over your word processor and place the drawing in the secondary application for editing. Rather, Ami Pro's button bar and menu tools change into drawing tools to allow you to edit the drawing. This is called "in-place" or "in-context" editing and is the current OLE 2 technology in seamlessly integrating applications.

> This is also called "object-oriented" computing. In "object-oriented" computing, the user is concerned with the document and not with the applications and tools needed to complete the document. In an effective "object-oriented" environment, producing a document containing text, pictures and calculated figures would require working in a single application providing the needed tools to produce the finished product. If capabilities were needed beyond those of the single application, the application would invisibly provide the tools from other applications.

Instead of viewing another application floating over your word processor, you view and work with all the document's contents within the one application.

Oops! I made a mistake...now what do I do? With Ami Pro, that's no problem.

Ami Pro also excels in other features. Perhaps the most important feature available on word processors is the "undo" command. With so many buttons and commands, it is inevitable that, at some time, the wrong button will be selected and your document will be painfully altered. Even if the wrong button is not selected, experimenting with the formatting and styling features of these word processors can produce some professional results...but only if you have confidence that you can retract the changes if the result is not as expected. While all these word processors provide at least one level of "undo", Ami Pro provides four levels of "undo". While seemingly unimportant, in the past I've missed the ability to retract more than the last change when formatting has placed unwanted changes more than one keystroke away. This is a big plus for Ami Pro. Another is speed. Windows products are notoriously slow when compared with DOS products. This is due to the large amount of processing necessary to produce the graphical view of the Windows product. Furthermore, Windows applications must process information for use with the Windows print drivers. The time it takes the application to process the document and return control of the application to the user is of paramount importance to most people. If the document is a long document, this time lag can be frustrating. Ami Pro is noticeably quicker to print documents than some other Windows word processors due to its built-in printing spooler. Ami Pro will process the printing instructions and return control of the application to the user quicker than some other word processors. While Ami Pro processes the actual printing in the background, the user can close the file and move on to other tasks. In most other respects, Ami Pro is on par or exceeds the capabilities of the other processors.

Microsoft Word for Windows gives Ami Pro a "run for its money"

Microsoft's Word for Windows is a very capable word processor. I personally have the most familiarity with this particular product having used it for more than three years. See Figure 9-4. This is the mainstay application on my computer and, with some time and effort, an extremely powerful and versatile tool. Most of what I will discuss about Word is equally applicable to the other Windows word processors.

Word's power and versatility in word processing are, in my opinion, without equal. While Ami Pro may provide better drawing tools integrated with the application and WordPerfect provides better spreadsheet versatility and file indexing functions within the program, Word excels at word processing. Word offers many of the function enhancements provided by Ami Pro such as OLE 2 capabilities (Ami Pro uses OLE 2-like capabilities in integrating its various modules but does not have actual OLE 2 capabilities when embedding non-Lotus objects), background printing, a 100 level undo function, automatic and reversible document formatting with change by change review options, strong mail-merge functionality, automatic spelling correction, good support for large and complex document management and a fantastically easy but powerful macro language. It has limited but capable support for toolbar customizing and makes effective use of the right mouse button to place object oriented commands (such as cut, paste, or format) within easy reach.

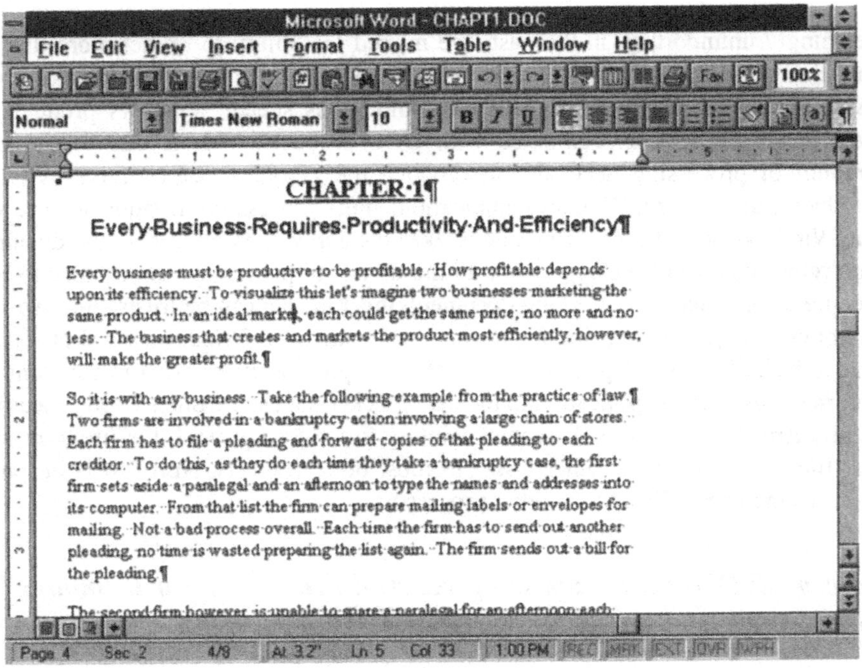

Figure 9-4 Word for Windows provides an incredible amount of power and functionality for drafting everything from simple letters to the very book you're reading now.

What are "Templates" and "Styles"?

Word uses templates which contain individual styles as the basis for new documents. Some of the templates that may be used are a normal style template, a personal letter template, a business letter template, a term paper template, a business proposal template, an overhead or slide template, a dissertation template and others.

Each of these templates contains styles which are appropriate for the templates purpose. See Figure 9-5. Most documents use the normal template which provides one inch margins and uses a 10 point or 12 point Courier typeface. Each paragraph is indented ½ inch on the first line and is single-spaced. Each paragraph, in turn, is separated by a blank line.

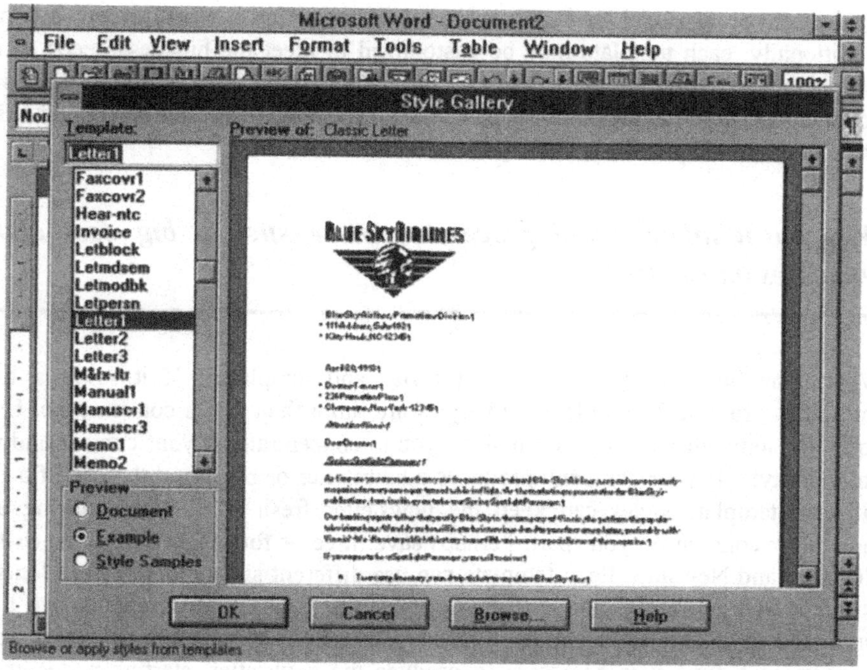

Figure 9-5 The Style Gallery helps you recall which of five different letter templates is most appropriate for your next letter. Even better, you can preview your actual document in different templates by using the Gallery, instantly reformatting correspondence, reports, presentations and memos with just a click of the mouse.

This "normal" template can be configured to your personal preference and the above example is only one example of what the normal template may contain.

The template is a combination of the style or the collection of styles that make the document appear different than others. In this example, the normal template is comprised of one style producing a single-spaced 12 point Courier typeface with a leading indent and one-inch margins. A letter template will differ from the normal template and will provide a place for the date, addressee, salutation and closing, each appropriately indented in the appropriate manner. The addressee may contain its own style while the salutation and closing are each separate styles. The overhead template will provide a title in larger type (one style), perhaps bold and underlined as well (a different style), followed by a bulleted list or numbered items for the business presentation (a third style). Each of these templates guides the user to produce a professional and appropriate document for their intended purpose. Additionally, each template may be customized to meet the business needs of the individual or custom templates can be created for unique presentations, reports or documents. These templates can be saved and new documents can be created based on a choice of templates.

Why do Windows word processors make such a big deal about templates and styles?

What's the big deal, you say, about styles and templates? If it saves a little formatting, so what? Templates and styles are more than just a convenience. Used correctly, templates and styles can allow you to concentrate on your content and not on your style. If your company produces a newsletter or brochure, the use of a few different template styles can keep the newsletter fresh while not requiring any thought or concern on your part. Perhaps save three or four templates as Newsltr1, Newsltr2 and Newsltr3. Each template can use different size type, different fonts, a different column layout and different graphics or logos. The templates are then circulated so that each template is used once every three publications. In this manner, each time it is necessary to produce the newsletter, starting a document based on a different newsletter template produces a product different from the prior publication...all without effort on your part. Finally, templates allow you to maintain consistency when you want to maintain consistency. By using the same template throughout your business, you can maintain consistent appearances even between different departments, employees and projects. Rather than cater to the individualistic whims of the moment, your templates will ensure that each letter leaves your company with a consistent format, salutation, closing, paragraph spacing, and margins.

One example of why you may want to use styles.

Finally, as an extreme example, Word uses styles for chapter headings, document headings and subheading that are appropriate for inclusion in a long report or document such as a thesis or quarterly report. See Figure 9-6. These styles act as internal markers to the application. The application can search through the document to sort the various headings and subheadings based on their style and produce a finished Table of Contents listing the headings and subheadings in the proper format.

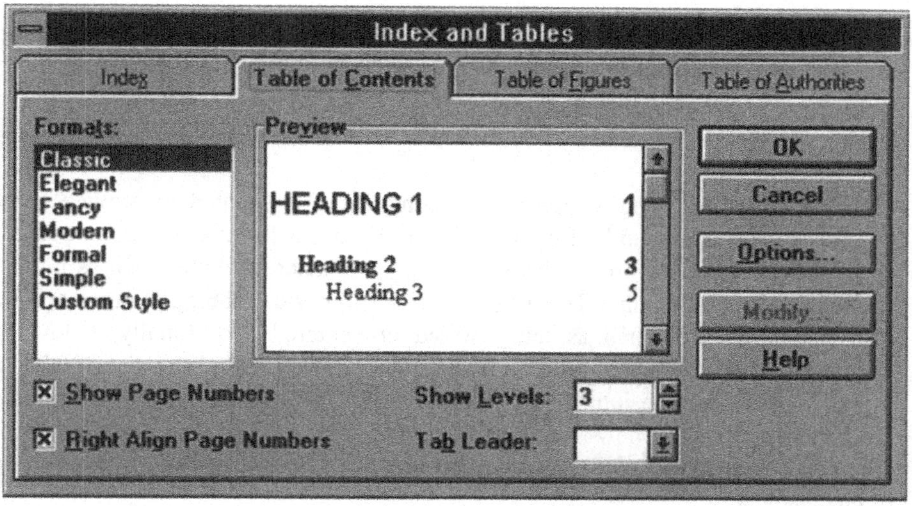

Figure 9-6 Styles are used to automatically format and "mark" text, pictures and tables so that you can worry about content and not worry about indexing or contents. By using styles, you maintain consistency throughout your document. Marking the text for automatic tabulation of tables and indexes also prevents the headache of manually re-indexing when the text is reorganized or page numbers change throughout the drafting stages of your project.

This use of styles is effective and productive. That is the "big deal". Finally, be aware that templates and styles are not documents upon which you place text, displacing text that may already be present. In many offices, this "poor man's template" is used to produce consistently formatted documents. These Windows templates are programmed by the application to format a blank document screen as you input text. The screen is initially clean and the text is invisibly formatted accordingly to the template.

Formatting in Windows word processors is easy.

Word and the other word processors provide simple and straightforward means to reformat single paragraphs or entire documents. These programs provide a list of menu items on the top of the screen. Just below the menu items, a ribbon

Microsoft calls each group of commands set out in a horizontal plane a "ribbon" of related commands. These may be variously called, button bars, icon bars or palettes.

of icons (graphical images representing commands) is situated to provide mouse access to many commands. Below this icon ribbon, a formatting ribbon provides mouse access to styles, fonts, character sizing, character attributes such as bolding, underlining and italicizing. This ribbon may also provide tabbing features and text justification features such as left justified or centered text. Finally, below this formatting ribbon, Word provides a scaled ruler showing the placement of tabs and margins which may be intuitively adjusted by grabbing the tab or margin markers and pulling them to new locations. Each time a change is made from these commands and ribbons, the application updates the screen providing an actual image of the changes.

The power of "selection" in Windows.

The theory behind these Windows word processors is simple... "select and change". Each command is premised upon the theory that the user will first select, in some manner, the text to be formatted or changed, and then the command is invoked to apply the change to the selection. The user may select a single character, a word, a sentence, a paragraph, a section or the entire document.

Documents may be invisibly divided into sections. Sections are commonly used to separate styles within the same document. I use sections to apply different column characteristics to my documents. If the document shall first contain an article set in one column and a second article is to be split into two columns, a section break is placed at the end of the first article and the second article may then be entered and formatted as a two column article.

The user can also select one particular style that is found throughout the document and reformat or change only the text using that style. Once a selection is made, the user can change the text style, or individually change the margins, font, text size, justification, add bold, italics or underlining, reformat the text into table format, a numbered list, a bulleted list, reformat the text into multiple columns or change the location of the text by cutting and pasting or simply "dragging" the text to the desired location.

This is "drag and drop" editing and is a very useful feature for intuitively reformatting the order of text in a document. Moreover, when the text is dropped into its new location, it automatically acquires the paragraph formatting of its new location while retaining any attributes that were applied to its characters. For this reason, it would acquire the margin settings of the new location but would retain its text size and attributes such as bold, italics or underlining.

Tables, lists and columns...never use them, you say? You will in Windows.

Tables are a particularly powerful feature which is maximized by these word processors. With tables, short columns of information can be easily formatted without using tabs. Text can be placed on both the left and right side of the page using a combination of tables and justification features easily accessed from the icon and formatting ribbons. Finally, tables can contain equations or fields which allow information contained in table cells to update other cells. This last function is very similar to a simple spreadsheet function however the table can also contain fields which do not include numbers. With fields, the user can place information about the document, including its revision date, history and author into the table. Custom fields may include any other data the user finds useful and the application can be told to prompt the user for information to be input into fields contained within the tables.

It's the finishing touches that separate the amateurs from the professionals.

Windows word processors also include a great number of integrated and useful features. All three mentioned here include spell-checkers which will provide suggested alternatives and add unidentified words to their dictionary for future reference. These programs also offer grammar checkers that can be configured for strict business or less strict personal styles and an integrated thesaurus for improving the range of vocabulary in your documents. All these word processors provide search and replace functions for finding text. Word also provides search functions based on styles, paragraph characteristics and text characteristics so if you wanted to see only the underlined text in your document, it could find each instance using the search function.

If you don't like the way it works, change it. That's the beauty of Windows word processors.

For those so inclined to "fiddle" with their word processors and to tailor the application to their own needs and desires, the Windows word processors are all very capable. Each includes its own commands and macro language to automate many commands and functions. These applications also include programs to design and build dialog boxes such as that below.

Windows word processors include macros and macro language for automating functions.

Building these boxes to hold items, checklists and options is accomplished intuitively and allows the user to program the word processor to request information for formatting the document, inputting information, and performing multiple function with one command. If you are interested in learning more about the ability of automating tasks with macros, contact the application manufacturer for more information. I know Microsoft provides, free of charge, a manual on WordBasic, the macro language used by Microsoft Word for Windows for all registered users of Word. Included with the manual is a disk containing the macros discussed in the book. If you are just curious about this language, Word has an entire section of "Help" devoted to the WordBasic Programming Language. The definitions and examples that are included in the help screen are those included in the written manual. Finally, if you like the idea of using macros to automate your work and provide functions not provided in the application, purchasing a mainstream word processing application such as the four mentioned in this book will allow you to purchase a great number of macros already prepared for your word processor.

Help...no problem in Windows. "I'll even teach you," says the word processor.

The above discussion highlights only a very few of the capabilities built into the new Windows word processors. The question is...how do you learn about all these features? The applications help you in two ways. First, these applications have tutors which are installed in the computer when you install the application. These tutors provide numbered lessons which start with the basics of manipulating the application, opening and saving files, traveling through the menus, toolbars and ribbons and progress through more advanced lessons such as formatting documents and using tables, columns, and lists. These tutors are a great means of developing a basic familiarity with the application and are well worth the few hours it may take to go through all the lessons.

What's "on-line" help and "context-sensitive" help and which do I want?

Finally, and perhaps most important, each word processor provides on-line help and, in some instances, "context-sensitive" help. "Context-sensitive" help is the ability of the application to open its help screen to information relating to the current task. For instance, if you were to begin setting tabs with the toolbar and did not understand all the listed options, selecting help would invoke a help screen already set to the issue of tab commands. I have found virtually the entire manual is available, with examples, through the help menus. The help screen, located in its own window, has its own search function and history function to locate those topics you can't find or commonly use. Of course, since the help command uses its own window, that means the help menu can be available even while you work in the word processing application by sizing the windows and placing them side by side. This is very useful for very complicated tasks...but the most recent applications have an even better way to help you. The future of help in Windows is "Coaches" or "Wizards". Coaches and Wizards are windows that pop up when you want to invoke a complicated or sophisticated function of the word processor such as embedding or linking a spreadsheet graph or chart to the document. The pop-up screen will guide the user through the steps of the task by showing examples of the task being performed. Alternatively, rather than use examples, the Coach or Wizard may request information from the user, as the information is needed, and apply the information in the correct manner to step by step perform the task. For intimidating functions such as embedding or charting, these tools help the average person utilize the full potential of these powerful applications.

After all that, which one do I get?

While I've discussed all these applications, you may be concerned with getting the "best" of the bunch. My advise is, don't worry about that. Each company is constantly updating their word processor to beat the competition. If one manufacturer includes a feature in their word processor that generates positive press, rest assured the feature will be incorporated in the next version of the competition. Pick a word processing platform and stick with it. If you are unsure of what is best, consider the manufacturer of your other applications. If you are a diehard Lotus 1-2-3 fan, get Ami Pro. If you have Microsoft Excel, consider Microsoft Word for Windows. Although all these programs can communicate to each other, each manufacturer will include macros or add-ins that allow an application to better complement its sister applications.

Chapter 10

Spreadsheet Software

An introduction to spreadsheets–the all-purpose tool of the software industry.

Next to word processing software, spreadsheet software is perhaps the most popular application used in business. Like word processing software, spreadsheets are flexible tools. A spreadsheet application combines analytical, presentation and database components in a single package. The analytical tools vary from the simple summation of rows and columns to the more advanced regression or correlations analysis, scenario management and even spreadsheet revision tracking. The database tools of most spreadsheet applications can manage both their own internally generated database files and pull database information from outside sources (such as dedicated database applications and their files) sort and filter this information and make it available to the spreadsheet's analytical tools. When the numbers have been sufficiently "crunched", the applications can then be called upon to chart the data and provide sufficient formatting control to wrap the figures and charts into a presentable package for "show and tell".

Spreadsheet application upgrades are predominantly a "Windows" thing.

Spreadsheets have become a prime example of the emerging (if not arrived) dominance of Windows-based application development. Even Lotus Corporation has revealed that Lotus 1-2-3 for DOS, its once-flagship product, will not see further, substantial development. Rather, Lotus will concentrate its upgrade efforts in the Windows (and presumably OS/2) market. Lotus isn't the only manufacturer to develop this "sit back" policy with its DOS product and, consequently, most spreadsheet competition and development will be situated in the graphical environments of Windows and OS/2. Accordingly, the focus of this chapter shall also be on Windows spreadsheet applications.

All the major spreadsheets provide many, although not all, of the same features.

When it comes to choosing a spreadsheet application, the choice is less a question of features than compatibility with other major applications and support for specialized tools and features of particular value to your business. All the major spreadsheets (Lotus 1-2-3, Microsoft Excel and Borland Quattro Pro) offer a rich assortment of analytical tools, charting functions and database queries and extracts. All the spreadsheets offer coaches, wizards and other types of context sensitive help features to better enable the end-user to utilize the advanced capabilities of these monster programs. Finally, all offer 3-D functionality to enable data to be reorganized and sorted within the spreadsheet while retaining functional integrity between ranges. Getting features is not the problem with any of these packages. Competition within the spreadsheet industry is not likely to disappear and, like the word-processing market, this competition will keep feature sets and functionality improving over time. Again, like word processors, pick your package and stick with it. If it lacks a feature or innovation found in another product, the next release will pick up on that innovation and "go" it one better.

If your spreadsheet must communicate with other software, purchase accordingly.

Compatibility is one issue you must address when deciding between the three heavy-hitters (and any others you may consider). If your spreadsheet information will come from a dedicated database, consider the ability of the spreadsheet to directly access the information. With new open database connectivity standards, this should not be a problem. *See* Chapter 11 Databases for a discussion of "Open Database Connectivity". If the spreadsheet charts or tabulated data is likely to be exported to documents or incorporated into a slide presentation, chances are that applications from the same manufacturer will make these information exchanges easier. While the workgroup functions of spreadsheet applications have improved by adding e-mail and routing capabilities along with revision tracking, some tracking features can only be implemented when the spreadsheet is routed within a mail application from the same manufacturer. Borland provides the Workgroup Desktop, a mailing/routing system for exchanging entire spreadsheet notebooks or individual pages with co-workers. The system is compatible across numerous mail platforms (MAPI, cc:Mail, MCI, WordPerfect Office, Lotus Notes). Lotus, on the other hand, provides workgroup features of a similar nature. Some of its more advanced features however, primarily rely on Lotus Notes. If I were to consider purchasing Lotus 1-2-3 for Windows for its workgroup capabilities, which are excellent by the way, I would carefully consider the purchase of Lotus Notes for my e-mail network.

Your investment in developing macros from a previous release may dictate your upgrade path.

Specialized feature support and specialized function capability should be another area of consideration when choosing among these packages. When I speak of specialized support I am speaking of the investment you may have made in a DOS spreadsheet and the investment other people make in providing add-in tools for your spreadsheet. If you've been using Lotus 1-2-3 for DOS and you are now looking to upgrade to a Windows spreadsheet, you may wonder whether this is the time to switch loyalties and consider Excel or Quattro Pro for Windows. The answer is both yes and no.

If your calculations heavily depend on customized templates and macros that you've developed for your Lotus spreadsheet, check carefully to see that those macros are supported in your new purchase. While Microsoft advertises Excel as compatible with Lotus macros and commands, Excel will only support macros and functions available through release 2.01 of Lotus 1-2-3 for DOS; quite an old release. If you do rely on a collection of macros for your 1-2-3 spreadsheet, then the logical choice would be to upgrade to Lotus 1-2-3 for Windows, regardless of what other applications may be on your computer. The additional work to regain the automation of those macros is unlikely to equal the small but discernible integration issues that may arise in exchanging information between your spreadsheet and word processing applications. On the other hand, if you don't have an investment in macros or templates that would otherwise be lost, now is the time to make the switch if you are so inclined.

As I've discussed throughout this book, in some instances it's better to let others do the custom design work to make your applications more productive. With mainstream applications, their is a whole universe of customized macros available through on-line services and electronic bulletin boards. Commercial products are also available for the heavy-hitters and the spreadsheet market is one of the more crowded add-in markets. There are many companies that provide add-ins designed to customize your spreadsheet for easier business use and whole catalogs of Excel and 1-2-3 add-ins, some at more reasonable prices than others. Although I don't expect you to shop for add-ins or peruse your BBS for macros before deciding on a spreadsheet, be aware that these mainstream products are more likely to have this third-party support than other spreadsheets.

When considering a spreadsheet purchase today, it's best to consider, not only the traditional spreadsheet uses, but new capabilities as well. In my interviews of spreadsheet users, I was amazed at how many people used their spreadsheets for nothing more than summing columns and rows of business expenses, converting differences to percentages and charting the results on a bar graph or pie chart. ***Even my word processor can do that!*** I kept asking these people...why do they continue to upgrade their spreadsheets when most of the improvements are in enhancements to the spreadsheet's analytical tools collection and better modeling capabilities? The answer, most times, was that these tools were not needed. Let me show you why they were wrong.

What good are "multi-dimensional" spreadsheets?

Multi-dimensional spreadsheet capabilities have been a strong source of competition between the manufacturers...and for good reason. The addition of multi-dimensional capabilities overcomes one of the major shortcomings of the traditional spreadsheet. True multi-dimensionality means more than just grouping related spreadsheets together or cross-referencing the data between spreadsheet pages. Spreadsheets have traditionally relied on placing data on a grid and referencing that data by position. With new modeling tools such as Quattro Pro's Data Modeling Desktop and Microsoft's Pivot Table, once rigid spreadsheet models can now easily be re-arranged dynamically. Data is grouped, not by positional references, but by categories or field headings and calculations are determined, not by positional references, but by relational references between data categories (Profit=Sales-Cost). Drag a category or field heading to a new axis and the data model changes.

A practical example of multi-dimensional modeling.

So why would this be useful to a small business? Let's assume you just opened a bicycle shop. You stock bicycles and you stock accessories and parts. As business progresses, you will probably want to know how your sales vary by inventory product. You may also want to know, for instance, whether inventory sales are primarily parts sales or bicycle sales. Finally, you want to know what your market is so that you can better allocate your advertising dollars. Your traditional spreadsheet would show each product's monthly and total sales in dollars and as a percentage of total sales. See Figure 10-1. This would give you a fair amount of information about whether the bicycles are selling more than the accessories or, if the spreadsheet were detailed enough, which accessories are selling better. If the spreadsheet is properly set up you can even collapse or expand your view of the data using the outline feature of your program to collapse accessory sales to a grand total or monthly total (Figure 10-3) or expand them to show daily sales as in Figure 10-1.

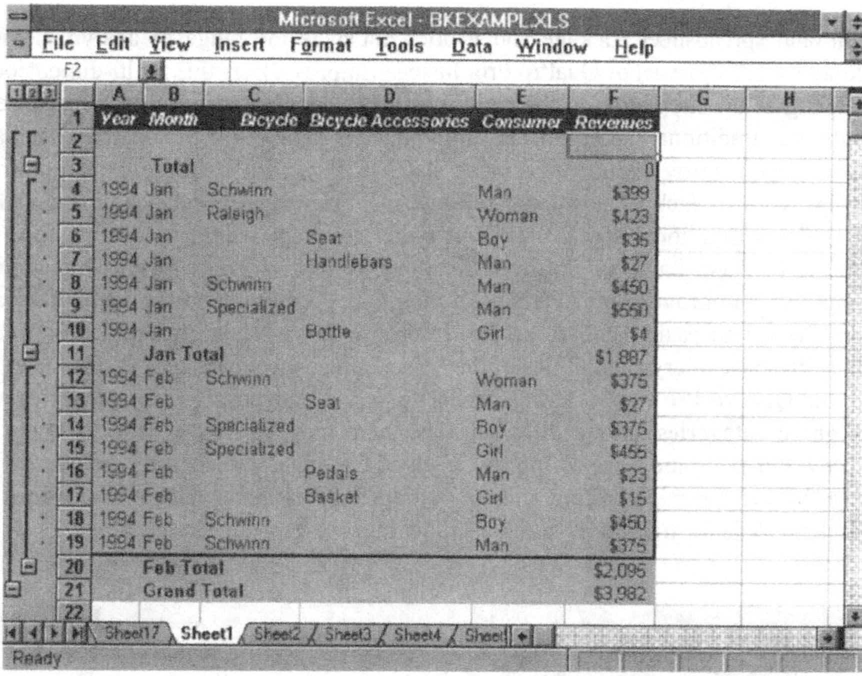

Figure 10-1 Bicycle and bicycle accessories sales are shown, sorted by month. The figure also shows outlining and subtotaling by month with a grand total, all automatically calculated and generated by Excel with a few mouse clicks.

But let's go one step further. Let's add a third dimension...is your market men or women, boys or girls? By adding this dimension (category, field heading...get the picture?) to the spreadsheet, you can now see where your advertising dollars are better spent. If the market category is placed with the inventory categories, a breakdown of inventory sales by market type (man, woman, boy, girl) let's you know if one market is interested in bicycles or accessories. If the market category is aligned with the time category (month, quarter, year), then the data is dynamically transformed and you can gauge the consistency of purchases by market type. See Figure 10-2. If, over time, one market has shown a decline in purchases, perhaps your advertising dollars need to be reallocated to "win" back that market. It's this type of dynamic modeling that makes good use of your computer's power.

What is Lotus Improv and can it replace my spreadsheet?

Interestingly enough, Lotus Corporation took its time including similar features into 1-2-3, preferring instead to offer Lotus Improv for Windows. Improv is not a traditional spreadsheet package and it does not have the range of analytical tools offered by 1-2-3, Excel or Quattro Pro. Instead, Improv offers this multi-dimensional modeling as an alternative to the rigid, position-oriented approach of spreadsheets. While the traditional spreadsheets apply queries and sorts to existing database information, Improv starts with a clean slate. It is its own database constructor. In keeping with its lack of positional referencing, formulas are not positioned within cells, like a traditional spreadsheet, but rather are kept within a separate formula pane. If it offers basic spreadsheet functionality and includes this 3-D modeling capability, is Improv for me? Perhaps, if your data doesn't already reside in database files. Even with basic database access, Improv is not intended to replace the more robust database query capabilities of the newer spreadsheet packages. With Excel, 1-2-3 and Quattro Pro now offering similar tools for transposing data categories and realigning categories among different axis, there may be little reason to invest in Improv. For the same price as Improv, each of the other spreadsheets includes more powerful and flexible charting and formatting features along with a heavy load of analytical tools for traditional number-crunching.

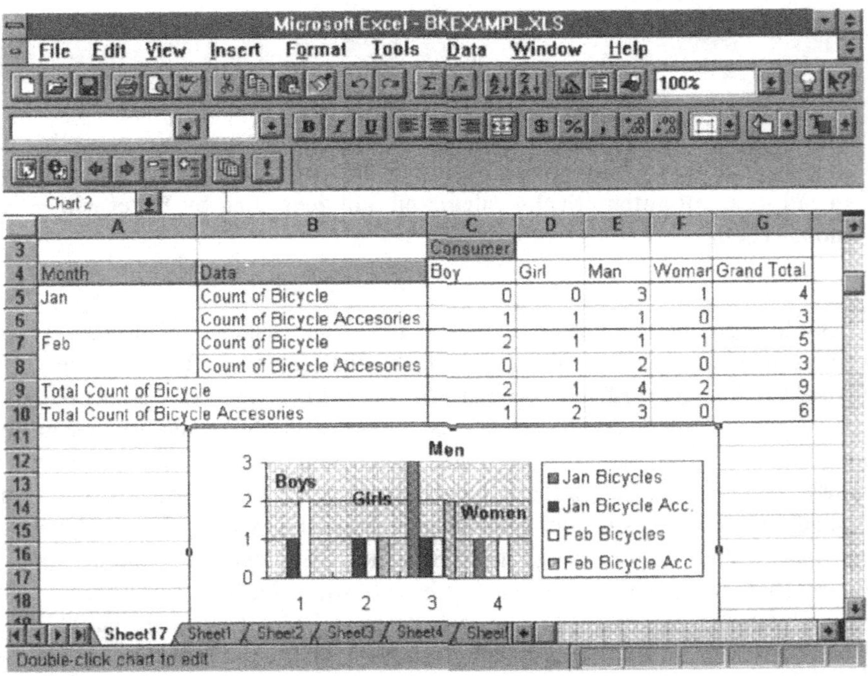

Figure 10-2 Excel's PivotTable feature shows comparisons in market share for bicycles and bicycle accessories by consumer type. With this feature, the month field could be dragged over to the column heading and transform the table to show consistency of purchases by consumer type. The text explains why this may be important to your business.

Microsoft Excel's outlining feature is a good tool I've found is often ignored.

Another very simple but effective feature that sees too little use from what I have found is Excel's outlining feature. With this feature data can be collapsed and expanded at will or rearranged by heading. All too often with large spreadsheets (large being a relative term), you can't see the forest for the trees. Sometimes, its easier to note trends by viewing quarterly sales rather than monthly sales or determine product popularity by regional sales rather than as a product of individual store sales. With outlining, the information, all contained within one worksheet, can be expanded or collapsed as necessary to cull through the totals and sub-totals and display information and reveal trends that would otherwise be lost in a jungle of numbers. Using our Bicycle Shop example above, the spreadsheet has been outlined to provide subtotals by month and a final, grand total. By picking each of the three outline levels on the far left side of the worksheet, we can expand or collapse the spreadsheet figures to our content as in Figure 10-3.

Figure 10-3 Excel's outlining feature provides flexibility and focus. Clicking on the level buttons to the far left of the data will expand or collapse the rows to show daily, monthly or annual figures. Note that the row numbers are not sequential in this example of monthly subtotals.

While this is an extremely simple example, a much larger spreadsheet would greatly benefit from this summary outlining. Furthermore, by sorting the data using Excel's filters, I can create subtotals and outlines, not just by month, but by other categories as well, creating subtotals by consumer categories, for instance, or by product. See Figure 10-4. Consequently, I can quickly summarize the subtotals of bicycles or bicycle accessories or similarly subtotal purchases by men, women, girls and boys.

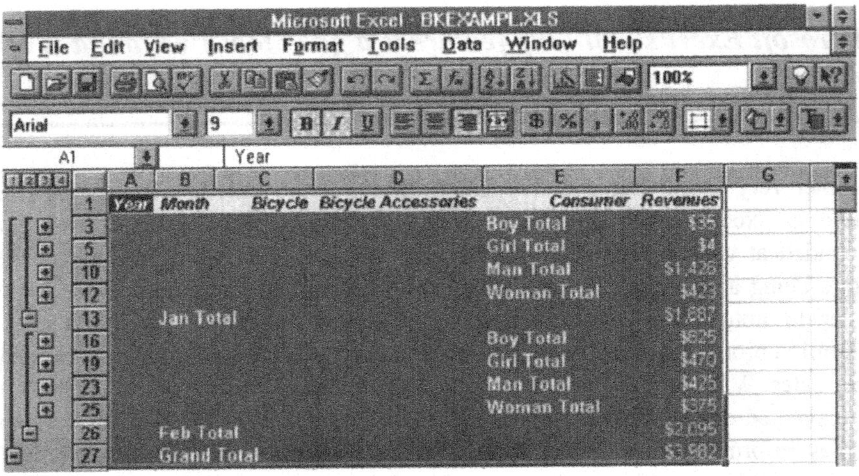

Figure 10-4 A combination of sorting, subtotaling and outlining features in this Excel spreadsheet provide just the facts this business needs to see where their income is being generated.

Lotus 1-2-3 for Windows offers great workgroup support and a unique mapping feature.

Lotus Corporation's 1-2-3 for Windows builds on the excellent reputation of its DOS sibling and provides a comparable range of power and functionality as that found in any other Windows spreadsheet while remaining compatible with existing 1-2-3 for DOS macros, menu and keyboard commands. See Figure 10-5. If you already use the DOS version and have a heavy investment in your collection of macros and templates, you can feel secure that upgrading to the Windows version won't be a traumatic experience or require you to "settle" for less spreadsheet than offered by its competitors.

1-2-3 offers great workgroup functionality, scenario management and query mechanisms for both internal and external databases. Its usability quotient includes a fully and easily customizable toolbar and icon palette (Figure 10-6), in-cell editing to retain focus on the spreadsheet and not on the formula bar traditionally located at the top of the spreadsheet and in-place chart and database manipulation (a la OLE 2).

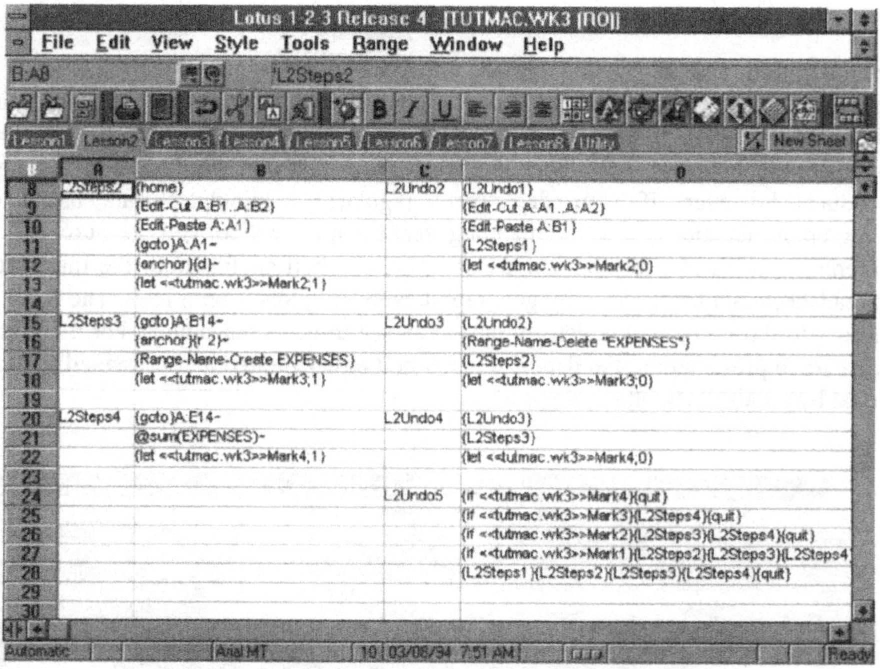

Figure 10-5 Lotus 1-2-3 uses tabs to keep track of the different worksheets in this single workbook file. Combined with Lotus Notes, its workgroup capabilities and backward compatibility with existing 1-2-3 files and macros makes it a great corporate product.

If you often work within a group manipulating spreadsheet data to review alternative scenarios or proposals, the workgroup features of 1-2-3 will make your day. Ranges, their values, formulas and even formatting can be named. Each of these separately named ranges is then identified by date, time and author and comments can be added to remind the workgroup of the range's purpose. Different versions can be moved in and out of the worksheet at will and combinations of these named ranges can be identified as alternative scenarios, effectively providing scenarios within scenarios. With Lotus Notes, 1-2-3 provides these capabilities concurrently to others in the workgroup (video conferencing anyone) automatically flags changes and provides multiple access levels to the worksheet functions.

What doesn't 1-2-3 provide?

Earlier I said that 1-2-3 had a comparable range of power and flexibility but you'll notice I didn't say the same range. This is because, in some respects, Excel and Quattro Pro provide functions not found in 1-2-3. While 1-2-3 uses the notebook metaphor to allow easy tabulation of pages in a worksheet, the function is limited to identification and navigation. 1-2-3 does not provide page rearrangement or grouping as in Quattro Pro or Excel. Lotus also fails to provide the outlining function so useful in Excel and doesn't provide the capability to open multiple, independent windows. 1-2-3 does include features that you won't find in the other products however. If your department regularly manipulates data based on geographic locations, 1-2-3's mapping feature may entice you to purchase it. Operating much like any other type of graph or charting function, the map takes spreadsheet data categorized by geographic area and plots it on a map. The result is similar to those population density maps you see in news magazines. For a national sales force presentation, the data is quickly and easily plotted and presented without equal by either of the other two products.

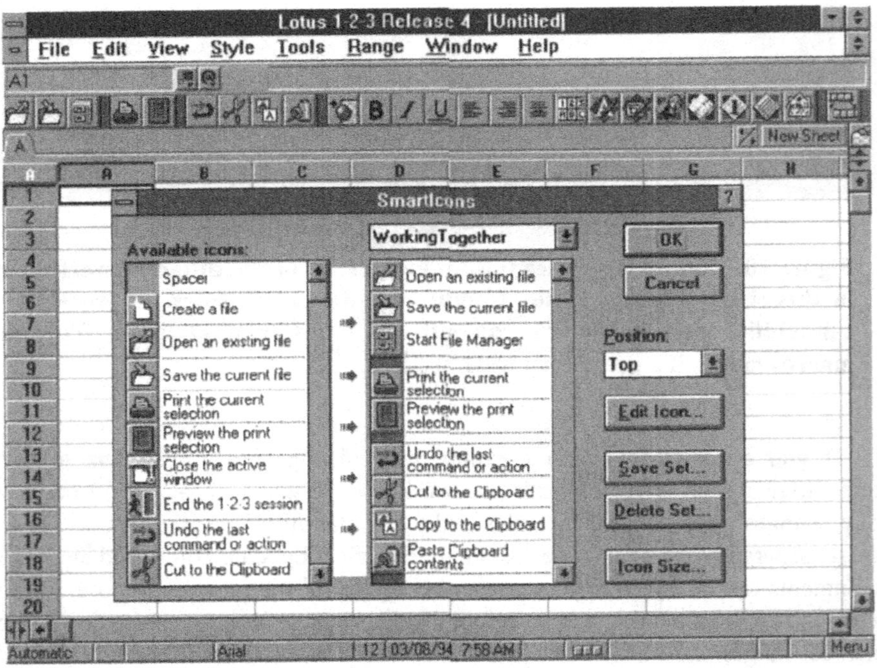

Figure 10-6 Lotus SmartIcons makes it easy to assign menu functions to icon sets that can attach to the top of the screen or "float" over your spreadsheet for easy access.

What does all this feature-listing mean to you? Just that you will have to decide which spreadsheet includes the work features that you find useful. If you constantly share worksheets across your network, then 1-2-3's ability to document authorship is probably a feature worth noting. If you think you will constantly use outlining but you don't need extensive workgroup capabilities, maybe Excel is a better choice. As I review the other spreadsheets, remember that all of these products will have similar analytical capabilities and all have capable database access but it is the few differences in usability designs that will make your spreadsheet choice work for you or not.

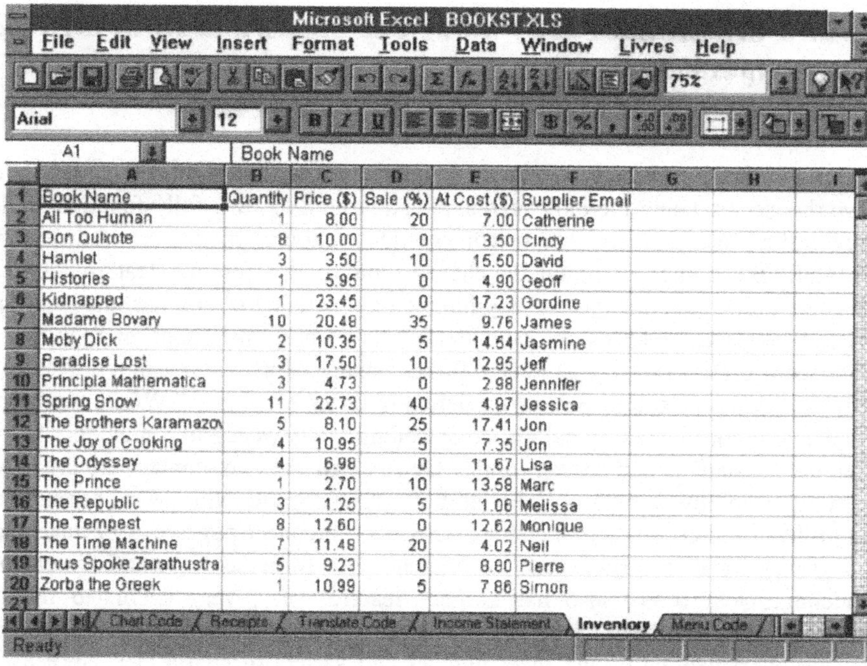

	A	B	C	D	E	F
1	Book Name	Quantity	Price ($)	Sale (%)	At Cost ($)	Supplier Email
2	All Too Human	1	8.00	20	7.00	Catherine
3	Don Quixote	8	10.00	0	3.50	Cindy
4	Hamlet	3	3.50	10	15.50	David
5	Histories	1	5.95	0	4.90	Geoff
6	Kidnapped	1	23.45	0	17.23	Gordine
7	Madame Bovary	10	20.48	35	9.76	James
8	Moby Dick	2	10.35	5	14.54	Jasmine
9	Paradise Lost	3	17.50	10	12.95	Jeff
10	Principia Mathematica	3	4.73	0	2.98	Jennifer
11	Spring Snow	11	22.73	40	4.97	Jessica
12	The Brothers Karamazo	5	8.10	25	17.41	Jon
13	The Joy of Cooking	4	10.95	5	7.35	Jon
14	The Odyssey	4	6.98	0	11.67	Lisa
15	The Prince	1	2.70	10	13.58	Marc
16	The Republic	3	1.25	5	1.06	Melissa
17	The Tempest	8	12.60	0	12.62	Monique
18	The Time Machine	7	11.48	20	4.02	Neil
19	Thus Spoke Zarathustra	5	9.23	0	8.80	Pierre
20	Zorba the Greek	1	10.99	5	7.86	Simon

Figure 10-7 Excel uses labeled tabs to tracks the sheets in a single workbook file and provides enough analytical power and helping hands to satisfy anyone from a novice through a rocket scientist.

Excel provides plenty of power and plenty of help for its advanced features.

Microsoft's Excel is a powerful workhorse designed with the idea that behemoth spreadsheets are no good to people unless they can use the advanced features. For this, Microsoft has provided help...and lots of it. In addition to the wizards and coaches that guide people through charting functions, database queries and the formulation of Pivot Tables for multi-dimensional data modeling, Microsoft pioneered the concept of automatic report formatting and simplified the process of charting data and applying revisions to the charts through the use of drag-and-drop revisions. Excel even keeps track of work patterns and offers its TipWizard at points to suggest how tasks could be better accomplished. Excel provides automatic sum features for totals and sub-totals and is smart enough to provide automatic outlining even for subtotaled columns. Like 1-2-3, Excel offers in-cell editing and provides perhaps the best multi-dimensional modeling tools next to Lotus Improv.

Quattro Pro provides good workgroup support and will even help you chart your data.

Borland's Quattro Pro for Windows stands out in this triad of spreadsheet powerhouses by being the only such application with its own fully functional slide-show utility. This alone may be reason enough to choose Quattro Pro if slide shows are your likely output. If you do choose Quattro Pro for this feature, don't be concerned that you are giving anything else up. Quattro Pro has the analytical strength of its competitors, an excellent built in workgroup manager requiring no other software (as does 1-2-3) to take full advantage of its features and the ability to provide similar multi-dimensional modeling to Improv and Excel. While workgroup changes are not tracked by author, color-coding alerts workgroup members to both altered cell contents and altered results. Quattro Pro does not contain the breadth of charting capabilities found in Excel but makes up for this with considerable flexibility in other areas. Its notebook tabs for worksheet pages can be rearranged and grouped and tab names can be referenced in formulas for multi-dimensional modeling. Quattro Pro also has another feature, very, very useful to budding spreadsheet analysts, that I have yet to see in any other product. If you are like me, you are overwhelmed by the sheer number and variety of charts these spreadsheet programs offer. With everything from pie charts to bar charts to line charts to donut charts (and numerous other options), how do you pick the chart that *best* graphically depicts your data and provides meaningful visual feedback to your audience. This is the purpose of charting but, too often, the pie chart or bar chart wins out over a potentially better alternative. Even among the pie charts and bar charts there are numerous options. Do you pick the vertical bar chart or the horizontal bar chart? Should sales be stacked or not? Quattro Pro provides a Presentation Advisor that reviews your data and suggests the best charting alternative. I've always thought this was a good idea and, if you're new to charting, this feature alone may be worth the price of Quattro Pro.

Chapter 11

Database Software

Database applications help you collect information.

Every business collects information. If its a service business, the information is client information, job or project information, and in-house employee information. If the business is sales-oriented, the information will include all of the above *and* inventory status. All of this information is traditionally kept in database files and accessed by any one of a number of different applications. The accounting and billing departments will use this information to prepare invoices using the billing or accounting software. Marketing will use this information to prepare advertising and marketing materials for existing or potential clients. Human Resources will use employee information to track employment practices and employee productivity.. Finally, inventory status will be tracked by shipping and receiving to ensure an adequate supply of product for pending sales perhaps using a dedicated inventory database application or an accounting application (maybe even a spreadsheet file).

While each department can prepare, manage and maintain its own database files, the efficient use of this information requires that all the information be integrated between departments. By allowing shipping and receiving access to information regarding sales, they can better advise manufacturing of product needs *before* there is a backlog of orders. By providing client information from the sales department to those in marketing, the marketing department's efforts will be targeted appropriately. This is the purpose of the dedicated database application.

Database applications do more than just hold or sort information in tables.

Database applications provide the integration, functionality and flexibility not provided by your word processor or spreadsheet application. While any decent word processor application can prepare a mail-merge using its own database files or external database files saved in universally accepted formats, the power to combine separate database files or reorganize data between separate database sources is probably beyond the capabilities of the application. The same goes for spreadsheet applications and virtually any other application that can make use of database files (such as accounting and inventory applications). The database functions, searches and field definitions are tailored to that application's needs, not your business needs. The dedicated database application, on the other hand, is an open book just waiting to be written. Collecting data from multiple source (parent) files and creating a child file containing the information you need for a specific purpose is a simple and straightforward matter. If you update the information in the child database, your source files are likewise updated without the need to search through the files and update information on a file by file basis.

An everyday use for your dedicated database application.

Why is this important? Let's assume that you've established a number of child databases for your business, each tailored to provide information for a specific purpose. One database provides information on customer sales showing orders by customer, product and salesperson. Updating this one database to reflect a sale of 100 widgets to Carl Customer by Sam Salesperson will similarly update shipping and receiving's inventory database (a parent database), marketing's customer database (a parent database) and Human Resources' employee database files (also a parent database). By using this one product, shipping knows it has 100 less widgets, marketing knows that Carl Customer has recently made a purchase and Human Resources knows that Sam Salesperson is doing his job. Similarly, a database can be created to track unpaid receivables, automatically culling through Accounting's database and Human Resource's database to match unpaid orders with salespersons. The salesperson can then be prompted to follow-up on collection or the task delegated to another department.

By now you can probably tell if a database application would be useful in your business. On the other hand, maybe you're wondering why you can't use your spreadsheet for these functions. It may be possible. I know people that use their spreadsheet program for everything from word processing to maintaining mailing lists to crunching numbers. Spreadsheets however, do have their limitations when it comes to performing database functions. While the new 3-D spreadsheets will allow you to store multiple tables of data within one notebook file, spreadsheets still depend, in most instances, on criteria-range approaches to filtering data. Some spreadsheets, most notably those from the big three, Microsoft, Lotus and Borland, now come with database query "engines" very similar to those within their dedicated database applications. With these more sophisticated database extractors some, although not all, of the functionality of a database may be found in your spreadsheet.

Still, these "query" functions don't allow you to access and modify the tables but just extract data from them. Some other application still has to allow you to maintain, alter and update your database files. The database application provides all these maintenance and extraction tools in one integrated package. Databases applications also excel at easy design of on-screen forms and generating reports depending on linked information from several data files.. Data entry and automatic updating are designed into the database application for easy use. While these functions can be accomplished with the spreadsheet, most spreadsheets won't provide you with the "running start" that database applications do and may require some programming effort on your part to get "up and running".

Up to this point I've mentioned a few terms (and there are a few more) that describe the components and functions of databases. Before we discuss and compare the different database products, let's discuss database designs. For instance, when you are shopping, do you know if you need a "flat-file" database or a "relational" database? Should you be concerned with its programming capabilities? What do "ODBC", "IDAPI" and "SQL" mean? For that matter, what do "Parent Table", "Child Table", "Record", "Keys", "Query" and "Referential Integrity" mean? Finally, how will you know if the database application will meet your needs?

Relational databases should be your only choice.

First of all, any database application you purchase should be "relational". While "flat-file" databases can work with more than one table at a time, they are not designed for this purpose (primarily being designed for work within one table) and would require manual cross-referencing between tables. While a flat-file database would be a good choice for mailing lists, this need is easily met by any word processor or spreadsheet application in today's market. In that case, you don't need the separate database application (although I'm willing to bet, if you are in a retail or manufacturing industry, you will need a database application). "Relational" databases allow you to link multiple tables, as we've discussed, by using common elements called "keys". With the relational database, the updates cross-referencing and report generation that introduced this chapter are easily integrated into your business. Even if your first use for the program only requires one table, I'm confident that you will soon make good use of the relational power of the database application.

Primary keys are the tools which give your database flexibility.

The "keys" are like the column and row headings of your spreadsheet. "Primary keys" are the foundation of your database. Primary keys, such as "account number", "product identification number" or "customer number" are the starting point for the design of your "parent table" These keys uniquely identify one item so that item can be referenced in other tables by reference to its primary key. The primary key should be a fixed value and some database applications provide for automatic and sequential tagging of information with "primary key" numbers. Automatic numbering of orders is a good example of "primary key" tagging. When an order is entered into the system (most likely by using an on-line form designed with the application and contained within the database set), its identification number is a unique number (when compared to other order numbers). This is its primary key. When these keys are referenced in subordinate "child tables" (also called linked tables), they are called "foreign keys". They provide the links between two or more tables. "Records" constitute each row of each table and may contain both primary and foreign keys in any number of combinations. The name, address, phone number and customer identification number (primary key) of each customer in your customer table constitute one record.

Figure 11-1 is a screen shot of Microsoft Query (Query is a mini-database application supplied with Microsoft Excel and operates much like Microsoft Access) which shows several database tables with their field (column) headings contained within each window. The field heading in bold is that table's primary key. The combination of all field headings in each table window represents information to be found in a single record. As you can see, these separate tables also have lines drawn from one to the other. Those lines are graphical representations of the links between tables (also called table relationships). In each case the line runs from the primary key (bold) of one table to the foreign key of the same name in another table.

Referring again to the example at the beginning of this chapter, your database may have two tables, the Salesperson table and the Orders table. Each salesperson at your company would be assigned an identification number. The column containing these identification numbers is the primary key for the Salesperson table. The Orders table would have a column containing salesperson identification numbers (primary keys) for each order in the table. In the Orders table, this column is your foreign key column and serves as the link between the two tables. When you, sitting at your computer, ask your database application to summarize each salesperson's sales for the month (or YTD), the application enters the orders table and connects orders to salespersons by using the foreign key to access the salesperson information contained in the separate salesperson table. Why not just include all this information in one table then? What if you instead want to see the relationship between your receivables and salespeople? Since each table can hold only one primary key, if the Orders table already has order numbers as its primary key, then salespeople could not be "keyed". You couldn't then establish a column in your receivables table containing salespeople "keys". The result would be numerous "flat-file" databases unable to cross-reference information between tables. The functionality and flexibility of your database application would be lost.

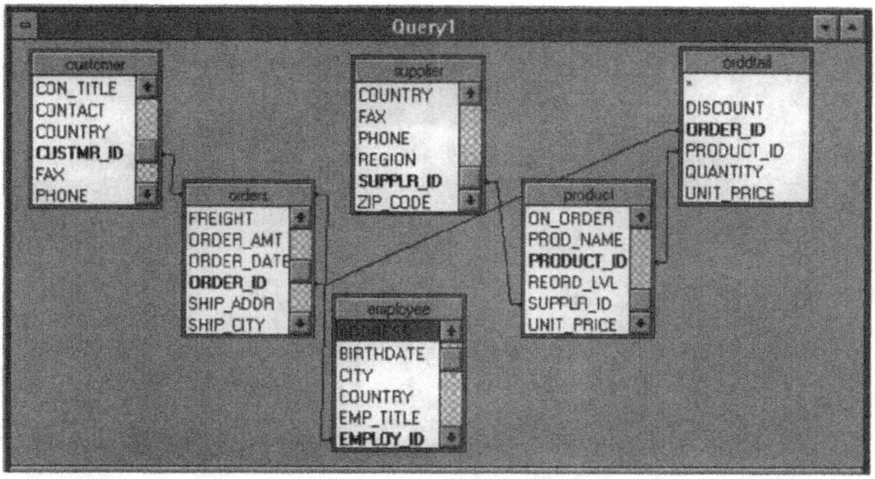

Figure 11-1 A database is comprised of sets of tables, each table containing its own combination of data. The tables are linked to each other by keys. The links are called relationships and are graphically displayed in the application window to aid in understanding and editing complex databases.

What's a "one-to-many" relationship?

From the example its apparent that a single record in one table may be referenced by many records in other tables. In this example, the Orders table will contain many records for each entry in the Salesperson table. This is called a one to many relationship and is the most common type of table relationship encountered in relational databases. One to one relationships may also occur between particular tables in a database set (such as when you have one salesperson for each customer or one shipper for each supplier) but are the exception rather than the rule. If one to one relationships permeate your database set, a review of the database design may be in order. One or two such relationships in a database set may be entirely proper however, since the records of one table may enjoy a one to one relationship with one table (supplier to shipper) but have a one to many relationship with other tables (supplier to product). In Microsoft Access, these table relationships are established and amended via the relationship window. The lines drawn between tables in Figure 11-2 link a primary key of one table with its foreign key in a second (dependent or child) table. The symbols indicate that these relationships are one (record) to many (records).

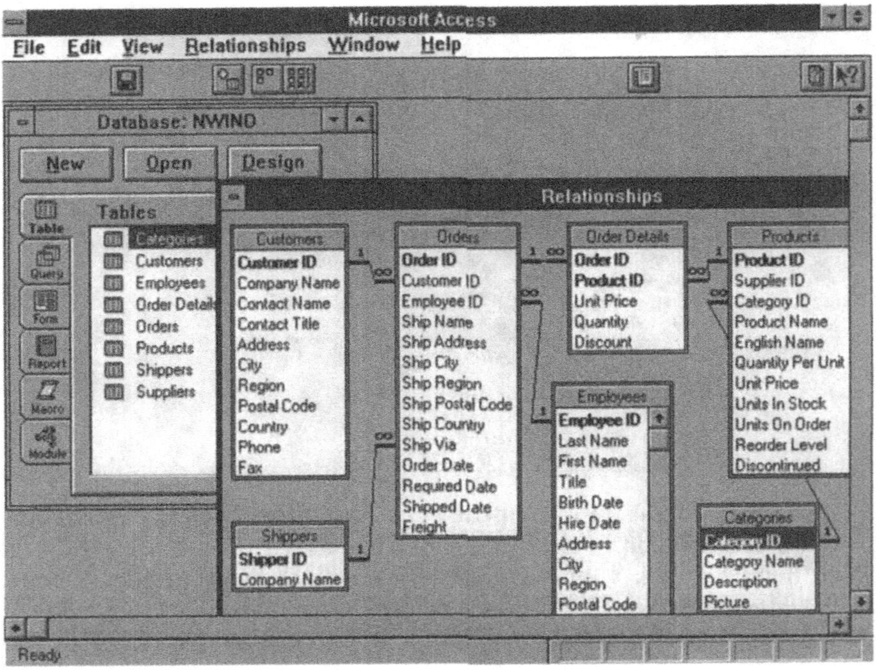

Figure 11-2 Primary keys in bold provide the link between tables which allows a query (or another table) to know where to find data. From the relationship window, its easy to see that the table containing orders matches order numbers to customers by using the Customer ID key, linked to the Customer table, to identify the name and address of the customer .

Using the application's forms feature to input and update information without direct table access.

Once table relationships are set up, the database is then prepared to earn its keep. Using these relationships, the database can accept information, input from on-line forms in the database, and update each database table. A typical business may use an orders form to take customer orders and input the information into the computer. The orders table is updated and, if its a new customer, the customer table may similarly be updated with the new entry.

By using an on-line form integrated with a database enforcing rules of referential integrity, the salesperson knows which information must be gathered to process the order. The computer can confirm the order is complete by enforcing "rules" which would otherwise prevent the order's entry if any pertinent information is omitted. If it is a new customer, the salesman cannot finish the order until all information necessary to update the customer table is obtained (so that a customer ID can be assigned).

What's a "query" and what can I do with it?

These table relationships also provide the power to sort and cull data from many different tables using queries. A query is a request for information that is obtained by combining data from one or more tables in the database. The result is a "temporary" table of data containing all the records meeting the query's criteria. If you want to know how many widgets sold during a period of time by a particular salesperson, you would request the information using the application's query function. The result would appear as a table containing records of only the widget orders for that particular salesperson during that time. Queries may also be used to act upon data contained across multiple tables in the database set. For instance, rather than accessing and manipulating table records directly, a query can instruct the computer to search through all the tables and records in the database and update or delete records.

> While similar to the cascading functions provided as part of an application's enforcement of referential integrity, discussed later in this chapter, the query used to update or delete table records is different in function since it is designed to update or delete information contained within one or more "non-key" fields of your records rather than updating or deleting primary key fields. Consequently, if you wanted to delete a customer from your database, you would invoke the cascading feature of your application since you would be deleting the customer ID field number (primary key) when you deleted that record. In contrast, if you just wanted to update the customer's address wherever it may be throughout your database, then you would invoke the update features through a query and instruct the computer to update the address fields for that customer.

A practical use of queries to update information across the entire database.

One example of the usefulness of this feature may be the need to update product pricing for your business. If pricing will be adjusted by a percentage (3% rise in retail prices, for instance), then your application can perform this function automatically by running a query which instructs the application to adjust all records in every table which includes product prices. If your prices will adjust solely for one product category, baked goods rather than frozen goods, for example, then the query can instruct the application to adjust only those records which contain pricing information for baked goods products.

Once you obtain information through your query, the application's report function may format the data, chart it and generate reports which summarize the information for you. In Figure 11-3, a relational database application (Microsoft Query) has been used to access multiple database files (customer, employee, orders, suppliers, etc.) and from the information, quickly determine which customers have pending orders and when those orders are due, whether the product is on order with the supplier and, if so, identify the supplier and their telephone number. From the query result of Figure 11-3, I know to be worried if it's June 10, 1989 and Foodmongers, Inc.'s order hasn't been shipped. I also know who to call about the product still on order. This is just one example of the everyday use you can gather from your database application.

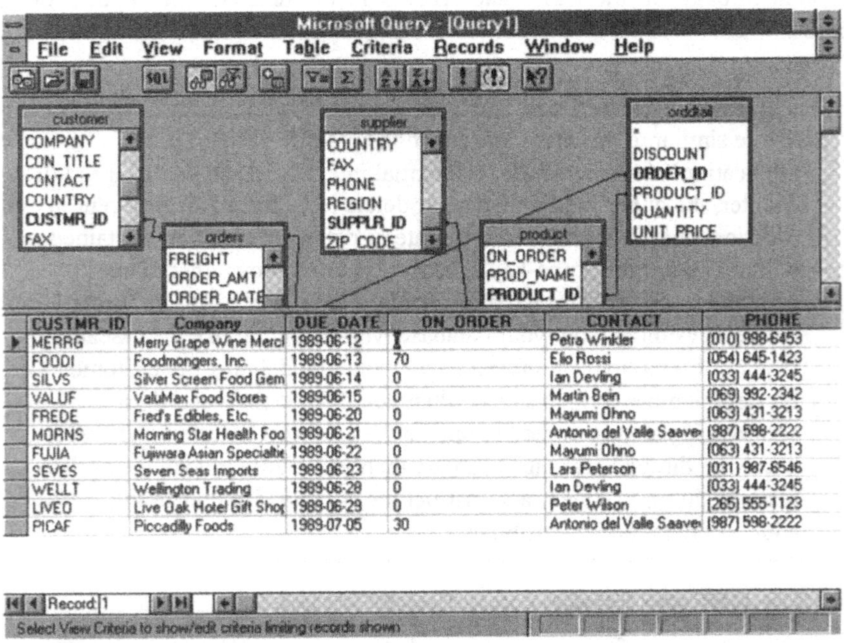

Figure 11-3 Queries extract data from your tables by using filters to collect data from across the entire database. Once the data is collected, it can be charted, exported for mail merges, updated or deleted, depending upon the capabilities of the database application.

Designing your database takes some thought and effort.

There are a few lessons to be learned from the prior examples. Database design, particularly for maximum efficiency, is not necessarily an easy task. First decide what information you want to access and how you want to access it. Orders and salespeople, orders and customers, salespeople and customers, receivables and customers, receivables and salespeople, orders and inventory, inventory and receivables and inventory and customers. From this, you identify the separate subjects. *Each subject belongs in a separate table, each with its own primary key.* In this instance, the primary keys will identify each salesperson, each customer, each product in inventory, each order and, perhaps, each invoice. For each subject, determine what facts are related solely to that subject and then only place those facts within that subject's table. For salespeople, that may include name, address, telephone and departmental information. For customers, name, address and telephone information at the very least. Any information you want that can be calculated or culled from a combination of information sources should not be placed within these tables. This information is available by generating reports and queries (like the above example). For this reason, total sales should not be contained in inventory tables, customer tables or salesperson tables. It is also possible that some tables will contain very little unique data (other than their own primary keys) but will heavily depend upon information accessed through foreign keys. The invoice table, for instance, may only contain its primary key (invoice number) and the invoice date. All the other columns may contain foreign keys such as customer number, salesperson number and product number. Finally, the information contained within each table should be separated into its smallest useful component and each component placed in a separate field (column heading). Names should be separated into first name and last name. Addresses should be separated into address 1, address 2, city, state and zip code. If there is more than one address for a customer, use separate records (rows) to store both addresses.

"Referential Integrity" is an IMPORTANT tool...USE IT !

"Referential integrity" is an often-used term in database descriptions and for good reason. This necessary feature protects you from yourself by protecting the integrity of your information. You want "referential integrity". "Referential integrity" will only allow you to add or delete records from tables if the addition or deletion will not violate the "integrity" of other linked tables. This means that you can't delete a record from your parent table, which may contain a product identification number or other primary key, if that record (key) is still being referenced in any other table. In this way, the application protects you from destroying cross-referenced information at its source. It will also prevent you from adding records to a child table if there is no reference to it at the parent level. This means you can't input a product number or customer number that is not already contained in the appropriate parent (master) table. This avoids "orphan" records, those records containing numbers and information that has no meaning to the database. By protecting links, the database application ensures that, when you generate a report, an "orphan" record (a sale, for instance) does not exist that would render your reports and calculations inaccurate.

Imagine what would happen, for instance, if an employee deleted a customer's name from the customer database table while that customer still owed money or had outstanding orders. Without referential integrity, any orders or accounts receivable tables would contain records for which there existed no customer information. Just try and collect your money then.

Any competent database application, and we'll discuss a few in this chapter, will provide automatic referential integrity as an option. Use it. USE IT! It's there to protect your business. Most competent database applications also recognize that you may have a valid reason or need to amend or delete records that would otherwise violate the referential integrity of the database. Consequently, these applications allow you to define the rules which will govern the referential integrity of your database. By picking those rules which will govern your database, you gain flexibility (perhaps at the cost of security. More on this later.).

Using update functions to maintain your database tables while maintaining referential integrity.

Suppose, for instance, a customer goes out of business. At this point, you may want to either enter information into the database to document the event and keep the customer information otherwise intact, or you may want to just delete that customer from your database. If you delete the customer from your customer table, imagine the pain it would be to similarly open up each linked table (sales, orders, invoices, etc.) to delete the "orphan" records pertaining to that customer. This is where referential integrity takes over. If referential integrity is strictly enforced, the application won't let you delete the customer's record. However, if you elect certain rules which maintain integrity within the database while permitting deletions, the record may then be deleted. Recognizing that the customer has been deleted (along with the customer's primary key-customer ID), the database application then maintains referential integrity by automatically deleting all related records from linked tables within the database. This is called a cascading function. Similarly, you may wish to update primary keys or alter a table's structure in such a way that the primary key's value as a reference tool would otherwise be destroyed. In this instance, you would elect a cascading update function that would protect the database's referential integrity by automatically updating all other linked table records.

As I stated earlier, while these cascading functions certainly may prove helpful in maintaining your company database, your security may be compromised. Strict referential integrity is a great tool for preventing mistaken deletions or changes to table records. By "softening" the rules, you may open the door for a mistaken deletion with disastrous results. If your bookkeeper mistakenly deletes a customer record with the cascade delete function enabled, the shipping department won't know that the customer is still expecting shipments since the orders will also be deleted. A better solution may be to stick with strict referential integrity and, if database maintenance requires cascading deletions or updates, alter the rules at that time, and only during that time, to permit careful maintenance tasks. Most database applications will allow you to alter the rules either globally or by amending the relationships between tables, including the enforcement of referential integrity. It may be more work for the supervisor, but you are better safe than sorry.

Exchanging database files and information across platforms with "ODBC" and "IDAPI".

"ODBC" and "IDAPI" are acronyms for two database standards. The first is "Open Database Connectivity" and it's been spearheaded by Microsoft. The second is "Integrated Database Application Programming" and it's spearheaded by Borland International. These standards are like the conversion filters in word processors that allow one word processor to read another's file. ODBC and IDAPI allow database applications to transparently access and import database files and information. Rather than depending upon a conversion of the database file, however, these standards allow the database application to access multiple database application files and manipulate their data, generating reports which may be based on datafiles created in disparate environments and using many different programming languages. "SQL" stands for "Structured Query Language" and is one such programming language commonly used when database applications involve networked or distributed databases (database files situated in different physical locations). With ODBC or IDAPI compliance, a database application can seamlessly work with all your database files and even share these files with your spreadsheet application. While ODBC appears to have the edge in terms of manufacturer support, either standard will allow work with disparate file structures.

The three heavy hitters, Microsoft, Borland and Lotus all provide Windows and DOS-based database applications. Unlike spreadsheets, feature sets may dictate which package you want or need. While each product will sort and query information, not all the database products automate tasks to the same degree, not all provide sophisticated programming language for added flexibility and customization and not all the packages support features to the same degree. Referential integrity is one feature which is provided in virtually every database application offered today but you may find the availability of integrity functions (such as the cascading functions discussed above) varies from product to product. Finally, the ability of your chosen database application to integrate with your spreadsheet or word processor application may be an important, if not critical, consideration when making your choice.

Lotus Approach can make your design choices for you.

Lotus Corporation's Approach database application is the simplest application of the three popular Windows applications. Approach is non-programmable meaning that it has no scripting capability, relying instead on macros to perform automated functions (this means you lose the "logic" operators and functions generally found in scripting or programming languages). In place of programming capabilities, however, you get a database application that pre-supposes you want to perform many of the more common database functions such as creating forms, reports, letters and labels and then goes about providing templates and guidance to get you started. It supports a wide variety of database file formats, including ODBC and SQL, and referential integrity however Approach include no charting capabilities depending, instead, on other applications (perhaps Lotus or Excel) to provide that function.

Microsoft Access is a solid, safe and powerful application with all the "bells and whistles".

Microsoft markets two database products, FoxPro and Access. Of these two, FoxPro will cater to a very limited segment of the market while Access is the mainstream product you are more likely to want. FoxPro supports the Xbase programming language and provides good development tools for those capable and willing to develop their own database structure. On the down side, FoxPro doesn't provide ODBC support and lacks referential integrity. It's a powerful tool for the database developer and for those interested in cross-platform support (IBM PC to Macintosh or UNIX systems) but lacks the civility most new computer users have come to expect from Windows applications. Access, on the other hand, provides ample hand-holding and sufficient programming power to meet most beginner, intermediate and even advanced user's needs. With Access, virtually any database file is accessible (pun intended) and it supports Xbase, Btrieve and Paradox file formats as well as ODBC and SQL capabilities. It includes referential integrity and its Wizards guide the end-user step-by-step through the process of generating reports and forms.

The Wizard or Assistant feature is perhaps the most important consideration of all, particularly to those that are new to databases or just feel that there is so much more they should be able to do with their database information. Each Windows product has its own combination of wizards, assistants, coaches, and "quick" forms or reports. If you need help in deciding what tables you need to set up for your business, open the table wizard (Figure 11-4).

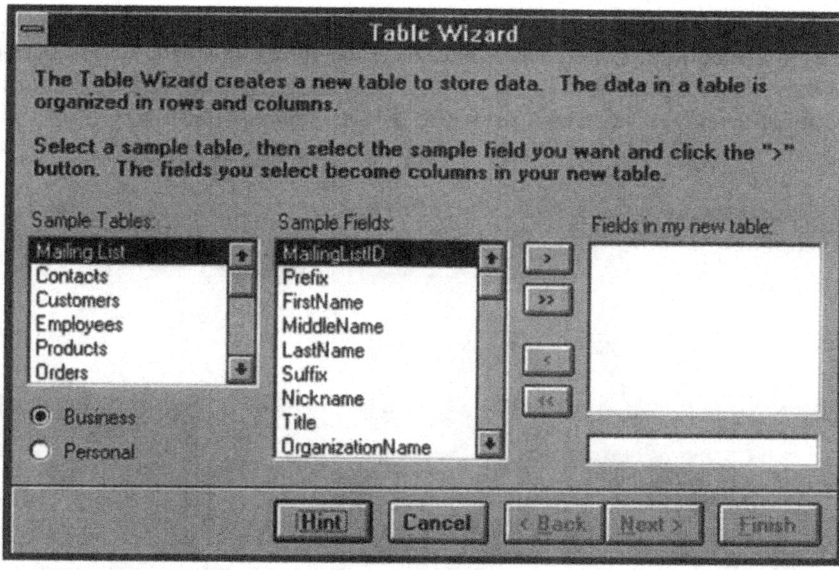

Figure 11-4 Wizards and Assistants help you see the elements of good database design...not always an easy task. By presenting the majority of useful business choices, these applications reduce your development time and help you design your database right the first time.

If you are wondering how queries can be useful, try the query wizard or click on the design button to begin a query design. Either way, the application provides you with guidance and help in combining your database tables to give you back meaningful data. See Figure 11-5.

The same goes for on-line forms and reports. If you want to generate a report or set up a form, either run a wizard to guide you through to a semi-custom product, begin designing the form with on-line help or just click on a button to automatically generate a default form or report (Figure 11-6).

Borland's Paradox provides excellent programming power but lacks ODBC support.

Finally, of the three Windows products, Borland's Paradox (also available in a DOS version) is a true heavy-hitter. Fully programmable, this is one of the more powerful mainstream Windows applications. It has one oversight, lack of support for ODBC;

Borland instead opting to include their own cross-application standard, IDAPI. With Paradox, powerful report and form capabilities are accessed using object-oriented construction techniques. All this means is that each item on the screen is treated as an object which can be manipulated or formatted by accessing its menu using your right mouse button. It also means that designing forms is both easy and extremely flexible. Paradox also handles very large databases and performs searches and queries with aplomb when compared with the less complex Lotus Approach.

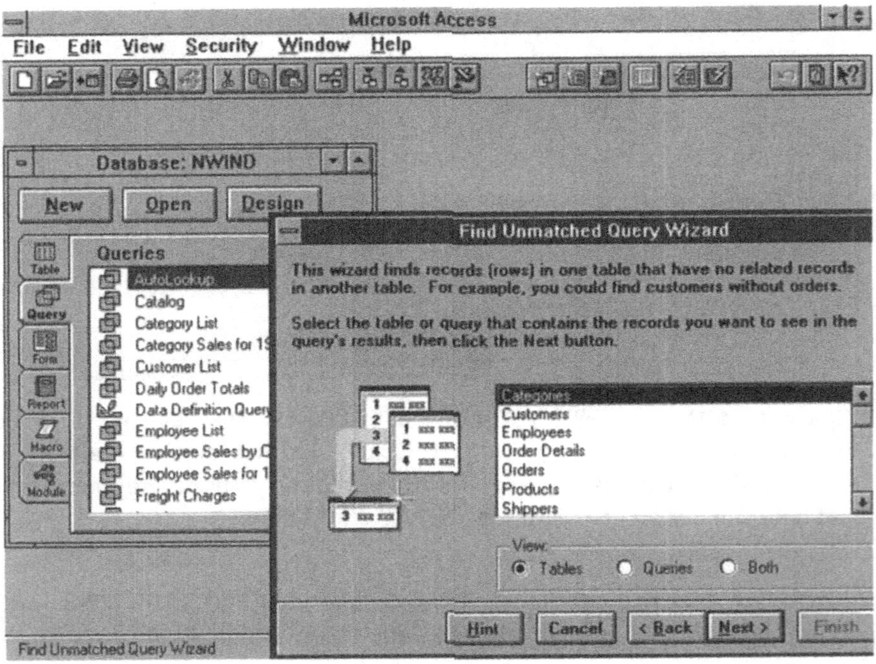

Figure 11-5 Queries are such powerful tools that you may not even know something is possible unless the application shows you. So it shows you.

Alpha IV is a well supported DOS application with good database development tools.

For those of you looking for a powerful DOS relational database application, check out Alpha IV from Alpha Software Corporation. This is one DOS application which has an apparent, continuing commitment from the manufacturer for its continued

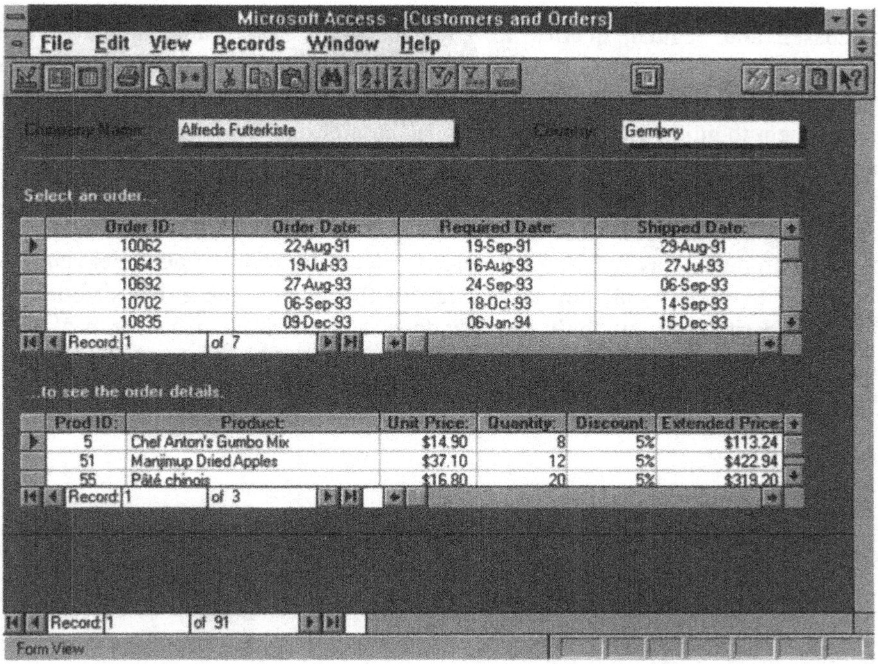

Figure 11-6 On-line forms are a safe path to and from your precious tables. Forms allow people to access and update data in the underlying tables by guiding them through menu choices. Database rules governing form use can require information to be entered in standard formats and prevent an incomplete entry in the system.

development. With Alpha IV, menu-driven and mouse-supported database front ends, reports, and forms are easily created. Referential integrity is maintained between database files and tools such as auto-skip and auto-advance speed up data entry when the application is used to fill in on-screen forms. Alpha IV uses "sets" to link up to 10 database files together for relational referencing. To build on-screen forms and reports for data entry, Alpha IV uses an outline feature, called the Application Editor, which allows the user to establish menu hierarchies and incorporate keystrokes, macros or scripts into the application. The application simulator then allows the user to test the application's development. With much of the functionality of the Windows databases without the graphical overhead, Alpha IV may be a good alternative for those concerned more with on-screen entry and retrieval than printed reports.

Which of these products is right for you is going to depend on how much power and flexibility you want or need. Paradox is extremely powerful and flexible while remaining relatively easy to use but lacks ODBC, an oversight more important if you must access other database sources or you are upgrading from another database application using a file format not supported by IDAPI. For particularly large databases and regular queries to large database sets, Paradox may have a performance edge over the other two Windows products. Microsoft's Access retains much of the power of Paradox while including ODBC and Microsoft's extensive help system to guide users through their database design. Its wizards, autoreport and autoform features may provide you with more database options than you want or need but it maintains database integrity, including referential integrity, while providing powerful referential tool options such as cascading functions. Still, either of these products may not be as simple as you really want or need, leaving Lotus Approach to perform all the basic database functions while still protecting your data's integrity. If you don't run Windows and have no need for a Windows database, Alpha IV is noted for its easy front-end development (on-screen forms) and effective data entry and retrieval.

Chapter 12

Accounting & Finance Software

INTRODUCTION

The focus of this chapter is on small to medium accounting and finance needs.

Accountants are called upon to crunch numbers for their clients and give meaningful feedback to the clients regarding cash flow, receivables and account reconciliation. While there are a number of higher-end software applications designed to meet the particular needs of accounting firms, I'm going to assume that the CEO of Ernst and Young is not reading this book but, rather, someone interested in starting a solo or small accounting practice or needing financial software to manage their own business. Let's start by reviewing the advantages of first the DOS environment and then the Windows environment when considering an accounting package. Then let's review some accounting packages for the DOS and Windows environments. Finally, we'll review some tax software packages that can import the careful accounting you've kept all those months and make tax season a little less hectic.

Do I want a DOS or Windows accounting application?

The advantage of DOS accounting applications is two-fold. First, DOS applications require less processing power, memory or hard disk storage than Windows applications. With the same processing power and memory, the DOS applications will provide "snappier" performance. The second advantage to the current DOS applications is their sophistication level. While some accounts won't require serialized inventory, consolidations and LIFO and FIFO costing, others will. The DOS applications also provide strong multi-user capabilities and may offer greater flexibility in servicing a wider range of commercial accounts.

Alternatively, Windows applications offer their own advantages. One key advantage to Windows is the ability to access multiple nodes of an application and simultaneously display information from diverse program areas. The manipulation of graphic images, if important to your business, is an art in Windows unequaled by any DOS application. Windows applications also provide detailed reports and transaction lists easily retrieved and formatted from either account files or graphic charts. Finally, the learning curve is almost always less steep in Windows applications, primarily due to the combination of tutorials, computer based training modules, on-line and context sensitive help and "wizards" found to varying degrees in Windows applications. If you are new to computers, this may be something to consider before purchasing a sophisticated DOS application with little or no hope of getting up to running speed in time to service your first account.

I realize that, in addition to those wanting to establish their own accounting practice, there are those that will read this chapter for hints on setting up their own internal accounting system. For this reason, I have not limited this chapter's discussion solely to those features of interest to the professional accountant.

Generally Accepted Accounting Principles...do I care?

Accounting applications designed for small businesses take two routes. There are those that adhere to GAAP (Generally Accepted Accounting Principles) and those that don't. Of those that don't, auditing functions and transaction correction are two features that accounting professionals may feel uncomfortable giving up while the small business owner may benefit from the simplified procedures offered by these non-GAAP compliant applications. Accordingly, accountants may want to pay special attention to the Peachtree, Service Industry Accounting, Computer Associates International and Microsoft applications while the QuickBooks application will appeal to small business owners managing their own accounts (particularly those already familiar with Quicken). When comparing products also keep in mind that security features will differ and file compatibility may differ. While security features may not be of great concern to the dedicated accountant, if you will be using these applications to manage your own book-keeping, you may want to limit employee access to account information. Similarly, you may wish to provide multiple levels of access, reserving payroll, transaction reversal and auditing features to yourself while still providing substantial access to your accounting personnel. For this, you need an application that will let you selectively "lock out" staff from particular program modules and functions File compatibility, on the other hand, may be a concern of the dedicated accountant. If you already have an established client base, consider the accounting packages used by those clients when fixing your needs. If you can import your client's financial data without reservation, then you can better serve your client in the least amount of time.

Why not get a personal finance application like Quicken?

What will an accounting application do for the small business owner that a personal finance application can't? Accounting applications can manage inventory, track orders and shipping status, provide receivables information and include the graphics, reports and analysis tools to track these items. Finally, if you operate on an accrual rather than a cash basis, personal finance applications are designed with the individual, cash-basis, taxpayer in mind. While the personal finance packages do provide some reporting functions geared towards business interests, support in some packages is sketchy.

DEDICATED BUSINESS ACCOUNTING SOFTWARE

CA-Simply Accounting for Windows.

Computer Associate's CA-Simply Accounting for Windows is a reasonably priced accounting application from a well known company. CA-Simply Accounting is tailored to those utilizing double-entry accounting practices (such as accountants) and supports both cash and accrual basis accounting. In addition to its double-entry capabilities, Simply Accounting provides an audit trail and capable accounts, ledger, inventory, payroll and project modules. Its short-comings, however, should be closely scrutinized before deciding on this package. Simply Accounting is limited in the number of accounts it can handle (of greatest concern to the dedicated accountant), and has severe limitations in defining such potential variables as sales tax, age periods and accruing finance charges. The payroll module adequately handles post-tax deductions but fails to account for pre-tax deductions (such as those found in a qualifying retirement plan). Finally, posting of entries cannot be automatically reversed or programmed to recur On the plus side, Simply Accounting provides multiple level password protection (as we previously discussed) and file compatibility with its higher-end sibling, AccPac Plus Accounting. Accordingly, if you later upgrade your practice, your information can go with you to Computer Associate's more sophisticated applications. Of all the reviewed applications, it is the least expensive with a clear and capable upgrade path.

Peachtree Accounting for Windows.

Peachtree Accounting for Windows has the ease of use offered by Simply Accounting but includes a host of additional features that make it a better choice for small accounting firms and medium-sized businesses. It provides account, ledger, payroll and inventory modules. It supports an unlimited number of bank accounts and provides flexibility in its account and vendor tracking tools not otherwise found in Simply Accounting. Finally, its analysis tools are easy to implement and give a quick preview of the cash, payable and receivable status of the business. Whether you are a business owner or accountant advising the former, you want an easy way to ferret these status reports from your application and Peachtree gives that to you. For the business owner, Peachtree will provide basic inventory management features but, if you operate from more than one location and want a package that can centrally manage all locations, neither this nor any other package discussed in this chapter is likely to meet your needs.

Microsoft Profit for Windows.

Microsoft, never one to sit on the sidelines, markets Profit for Windows. Like all Microsoft products, Profit places tutors and wizards between you and your data, making every effort to help you avoid accounting errors. For experienced accountants, these features may not be particularly welcome but, to the new business owner, they can be a blessing. Profit first guides you through installation and setup with a series of questions about your business designed to help the application set up proper accounts. Common accounting functions such as reconciliations and budgeting are also aided by wizards and entries are aided by questions designed to help place the data in the correct module. Like its brethren, Profit provides graphs and reports to aid in deciphering the "true" status of your financial accounts using cash flow, receivables, payables and sales summarizations. Are there any drawbacks? Profit supports only 10 bank accounts, perhaps limiting its usefulness to an accounting business, it has no clear upgrade path and does not allow cash basis reporting. Finally, Profit, like all Microsoft products, will eat up a lot of disk space (although, in all fairness, most Windows programs have this drawback).

Sybiz Service Industry Accounting.

Service Industry Accounting, by Sybiz International, is a capable accountant's tool. It can handle an unlimited number of accounts and has all the usual modules such as ledger, accounts, payroll and inventory. It provides an auditing trail, and automatic entry reversing but does not provide the necessary on-line help novices may need to understand the proper use of these accounting features.

Intuit's QuickBooks for Windows.

QuickBooks for Windows is marketed by Intuit and adopts the familiar face of Intuit's personal finance application, Quicken. Since I use Quicken for Windows, I find QuickBook's interface very comforting. While QuickBooks offers enough power for the small business and small accounting practice, it cuts corners on GAAP, making life easier for non-accountants. There is no auditing trail or strict entry reversal feature. Neither will the package provide 1099 forms as Peachtree and Service Industry Accounting applications do (but not Profit or Simply Accounting). Finally, if you need to calculate finance charges, QuickBooks won't make you happy. In most other respects, QuickBooks meets or exceeds the capabilities found in the other packages. If you or your business already depend on Quicken to manage your finances, QuickBooks provides an easy transition to more traditional accounting tools for business, as opposed to personal, financial analysis.

DacEasy Accounting for DOS.

In the DOS arena, DacEasy Accounting, Pacioli 2000 and Peachtree Accounting provide capable choices. DacEasy Accounting provides features well suited to manufacturing businesses or others needing detailed inventory and parts tracking as part of their accounting services. It provides reversed and recurring entry control and takes care of an auditing trail. Finally, DacEasy provides ledger, accounts, billing and cash management, and order and inventory modules. Add-in modules are available to meet growing business needs in the areas of order entry and payroll.

Pacioli 2000 and Peachtree Accounting...two other DOS applications

Pacioli 2000 has many of the features offered by DacEasy, although not all, but excels in one area...price. For the price, it provides all the basic accounting functions necessary to a small business. Peachtree does not offer the low price of Pacioli or even DacEasy but makes up for this with a powerful package more capable at managing medium businesses in its basic configuration than the others. Consolidated financial statements, flexible budgeting, invoicing and costing alternatives and automated data entry make this package a flexible option for small to medium businesses.

FINANCE MANAGEMENT & PERSONAL FINANCE

There is another class of accounting packages, called finance managers or personal finance software. Programs like Quicken for DOS or Windows, Managing Your Money or Kiplinger's Simply Money are targeted at the individual but offer such a wealth of financial services that these programs are equally effective at managing the finances of a small business.

Consider these caveats if you decide on a personal finance package.

There are a few caveats to consider, however, if you will be using these packages for your business. First, your business must use a cash basis accounting method and not the accrual method. Since these packages are designed for individual finance management, they do not provide tools for managing accounts on an accrual method. Second, these packages do not conform to GAAP and do not employ double entry accounting or audit trails. Don't count on payroll deduction capabilities or the ability to print invoices with these packages. With the emphasis on personal finance management, the manufacturers didn't see the necessity of incorporating these features into these packages. Third, these packages do not provide the usual business accounting modules as part of their design. Payroll modules, inventory tracking, accounts receivable and payable, general ledgers, and invoicing modules are not already set up and configured for immediate use. Many, although not all, of these features can be designed into these packages but this takes time, effort and at least a little knowledge about the product before you can be "up and running". As an alternative, you can use categories and class identification (such as customer, client, expense or income) to enable the collection of accounts payable, receivable, payroll or job costs information in pre-defined and customized reports. The few inconveniences, however, may not be an issue for your business or, you may consider these an acceptable offset for the lower cost and greater simplicity of using these packages rather than traditional accounting software.

On the flip side, these finance managers may provide features not included in the prior packages that you or your business can really use. If your business is finance-based; you invest in or provide stock or mutual fund advice to others, these packages provide tracking and reporting features that are not included in the traditional accounting packages. The packages also provide simple budgeting functions for individual accounts or small business needs and provide category features for tracking expenses and tagging transactions for inclusion in your year-end tax return. Simple financial advice is available in various measures from each package and financial calculations (such as loan amortizations and schedules) are available through built-in calculators. These packages try to streamline transaction entries by providing "quickfill" features which anticipate an entry based on your keystrokes and offer to finish the entry or provide a drop-down box containing entries that match your initial keystrokes. Quicken even provides a monthly calendar on which you can drag prior entries (sorted by payee) onto the calendar to begin register entries. This feature could be very useful for recurring, fixed sum payments or receipts. While any of these packages can write checks and maintain separate accounts and balances, their real strength lies in the capability to sort financial activities and help you review trends in account activities that can help your business. While each package has its particular strengths, any one of these would meet the accounting and budgeting needs of a sole proprietorship or small business.

Quicken is the standard in personal finance management.

Intuit's Quicken is a market leader in finance management and it shows no sign of surrendering its well-earned lead in this market. Quicken for DOS and Quicken for Windows both provide many of the same features although Quicken for Windows shows a marked advantage in its graphing capabilities and access to companion programs for pre-defined business accounting functions. I've used both products and prefer the more powerful reporting features of the Windows version. This is what I use in my business.

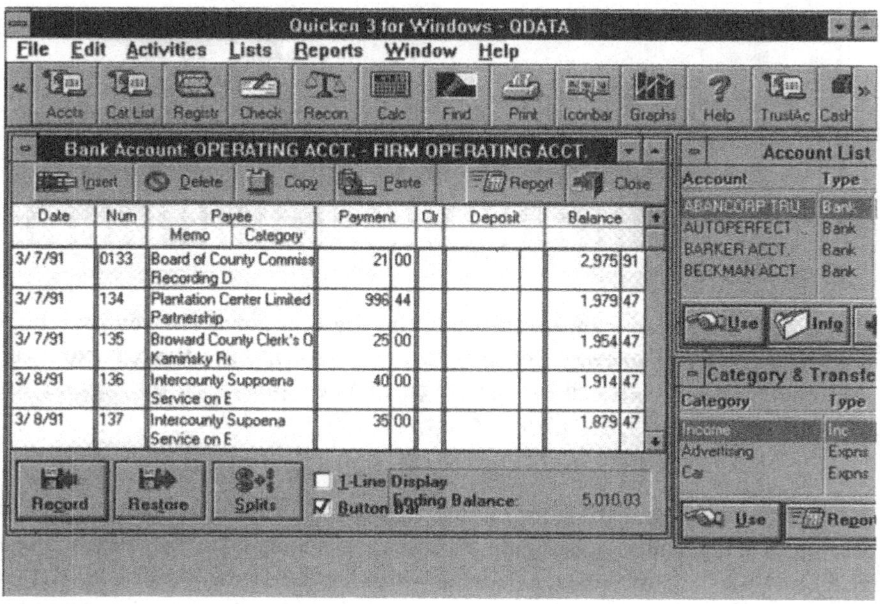

Figure 12-1 Quicken for Windows is not just an electronic checkbook just like a database isn't just an electronic rolodex. Quicken can tabulate and report on income and expenses to let you know where the money is and where it's going.

A wealth of features make finance software as powerful as a team of accountants.

Quicken provides the ubiquitous check register, memorizes recurring transactions, reconciles accounts, provides help in setting up budgets and categories, tracks loans and investments, imports and exports financial data and tax information and provides help all along the way (Figure 12-1). It also provides quick and easy (very important) reporting and break-downs of your financial information. There are a number of pre-defined reports for individual or business use including cash flow, budget, net worth, and period comparison reports. See Figure 12-2.

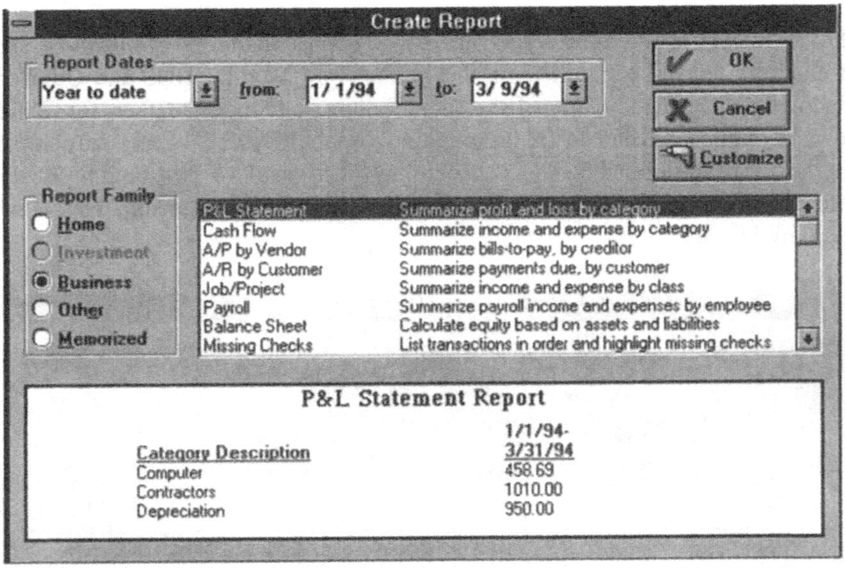

Figure 12-2 Quicken can provide many of the functions that you may have thought were the province of spreadsheet applications. Each report and statement in the standard list can be customized and saved for regular use or you can design a report from scratch. See Figure 12-3.

Pre-defined reports for profit & loss statements, job or project accounts, receivables and payables, payroll and balances are available for your business needs. See Figure 12-2. These reports pull their information from account registers and depend heavily on the proper categorization and class identification of transactions.

In effect, Quicken centralizes the input of information rather than dividing input by module, as in traditional accounting packages, but requires more care in proper identification of each transaction so that meaningful reports can be generated at a later time. When I first started to use Quicken, I didn't give enough thought to categorizing or classifying my transactions and depended more on the search function of the program to pull the information into reports. This was a mistake. By taking the time to define customized categories, I am able to better see where and when income and expenses are generated. Finally, by assigning each category to a line on my tax return, hundreds of transactions are immediately input into my tax software with minimal effort.

Once categories and classifications are assigned, the pre-defined and customizable reporting and graphing features of Quicken will enable periodic review of account income and expenses.

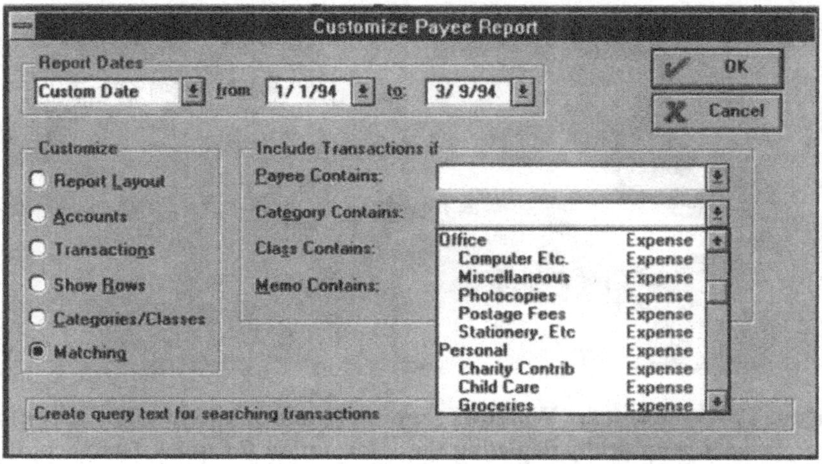

Figure 12-3 Customizing reports by date or by categories lends itself to financial comparisons and allows the same report to be used for different accounts and transactions.

The graphs provide some visual cues and break categories down into percentages to give you immediate feedback on your business finances.

If the income portion of your bar chart is less than the expense portion of the chart, then you know right away you spent more money than you earned for that period. See Figure 12-4. The graphs provide more than generalized information however. If a particular category draws your attention (you can't figure how you spent 18% of that month's expenses on business meals, for instance) clicking on the pie segment for that category will produce a "quickview list" of the data represented by the segment. See Figure 12-5.

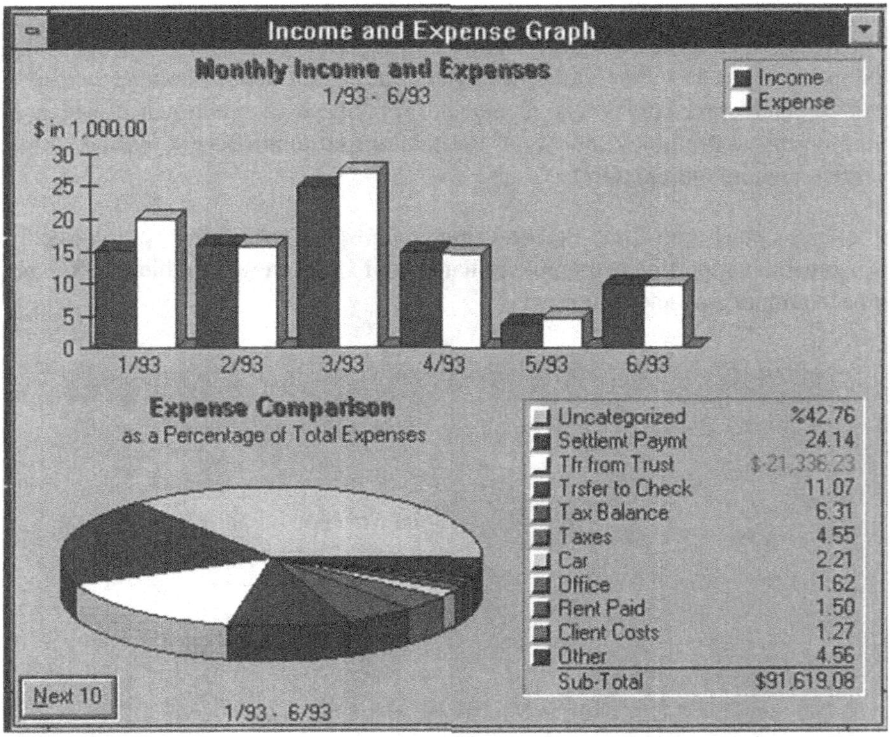

Figure 12-4 Quicken for Windows graphs are one or two mouse clicks away and, besides graphically depicting the information for quick feedback, they provide item-by-item breakdown reports on each category of income or expense just by clicking on that category.

Reports and graphs help you understand your business' financial trends.

The date, amount, payee, memo and category information is all displayed without searching through the account registers for the pertinent information. This feature can also be invoked from the account register to pull up a list of payments to or from a client, customer or vendor. This is one quick and easy way to collect account status information or pull together payments to various and diverse sources by categorized income or expense or related to a particular job or project.

Some features that don't receive as much attention as the graphing and reporting features but are, all the same, necessary to manage your finances are Quicken's ability to link loans to checking accounts while maintaining separate loan registers, allocate principal and interest categories to loan payments and track principal reduction, allow custom categories for expenses and income and allow each category to be individually tagged for inclusion on a particular line of your tax return schedules. Finally, Intuit provides an add-on program for Quicken, called Quicken Companion for Windows, that provides invoicing and payroll capabilities.

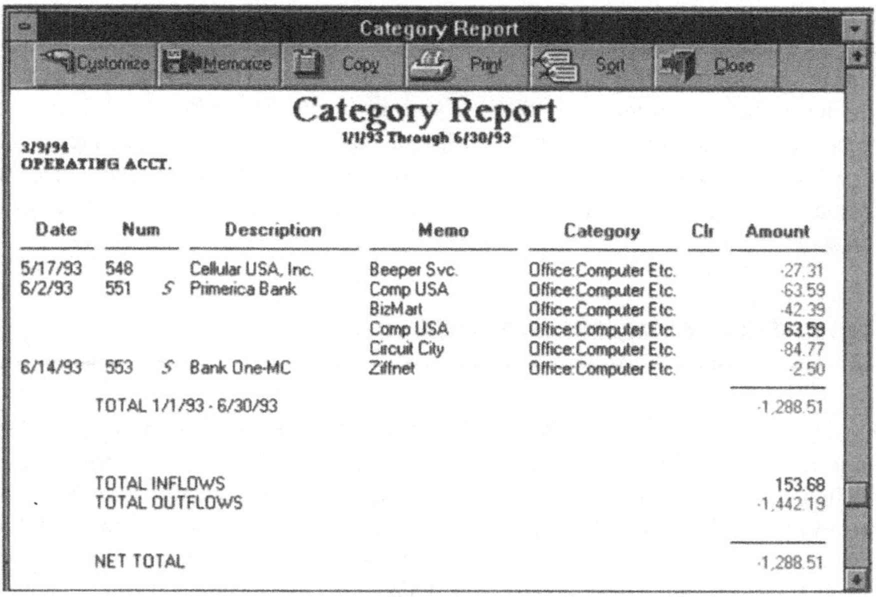

Figure 12-5 This is the result of clicking on the "Office" category in the expense column of Figure 12-4. The resulting report can be customized or printed among other things.

Banking by modem is offered by most personal finance packages.

In addition to the many banking, budgeting, reporting and loan tracking features found in Quicken (and the other packages), Quicken offers electronic payments and credit card statements. Using both these services (available through third-party companies at an extra cost), Quicken becomes the Grand Central Station of your financial activities. The electronic payments option works by forwarding a payment entered in the account register to the processing company by modem. The processing center (Check-Free) pays the bills which are reflected in the following bank statement. This eliminates the need to print checks or mail payments however, over a pre-defined number of payments, additional costs per transaction are incurred. This feature allows the flexibility of automatically scheduling recurring payments while still enabling you to enter non-recurring payments as necessary.

Quicken also has its own VISA *credit card.*

By using this card, itemized card statements are automatically categorized and input into your Quicken account register by disk or modem. A major drawback to this feature however, is that transactions are grouped according to generic, pre-defined categories such as dining, travel, clothing or miscellaneous depending upon the transaction source. This means that you cannot define your own categories for purchases unless you manually re-enter your own categories after the information is placed in your account register...but why pay for the service, then?. Since I try to take full advantage of Quicken's ability to define categories and allocate categories for tax treatment, the credit card service would be counter-productive in my instance.

You can even print your own company checks.

Finally, if you're a traditionalist, Quicken also offers the ability to print checks from your laser or dot matrix printer. Computer generated checking supplies are also available through many other office supply companies and catalogs other than those recommended by Intuit. If you are so inclined, there are even programs that will enable you to print your own checks and include the MICR account number on the check for electronic processing at your bank. If this is your preference, you will need a MICR toner cartridge for your laser printer. While I don't think it's likely to be a cost-effective method of printing your checks after taking into consideration the cost of the MICR cartridge, the downtime in switching cartridges and the necessary cost of the paper for the checks, you are welcome to do your own cost-benefit analysis. If all your checking is done at one time or you can dedicate a laser printer solely to printing checks or you do a lot of "check-cutting", it may be worth it.

Managing Your Money is another powerful finance manager.

MECA Software's Managing Your Money is another finance manager with flexible account and register maintenance and powerful reporting features to help you manage and track your money. As a DOS only product it keeps pace with Quicken in most instances. Its charting and graphing capabilities are on par with Quicken's DOS version (Quicken for Windows provides prettier, though not more accurate, graphing functions than the other programs) however Managing Your Money doesn't provide you with a break-down of the register entries that comprise a report or graph segment (perhaps its most serious flaw when compared with Quicken). Managing Your Money does make up for this shortcoming, however, with three times the number of predefined reports, more than three times the number of financial calculators (whew!) and the ability to generate invoices. Its real strength, when compared to other similar packages, lies in its strong portfolio and financial management capabilities. It's designed to dial on-line services and download stock or fund quotes. The package will track these quotes and alert you to price floors and ceilings when these are reached. Finally, Managing Your Money provides electronic bill-paying (but not automated input of credit card transactions) and more financial and tax planning advice than Quicken; a helpful feature for those new to financial management.

Kiplinger's Simply Money for Windows uses icons to the "max".

Kiplinger's Simply Money for Windows is a third alternative that incorporates an icon-based approach to finance management. While some may find this a little too cute for serious business use, Simply Money allows you to set up an icon, representing financial transaction such as the payment of office rent, and drag the icon to the check register for each payment. This is in lieu of manually entering the transaction into the register and is akin to Quicken's calendar feature for "drag and drop" financial management. In practice, unless you have a lot of recurring transactions involving the payment of fixed sums, I've found the "quickfill" feature (memorized transactions) of each package to be a better alternative for entering transactions into the account register.

Simply Money provides most of the features found in the other packages and is particularly easy to setup for personal finance management. It offers the banking, reconciliation and budgeting functions found in the other products and includes loan tracking and financial calculators for extended financial planning. Simply Money also provides a good number of predefined reports but, like Managing Your Money, it doesn't allow you to view a break-down of register entries comprising a report or graph. It also lacks both the automated credit card transaction entries (no great loss in my opinion) and the ability to opt for electronic payment. Simply Money provides the coaches and pop-up financial advice that may be helpful to users unfamiliar with managing finances by computer but it lacks some of the business versatility found in both Quicken (including its Companion product) and Managing Your Money since there are no provisions for invoicing or payroll functions. For a sole proprietorship however Simply Money may be an effective means to manage both business and personal accounts for the person new to or unfamiliar with computer finances.

One final note on personal finance software...

These packages will save an enormous amount of time if used to their potential. However, no software package can help if you don't take advantage of its feature set. From the beginning, set up expense categories that make sense in your own business and don't depend on the package's "generic" categories to tell you what's going on with your company's money. Similarly, set up accounts and design reports which make sense to you and not to the software developer. Taking advantage of these features and using the reporting functions will provide you with feedback that is important to maintaining your business health.

TAX PREPARATION SOFTWARE

If you've diligently categorized your income and expense for the year on one of the accounting packages I've discussed (and perhaps others), you can now be rewarded with almost effortless tax filing by using a tax preparation package. Even if you didn't use a computer-based finance package to manage your accounts (or didn't categorize your transactions), you can still benefit from a tax package. Just a few of the benefits include the following:

⇒ No need to search for IRS approved forms or schedules;

⇒ Automatic and accurate math calculations;

⇒ Automatic and accurate carryforwards from one schedule to another;

⇒ Alternative filing scenarios and "what-if" capabilities to test tax-planning strategies;

⇒ Automatic and accurate penalty or alternative tax calculations;

⇒ Auditing of returns, comparison to national averages, "flagging" of suspicious or unusual entries and deductions and prompting for missing information;

⇒ Tax tips and advice for the current return (including an audit for commonly missed deductions), tax planning advice for the following year; and

⇒ The option of selecting electronic filing (at an additional cost through a filing service) from the convenience of your business or home.

For the very reasonable cost of these packages, any one of these would be a good reason to do your taxes by computer if you don't intend to hire a professional for the service. I do have one caveat however. While these packages provide ample oomph for personal tax preparation, they are not designed with the intent to guide a business through the preparation of its tax schedules. These packages are sufficient, however, for almost any sole proprietorship or small business entity (perhaps a subchapter S corporation or partnership) relying primarily on the Schedule C and Schedule K for listing business income and expenses.

Windows tax programs have some very real advantages.

The same reasons that I've recommended Windows products throughout this book are the same reasons I'll recommend the Windows versions of tax packages. In properly designed applications, you can keep multiple windows open and switch between them or tile them side by side and navigation and access to help features generally exceeds that available in the DOS versions. Universal printer support in Windows also means that you will have no problem printing your schedules and forms on whatever printer you happen to own.

Most tax packages solicit tax information by three alternative and concurrent means: direct entry on the form/schedule, interview process by topic(s) and "shoe-box" entry on a category, schedule-line or item basis. These are concurrent methods because all three methods can be used, at your discretion, to prepare and update a single tax return, allowing you to switch between methods "on-the-fly" as you wish. This way, if you run across a collection of cash receipts which are not already sorted or input into your accounting package, you can skip to the shoe-box feature and start inputting the receipts before continuing with your interview. The "shoe-box" method improves on direct data entry by guiding you to the correct schedule and line entry from a list of choices and tabulating the totals with information already input at other times or by other methods. The Interview feature is the best method to import W-2 and 1099 information in an organized and comprehensive manner. The Interview will also prompt you for information you never considered (or forgot) that should be included in your return (like income from an estate, trust or foreign source).

Your ability to import financial data into your tax software is a very important consideration when deciding on a program.

The three heavy hitters in tax packages are TaxCut, Personal Tax Edge and TurboTax. Computer Associates also offers Simply Tax to complement its Simply Money financial management software and is now a contender to the other three. Before you decide on one tax package over another, there are at least two things to keep in mind. If you are importing data from your accounting package, consider the tax software's ability to import the data in a compatible format. Most personal finance and financial management packages have solved this problem by incorporating the ability to save their information in TXF (Tax Exchange Format-developed to be a universal tax format to ease transfer of data between finance and tax packages), others may not. See Figure 12-6. If so, you will need a tax package that can import the data in its native format.

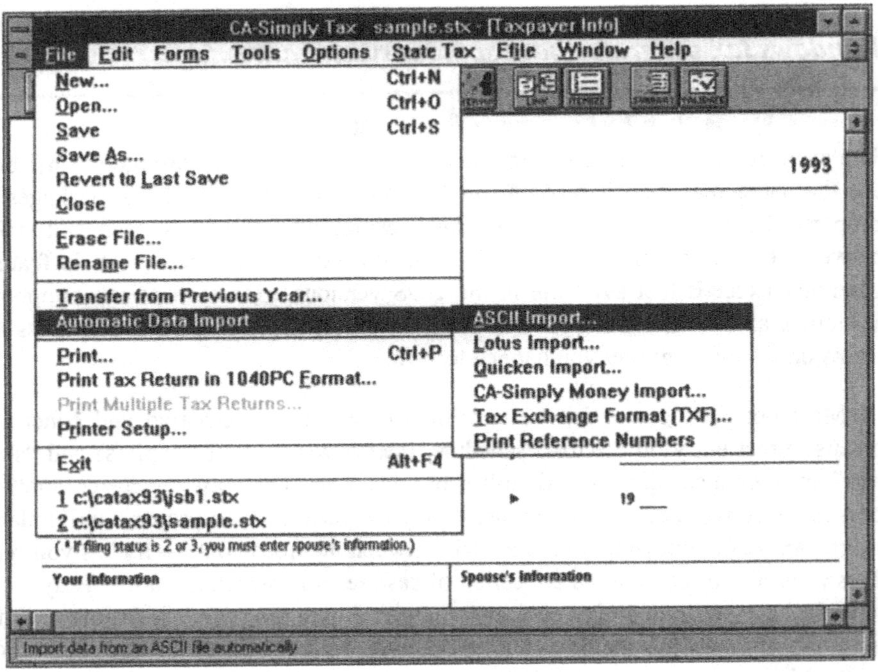

Figure 12-6 Simply Tax is obviously not going to have a problem importing financial data from any number of sources. In practice, it import my Quicken data without trouble categorizing all my expenses and placing them on the correct forms and lines.

Both TaxCut and Simply Tax include the ability to import data in other applications' native formats while TurboTax will automatically extract the financial data from Quicken. On the flip side, some tax packages don't even offer the ability to import TXF files, a decided deficit if you already keep computerized financial records. Of secondary concern, some tax packages offer a greater selection of IRS approved forms than other packages. While Personal Tax Edge offers 60 or so forms and schedules, TurboTax offers more than 100, with the other packages falling somewhere in between. If your return is likely to contain some less popular forms (like Form 2119 for the sale of a home) check first to see if the necessary forms are included in the package. Finally, if you will be filing a state tax return, confirm a tax package is offered by your chosen vendor for your state (and check the price of the state package which may affect your total cost and influence your buying decision).

TurboTax is an excellent product in both its DOS and Windows.

ChipSoft's TurboTax has been a perennial leader in the tax software race and it continues this trend with excellent DOS and Windows products. TurboTax offers more forms and schedules than any of the other programs and even incorporates a deduction finder feature to search for commonly missed deductions. It uses the same three methods as the others to input data and automatically places the information in the correct forms, calculates totals and carries these totals forward to other forms as necessary. It incorporates audit features to search for missing information or questionable deductions and provides the capability to perform audits on a form by form basis. Finally, help features enable you to view IRS instructions or plain English instructions (there is a difference between the two, you know) and the package outputs via IRS approved forms or electronic filing.

Simply Tax is a good complement to Simply Money

If you use Simply Money as your finance package, Simply Tax may be your logical choice for tax software (although not the only choice). Simply Tax is a newcomer to the tax market when compared with TurboTax and TaxCut but it still offers the same features and many of the tips offered by its older competitors. The interview, "shoe-

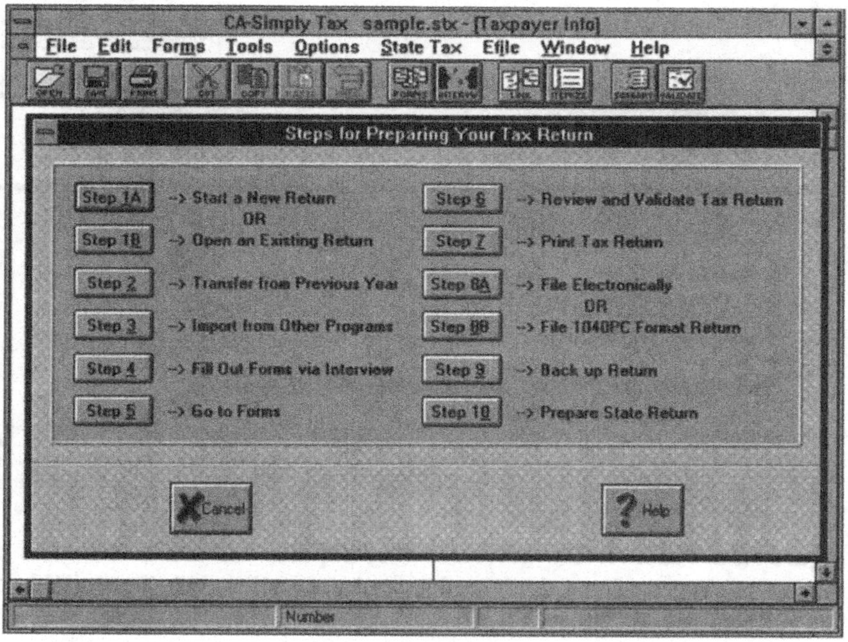

Figure 12-7 If taxes scare you and tax software intimidates you, let the software take your hand and guide you step-by-step through the process. Although by no means the only way to do your taxes, the step-by-step approach helps you grasp the entire process and keeps things in order.

box", and direct entry features are all present and work similarly to the other packages. The program features can be individually accessed by selecting items from the top menu or by choosing methods from a master step-by-step guide for preparing, auditing and printing the return (Figure 12-7).

Interviewing prompts you for information to calculate your return.

In the Interview, you can begin at the beginning, hop around by category or schedule and stop and continue the interview process at will. While the top of the screen provides a list of questions based on your interview category, the lower screen half displays the appropriate schedule. See Figure 12-8. Buttons are available to bring up a list of interview topics, forms or help.

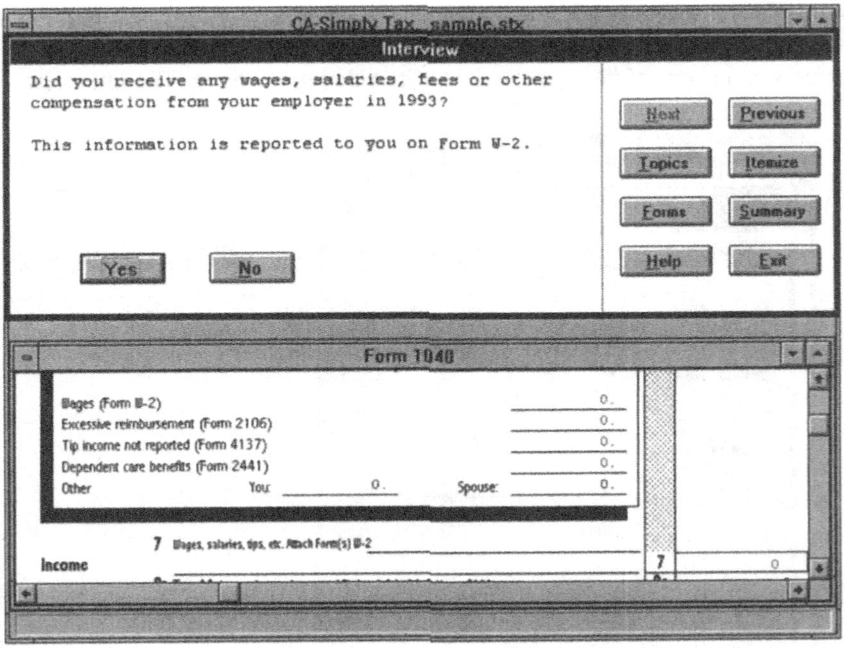

Figure 12-8 The interview process is very popular and can be found in all the tax packages. If you don't understand a question, help is available or you can skip it and return to it later.

You can also proceed to the next topic or question or travel, question by question, all the way to the beginning of the interview process. The package, again like its competitors, provides worksheets to itemize deductions and a memo pad to keep notes. The "shoe-box" feature enables you to input information by selecting a tax category or subject or selecting a particular tax form or document (Figure 12-9).

Tips and help are abundant throughout the package and you can even cross-reference a number to locate its source data. Finally, the audit feature looks for missing information or flags unusual deductions (when compared to national averages) and the package prints IRS approved forms or offers electronic filing.

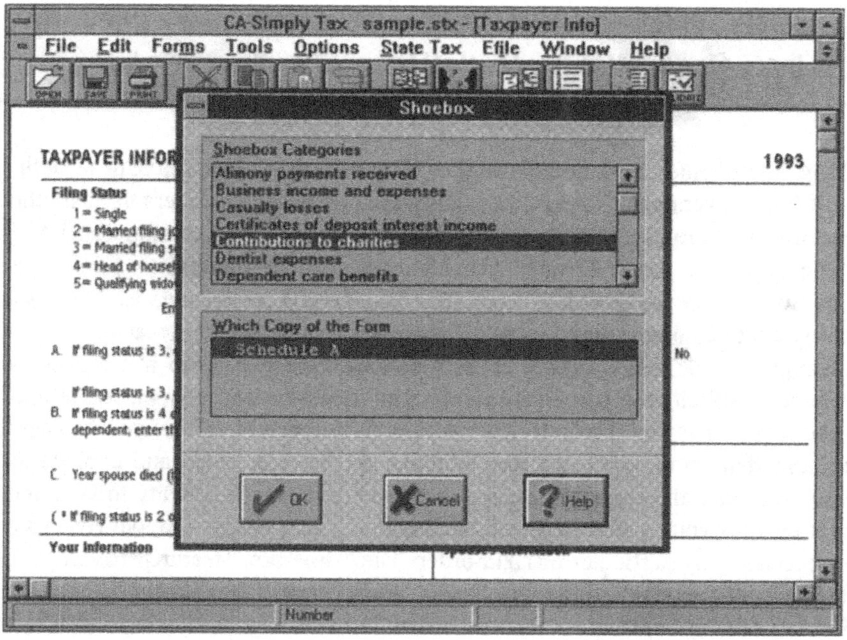

Figure 12-9 Reducing computer help to human form, the electronic shoebox, a surprisingly popular feature, lets you tell the computer (for a change) what you want to tackle next.

Personal Tax Edge provides a good range of features and is a worthy competitor to other tax packages on the market.

Personal Tax Edge also provides the three traditional methods of tax preparation. Its interview process is capable although slightly more rigid and not as flexible as the others. Its "shoe-box" feature, though useful, doesn't provide the depth of topics and prompts to enable a user to navigate unfamiliar tax territory. Useful features include color-coding (on-screen only, of course) to provide visual cues on data entry (identifying program calculated sums or user-input sums over-riding program calculations) and the ability to place "estimated" figures in fields, reviewing and updating the estimates at a later time. Personal Tax Edge also offers the usual assortment of financial calculators, worksheets and memo forms. It offers depreciation capabilities and generates amortization schedules. At the end of the process, auditing checks for omissions, errors, fields marked as estimates, offers comparisons to prior filings or national averages and performs "what-if" scenarios to help you determine your most advantageous filing status. Printing IRS approved forms or electronic filing rounds out the package.

TaxCut is also available in both DOS and Windows versions.

MECA, the people that market Managing Your Money, offers TaxCut in both DOS and Windows versions. As previously discussed, the package offers three methods to input information and a number of alternative methods to access appropriate forms or schedules for "hit and run" tax preparation. The interview process in the Windows version provides large icons for categories of tax related expenses such as employment income, home-related deductions, stock and investment income. Selecting each of these, in order or out of order, brings you to a list of questions designed to solicit the appropriate information and automatically place the totals on all the required forms. The interview process is designed to allow you to skip those questions that do not apply to your situation and provides help and explanations to help ensure that all pertinent questions are answered. The flexibility to skip between topics enables you to work with information in logical groups without requiring you to proceed in any particular or rigid order. The "shoe-box" feature provides a list of categories and people (employer, bank, stock broker, for instance) and allows information to be input in any random order. The package will easily skip from one category to another as you proceed from one receipt or form to another, soliciting the information and placing it in its correct place. If you think the interview process missed something, traveling down the list of categories (which can also take you directly to the form and line-item) will likely provide the answer. As with the other products, you can also skip from form to form inputting information directly or via worksheets which total the entries, and audit functions will check your work for accuracy, completeness and comparison with national averages (to forestall that ever-present audit threat). Finally, as with the other packages, you can print the schedules in IRS approved format, print out close approximations for manual reference when preparing IRS forms by hand or file your return electronically.

A final note on tax software...

As with the personal finance packages, any of these tax packages will save you time...and therefore money. All the major packages will accept your financial data in a number of formats and will provide more guidance than you are likely to get if you regularly plan your own taxes. The ability to "experiment" with return options, filing either jointly or separately with your spouse, for instance, and allocating expenses accordingly to maximize your itemized deductions may even save you the nominal cost of the software.

Their use as a business tool, however, is limited by their focus on individual, rather than corporate, returns. Most will not provide any of the necessary forms for even a moderately sized corporation but will handle partnerships and sole proprietorships with aplomb. Even if you need a professional to guide you through the state and federal maze of corporate tax filings, consider that experimenting with tax software on your own personal return may give you ideas on how to better manage your company's compensation programs to better your own personal tax position.

Chapter 13

Schedulers & Information Managers

What's a PIM?

After word processing software, perhaps the application with the greatest general business potential is scheduling software and information managers. Known variously as Personal Information Managers ("PIM"), Contact Managers or Free-form Databases, these applications are supposed to replace, to varying degrees, your rolodex, desk calendar, daybook, notebook and the scribbled notes of "to-do" items and return calls. Some such applications may also include more sophisticated features such as Gantt charting, concurrent or network scheduling, invoicing and time-keeping and even generate form letters and financial status reports. I will refer to all these products generically as "PIMs".

Like your Rolodex, your PIM must organize and work with data the way you want it to work.

I am going to give just one piece of advice about PIMs...make sure the application complements your working style. Each product emphasizes different priorities and collects and presents information in a different manner. Unlike other software applications that remain useful even if not designed exactly as desired, a PIM will only be useful if it facilitates easy input and allows easy output for your reference. I have found, through experience, that the most sophisticated PIMs aren't necessarily the best for quickly inputting an appointment or note and painlessly accessing the information later when it is needed. If it isn't easy and quick to use, you will soon revert to your scribbled notes and pocket-size appointment book.

Because PIMs are individualistic in their approaches and every PIM may not appeal to every person, it would be helpful if a person could test the product before committing to it. In most instances this is not possible. Even the computer superstores will not accept open software returns. For this reason, I find the PIMs available through mail order or on-line services to be a great bargain. Some of the PIMs I will discuss in this chapter are shareware software. Shareware software, discussed in greater detail in Chapter 8 is a software sales concept. The software is licensed to a person for a temporary period (usually 20-30 days) for testing and compatibility. Most such software is completely functional and is not handicapped in any way however, registration reminders will appear at times to remind the person to register the software if the software continues to be used after the trial period. If the person finds the software useful, a registration fee is paid to the software developer by check or credit card and a "key" or code is provided to disable the registration screens (also known as "nag" screens for their propensity to nag the person into registering the software). Registration of the software may also provide the registrant with a written instruction manual, disks with updated versions of the software and update notices from the developer. Such shareware is generally very inexpensive and offers substantial savings over comparable commercial products.

In fact, shareware is so good in many instances, that it develops a strong following and may even be offered commercially at some point. One of the shareware products I will recommend in this category has since "graduated" to the "big time" and is now a commercial offering at local computer stores.

Test-driving PIMs even if the store won't let you return software.

The great advantage to this product is the ability to review the software's features and interface. As I've said, the PIM interface is a very personal item and I highly recommend reviewing the shareware products before investing money in commercial products.

Time & Chaos works like I want a PIM to work.

To date, my vote for best PIM is Time & Chaos.

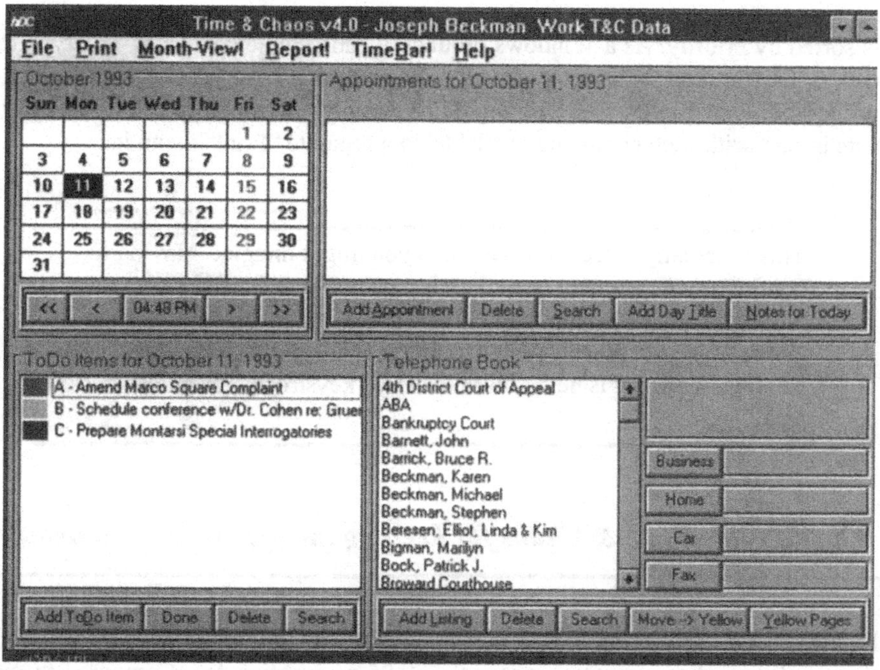

Figure 13-1 Time and Chaos makes it easy to see and access most everything you need on a day to day basis. The Appointment list, to-do list and rolodex are all displayed on one screen so you don't have to "dig" for them. In actual practice, this feature is more important than you might imagine.

A good PIM should do more than just keep names, addresses and calendar dates.

This is a Windows product and incorporates the menus, buttons and screens used in Windows products. See Figure 13-1. If you want a capable appointment calendar, "to-do" list and simple but effective contact manager, this is it. In addition to these basic items, it also provides bar charting to see blocked time for the entire month at a single glance, and group scheduling by superimposing the timebars for one or more people. It provides quick and easy status reports of appointments or "to-do" items and its combination rolodex/contact manager integrates with your word processor to print form letters. It provides separate white page and yellow page rolodexes to separate personal contacts from business contacts and prints a wide variety of reports and calendars. Like all good PIMs, it provides conflict checking, notifying you if you attempt to overlap two appointments and provides a configurable alarm to notify you of upcoming appointments. Appointments and tasks can be color-coded to reflect their importance and priority (red representing high priority) and the to-do list is sorted by priority. As a Windows product, it can take advantage of Truetype fonts and prints through Windows virtually guaranteeing that your calendars can be printed on your printer. And printing daily, weekly and monthly calendars and task lists is easy with each command available on a separate "Print" menu list.

This is actually more important than you might imagine. Having to configure your printout each time is a pain that will reduce your willingness to rely upon the PIM. Selecting one menu item in Time & Chaos however, reveals each list option available for immediate printing. Your list is never more than two keystrokes (or mouse clicks) away.

Why do I like Time & Chaos for keeping my appointment schedule?

Finally, as a shareware product, it can be acquired at no initial cost to try free for 30 days and thereafter requires a minimal $29.95 registration fee. Compared to many commercial offerings it is a genuine bargain. While it won't print fancy graphics, icons or clipart and it doesn't print particularly fancy calendars, as a business tool, it is among the best. In my opinion it's the best for one simple reason... it places appointments, the "to-do" list and the rolodex/contact manager all on the desktop at once where any particular item is immediately available. It also displays the appointments and to-do items in a legible manner rather than forcing appointment notes into monthly calendars covering the desktop. Its interface is clean and uncluttered and the important information is not lost in the jumble of icons, buttons and other graphics on the screen. Perhaps the only addition I would make to Time & Chaos would be a time bar to set appointments by dragging the mouse pointer across the appointment times on the bar. Recently, Time & Chaos was released as a commercial product, for the same price, as The Computer Organizer and is available through Impulse Software, Inc. at 214-437-2849.

Almanac is another good PIM and Calendar application.

Another good shareware PIM is Almanac.

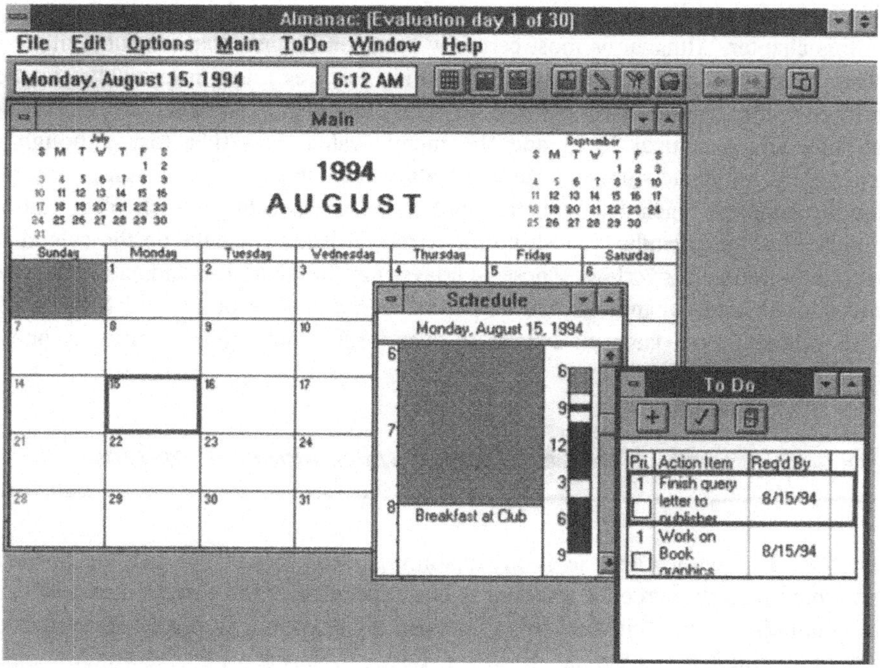

Figure 13-2 Almanac lets you see your schedule and to-do lists all at one time. Unique to Almanac are overlays which can personalize the calendar by "overlaying" an included holiday calendar, jewish calendar or a customized calendar for your own anniversary and birthday reminders. You can also customize Almanac to operate in foreign languages.

Calendar overlays allow birthdays, anniversaries and holidays to be displayed or hidden at will.

It provides the time bar mentioned above to set appointments. It also includes many of the features found in Time & Chaos including the calendar, "to-do" list and appointment alarms. The calendar is configurable to show daily, monthly or annual calendars (but lacks a weekly calendar option). The "to-do" list may be sorted by priority or due date (an advantage over Time & Chaos) however the entries are not color-coded for quick reference. The calendar, "to-do" list and scheduler each reside in individual windows capable of being sized to share the screen or maximized to monopolize the screen. The rolodex/phonebook categorizes entries for indexing so that personal phonebook entries can be listed separately from client or business entries. The phonebook entries can't be password-protected or linked to anything else except an auto-dialer although an address can be copied to the Windows

Clipboard for use in other applications. When compared to the other PIMs discussed in this chapter, Almanac is most certainly intended for personal or stand alone use since it does not include the group scheduling features found in products intended for network use. In terms of its usability, many features in Almanac may be invoked by selecting graphical icons and the menu system is satisfactory although not exemplary. Almanac's one outstanding feature is its ability to store multiple overlays for the calendar. Included with the application are overlays which place national holidays on the calendar, jewish holidays and christian holidays on the calendar as well as other such overlays. These overlays may be altered to indicate other dates and anniversaries of interest and additional overlays may be created from scratch. With Almanac, you have no excuse to ever forget your spouse's birthday or your wedding anniversary.

My problem with Almanac is screen space and print options.

One problem with Almanac is my inability to comfortably fit all the necessary information on the screen at one time. I like a calendar of the current month with my daily appointments, a current "to-do" list and my telephone directory all available at one time. Almanac's calendar, however, does not shrink when the window size is reduced and fitting the entire monthly calendar on-screen requires a large percentage of screen space. Consequently, very little space is available for the appointment time bar and the "to-do" list. Furthermore, detailed notes about appointments are not available except after selecting the appointment and the appointment text contained in the calendar is too small to be useful. Finally, unlike Time & Chaos, the menu does not provide instant access to all printing options for the calendar and "to-do" lists. Almanac's registration price is $49.95 through Impact Software at (909) 590-8522.

Above & Beyond is another sophisticated PIM.

A third shareware PIM that I've experimented with is Above & Beyond.

Above & Beyond is less intuitive than the prior two shareware products but it sports a number of powerful features which rate it high marks for workgroup use. The program makes use of graphical icons to select prior and later dates, daily, weekly or monthly calendar schedules, the priority list, modify appointments and tasks view or modify notes, juggle schedules and print a daily schedule list. Its menu allows considerable flexibility in scheduling, its search and sorting capability is decent and its notes feature for quick reminders is easy to use. For network use, Above & Beyond has a nice feature called Meeting Maker which allows an

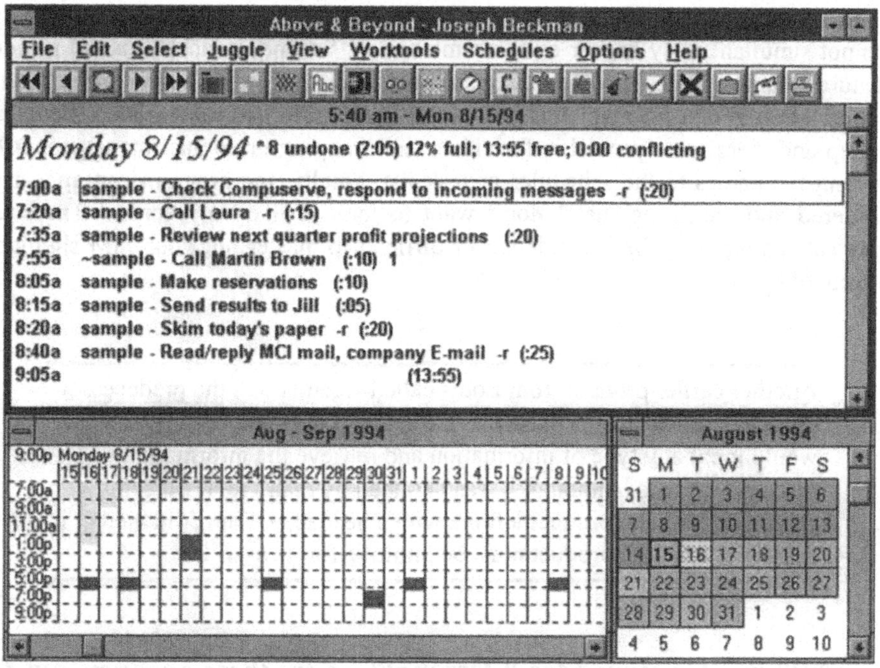

Figure 13-3 Above & Beyond has a lot of features and information packed into its menus and screens. Pulling up the main screen doesn't give you a clue as to how to do anything however, if you are willing to take the time, it can do almost anything and offers great network capabilities for a shareware product.

administrator or supervisor to set meetings by inputting the date and time range while all intended attendee's schedules are open on the screen. The application then searches the open calendars and reports available slots for the meeting. Once a time is set, the application places the meeting description in all calendars. This is certainly one step ahead of Time & Chaos' superimposed timebars which require the administrator to review the information and pick available time slots. In addition to the Meeting Maker, Above & Beyond has a (sort of) file synchronization feature for maintaining current copies of your schedule between your desktop and portable computer, networked conflict checking, networked task management and automatic backup of critical scheduling files. For those regularly needing to coordinate schedules and meetings or track and assign tasks across a network (workload management in Above & Beyond terms), this product beats the prior two PIMs, "hands down". For your business, its strength in this area may be enough to justify the steeper learning curve I encountered when comparing it to the prior two products.

Now for the downsides to Above & Beyond. First, the calendar and "to-do" list cannot simultaneously appear on the same screen. Second, it lacks a useful rolodex feature. While it does have an address/phonebook tool, it's nothing more than a combination of text files which can be searched by word. No categories or fields are set up and there is no provision for either mail merging or contact management by linking the names to the scheduler or task list. Finally, the program can appear so cluttered and confusing that I don't want to look at it on my screen. There are applications that may be intimidating or difficult to master but your PIM shouldn't be one of them.

Another earlier product from Lotus called Agenda was the predecessor to today's PIMs. It was known as a free-form database because the user would input any type of information and retrieve the information through searches. Although it was heralded by many reviewers, my short stint with the product left me with a headache. I never looked at it again. I repeat, the product must be intuitive for its user.

The "P" in PIM stands for "Personal", so try these products out for yourself.

In all fairness however, Above & Beyond does provide some great network features I haven't found in any other shareware product. As shareware, its initial cost is nominal or free. In Chapter 8, I showed you how to initially acquire these shareware programs for free rather than pay commercial on-line services or mail-order software houses for the privilege of reviewing the software. Although I don't find it to be my best business tool, Above & Beyond may be just the product to meet your needs and my prior criticisms shouldn't dissuade you from reviewing it for yourself.

Similarly, my reviews of the other products shouldn't sell you on those products since each person has his or her own expectations and needs in keeping an organized calendar and task manager.

The fourth and final shareware PIM product I'll review is from Wilson WindowWare and is called Reminder.

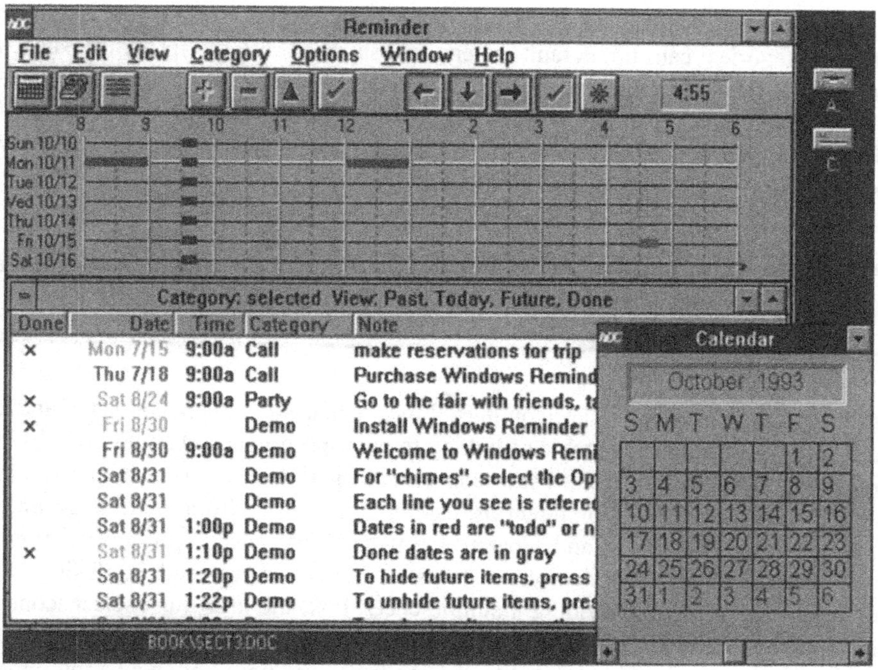

Figure 13-4 Reminder makes use of timebars to visually display scheduled appointments. Information is entered through the floating calendar displayed in the lower right corner of this screen.

WindowWare's Reminder is a capable PIM easy on hard disk space but with the advantages of Windows.

Wilson WindowWare provides a number of very capable windows shareware products and Reminder is no exception. Reminder is actually two programs, a calendar and a scheduler. See Figure 13-4. The calendar is a small, self-contained monthly calendar screen from which the user accesses the scheduler. The calendar can be advanced or regressed one month at a time by selecting the arrows or in annual increments by selecting the title bar. Once the user is within the desired month, selecting a particular day with the mouse calls up a schedule box. In this box, an appointment, task or contact can be input. The user can review a sorted list of tasks and appointments by selecting the second program, the Reminder. This second program uses a selectable bar graph of the current week to reflect scheduled appointments and a text list of both tasks and appointments in the lower half of the screen. The list can reflect past, present, future or completed tasks and appointment or any combination of these items. The list can be further limited by categories which are selected at the time the appointment or task is input to the computer. These categories can be default categories supplied by the program such as "meeting", "report", "call", or even as personal as "birthday". The program also allows custom categories to be input and added as a sort option on the menu list. Finally, the program requires very little hard disk space compared to many Windows programs. A minimal installation used just 230K!

Reminder is another PIM without a rolodex or capable means of maintaining contact logs.

Still, the program has its shortcomings. First, it has no rolodex/contact manager. Although the program is capable of linking to other programs and could probably be programmed to invoke a client list or contact manager, its more work than should be necessary. Second, the appointment list cannot be separated from the task list unless categories are used to sort and separate the two. Third, selecting a combination of past, present, future and completed tasks is more difficult and confusing than necessary. Rather than providing a simple check box, the user must select icons or menu items individually to set preferences for the task display. Fourth, the appointment and task list is limited to starting times and does not show appointment or task lengths. This information is only available graphically on the time bar. Fifth, the Reminder and Calendar windows cannot be resized, only moved. When juggling more than one screen of information, this limitation can become frustrating. Finally, the printing options for the program do not include simple daily, weekly and monthly calendar and task list printouts. Again, the user must select from menus for the categories and time periods of the desired report rather than merely selecting a single print command on the menu as in Time & Chaos. The registration fee of $59.95, however, does include a print program for printing monthly calendars (although you have to pay to find out how well it works). Although a capable program, Reminder hedges on features standard in some of the other PIMs.

Polaris Packrat is a task manager for your computer as well as your life.

Polaris Packrat is a commercially available PIM that goes beyond the simple PIM function of calendaring to provide a shell from which all files, applications, data and information can be input, organized and retrieved. In this capacity, it acts almost like the disk management utilities I will discuss in the next chapter. If this is sounds like it is more than you need in a PIM, you may be right. Besides costing ten times more than Time & Chaos, even at discount prices, it requires 8 MB of hard disk space to store all its files (this is compared with Reminders 230K and Time & Chaos' 600K!).

The math calculates as follows: 1 MB=1024K, so 8 MB=8,192K ! That means Packrat requires 35x as much space as Reminder and 13x as much space as Time & Chaos.

Packrat is not only a PIM, it's a complete computer organizer.

Packrat uses a "file folder" metaphor to hold related information, whether data files or applications. The information can also be organized by form or category for later retrieval. This input of data into folders or categories allows the user to place tasks and appointments into appropriate folders and collect all the tasks through sorting commands. The product is a capable PIM but may be more than you want or need.

ACT! is for logging client and customer contacts...a sophisticated contact manager more than a PIM.

The next product is more dedicated contact manager than a simple calendaring program and may appeal more to those persons who desire to keep their daybook and rely on the computer to log call histories and collect and collate sales and marketing efforts. ACT! for Windows ($395.00 from Contact Software International Tel: 800-365-0606) requires 2.5 MB of hard disk storage which is quite reasonable for its features.. A DOS version is also available for the same price which incorporates many of the functional features of the Windows version without the human interface advantages of the Window product such as linking to other applications and "drag and drop" scheduling. The product interface is generally uncluttered and it makes good use of icons and pull-down menu commands to accomplish many tasks.

When reviewing the prior calendaring programs with these contact managers, keep in mind that I place a very high priority on the simple interface of the calendaring programs and detract points for any extraneous screens, icons or actions necessary to set an appointment or task. In contrast, I allow more leeway to the more sophisticated contact managers which, by their nature, are not intended to be calendaring programs but to record sales and contact history. Accordingly, the need to go through two or more screens to input all the data in a calendar program or to get a printout of the weekly schedule is a minus while the need to suffer through screens in a contact manager may be sufferable.

The application is customizable and can be set to display more or less information depending upon your preference but retains powerful search and sort features necessary to separate the multitude of contacts even within one company.

The scheduler allows scheduling using the mouse to drag, drop and click entries. With all your contacts on file, it only makes sense that the program allow you to communicate with those contacts and ACT! does this with alacrity. While it includes an internal word processor that supports formatting and graphics it also links to other Windows word processors, sports mail merge capabilities and exports to Windows fax software providing the name and numbers from its internal database of contacts. Finally, predefined reports are immediately accessible to the user for updated written reports at the click of a mouse button. If you like what you've read about ACT! but can't justify the price, consider 1stACT!, available in both DOS and Windows versions for less than half the price. While the feature list is more limited, much of the functionality found in the full versions remains in these "lite" products.

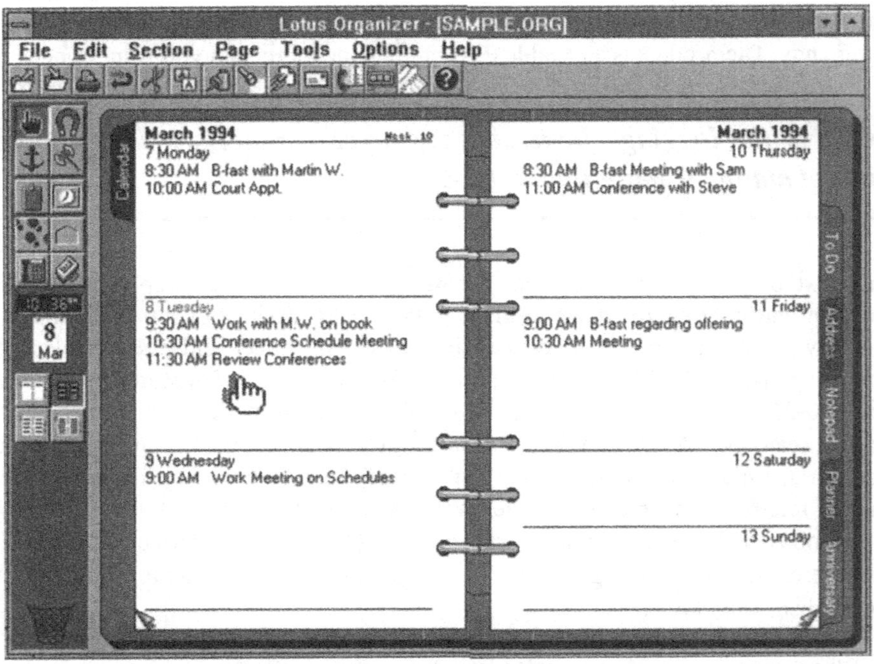

Figure 13-5 Lotus Organizer goes to great pains to simulate the Day-Planner you may carry around with you. Hidden behind this familiar look however, are some very powerful features for updating, linking and accessing information you won't find in the paper copy.

Organizer is just like your familiar daybook organizer.

Finally, one very, very popular PIM is Lotus Corporation's Organizer pictured in Figure 13-5. Lotus combines the familiar with the cute and includes some nice pluses to boot. The Organizer desktop is set up with a Filofax or Organizer book metaphor, complete with tabbed pages for separate appointment, to-do list, address, scheduling and notes sections. The left side of the screen holds the trashcan and navigation icons for switching between daily, weekly and monthly views when reviewing appointments.

When an item is to be placed on your "to-do" list, the Organizer pops up a fill-in box with sufficient flexibility without overloading you with options. See Figure 13-6. The Organizer also contains tools for linking items and contacts between your address list, notepad, calendar and "to-do" list allowing you to link a contact's address with an appointment, for instance.

As with some of the other choices, my "beef" is with the inability to place all daily items, both calendar and "to-do" items simultaneously on-screen for quick review. Like the daily organizer book it simulates, you must turn to the appropriate section to see those items. Still, Organizer is "network friendly" and, for those using other Lotus products, it provides good workgroup scheduling abilities (if your network software doesn't already provide this).

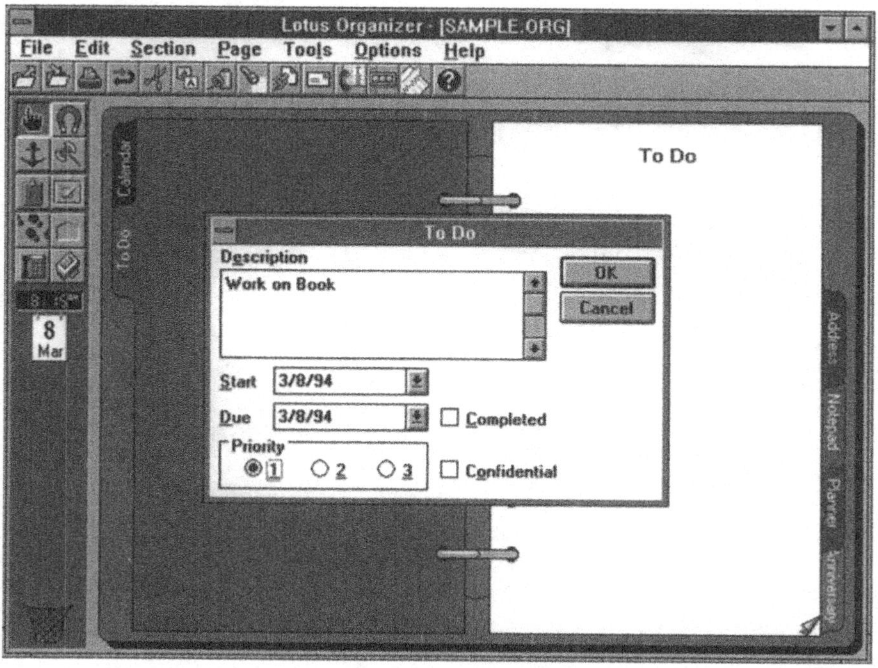

Figure 13-6 The "To-Do" input box lets you decide how important the task is and whether it should be held "confidential". The only problem I have with the list is that it can't be placed side-by-side with my appointments. This limitation of the paper version was unfortunately carried over into the computer product.

My final caveat: Don't get more PIM than you need...it will just take up storage space and throw more information at you than you want or need.

Remember my advice at the beginning of this chapter. If you will only use your PIM to keep appointments and tasks handy or keep simple notes regarding contacts, I do not suggest you purchase the most sophisticated PIM you can afford. I have found that less clutter and extraneous information allows greater focus on the information you want to extract. Look for a product that will place this information on your screen by default or no more than one keystroke or mouse click away. Any more than that, and I guarantee you will reach for your daytimer.

Chapter 14

Utilities & Disk Management Software

What's a "shell", "utility" or "add-on" and what will it do for me?

So many software products are available that profess to improve DOS, Windows or any other working environment. These products are advertised as shells, utilities or add-ons to DOS or Windows and promise to make DOS and/or Windows easier to use, more reliable, and more secure. While some such products are single tools for single applications, many of these products are a conglomeration of tools and utilities designed to organize, protect, analyze and, if necessary, recover your data and applications. These utilities may

- free RAM memory to run larger applications or files;
- double the apparent storage capacity of your hard disk;
- backup data;
- search data and files for computer viruses;
- reorganize data or search for lost files and data; and
- analyze the interior of the computer or its files and fix any errors.

In this chapter I will discuss some of the more popular utilities and shells available to increase your computer's efficiency and organize and protect your applications and data. First, I will start with some single purpose utilities for increasing the computer's capabilities and protecting data and finally I will close with a discussion of a few all-purpose utility packages.

A little history...why are utilities so popular now?

When DOS was first released in the late seventies, hard disks were nonexistent and most computers used floppy disks to operate applications and store files. Applications would run in the 64K of RAM memory that was then available and computer viruses were unheard of. As time progressed, hard disks became the norm and began to grow in size to accommodate the growth of more sophisticated applications. With the storage of applications and data on the hard disk, people needed a means to safely store the information in case of a computer or human operator failure. Subsequent versions of DOS included a "backup and restore" function for storage of the hard disk data on floppy disks and its restoration to the hard disk if the original data was lost or damaged. During this time, some applications were then designed to remain in RAM memory for immediate recall at the push of a button. Other such applications were designed to be stored in RAM memory while the computer was on and to monitor the storage of files and test for the presence of computer viruses.

> These both are called "TSR"s or "Terminate and Stay Resident" applications, so called because the application remains operative in RAM memory even though the computer may have other applications being utilized at the same time.

In conjunction with the growing sophistication of applications which demanded even more memory to operate, people began to look for a way to manage memory, RAM memory, to simultaneously accommodate all these applications in memory. Even before DOS included a "memory manager", manufacturers began to address this need with their own products. Some manufacturers addressed the need for applications to check for computer viruses and others supplied software to repair damage to files through computer error or human error.

Doesn't DOS come with all the utilities I need?

With the release of Microsoft DOS 6, IBM's PC-DOS 6 and Novell Corporation's DR-DOS 7, the three leading disk operating systems, most persons now receive many of the utilities discussed and listed above with the DOS of their choice. In most instances, this will be Microsoft MS-DOS and it will usually be pre-installed in any computer purchased today. Received with MS-DOS (and the others) are the following:

- RAM Memory Management;
- Backup and Restore software;
- Hard disk compression software;
- AntiVirus software;
- Undelete utilities (allowing the recovery of accidentally deleted files); and
- Disk management utilities for file searches and task switching.

Why add to DOS? Are other utilities really that much better?

Even while DOS includes all these utilities, manufacturers still provide such utilities as stand-alone products or as part of comprehensive packages. These stand-alone packages will generally include features not available in the generic DOS product. These features may include:

- Greater customization and flexibility for advanced users;
- Greater compatibility with other products;
- Intuitive interfaces for ease of use; and
- Better results than the generic DOS products.

When reviewing these utilities, keep in mind that your needs are paramount and, if you will not benefit from greater customization or do not need that extra 10% of the stand-alone product, then invest your money elsewhere and rely upon the utilities included with your DOS.

Memory Management allows your computer to efficiently use its available memory.

Memory management is the means by which a utility will reallocate the memory on your computer to regain memory that the computer does not presently use. Most people have heard of the 640K limit of DOS and how Windows and newer operating systems allow the computer to access much more memory. It is this 640K limit that I speak of when I talk of memory management. Most computers, in addition to the 640K of memory have other memory located above the 640K that is reserved for uses other than use by applications. Memory management software "remaps" this high memory to allow the computer to access that memory for use by applications.

The computer can then place small applications in this memory area above 640K and free the 640K for larger applications and uses. The process of memory management can be advanced further than this but, the beauty of memory management software is, you don't need to know a thing about computers or memory to use the software.

Why wasn't MS-DOS 5's Memory Manager good enough?

Microsoft first provided a memory management utility in MS-DOS 5. The utility was marginally effective but could not compare to specialized memory managers by other manufacturers. In addition to providing less functionality than other products, MS-DOS 5's memory management utilities had to be installed and configured by the user and eking out maximum gains was not an easy process. MS-DOS 6 solved many of these problems. MS-DOS includes MemMaker, an updated memory management utility. MemMaker is installed by typing "memmaker" at the "C>" prompt and following on-screen instructions. Configuration choices are determined by answering questions regarding your system use and on-line help gives the installer more information and guidance on the proper choices. The utility then installs itself after reviewing the applications, utilities and computer system. Best of all, the setup is completely fool-proof and reversible if something goes wrong. With MemMaker alone, I increased my system RAM from 508K to 614K

> This means that, before MemMaker, my TSR utilities and other applications that remain in memory reduced my 640K of conventional memory to 508K. MemMaker reallocated all those applications into high memory and I regained 106K of RAM memory.

With its ease of use and bullet-proof reliability (not to mention its free with MS-DOS), MemMaker is probably sufficient for all but hard-core users. If you don't think so, then consider its competitors.

386MAX improves upon MemMaker but it will cost you money. By the way, despite the name, it can be used on 486 computers.

386MAX is one such product. Like the other competitors, 386MAX takes a more aggressive approach to "re-mapping" memory and, in the process, regains memory not available with MemMaker. In the process, it also has a greater potential to cause problems by reallocating memory space it shouldn't touch. For instance, the computer uses "ROM BIOS" memory to store start-up and operating information even when the computer is off. These products search that memory for free space which is then converted to free more conventional memory. If the utility is too aggressive however, it may overwrite information or take up "ROM BIOS" memory needed for proper computer operation. The result is a "freeze" or "lockup" of the computer. While this situation is not the usual result, the point is that these more aggressive techniques pave the way for greater conflict. Like they say, no pain...no gain. One place 386MAX doesn't provide pain, however, is in the setup

> Actually, all these competitive products beat Microsoft's MemMaker to the market with easy and automatic installations by years.

It installs as easy as MemMaker and provides even greater flexibility in the use of memory for persons using both DOS applications and Windows applications. In addition to recovering more memory, 386MAX will check installed memory for certain defects and works with hard disk compression software.

NetRoom is a very advanced Memory Manager using "cloaking" technology.

NetRoom provides the functionality of 386MAX and then some. NetRoom regains additional memory space using a "cloaking" technology. This technology replaces the ROM BIOS discussed above with a marker. The marker redirects attention to high memory where the ROM BIOS is moved. This, of course, frees the prior ROM BIOS memory for use as conventional memory. While this technology is not compatible with all computers, NetRoom tests the computer before using "cloaking" and so avoids potential problems. The manner in which NetRoom "swaps" memory is also conducive to quicker performance when compared with other memory management technologies. Like 386MAX, NetRoom provides memory analysis capabilities but also includes virus protection for its BIOS code and caching programs to speed data access and perceived performance. With an easy installation and intuitive interface, NetRoom is a great tool for those needing maximum conventional memory.

QEMM-386 is a 32 bit Memory Manager using "Stealth" technology.

Quarterdeck Office System's QEMM-386 provides the functionality of the above products, analysis programs and easy and automatic installation. It also provides a 32 bit memory management program optimized for the new Intel Pentium processor.

QEMM uses "Stealth" rather than "cloaking" to "swap" memory and free conventional memory for use. It also uses a feature called "DOS-Up" that performs the same function as NetRoom's "cloaking" to place markers for DOS files usually loaded in conventional memory. With "DOS-Up", 60K or more of memory can be freed for conventional use.

Which Memory Manager do I need?

Again, when considering MemMaker, included free with MS-DOS, and the three other utilities, consider your real needs. If you work exclusively with Windows applications or do not use large data files with newer DOS applications, then MemMaker is probably sufficient. Also consider that the other three programs will cost you 1-2 MB of hard disk space and $50.00-$100.00 for the additional memory eked out by these advanced memory managers. If you need the memory, they're worth the money; if not, then spend your money elsewhere.

Backup Applications let you protect your investment in your business data.

As I mentioned earlier, backup utilities are necessary to store copies of data files and applications kept on your hard disk in case the data is lost. If you think backup software is only to protect you from a mechanical failure or computer error, think again. Natural disasters can wipe out your entire office, including your computer and, although you can order a new computer, its the data that's vital to your business. With a backup kept in your home or another office location, you can order a new computer, restore the data and be back in business in 24 hours. The alternative, if you can even recover the actual computer, is to retain data recovery experts to recover the data off your "dead" computer and hard disk. It takes time and is more costly than backups. Also consider less exotic means of losing data. Theft is not only possible, in some areas, it is likely. I'll bet your business insurance won't cover the damage caused by data loss. Also consider that malicious action by a fired employee can render your data non-existent. If your employees are human (and I assume they are) consider that a mistaken deletion or overwrite can render critical files irretrievably lost. These are all very real reasons for backups on a regular basis. I have needed backups to restore system settings during experimentation and to recover data files that I mistakenly thought I no longer needed. Having the backups kept a moment's error from resulting in a long and tedious afternoon of reconstruction.

Backups can be difficult with great amounts of data...but there are solutions.

The problem with backups is that newer applications are so much larger that the total amount of data to be backed up and the time involved in such backups approaches intimidating numbers. Even personal computers are likely to approach 200 MB of application software and data storage. Transferring that much data to floppy disks can take hours and over 100 floppy disks. The time and aggravation involved begin to justify not backing up the data. There are a few solutions however. The proper solution depends upon your circumstances, budget and inclination.

Tape drives will back up large hard drives at a reasonable cost.

The hardware solution is tape drives. Tape drives replace floppy diskettes with tape cartridges similar to cassette tapes in design. These tapes can hold 40-120 MB of data on a single cartridge. With the use of compression techniques, most backup utilities can effectively double these capacities to 80 -240 MB of storage. Tape drives are a reasonably priced solution to large storage needs and most backup applications and utilities can support the few tape drive standards promoted today.

What's a "full" backup and how does it differ from "incremental" or "differential" backups?

The software solution to large backup needs is to use "incremental" or "differential" backups jointly with a "full" backup. What does that mean?, you say. Simply put, a "full" backup is a backup of all files on your hard disk

> In many instances, "full" is used to describe backups of all files on a hard disk. Actually, a "full" backup is a backup of all files within a group or set of files regardless of whether a file has changed or remains unchanged since the last backup. Files can be part of more than one backup set and each set can constitute a "full" backup of all files within that set.

An "incremental" backup is a backup of all files that have changed since the last "full" backup or "incremental" backup. A "differential" backup is a backup of all files that have changed since the last "full" backup. What is the practical difference between "incremental" and "differential" backups? First, at the start of your business, you would perform a full backup and consider performing a full backup on the 1st day of each month. Assuming your data changes daily (such as orders and inventory databases), you should then strongly consider backing up the data each workday in case of theft or damage during the night. Each incremental backup will record the files that have changed from the previous day. At the end of the monthly period, you will have one full backup and 20 separate incremental backups (assuming 5 workdays for four weeks), each recording the state of your datafiles for that workday. If you were to instead follow the full backup with a differential backup, at the end of the month you would have one full backup with one separate differential backup set.

Which type of backup do I want to use?

Which do you use then? If the only files that change on a regular basis are a few database files, then the differential backup is quicker and requires less juggling of backup disks. Its one disadvantage is that each workday, the prior day's files will be overwritten. If, five days later, you need to access the datafiles for a particular workday, they will not be available with a differential backup.

> They would be available with an incremental backup. This may be more important if you accidentally delete a file that has changed since the full backup and don't discover the error for a few days.

If a large number of different files are changing daily, then the incremental backup will record only those changes and will be quicker than the differential backup as the end of the month approaches. Its chief disadvantage lies in restoring data to the computer. To properly and effectively restore the computer's files in case of a total loss, the incremental backup method requires you to first restore the full backup set and then restore each incremental backup set starting with the first such set after the full backup and progressing through each incremental set to the present. If a restore is necessary on the 30th day of the month, this requires one full restore and 20 subsequent incremental restores. Its advantage is the differential backup's disadvantage, discussed above.

With 140 MB of data, what's my solution to backing up my computer? How about two different "full" backups.

Finally, consider my solution to the problem, discussed in greater detail in Chapter 22, Practical Tips and Tricks. I separate my files and directories into application files that do not change regularly and client data files and directories that change on a regular basis. My backup utility allows me to define more than one backup set with a description and I have two such backup sets "Application Files and Forms" and "Client Files"; each being a full backup set. Very infrequently, I will perform a full backup using the "Application Files and Forms" set and backup all my applications and form files. This takes approximately 40 disks and 30 minutes but I only perform this type of backup every three months. The "Client Files" set is a full backup set requiring 3 disks and 2 minutes time. It holds all my client files and other regularly changing files (such as template files that change due to the addition of glossary entries and macros) and can be backed up daily. The advantages to this backup system are two-fold. First, I have no investment in a tape backup system. Second, I can perform full backups of directories thereby catching all files added in that workday in addition to those files altered during the day...and it takes only two minutes. This is even quicker than using a tape drive. Moreover, if I need to restore a single file or all the files I know where to find the file depending upon its nature as an application file or data file and a full restore would not require me to keep track of differential backups or incremental backups. The only disadvantage to this system is that new applications would not be backed up until the next quarterly full "Application" backup. In most instances, this drawback would be minimal since most businesses do not regularly add applications to their systems and, in any event, the application is available on the original disks and can be easily re-installed. Overall, I think its one slick solution if it meets your needs.

How do backup utilities differ and what do I look out for?

Why have I discussed backup methods before discussing currently available backup utilities? If you require tape drive backups, some utilities will not work for you. Additionally, some utilities make multiple backup sets easier to manage than others. Microsoft includes a backup and restore utility with MS-DOS. The backup and restore functions have been available in MS-DOS since version 2. The newer versions however, have provided more functions, flexibility and dramatically improved user interfacing(i.e. they're easier to use). I will limit my discussion to the most recent and most capable version in MS-DOS.

Although it is a dramatic improvement over prior versions, Microsoft's Backup will not work with tape drives or many other backup alternatives. If you can effectively backup to floppy disks however, it may meet your needs. Microsoft includes versions for both DOS and Windows operating environments and the new use of graphical and menu-driven interfaces greatly increases the utilities productivity over prior versions. See Figure 14-1.

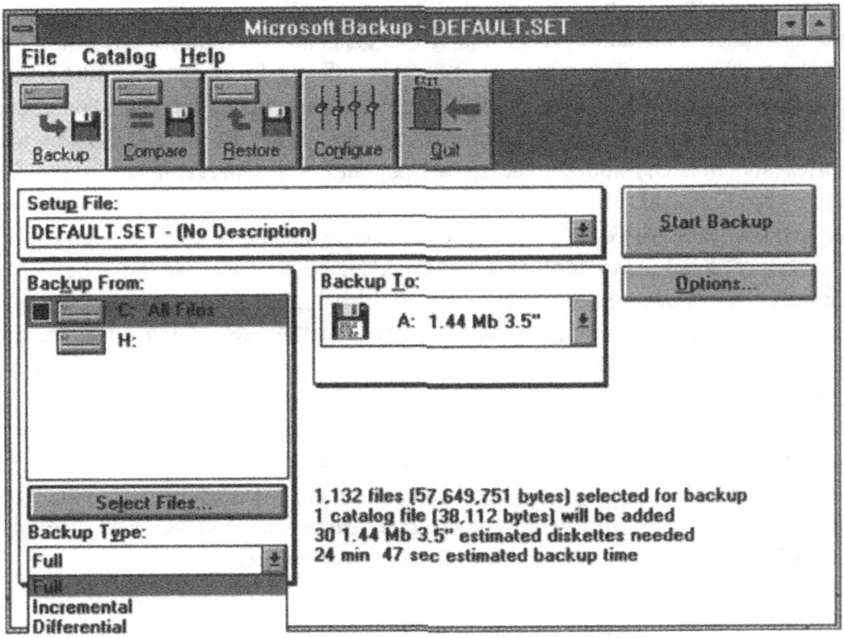

Figure 14-1 The Backup program included with MS-DOS is a great improvement over prior versions but lacks tape support for larger systems.

MS-DOS Backup is actually based upon the Norton backup utilities sold by Symantec Corporation and uses Norton Backup's master catalog system to store catalogs of multiple backup sets on the computer's hard drive and the backup disks. It also incorporates compression to effectively reduce the number of diskettes needed for a backup. Compared to the stand alone products however, MS-DOS Backup is slower to backup and restore files and does not provide the customization or options available in the stand alone products.

Norton Backup for DOS and Windows makes backups easy.

Norton Backup for DOS and Norton Backup for Windows are full featured backup utilities providing intuitive interfaces, a wide range of options and automatic configurations and very quick backup speed and compression. See Figure 14-2. While these utilities can backup to tape drives, only certain tape drives are guaranteed to work and the utilities will not work with parallel port tape drives used by portable computers.

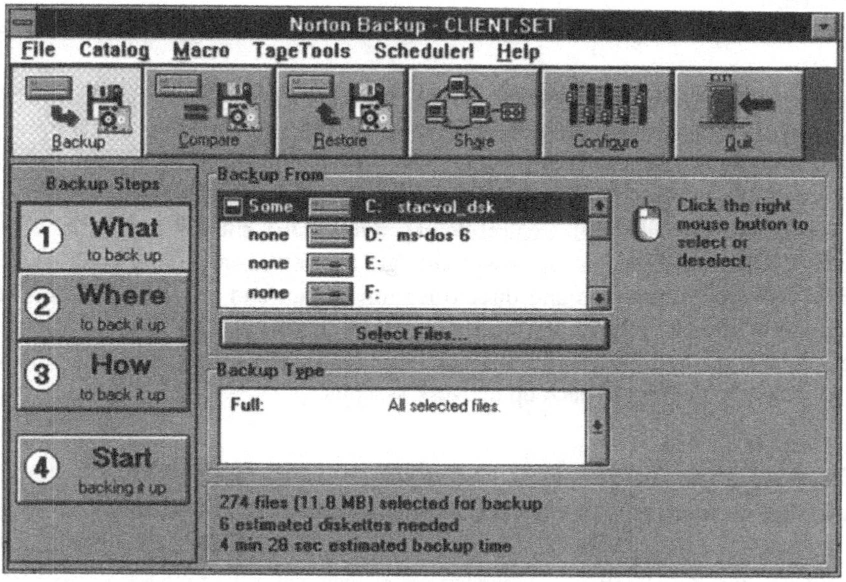

Figure 14-2 Norton Backup (Symantec Corporation) includes support for high-speed tape drives and includes the tools to maintain your tape drive collection. The entire program is amenable to point and click operation.

It would amaze you how diskettes are mistreated, either intentionally or by accident. Although manufacturers attempt to render them durable, people still manage to destroy diskettes with alarming frequency.

Norton Backup has been rated as 150% faster than MS-DOS Backup, primarily due to its ability to directly access memory during the backup process. Norton Backup can also manipulate data on tape cartridges, deleting portions or overwriting the data for increased security. Norton and Microsoft's storage of catalogs on the hard disk also provides a measure of security in those instances when file information is not available from the last disk or tape in the backup set. In case you think it unlikely that a disk should be lost, consider that the data can be lost through faulty diskette media or by dropping the diskette during a backup and running your chair over it.

Finally, Norton Backup can read and write using Microsoft's backup compression standard. This makes it the most feasible upgrade choice for those persons continuing backups started with MS-DOS.

Central Point Backup for DOS and Windows is on par with Norton Backup.

Central Point Software's Backup for DOS and Backup for Windows are direct competitors to Norton's products. Both backup with similar speed and restore from diskettes with similar speed (although Central Point's utility is noticeably quicker to restore individual files from tape drive cartridges). Both provide password protection to secure backups (although Central Point provides DES encryption), a file viewer to view files before selection for backup and graphical tree and file directories to pick or exclude individual files and directories for backup and restore. While Norton is marginally quicker in most instances, Central Point provides optional virus scanning during backups and Central Point works with SCSI tape drives, an optional backup drive likely to be used to back up network systems.

Fastback Plus has features of benefit to network systems.

A third popular, dedicated backup program is Fastback Plus for DOS (also Fastback Plus for Windows). In addition to innovative features useful for network use, Fastback Plus provides many, although not all, of the file selection features of Norton and Central Point. If Fastback is a consideration, be aware that the DOS and Windows versions vary in features, options and flexibility with the DOS version being the more capable of the two.

Which backup utility do I get? My suggestion is Norton Backup.

Of these three products, Norton is my choice for a backup program. With marginally quicker speed, a feature set not exceeded by either of the other two products and the ability to read MS-DOS backup sets, Norton is a logical choice. If you are considering either the Norton or Central Point products, also consider the packages offered by each manufacturer and discussed later in this chapter. At the price of a single utility, these packages include the full-featured backup programs in addition to a slew of other capable utilities.

Hard disk compression...you can really get twice the capacity from your hard disk!

This is called "on-the-fly" compression and differs from compression utilities such as PK Zip, ARJ and LHZ which compress files for storage or archiving. Files compressed with these "archivers" must be manually de-compressed before use.

How does compression work and what is "on-the-fly" compression?

Hard disk compression utilities have become mainstream utilities today, primarily because of Microsoft's first foray into this market with MS-DOS 6 DoubleSpace and the large, installed customer base using MS-DOS and DoubleSpace. Hard disk compression utilities invisibly double the apparent size of a computer's hard disk storage capacity by compressing files stored on the disk and uncompressing the files when the files are "read" into RAM memory for use.

Prior to MS-DOS 6, these utilities depended upon software drivers (like video drivers or printer drivers) to be loaded into memory during start-up and redirect the file searches to a compressed file containing all the compressed data on the disk. The machine was then fooled into thinking this compressed file (called a CVF for Compressed Volume File) was the entire hard disk drive.

> Disk Compression can create problems but DOS 6 has addressed these problems and increased the safety and reliability of disk compression utilities.

If the compression drivers were accidentally deleted or damaged however, the computer would not know where to access its data and the data would be "lost". While these utilities have previously required careful installation and setup to prevent such data loss, Microsoft changed the face of compression utilities by incorporating these utility drivers into an earlier part of the computer start-up process. By incorporating this search for the utility driver before user intervention is possible and before any other application or utility could be placed in memory, Microsoft both simplified the configuration process and reduced the opportunities for machine or human error.

DoubleSpace is a disk compression utility included in the price of MS-DOS.

As part of MS-DOS 6, Microsoft included DoubleSpace, a disk compression utility. With DoubleSpace, a 40 MB hard disk could become an 80 MB hard disk. The greatest advantage to using Microsoft's DoubleSpace is the price. Rather than pay the $100.00 or so for another dedicated utility, DoubleSpace is included in the price of MS-DOS (about $50.00 where discounted). Its disadvantages when compared with the other dedicated utilities are numerous however. First, DoubleSpace does not include as capable and comprehensive a set of organizational and maintenance as other compression manufacturers. Since the data is stored in a compressed format on the disk, some utilities developed to maintain and organize a hard disk populated with uncompressed data do not operate correctly...hence the need for such dedicated utilities. While DoubleSpace provides functional utilities to meet these needs, the utilities are not user-friendly, lack features and customization available in other products and lack the performance and results attained with these other products. DoubleSpace also lacks a sufficiently capable Windows interface for accessing its utilities and providing feedback on the status of the compressed disk and data. The better products provide this convenience and efficiency which, after all, is the purpose of Windows. Finally, other products will generate slightly greater compression than DoubleSpace for a given performance level and provide utilities to read and write to compressed data on floppy disks even if the current computer does not use the compression utility. Still, Microsoft is committed to DoubleSpace and, in the future, should provide updates to its native compression utility to match its competitors and up the ante in the disk compression arena.

Stacker provides a margin of safety and performance unequaled by other disk compression utilities.

Stac Electronic's Stacker product is the standard by which all other compression products are compared. Currently Stacker for DOS & Windows provides the best combination of integration, maintenance, ease of use and results of any disk compression product available today. Stac also provides a very capable version of Stacker that does not use Microsoft's MS-DOS 6+ integration feature but provides very reliable compression with the updated utilities and interface of Stacker. In addition to compression rates generally exceeding DoubleSpace's by at least 10% for a given performance level, Stacker can be installed and maintained from either DOS or Windows using a very clear menu in DOS, icons and menu selections in Windows and on-line help system to guide the user through new operations. Figure 14-3 is the Stacker Toolbox, from which all Stacker functions can be controlled monitored in Windows.

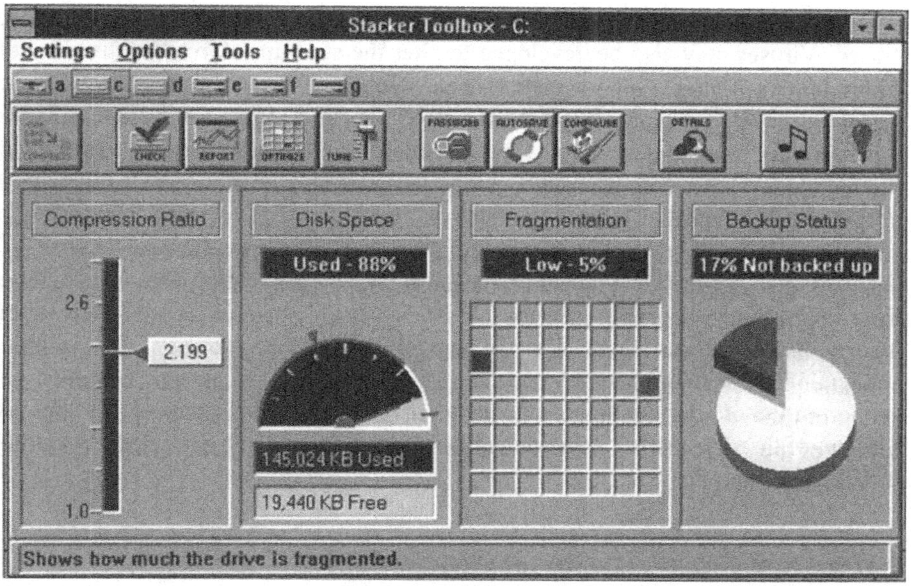

Figure 14-3 The Stacker Toolbox provides immediate graphical feedback on the status of your hard disk system. As you can see from the graph, this hard disk is relatively full, has a fair chunk of data that needs to be backed up but doesn't have much file fragmentation. With the Toolbox the speed and compression ratio can be adjusted, defragmentation can be commenced and readouts of file compression by directory or type can be accessed.

Stacker provides automatic checking at start-up, prompts the user through its menu to fix any problems encountered with the compressed data and provides flexible options in organizing the data on the compressed disk. Stacker also makes good use of graphs to indicate disk usage, disk fragmentation, increased space and the percentage of data that has not been backed up. Although it is not perfect, Stacker is the best of these utilities currently available.

What are computer viruses and why are Anti-Virus utilities a "must" for all computers.

AntiVirus utilities protect computer data from damage or loss due to computer viruses. Computer viruses are applications that are developed to infiltrate a computer through its memory and attach themselves to executable files. These viruses infiltrate the computer memory when a person unknowingly copies infected files from floppy diskettes or transfers infected files from another computer through a modem or laplink cable. The virus may alter data by replicating itself or other data within the file and thereby destroy the file or alter the manner in which the computer operates.

By altering the computer's operation, application and data files may be altered or erased. Viruses may also be developed to alter the start-up information used by the computer to configure itself on start-up or viruses may alter or destroy the file index system used by computers (called the FAT or File Allocation Table) thereby rendering the computer's data inaccessible. While some viruses have been catalogued and their computer code can be recognized by most competent anti-virus utilities, newer viruses have been developed known as "stealth" viruses or "polymorphic" viruses. These viruses actually alter their appearance over time and disguise their presence by metamorphasizing thereby preventing anti-virus utilities from identifying them by reference to a particular string of code. Why some renegade software developers feel the need to prove their prowess by developing applications to damage people's data is unclear, one thing is; in this computerized version of the old missile-antimissile game, using last year's technology can get you shot out of the sky. I always recommend a top-of-the-line anti-virus utility. Anything less is false insurance.

Norton Anti-Virus is a top-notch virus fighter.

There are two top anti-virus utilities on the market, Central Point Anti-Virus and Norton Anti-Virus. Year after year, these two companies consistently rate high marks in the industry for their anti-virus utilities. Norton's AntiVirus, available as a stand-alone utility or as part of a package (discussed below), is composed of two separate components, Virus Clinic and Virus Intercept. Virus Intercept remains in the computer's memory at all times and constantly guards against the presence of a virus. If a virus is detected, Virus Intercept interrupts any application in current use to warn the operator of the possible presence of a virus. What Virus Intercept does and what it will allow you to do are customized via the screen in Figure 14-4.

How do Anti-Virus utilities identify and protect against viruses?

How does Virus Intercept know if a virus exists? Two methods are available. First, known virus codes are recorded in memory with Virus Intercept and are matched against other application codes to detect the presence of a virus. Since new viruses are constantly being released and new strains of old viruses (virus computer code subtly altered through interaction with other application code) are being discovered, these virus codes are constantly updated by Symantec and are available through AntiVirus upgrade disks purchased through Symantec or virus code updates available through Symantec's BBS service. Virus codes can also be updated manually. The second method involves a process of inoculation and is currently used to seek and detect unknown viruses that may be on the computer files. AntiVirus

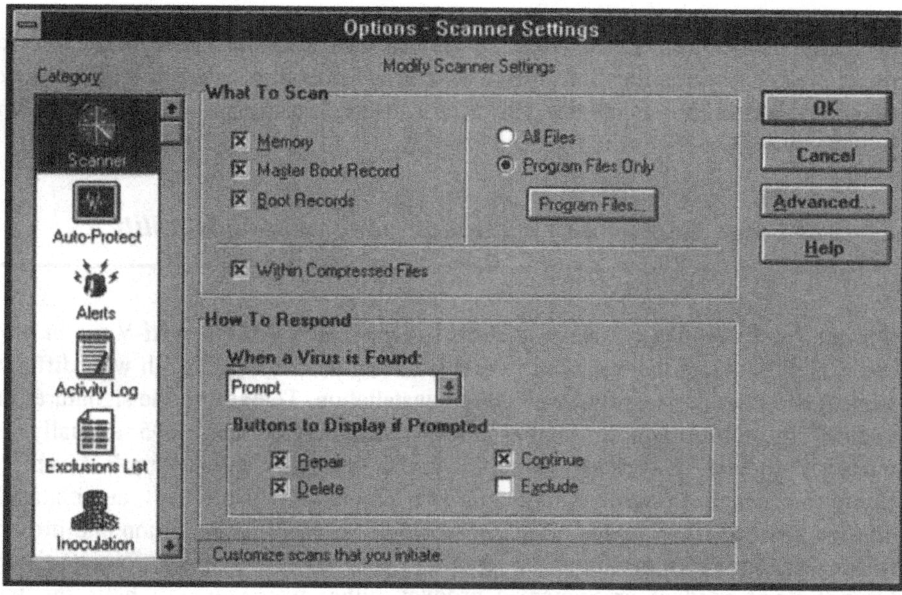

Figure 14-4 Depending upon how you use your system, you may want Norton Anti-Virus to monitor all or just some of your files. For network compatibility, you can define which actions an employee can take when the warning is displayed. In this way, if you don't want employees deleting files which are "flagged" as possibly virulent, you can remove that choice until a manager or network administrator assesses the situation

scans all files on the computer and assigns inoculation values to each program file on the computer. If a file is scanned later and reports a different value, AntiVirus reports that the file has been altered and may be infected by an unknown virus. Unfortunately, this is not always the case since application files may change size for a number of reasons unrelated to computer viruses. If the application is updated, the old values are invalid and the files must then be reinoculated to assign new updated values. Accordingly, this method is not ideal. Still, it provides at least some level of protection against new, undiscovered or "stealth" viruses.

If a virus is detected, Virus Clinic, the second component, is then used to either repair the infected file and remove the virus or delete the entire file to cleanse the system. Whether a file can be repaired will depend upon Virus Clinic's ability to identify the virus and the manner in which the virus infected the file. Some viruses merely append themselves to program files and so their code can be identified and removed. Other viruses may delete the file's code and replace it with their own code. Such files are generally not repairable and the file must be deleted and a clean copy restored from backup sets, if possible.

Virus Clinic may also be used to selectively scan the entire disk, selected directories or selected files for viruses when, for instance, a new file or directory of files is placed on the computer. This scan can confirm the absence of viruses and provide the values for inoculation protection.

Central Point's Anti-Virus is another good anti-virus utility.

Central Point's Anti-Virus is comparable to Symantec's Norton Anti-Virus in most respects. It provides the same sentry and scanning modules (although with different names) and provides easy and well guided installation. The virus code signatures are updated by subscribing to Central Point's disk service at $79.95 annually for quarterly updates or updates can be acquired through Central Point's forum on CompuServe for a log-on charge. Central Point Anti-Virus will automatically remove infected files or alter the file extension to prevent its execution and provide full reports on screen or output the reports to your printer. Whether you choose the Central Point product or Symantec product, either way you will have the best combination of anti-virus defenses offered today.

What do I do if a file is accidentally deleted? Use an undelete utility.

Sooner or later, you will delete a file you later want or need. Perhaps you deleted the file with a DOS command you didn't understand or perhaps you overwrote the file with another file of the same name. In any event, most times such files can be recovered. Contrary to popular belief, when a file is deleted or replaced with another file of the same name, the information is not erased from the hard disk (or floppy disk). Rather, DOS goes to the file index table (called FAT for File Allocation Table) and erases the first letter of the filename. Without a full filename in the index, DOS does not know where to search for the file on the hard disk and it is effectively "lost". Undelete utilities operate by keeping records of these "deleted" files and their location on the hard disk. By invoking the undelete utility, a person is presented with a list of filenames missing their first character. By replacing this character, the person then provides the information necessary for the undelete utility to recover the file. Pretty neat, huh?

How long after a file is deleted can I recover it?

As time progresses however, new files and data are placed on the hard disk and may eventually overwrite all or part of a "deleted" file. When this happens, the ability of the undelete utility to recover the file is degraded. For this reason, undelete utilities are tools best suited for immediate or recent file deletion recoveries. To enhance their effectiveness, some undelete utilities can be configured to protect "deleted" files from being overwritten by new data until a period of time has passed or unused hard disk space is no longer available for new data.

MS-DOS includes an Undelete utility. Why buy another?

Microsoft's MS-DOS Undelete utility (included free with MS-DOS and pictured in Figure 14-5) is licensed from Central Point Software however, Central Point includes greater flexibility and an improved feature set. Microsoft's Undelete provides Delete Sentry, which is the utility's means of protecting data from being overwritten.

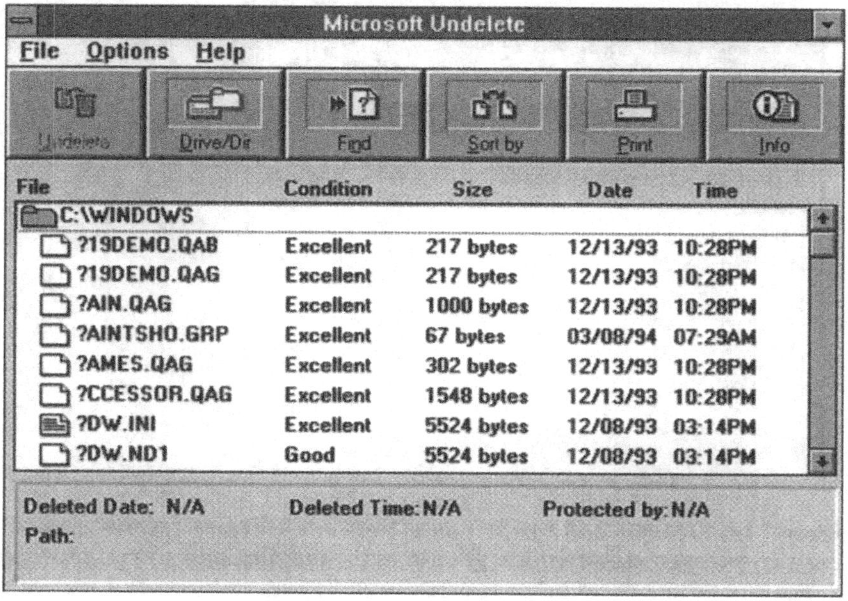

Figure 14-5 The Undelete utility included with MS-DOS is effective and "free". Although it doesn't have the extra protection offered by third party products, it will recover files recently deleted by an inadvertent slip of the fingers.

The utility will default to protecting deleted files for 7 days and will not use more than 20% of the hard disk space to store such protected files. Once the 7 day period or 20% limit is reached, the oldest files are no longer protected although they may not be immediately overwritten. These defaults can be changed. The Windows version of Microsoft Undelete provides a menu of deleted files available for recovery but little else. Still, the utility is effective and serves its basic purpose.

Central Point's PC Tools includes an Undelete utility with file viewers and manual recovery.

Central Point's Undelete, included only in its utility packages PC Tools for DOS and PC Tools for Windows improves upon the licensed Microsoft version by providing viewers to view deleted files in a menu for undelete selection. The file can also be manually reconstructed in the event automatic recovery is not possible. Manual recovery is likely in instances where most but not all of the files fragments remain untouched and can be recovered, resulting in a damaged but recovered file.

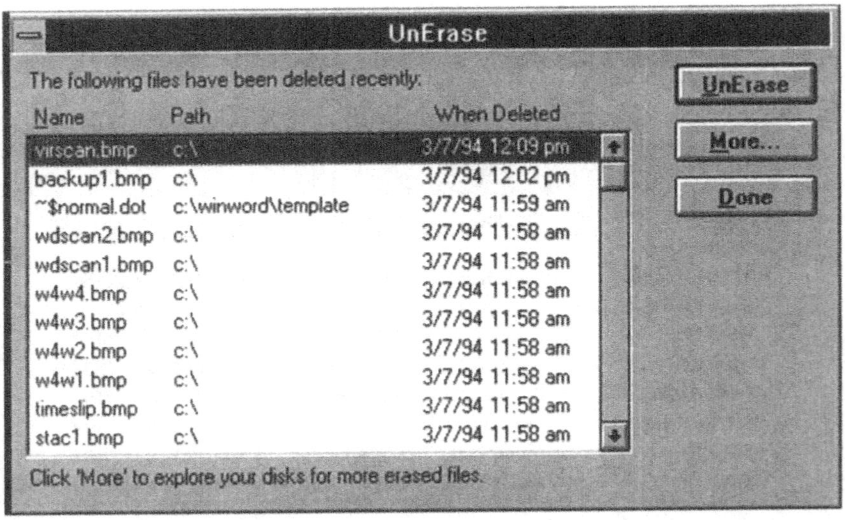

Figure 14-6 Straight and to the point, Norton's Unerase feature makes it easy to recover deleted files. Its strength and flexibility are hidden but accessible to fine-tune the system resources it uses to track and maintain a list of recoverable files.

Norton Utilities and Norton Desktop also include a full-featured Undelete utility.

Symantec's Unerase utility is available in its utility packages including The Norton Utilities, The Norton Desktop for Windows and The Norton Desktop for DOS. See

Figure 14-6. Symantec's product is directly competitive with Central Point's by providing file viewers and the ability to manually reconstruct deleted files. Norton Unerase can also utilize markers left by MS-DOS to mark the location of deleted files and undelete files protected by MS-DOS's Delete Sentry. Finally, Unerase can use file location data stored by the Norton Image utility, also included with these utility packages, to recover files even without the benefit of the other deleted file depositories.

"Shells" provide a number of advanced utilities at a reasonable cost.

Many of the above utilities are packaged with disk and file management shells by their respective manufacturers at a cost nominally exceeding the cost of a single utility. Symantec markets The Norton Utilities, The Norton Desktop for Windows and The Norton Desktop for DOS.

What is Norton Utilities and what does it include?

The Norton Utilities is a conglomeration of many disk maintenance and repair utilities, including Norton Disk Doctor, a utility for analyzing and repairing the file and directory structure of the hard disk and the index table (FAT) used to store file and directory locations (shown in Figure 14-7).

It also includes the Unerase utility (Figure 14-6), a disk editor for dissecting the hard disk's contents (not for the faint of heart) and Speedisk, a utility for physically relocating files on the hard disk for better access and performance. The current version of The Norton Utilities works in the special environment of hard disk compression and is capable of recovering and maintaining data on hard disks compressed with Microsoft DoubleSpace and Stac Electronic's Stacker (among others). However, The Norton Utilities, while considered the best for maintenance and repair duty, lacks the broadness of scope of the other utility packages.

PC Tools allows customization of DOS and Windows to work with you...not against you.

Central Point's PC Tools for DOS and PC Tools for Windows are well rounded packages for everything from file access and disk management to disk repair, backup and anti-virus protection. Both provide a clear directory tree and file window with access to many file and directory functions, file viewers for viewing files without

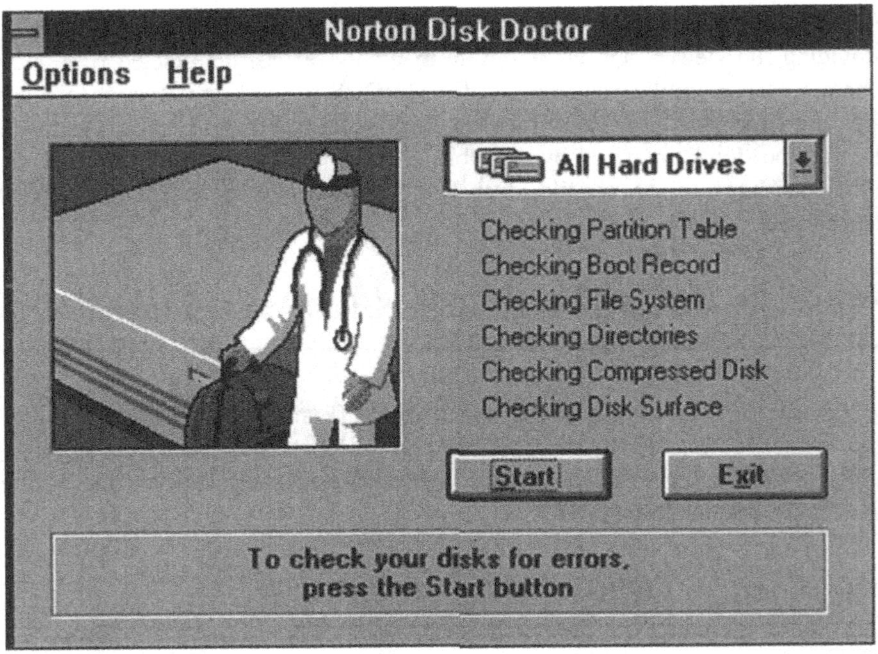

Figure 14-7 Its powerful but Symantec makes it easy to use. Norton Disk Doctor provides a host of functions designed to repair very serious hard disk and floppy disk problems with little or no knowledge on the user's part about computers. Even most brands of compression software don't bother it.

taking the time to actually launch the file's application and load the file, and the ability to switch between applications. PC Tools also provides the same capable backup and anti-virus utilities that are available as separate packages.

Since each separate utility's list price is approximately 70% of the list price of the entire PC Tools package, PC Tools is the logical choice for anyone considering purchasing one or more of these separate utilities.

The Windows version provides a multiple desktop utility that provides the option of placing full-screen applications in separate virtual desktops and switching from one to the other as needed. The Windows version also makes good use of "drag and drop" interfacing to allow desktop customization and arrangement. The icon toolbars are customizable and include text as well as graphics images to help the user keep track of functions. PC Tools also provides disk diagnoses and repair functions even from within Windows and can automatically defragment the disk even while the computer continues to be used. Finally, for you Windows users, PC Tools offers configuration advice to help eke out that last ounce of performance and continues to keep track of your resources with its "Crash Recovery Guard" feature. In the event of a system lockup or crash, PC Tools can place you right back in the driver's seat with no information loss.

Norton Desktop for DOS and Windows includes many Norton Utilities and additional enhancements to the DOS and Windows desktops.

Symantec first released its Norton Desktop for Windows, one of the first full featured Windows shells to replace the Program Manager and File Manager programs and allow a greater range of customization and control over the Windows environment. Later, Symantec released Norton Desktop for DOS. Although the interfaces are similar, the DOS environment places limitations on the flexibility of the DOS product not found in Windows. Symantec's DOS product is competitive, however, with PC Tools for DOS. Norton took the functions of the Program Manager, File Manager and the Accessories groups found in Windows and placed them on the desktop. Icons representing drives are placed directly on the desktop and may be selected to reveal a directory and file window (called the drive window). From the Norton menu or the customizable button bar on the bottom of the drive window, a person can perform many powerful file management functions. Selecting a file within the window will launch the file's native application and load the file. From these drives, you can copy, move and delete a single or discontinuous range of files, directories and subdirectories. Tool icons can also grace the desktop, enabling you to perform any number of disk management and file management functions just by dragging and dropping filenames from a drive window or drive icons from the desktop. If you want to print a file, drag it from the drive window to the print icon. If you want to delete or shred (irretrievably delete) a file, directory, or subdirectory, drag it to the SmartErase icon or Shredder icon. If you want to backup your C: drive, drag the drive icon to the backup icon. You get the idea.. In addition to file and disk management however, Norton Desktop also includes an assortment of mini-applications (mini-applets?) like a Personal Information Manager (PIM), three calculators, an icon editor, a very powerful text editor and a very capable cross-application macro language (meaning it can run not only Norton Desktop but other applications as well).

Norton also pioneered the concept of "groups within groups". With this concept, groups of icons, representing either applications or data files, can be placed in one group and that group can further be placed within other groups. This hierarchical organization allows greater flexibility in grouping related files and applications. For instance, if your company had east, west, north and south regional accounting reports a group could be established to hold accounting reports and then four subgroups could be placed within that group for each of the four regions. If you were so inclined, each of these subgroups could contain groups for the divisions within each region. In this way, a single report would be placed logically within the hierarchy of the organization. In contrast, Windows only allows single groups within Program Manager. Accordingly, using Program Manager, all the division reports and region reports would be contained within one group making retrieval a harder proposition.

If this isn't enough to convince you that you may want such a product, consider that Symantec also includes many of the disk repair and maintenance utilities (although not all) it packages in The Norton Utilities, includes its full featured backup program and further includes its full featured anti-virus program. Purchase this one program and continue updating the program, and you stand a good chance of receiving updates to all the other products (repair utilities, backup and anti-virus) as well. I consider it a fantastic bargain.

In addition to the utilities we've discussed, there are also a great number of shareware utilities that are available to manage your files and organize your desktop. The following shareware utilities run the gamut from archiving utilities which "crunch" your files into smaller packages for storage and transmission over modems to products that give you virtual desktops and others that manage those desktops, launch applications and locate files.

PKZIP compresses files and directories of files for efficient storage (called archiving) by using a compression scheme similar to those used by "on the fly" compression utilities like DoubleSpace and Stacker. With PKZIP, the files cannot be accessed (although they can be viewed with some other utilities) until they are "unzipped" using its sister program PKUnzip. Over the years, PKZIP has been improved to provide more features and now provides compression of files over multiple floppy disks. Available as freeware to individuals, but not businesses, an enhanced version is available at cost from the author. The program has many advanced features which can be accessed through a DOS command line (Figure 14-8) although many utilities are now available for intuitively accessing these features. See WinZip and Figure 14-9.

Registration: PK Ware, Inc.
9025 North Deerwood Drive
Brown Deer, WI 53223
Voice (414) 354-8699
BBS (414) 354-8670
FAX (414) 354-8559
$47.00 registration fee includes disk, printed manual and free upgrade

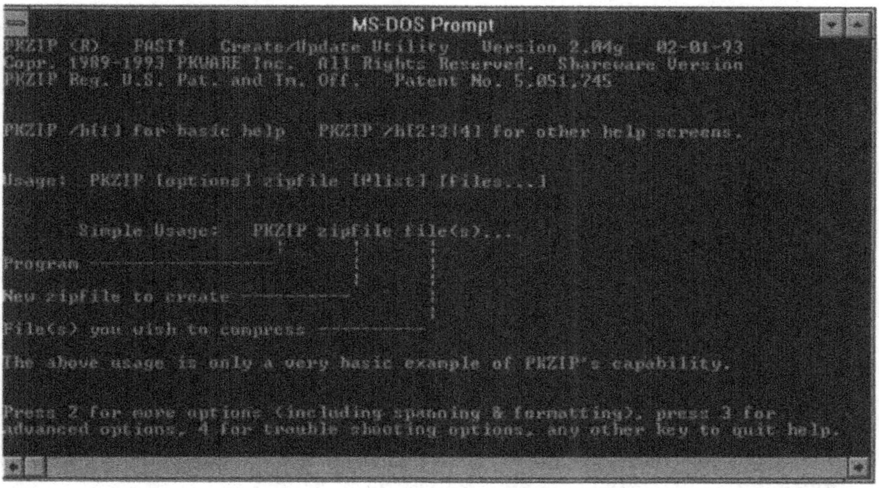

Figure 14-8 PKZIP is the standard by which all other archiving programs are measured. After numerous revisions, the program can archive large files that require two or more floppy disks and it can even be used to backup your hard disk in the absence of any other backup software. Its functions can be accessed by using the DOS command line (pictured) or by using a Windows utility with menus and buttons for each function. If the latter option appeals to you, I recommend WinZip.

ARJ is a direct competitor to PKZIP. It provides comparable performance but requires registration for its continued use. This compression utility also contains many advanced features intuitively accessible through many file compression "shells" including WinZip.

Registration: Robert K. Jung
2606 Village Road West
Norwood, MA 02062
Registration not mandatory for personal (nonbusiness) use. $35.00 registration fee for business, commercial or institutional use after 30 days.

WinZip is a Windows "front-end" and file archive management tool for compressing and uncompressing files or entire directories using PKZIP, ARJ, or LHZ file compressors. See Figure 14-9. It allows updating of compressed files, viewing capabilities and a unique check-out facility that decompresses a list of files into a temporary directory for testing and review before actual decompression and installation on the hard disk.

Registration: Nico Mak
P.O. Box 919
Bristol, CT 06011-0919
$29.00 registration fee

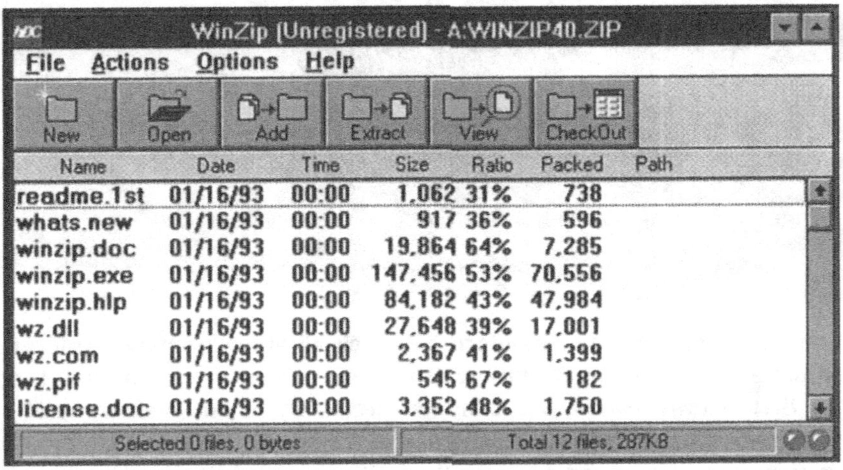

Figure 14-9 WinZip includes built in PKZip and PKUnzip features so you don't need separate copies of those files to manage your archived files. It makes it easy to access the powerful but buried features of pkzip. It's regularly updated and enhanced to keep up with new pkzip features and enhancements requested from registered customers.

PKLITE is an "on-the-fly" compression product which compresses executable files (files containing EXE and COM extensions) to 50-60% of their original sizes while allowing the files to operate as if uncompressed. In this respect, its purpose is similar to DoubleSpace and Stacker but it must be used on a file by file basis rather than as a means to compress an entire hard disk drive. It differs from PKZIP and ARJ which can compress all types of files (not just executable files) but can only store the files which must be decompressed before use. This product is marketed by the same people that market PKZIP and is also available in an enhanced version (PKLITE Professional) which may be used to distribute software in compressed form for commercial purposes.

Registration: PK Ware, Inc.
9025 North Deerwood Drive
Brown Deer, WI 53223
Voice (414) 354-8699
BBS (414) 354-8670
FAX (414) 354-8559

Free for non-commercial use. $46.00 registration fee includes disk, printed manual and free upgrade

Use for professional purposes requires registration of PK Lite Professional at $146.00.

LITEMENU is to PKLITE what WinZip is to PKZIP, an easy to use interface for using PK Lite by picking commands from the menu. This utility makes PK Lite's command-line features easy to use.

Registration: Borris Technologies
88 West 1485 North
Orem, Utah 84057
(801) 226-6525
$10 registration fee

METZ TASK MANAGER is a replacement for Microsoft Window's own Task Manager and so much more. This one product can virtually replace the Program Manager shell and act as an application launcher, file and directory management shell. See Figure 14-10. It provides system information at the click of a mouse button and can search through directories for files based on file name, extension or text content. Finally, it includes a nine button user configurable icon palette for one-click access to nine applications or commands.

Registration: Metz Software, Inc.
P.O. Box 6699
Bellevue, Wa. 98008-0699
(800) 447-1712

$49.95 registration fee after 30 days, includes Metz Utility Pack (4 additional programs working with Task Manager)

Figure 14-10 Metz Task Manager contains the functionality of both the Windows's File Manager and Program Manager while providing monitoring and system information functions generally required of third party utilities.

FONTSEE is a handy Windows utility to view and print a list of all fonts on your system (Figure 14-11). Each font is printed by name in its actual typeface. If your system has over 100 Truetype fonts installed, as does my system, then this utility can help you see, at a glance, what you may have forgotten was there.

Registration: REEVEsoft
P.O. Box 1884
Clemson S.C. 29633
(803) 654-7378
$15.00 Registration for latest version. No manual is necessary

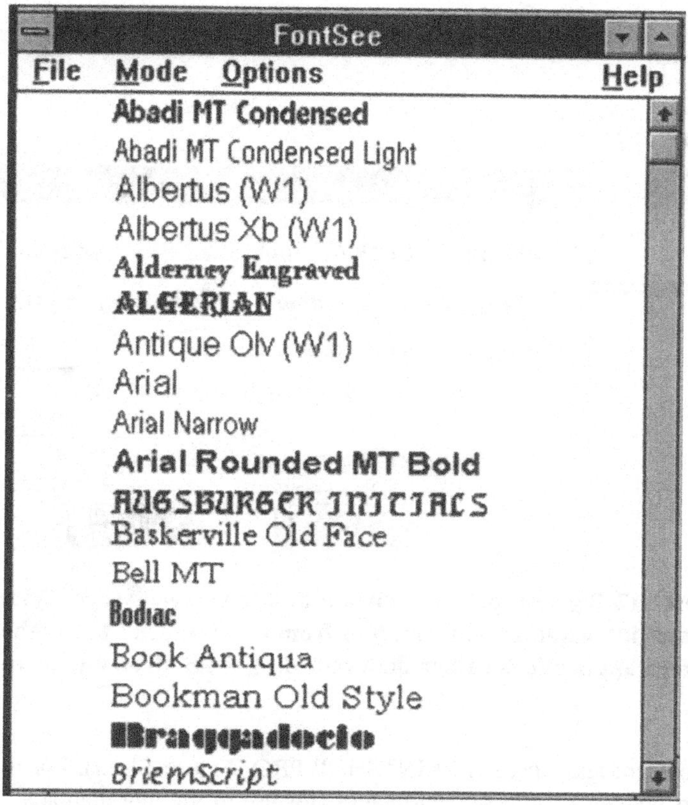

Figure 14-11 FontSee requires very, very little disk space but provides a sorely needed service for those with more font styles than they can remember.

BIG DESK is a Windows utility that allows you to set up and manage virtual screens or desktops so that multiple full screen applications can be simultaneously maintained. See Figure 14-12. What does this mean? You can run a full screen word processor on one virtual desktop while you run your spreadsheet on another. For fast and dirty switching between applications, it's more convenient than minimizing and maximizing your applications on your one desktop screen.

Registration: £20 Registration Fee (no manual necessary)
SP Services
PO Box 456
Southampton
United Kingdom
SO9 7XG

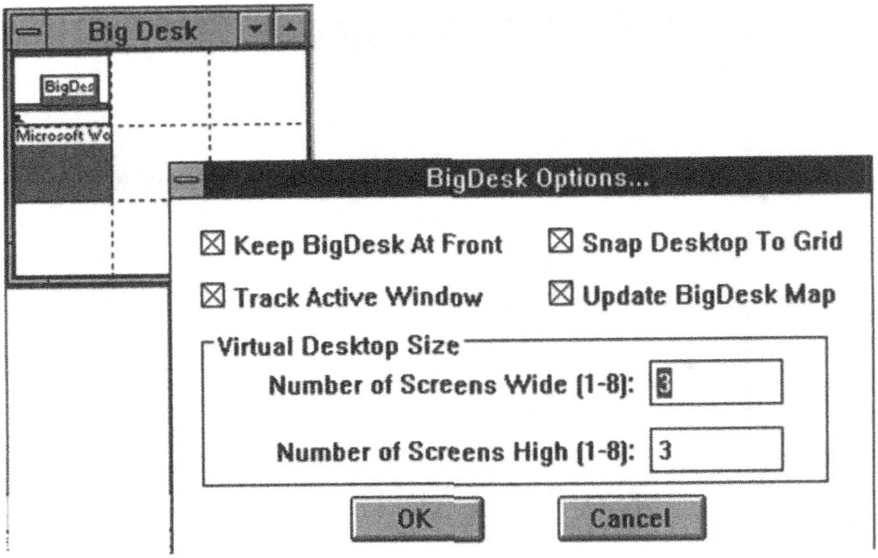

Figure 14-12 BigDesk provides virtual desktop screen space. With multiple screens of information, you can hop from one "screen" to another to view full screen applications rather than crowding them all on one screen.

Last but not least there is PAINTSHOP PRO (Figure 14-13). For those needing to convert images, capture screen images (for use in training manuals, for instance) or manipulate the size, colors or shading of an image, Paint Shop Pro is an excellent tool. The program provides graphics alterations including resizing without loss of clarity and definition, rotation, filtering and special effects such as solarizing. With PSP, the user can adjust the brightness/contrast, highlights/shadows, and color depth. It provides great image manipulation such as image cropping and other enhancement capabilities.

Registration: JASC, Inc.
10901 Red Circle Drive
Suite 340
Minnetonka, MN 55343
Tel.(612) 930-9171
Fax(612) 930-9172
$69.00 registration fee after 30 days, includes disk and bound user's manual

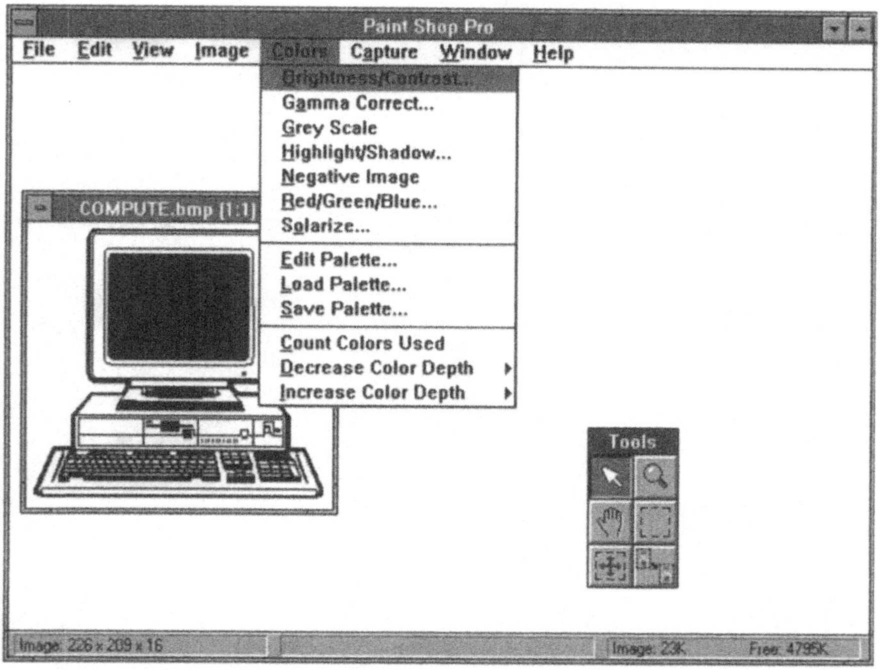

Figure 14-13 Paint Shop Pro provides enough features and versatility for the price to recommend it over a number of highly touted commercial software packages. It provides good graphics editing tools, format conversions and screen capture capabilities. Finally, it doesn't take up a lot of disk space (for a Windows program) and its memory requirements are acceptable.

SECTION IV

Chapter 15

Portable Computers

Why Portables now?

Portable computers are the fastest growing segment of the computer industry. The combination of potential productivity, changes in workplace structuring and corporate emphasis on flexibility has resulted in widespread acceptance of portables previously regarded as expendable "toys". Technological advances in recent years have resulted in truly portable computers capable of competing with powerful desktop systems as your primary computer. The industry has further advanced the portable as a viable system alternative by supporting portables through the development of peripherals and accessories that were previously available solely on desktop systems. Finally, the advent of Windows and the "user-friendly" graphical interface has resulted in software (most particularly, communication software) capable of allowing more effective use of the portable by salespersons or other field personnel that otherwise would be unable to reliably use the computer.

> This is not meant as a slight to those many field personnel that now use portables with DOS. It is true however that Windows and other graphical interfaces allow a user not otherwise intimately familiar or comfortable with computers an easier time in accomplishing many tasks. I regularly use my Windows modem and fax software to use my portable computer as a totable communications center. When I try to use my home computer's DOS software to communicate or send faxes, however, its never easy and the results are never as good.

Is a portable necessarily what your business needs?

Before discussing the available offerings and features that you will encounter in shopping for a portable computer, you must first decide if a portable meets your needs. As part of this analysis you must also decide how you will use the portable. These decisions will dictate the features and style of computer that will best serve your needs. For example, if your portable is going to be your only computer, its ability to store, operate and display all your applications and data is imperative. Furthermore, its communications options and ability to connect to networks may be an issue. If the computer must be capable of accepting expansion cards for a tape backup system, if you use a scanner as part of your regular work or if a sound card is needed for presentations, this will also dictate your options. Alternatively, if the portable is intended to solely be your traveling companion for business trips, your storage, communication and expansion needs may allow you to purchase a lighter, more portable system than in the prior example. Throughout this discussion, I will attempt to remind you of these alternatives when discussing a particular product or feature.

"Luggables" or "clamshell" portables are designed for heavy processing and sophisticated video presentations.

Portable computers are available in a number of sizes. The terms "luggable" or "laptop" are generally reserved for those portables exceeding ten pounds and approaching the size of expandable briefcases. Some systems may also be described as "clamshell" computers due to the manner the computer keyboard is hinged to and covers the computer box and display. Many such systems are extremely powerful, versatile systems with the ability to accept expansion cards for specialized uses. Such systems usually sport upper-end processors and color displays. Some are portable multimedia presentation systems, designed to accommodate and run the newest software and video offerings, for leading edge computer generated video business presentations or demonstrations. Such systems are also costlier and less portable than most mainstream businesses can tolerate.

"Notebook" computers are the most popular portables.

"Notebook" computers are the most popular portables available today due to the wide variety of configurations. Notebooks vary in weight from 5 ½ pounds to nine pounds and generally vary in size from the standard 8 ½" x 11" piece of paper to larger 9" x 12.5" sizes with every combination in between. The thickness of such notebooks varies between 1 ½" and 3" with the thicker designs generally required for the more complex color displays. This chapter will focus on these more mainstream choices and the subnotebooks described below.

What's a "sub-notebook" and is it better for me than a notebook computer?

"Sub-notebooks" will weigh from 2 ½ pounds to 4 pounds and cut the physical dimensions of notebook computers by a third. In return for their more diminutive size and weight, most sub-notebooks will exclude an internal floppy disk drive, reduce the keyboard and display areas and provide less storage capacity than their full-size counterparts. In recent years, however, the reputation of sub-notebooks as second-rate computing tools has been set aside in favor of today's more capable offerings. Subnotebooks are now available with powerful processors, increased storage capabilities, and much improved keyboards and displays. Many of these machines provide very capable computing power for a second business machine.

Personal Digital Assistants (PDA) are computers but their size limits their universal acceptance as necessary business tools.

The smallest group of portable computers are known as "personal assistants" or "pocket" computers. These computers are generally useful as replacements for daily planners and for retrieval of notes and addresses. Some have very useful interfaces including touch-screen capabilities (the ability to pick among on-screen menus and choices such as appointment books, calendars or notes by touching the on-screen icons representing these choices with a finger or supplied pointing device) however, many contain diminutive memories, displays and keyboards that make them unsuitable for word-processing or spreadsheet computing. For this reason, these computers will not be discussed further.

What equipment is included on a portable and how does it compare with a desktop computer?

The keypad is also called a numeric keypad and differs from the keyboard by offering only the numeric keypad usually found on the right side of most keyboards. A portable capable of accepting a numeric keypad would be a good choice for a traveling accountant or other financial analyst.

All portables consist of the same components discussed in Section II of this book. Portables are available with a wide choice of main processor chips, hard disk drive capabilities (permanent storage), RAM memory (temporary storage), and displays. In addition, most portables will include at least one external serial port, one parallel port, and an external video port. Many more will include additional ports including PS/2 mouse ports, external keyboard ports, external keypad ports, external floppy disk drive ports and, in some instances, docking station ports. Many subnotebooks will contain dedicated external floppy disk ports to accommodate the floppy disk drive that has been removed from the machine and provided as a separate unit. Some notebooks also contain these ports to accommodate floppy disk drive accessories available from the notebook manufacture. Such accessories may include tape units or 5 ¼" floppy disk drives since the portable will usually include an internal 3 ½" floppy disk drive. The PS/2 mouse port, keyboard port and keypad port can be the same port on some computers which reduces the total ports and only matters if you need separate ports for two or more such devices.

Portables will also generally include a second serial port (many are advertised as containing two serial ports) that is accessible solely from within the machine and is usually reserved by the machine for a communications device such as a modem or fax/modem.

Toshiba notebooks go one step further and even provide separate PS/2 mouse ports and PS/2 style keyboard ports. This feature is useful for two reasons. First, separate ports means each port can be configured for its particular device. If a single port is not dedicated to the function you need (for instance, a mouse), then the computer must be re-started to configure the port for mouse use. My PS/2 mouse port is internally configured to accept an external keyboard. If the machine is already running and I want to use a mouse in that port, I must restart the computer. On Toshiba's machines, however, the PS/2 mouse port is permanently configured for a mouse and the PS/2 style keyboard port is configured for keyboard use. If the machine is already running, I can connect a mouse at any time and the mouse will operate without further trouble. In the long run, this is a nice feature. Second, by using separate ports, the computer can accept both a mouse and a keyboard/keypad. This is nice if, like my wife, you cannot get used to the layout of a non-standard portable keyboard.

PCMCIA cards and PCMCIA slots...what are they and do I need one?

Today's portables should also include a port that will only be found on tomorrow's desktop machines. The PCMCIA slot advertised on some machines is a slot that accepts a "credit-card" containing electronics, miniaturized mechanical devices or even software. PCMCIA refers to the organization composed of multiple manufacturers that sets the standards for such devices so the consumer can be sure a card advertised as meeting a specification will work in a computer advertised as containing such a port/slot. The "credit cards" and ports come in a variety of thicknesses ranging from 5 mm. to 17 mm. PCMCIA Type 1 cards and slots are the thinnest and Type IV cards and slots are the newest and thickest available. The Type 1 cards are generally manufactured solely as temporary or "flash" storage cards. They provide non-volatile storage of information but have limited capacities.

Non-volatile or "flash" memory retains information for immediate use even after power has been turned off. Such memory, however, provides faster access than the traditional hard disk drive by using memory chips to store the information rather than the hard disk's platter of magnetic media. In this respect, the memory is equivalent, in use, to RAM memory. It differs from RAM memory, which is volatile, since information stored in RAM memory is lost when the computer's power is turned off.

Alternatively, these cards may be used to increase the RAM memory capacity (temporary, volatile memory) of the machine but at a very high cost. Type 1 cards are generally found and used on the "personal assistant" computers to store information outside the machine or provide software programs that cannot be stored on the machine due to its limited capacity. Type II cards and slots are used for communication devices of varying sorts. Modem devices, fax/modem devices or network interface devices are available to fit PCMCIA Type II slots. Such slots are generally found in subnotebooks and many older notebooks. The slot is particularly useful for subnotebooks which may not have the internal capability to accept an internal communication device (internal modem). The slot is also useful for those notebooks whose manufacturers do not offer internal high-speed communication devices. While 2400 baud modems were popular a few years ago, the newer, 14,400 baud or 14.4 Kbd modems are reasonably priced and offer greater productivity. While many manufacturers still offer 2400 baud internal modems as options or standard on their portables, such devices are out-dated for all but the most informal entertainment purposes. Type III cards and slots were developed to accommodate small hard disk drives for reasonably priced external storage capabilities. The thicker card is necessary to contain the miniature mechanical hard disk consisting of rotating platters and a read/write arm.

It sounds suspiciously similar to a phonograph player and it is.

Currently, PCMCIA Type III cards are available that will hold over 80 MB of data (on a credit card !). The advantage of many portables containing a Type III slot is that this same slot may be used to accommodate two Type II cards. *This capability may not be available on all machines so be careful.* When it is available, it would enable a user to, for example, connect to the company network using one card and fax information from the second card.

The Type IV standard was developed to accommodate even greater storage capacities than the Type III standard. The thicker ports will generally accept thinner cards in addition to their own cards. Accordingly, such ports are to be favored over the thinner ports for their increased versatility. If you are purchasing a notebook at this time, the PCMCIA Type III slot should be included. Subnotebook purchasers should seriously consider subnotebooks including two Type II slots or one Type III slot.

Look for 3.3 volt or SL enhanced processors in portables. Low power versions of main processor chips extend a portable's battery life.

When it comes to processors, virtually every possible processor available for desktop computers is available for portables. Portable, however, have also been marketed with low power versions of the desktop processor chips to conserve battery power and extend the portable's battery usage. As stated in Section II, Intel's SL series of processor chips was a direct response to the portable market's need to increase available battery life. Cyrix and AMD have also responded to the need for low power consumption with their own brand of chips. Low power consumption has been addressed by two methods however. Portables may include processor chips that require 5 volts to operate or may require 3.3 volts to operate. Some processor chips, advertised as low power versions of desktop processor chips are merely 5 volt chips that either have been designed for power conservation such as the early 386SL processor chips or are processor chips that require less voltage when compared with others in the same manufacturing run(but are still rated at 5 volts). The better alternative is the 3.3 volt processor chips. Intel now markets a 486 SL chip that operates at 3.3 volts. Intel, Cyrix and AMD also manufacture 3.3 volt versions of many chips found in desktop systems. At 3.3 volts, the same chip draws almost 40% less power than a 5 volt chip. This difference generally translates into a 30% increase in battery time. Coupled with power management features included in many prior systems (such as display blanking and sleep modes), 50% more computing time is possible. When shopping, be aware that low power may mean either the 5 volt or the 3.3 volt version and, where possible, confirm that the product does indeed, include the 3.3 volt processor chip.

When shopping however, you can't stop there. To receive the maximum benefit from the purchase of a 3.3 volt chip, be aware that the product must also contain devices and circuitry that also operate at this lower voltage. The display, hard disk drive, floppy disk drive and RAM memory may all be either 5 volt or 3.3. volt devices. Earlier machines containing the 3.3 volt chip did not contain these additional low power devices and so did not realize the maximum increase in battery life. Such machines are generally described as "hybrid" machines for their combination of 3.3 and 5 volt technology.

486 Portables are the practical minimum for a smart business purchase.

Of all the processor combinations available, your budget and perceived need for particular features and accessories will generally dictate the particular processor chip in your intended purchase. As a guideline however, do not purchase a 386 portable computer (nor a 286 portable, if you can find one still for sale). The 486 portable computer should be your minimum purchase. The small price difference between a 386 computer and a similar computer containing a 486 processor operating at the same clock speed (MHz) is more than offset by the performance difference. Due to the design differences between 386 chips and 486 chips, a 486 chip rated at the same speed will perform twice as fast as the 386 chip. This is because the 486 chip will perform an instruction every tick of the clock (remember the metronome analogy) while the 386 chip will perform an instruction every other tick of the clock. Prices for such portables are reasonable enough that the limited capabilities of the 286 and 386 chips do not justify investment of money in such machines.

While it may be nice to get the latest 66 MHz 486 portables, you may not need such a machine. I have recommended 20 MHz 486SX machines as good purchases for moderate budgets. While the processor chip was not nearly as fast as others on the market, for the same $2,500.00, that person received a large hard disk, excellent quality color screen, excellent ergonomic design and expandability. The purchase of a faster processor at the same budget would have required sacrificing features which increased the efficient and productive use of the portable. The difference between the high end portables containing 66 MHz 486 chips and the low-end 20-25MHz 486 chips is about double the performance. This is a noticeable but not frustrating difference in most instances. If the portable is to be your primary computer and you do processor intensive calculations or management of enormous databases, the faster processor may be advantageous. For general word-processing, a lower end chip will enable you to purchase more features for a versatile combination.

Finally remember that a faster processor, all other things being equal, will reduce the battery life of the portable and requires more advanced technology in its supporting circuitry and devices to take advantage of its faster speed. A machine optimized for such a processor will reflect in its higher price the cost of this advanced technology.

One last caveat. Although desktop machines have generally re-allocated video processing to their internal video boards, many portable computers today do not have advanced video subsystems. For this reason, unless the portable incorporates and advertises a direct bus or VL bus video system, the portable's processor chip will still be required to process the video signals. As discussed in Section II, this increases the processor's workload. If this is the case, a faster processor will be necessary to match the performance of a desktop system using an advanced video system.

The corollary to this is that a machine using a very fast processor but not engineered or designed to take advantage of the speed may perform no better than a machine using a slower processor. Texas Instruments manufactures a very fine line of portable computers. Its current offering includes a 50MHz 486DX/2 computer. In some instances, this machine outperforms 66 MHz 486 portable computers by other manufacturers. In those instances, it is obvious that the superior engineering skills of Texas Instruments have resulted in a product using mediocre engineering skills and relying upon an uneducated consumer to fall into the trap that faster is always better.

While portable's hard drives are smaller than desktop computers, you still want the largest you can afford.

Hard disk drives provide your permanent storage for data and applications. As I discussed in Section II, I recommend a hard disk of 200 MB. This does not mean that the various hard disks of 170 MB or 180 MB are necessarily insufficient. As with the processor chips, you must balance your needs with the combination of features found in portable's within your budget. While you can purchase a larger hard disk at a later time for your desktop system (or even install a second hard disk), portables do not offer this option.. Although companies will install larger hard disks in your portable, the cost is prohibitive. Some portable are designed, however, with removable hard disks. While hard disks are generally permanent installations in most desktop systems and many portables, some portables are designed with hard disks that are removed much like the portable's battery. These companies offer hard disks of various sizes as options to their machines and additional hard disks may be purchased as accessories from the manufacturer or reseller. The advantages of such systems include the ability to expand your personal storage capabilities by purchasing additional disks, expand the computer's use by allowing one computer to be used by a number of employees, each having his or her own hard disk with programs and data intact and secure, and by providing the capability to store the hard disk in a safe or fire box for security. If the security and ability to share one machine are of benefit to your business, by all means consider such a machine. If the machine is for private use however, and you are unlikely to spend the $700.00 or so for an additional hard disk to increase your storage capacity, then don't discount machines without this feature.

> Don't think that you are benefiting from the purchase of two 120MB removable disks over the purchase of a machine with one 180 MB or 200 MB disk. Unlike the PCMCIA hard disks that complement your internal hard disk storage, each removable hard disk substitutes itself for the other hard disk. You would have to install your application software on the second disk as well as the data you intended to use. In that case, storing two copies of your word processing software on two such disks just so you can work with the data on both disks effectively reduces your efficiency since Murphy's law dictates that the data you want will always be on the other disk.

RAM Memory upgrades for portables can be more expensive than desktop upgrades but just as important to effectively use today's large applications.

The RAM memory capacity of most portables is sufficient for their intended use. Most 486 notebooks are upgradable to 20 MB or even 32 MB of RAM memory. In Section II, I stated that graphical applications will generally show only incremental gains in processing speed beyond the installation of 8 MB of RAM. For this reason, even a notebook capable of expansion to only 12 MB would probably be sufficient for today's applications. This would not hold true, however, for the newer 32 bit operating systems and applications such as Windows NT or IBM's OS/2. These systems require substantial hard disk and RAM memory capacities. Currently, 8 MB RAM is the advertised minimum however, most users and industry insiders recommend twice this amount of RAM for smooth operation.

Subnotebooks, which are unlikely to be used as primary computers, will generally hold less than this. Some subnotebooks are upgradable to 12 MB however most will accept a maximum of 6-8 MB. Be particularly careful if you intend to purchase a subnotebook and intend to use the machine for everyday use. As I stated earlier, the use of graphical software will require a minimum of 4 MB of memory and everyday users will want 6 or 8 MB. Some of the more sophisticated features of some applications may require even more memory to operate smoothly (particularly if the application is operating concurrently with other applications).

Winfax Pro, a popular and very capable fax communication application with OCR (for an explanation of OCR, see Chapters 20 & 22) capabilities requires 6 MB to operate. When the OCR feature is implemented however, even the 8MB of RAM memory in my computer appears inadequate.

Software applications are increasing in complexity and in their memory needs. A software application that is released in the near future may require more memory to operate properly than may be available in your subnotebook. One workaround to this problem for those with portables containing PCMCIA slots is the purchase of flash memory cards. As I stated earlier however, these cards are very expensive. Better to avoid the problem than to correct it later.

When shopping, be aware that most manufacturers incorporate proprietary RAM modules or cards in their portables. Accordingly, you will have to purchase RAM upgrades from the manufacturer or a third-party vendor (usually mail-order vendors) offering compatible upgrades at significant savings. Also be aware that some vendors provide user-friendly upgradability with the simple removal of a detachable cover on the portable. Other machines, however, require surgical skills and may necessitate shipping the machine to the manufacturer to install a RAM upgrade

If the upgrade requires that the machine be returned to the manufacturer, it is most likely that the inconvenience, expense and lost productivity will tend to dissuade an upgrade at a later time. Such a feature is a liability and is generally not found on well-designed portables.

As a final caveat, before shopping, go back to Section II of this book and re-read that portion of Chapter 3 that deals with the available memory upgrade paths. Be careful that the notebook you purchase today can accept memory upgrades sufficient to meet your needs and without busting your budget.

When shopping for RAM memory upgrades to portables, don't shy away from the multitude of third-party vendors hawking upgrades at prices significantly lower than the notebook's manufacturer. I have used two of these vendors to purchase RAM memory for my notebook with excellent results. Look in the advertising sections of monthly computer publications like PC Magazine or PC Computing. Most guarantee full compatibility of the memory in both fit and function.

Do I really need a floppy disk drive on my notebook computer?

Notebook computers will include internal 3 ½" 1.44 MB floppy disk drives for storing data on floppy disks or exchanging information between computers. The floppy disk drive is also useful for backing up the computer's data in case the computer is lost or the hard disk is damaged or inaccessible. A very few notebooks are designed to allow the floppy disk drive to be removed from the machine (like the battery or removable hard disks) to substitute a second battery in its place. In such machines this effectively more than doubles the battery life of the portable and may be of interest to those persons needing long battery life in lieu of floppy disk storage. If this feature interests you, check out the line of Panasonic notebook computers, the NEC Ultralite notebook or the IBM notebook, all of which offer "plug and play" component interchangability. Although manufacturers and reviewers apparently think everyone is using these portables on intercontinental flights, this convenience may be useful for salesmen or consultants not wanting to detract from their flexibility by searching for electrical outlets every few hours.

Subnotebooks will usually reduce their dimensions at the expense of an internal floppy disk drive. Most, although not all, manufacturers will include an external floppy disk drive with the subnotebook as part of the price of the notebook. When the floppy disk drive is not attached to such computers, the computer may still communicate to other computers or transfer information through the use of linking cables as discussed in Chapter 17. In the long run, you will want access to a floppy disk drive. From experience, I will tell you that installing software, which is purchased on floppy disks, is more difficult and very inconvenient when using a second machine and linking cables. Expect the floppy disk on a standard notebook and I recommend you include the cost of the drive in any purchase of a subnotebook.

Color notebooks...what's available and what's the difference?

Other than the processor, portable display options are the greatest influence on the price of a portable computer. Notebook computers are now available in monochrome and color. Two technologies account for the range of display options. LCD (Liquid Crystal Displays) and TFT (Thin Film Transistor) technology. LCD technology accounts for most monochrome displays and also accounts for passive matrix color displays. While passive matrix color displays are more expensive than monochrome displays (commanding on average a $500.00 premium), they are generously less expensive than active matrix (TFT) color displays (which command a $1,500.00 to $2,000.00 price premium over monochrome models). Passive matrix LCD technology can be further divided into the earlier technology and the newer dual-scan or double-scan technology. LCD displays operate by activating individual pockets of crystals laid out in a flat grid pattern. TFT technology, utilized in the high-end color portables available today, uses a flat grid of transistors which are switched on and off by control circuitry to produce the display picture. In addition to involving more complex display circuitry and controller circuitry, the initial low yields of acceptable circuit boards for this product have kept the price at a premium.

Manufacturing failure rate isn't the only factor. Most such components are also subject to import tariffs which adversely affect the final price.

Within the monochrome market, all displays, with one exception, depend upon LCD technology to produce various shades of gray to simulate a color image. One computer, the Compaq LTE includes the option of an active matrix (TFT) display. The use of the active matrix display eliminates the disadvantages of LCD technology by providing a clear, bright image with no ghosting or bleeding of the overlapping images. Rapid movement on the active matrix screen (such as the movement of a mouse across the screen) does not result in the temporarily loss of image definition characteristic of LCD technology since the ability of the circuit board to refresh the image is vastly superior to the refresh rate of LCD screens.

Within the color display market, the three options are passive-matrix (LCD), dual-scan passive matrix (LCD) and active matrix (TFT) displays. Passive matrix operates similarly to monochrome LCD displays and active matrix operation has been explained above. The newest technology, dual-scan passive matrix can be expected to replace the older passive matrix color technology and, even today, there is no price premium for the dual-scan technology. Dual-scan displays tend to display brighter colors with less loss of definition during movement than the older technology. Such displays accomplish this by splitting the screen in half and refreshing each half at twice the previous rate. The result is a color display vastly superior to that of passive matrix but still not approaching active matrix quality. For most portable users however, including myself, this new technology is sufficient for portable and even everyday use.

Even among displays using the same technology, there are "winners" and "losers".

There is but one rule of thumb when considering the difference in displays...you must view the display for yourself. There are vast differences in display quality even among portables sporting the same type of display and all of the display types are prone to this individualism. I've reviewed active matrix displays that don't compare with passive matrix displays and I've reviewed monochrome displays that provided a more comfortable display than some passive matrix color displays. Depending upon your intended use for the computer the quality of the display may have varying degrees of importance. For the person using their portable's display even a few hours each day, the display must be clear and comfortable. A display that is difficult to view or otherwise makes operating the software difficult will reduce your productivity and, over time, cause fatigue and eye strain. Some people however, may use their portable's display only occasionally and will generally use an external display located at home and/or their office. In such instances, the display may not be of paramount importance when compared with other features. Consider your intended usage before deciding you can only live with the active matrix color screen at a cost of $3,500.00 to $4,000.00 instead of a monochrome display at less than half that price.

What else do I have to know about portable computer displays?

The size of portable displays varies greatly and will also contribute to the ease of use and perceived clarity of the display. Added to the equation is the choice of reflective display technology and backlit or sidelit display technology. Notebook computer displays are advertised in sizes measured diagonally (like a television set) and range in size from 8.5" to 10". While that size difference may seem insignificant, it is not. I repeat... that size difference is not insignificant. Again, consider how the computer is to be used and give this feature greater import if the display is to be used on a regular basis. Of course, display size is another feature in which subnotebooks come up short. Although subnotebooks are no longer manufactured with outdated display resolutions (older CGA and EGA resolutions), their displays are considerably smaller than the full notebook. Most subnotebook displays range from 6" to 7.5" in diagonal measurement.

> If you intend to use the subnotebook solely to transport work to and from the home and office, the lack of a usable display may be an acceptable tradeoff to the light weight and portability. By keeping an external monitor at home and at the office, the subnotebook's deficient display will not be a performance deficit.

This size is insufficient for full and productive use of most graphical software. Most notebook computers also include full backlighting, and may be advertised variously as including sidelit displays, backlit displays, CCFT displays (a form of backlighting) or others. Backlighting is the ability of the computer display to produce its own light. This light then provides a "back-drop" for the liquid crystals. The effect is not unlike the little lights contained in LCD display watches. Without the light, the LCD display is not visible in low light. With the light on, the dark crystals are visible against the lit background.

Backlighting increases the brightness and contrast capability of the computer display for easier viewing in both bright sunlight and poor office lighting (it can even be used for night reading with your bedroom night-light turned off) however backlighting uses power at a tremendous rate.

Most portables include power management features which turn off the backlighting when the computer power remains on but the computer sits unused for a period of time.

For this reason, some subnotebooks delete backlighting and rely upon reflective display technology. At this time, Dell Computer's 320lsi subnotebook is the best known example. Reflective technology is not new technology. Some manufacturers used reflective displays in older portables before the advent and acceptance of backlighting technology. Reflective displays rely upon the natural light available in the surrounding environment to pass through the liquid crystals in the display and reflect off the back of the screen. By reflecting off the back of the screen, this natural light provides a "back-drop" to highlight the liquid crystals much like that of backlighting. Newer displays have improved upon the older reflective technology however even today's reflective screens do not compare with backlit displays. Reflective displays heavily rely upon sufficient ambient light to provide a clear display. When I first looked at the Dell 320 inside a computer store, the screen was very dark and I could not adjust the screen to provide a better display. If your intended purchase contains a non-backlit display I strongly recommend you personally view that same display or similar displays at your local computer store before your purchase. My recommendation is to stick with back-lit or side-lit displays.

The notebook's keyboard design is VERY important. Really? What do I need to know?

The portable's keyboard probably gets less attention from the average consumer than it should. Most consumer's are understandably dazzled by the multitude of processor, hard disk and display choices and are concerned with purchasing the most powerful and colorful computer they can afford. Those of us that use our portables on a daily basis recognize that the portable's keyboard is probably more important than affording a processor with a marginally faster clock speed or a hard disk with 20 MB greater capacity. The keyboard, like the display, is the manner in which the user interacts with the computer. This interaction will directly affect your productivity. While even the worst keyboard can be tolerated, an efficient layout and comfortable response is key (pun intended) to the efficient and productive use of your computer. The marginally faster processor will do you little good if you constantly hit the wrong key, have to hunt around on the keyboard for keys in an unnatural layout or you are constantly irritated by a lack of tactile response from the keys. I consider the keyboard my "deal-killer" when reviewing portables for purchase recommendations

---

As I stated earlier, I believe Texas Instruments produces a very fine line of portables. T.I. portables are light, well equipped and well engineered. Until T.I. revamped its keyboards to a more acceptable design, however, I would not consider purchasing a T.I. portable because the keyboards used inferior layouts.

What are "full-size" keys and why do I want them on my portable?

Manufacturers utilize different methods to reduce the keyboard to the size of their notebooks. Two such methods are to reduce the size of the keys and to reduce the standard key spacing found on full size keyboards. Manufacturers reduce the key-spacing by reducing the unused space usually found between keys on the standard desktop keyboard while keeping the configuration and arrangement found on the desktop keyboard. Touch-typists used to the more standard spacing may require some adjustment period for reduced key spacing however it is reduced key sizes that really pose a problem for such people. In many instances, the manufacturer will reduce the size of certain oversized keys such as [Enter], [Backspace] or the [Shift] keys and will also reduce normal size keys (usually the function keys located along the top row of the keyboard) to 70 % of their normal size. In this way, the manufacturer can fit more keys along the top row and reduce the total keyboard dimensions. By reducing some keys sizes however, the layout and keyboard configuration is altered and a touch-typist used to reaching for and hitting the [F5] key may instead hit the [F7] key. If you are a touch-typist, visit your local computer store and spend a half-hour or more trying these different keyboards before purchasing. This trial time before the purchase may be time well spent in avoiding a frustrating purchase.

What's "tactile response" and do I care?

The tactile response of portable keyboards may also differ from that of desktop keyboards and requires some adjustment. Portable keys operate based upon direct mechanical manipulation rather than membrane (also called bubble) or spring technology. For this reason, portable keys may not provide the feedback of desktop keyboards that tells the operator the key has been sufficiently depressed to register on the computer. Portables also compound this problem by reducing the key travel distance from that encountered on desktop keyboards. The result may be a keyboard that feels unusually harsh and unresponsive. I personally find the reduced key travel distance to be a productive benefit. With reduced travel, my hands require less movement and my typing efficiency increases. While most manufacturers attempt to solve the first problem by providing an electrical keyclick to signal sufficient key depression, there is very little to be done about the second issue except to provide "full-travel" keys which solve the problem. Portables available with such keys will be advertised with "full-travel keys".

> The first problem may not really be a problem. Like the song says...silence is golden. A good portable will allow the user to set certain keyboard preferences including the presence or absence of the electrical click. In public, at meetings or in the courtroom, the electrical keyclick may be both an annoyance and an interference that results in you and your computer receiving unwelcome attention.

What are "embedded" and "dedicated" keys and which keys do I definitely want on my portable's keyboard?

Since manufacturers are always endeavoring to shrink the size of their computers for increased portability, most portables do not contain the full IBM standard 101 keyboard. Most portables "embed" a certain number of keys into others to "emulate" the 101 key keyboard common on most desktops.

"Embedded" keys operate in the following manners. For keys such as the [F11] and [F12] keys, the user will depress a special [Fn] key on the computer while depressing a second key which contains the embedded [F11] or [F12] function. The separate cursor keypad usually found on full size desktop keyboards is embedded in the center of the portable's keyboard and is also activated by depressing the [Fn] key with the appropriate embedded key. Portables also contain an embedded numeric keypad which may be activated by first locking the numeric keypad lock (by using the [Fn] key) and then using the [Fn] key as outlined above in combination with the embedded function key.

The importance of these keys cannot be understated. These keys see regular use on my computer for more than word processing and drafting. These keys are navigation keys which are commonly used by many applications to shift between screens and on-screen options. In my opinion, having eight cursor keys is indispensable for truly efficient computing.

The manufacturer may also provide the keys in a non-standard layout to meet the physical requirements of the portable. The following diagrams show how some manufacturers incorporate multiple key functions into the 78-82 keys normally found on portables. As a general guideline, those portables containing 82 or more keys have compromised less than those portables advertised with 78 to 80 keys. The first keys to be sacrificed are the function keys located along the top row of the portable keyboard. While the desktop keyboard provides 12 full function keys (F1-F12), some portables will contain only ten function keys, which may or may not be full size keys. In such instances the last two function keys (F11 and F12) are embedded in the F1 and F2 keys and can be activated only by depressing a special function key on the portable (usually marked Fn) while depressing the second function key. This is inconvenient at best. The second and more serious sacrifice that separates the well designed portable from others is the 78-80 key portable embeds the cursor function keys. There are eight cursor function keys. These are [Home] [End] [PageUp] [PageDown] and four arrow keys. The better designs will provide eight full size keys to aid the user in quick on-screen navigation.

The layout of these keys is also a consideration. Some manufacturers will place the keys in nonstandard configurations to meet the physical layout of their design while others will adhere to the more standard inverted T layout of the arrow keys and placement of the remaining keys in a single row along the right-side of the keyboard. The great advantage to purchasing a notebook with an excellent keyboard is that you can use that keyboard at all times rather than using the portable's keyboard when out of the office and relying upon an external keyboard when working in the office. In this way, you will not need to adapt to different layouts, key spacing and tactile responsiveness which invariably reduces your efficiency and productivity.

IBM's keyboard is acceptable although some of the cursor function keys are placed along the top of the board in a non-standard configuration. Compaq also markets a tolerable keyboard layout which, unfortunately relies upon reduced size cursor and function keys as does the Texas Instruments design. My final advice in this area is not to scrimp on keyboard features. In the long run, it's not worth it.

Using a pointing device with your portable.

As I've said earlier, the advent of graphical environments has resulted in the enormous acceptance of mice, trackballs and other similar devices for on-screen navigation and editing. Since most portables are now used with graphical software such as Microsoft Windows, manufacturers have attempted to incorporate a wide variety of mice and trackballs into their portables to provide a more compact travel combination. Of course, portables may also be used with mice and trackballs designed for desktop use, as explained in Section II, by using their serial ports and PS/2 mouse ports but, for extensive travel use (and for other reasons), the availability of an "on-board" mouse is most convenient. Since I have already discussed mice and trackballs in Section II I will not repeat that discussion here. Rather, I will focus upon some alternative pointing devices available in the portable computer market and the ergonomic limitations a consumer should be aware of when comparing portables.

Microsoft and Logitech make two good trackballs for portable computers.

I use the PS/2 version of Microsoft's Ballpoint Mouse. As I stated earlier, the Ballpoint Mouse was better shaped to my size hand and provided more convenient button placement. The lack of a serial connector is not a deficit since I always use my PS/2 mouse port for the mouse and keep my serial port available for linking cables. Since the PS/2 version does not use the adapter necessary on the serial version, I find it must easier to manipulate the cord and trackball body.

The Microsoft Ballpoint Mouse and Logitech's Trackman are two popular trackballs for external use on a portable computer. Each may be connected to either the serial port or, with their included adapters, to the portable's PS/2 mouse port. Microsoft also markets a Ballpoint Mouse with a PS/2 connector. This product cannot be attached to the portable's serial port however, I find it a more portable and convenient product than the serial version because of its shorter cord and reduced weight

What if I want something different from a mouse or trackball?

Appoint Corporation markets another popular trackball called the Thumbelina. At one quarter the weight and size of the other trackballs, this unit is extremely portable. Its drawbacks include non-convenient button placement requiring the operator to move her thumb or finger to operate the buttons and a very small tracking ball requiring multiple spins to transport the on-screen pointer across the screen with moderate precision. Appoint also markets the Gulliver pointing device. The Gulliver operates like a conventional mouse and provides convenient button location, a small size and short cord. While most companies market products that closely resemble, if not in looks then in design, either the standard mouse or trackball, Interlink Corporation had different ideas. Interlink markets the Portapoint, a mouse alternative that connects to the computer's serial port. Rather than moving a tracking ball as in the mouse or trackball, Portapoint uses a rubber button which is depressed to produce movement. The button, which senses the direction and pressure of your finger's movement moves the cursor accordingly. If the button is pressed hard and to the top, the cursor moves quickly to the top of the screen. If the button is pressed lightly and to the right, the cursor moves slowly to the right. In brief practice, I found the cursor movements to be sufficient for dragging and dropping objects or making choices on a menu however its precision did not equal the more traditional mice. With more practice, the Portapoint may provide adequate precision. It is an acquired taste and it does offer an interesting alternative to traditional products.

What about portable's with built-in pointing devices...are they all the same? Absolutely not!

The pointing devices included on-board most portables operate similarly to the trackballs described above. Most incorporate a tracking ball and two buttons. When shopping however, be aware that not all such devices are created equal. The position of the ball and its buttons varies tremendously from product to product and even within product lines. While a vendor may provide the on-board trackball in one location on its value-priced portables that same vendor may provide a more ergonomic trackball in its higher-priced models. Some vendors locate the tracking ball at the rear of the machine on either the left or right-hand corners while others place the mouse and buttons at the front of the portable, either centered or off-centered. One manufacturer, Compaq, even mounts its trackball on the right side of the display screen and places the buttons on the backside of the screen (effectively on the front cover of the computer). In practice this position offers excellent ergonomics (the buttons are easy to hit) and good cursor precision but long term use of the mouse in this position would probably be tiring.

Another type of pointing device is the "J Key" mouse. The computer's "J" key is designed to rock in any direction sending the mouse pointer moving across the screen. While I am tolerant of new ideas, the half hour or so I experimented with the J-Key left me totally frustrated. It seems like a "neat" idea but I strongly recommend you try it before buying it.

Some manufacturers may even put the trackball in one location and the buttons in another location on the portable. This effectively results in a two-handed mouse. In my opinion, such a mouse is an abomination and should be avoided. The centered or off-centered trackball and buttons appears to be the best solution to the placement of an on-board trackball. When comparing trackballs, also consider the size of the trackball. As I've discussed earlier, smaller tracking balls increase the need to move the ball multiple times to achieve large movement with reasonable precision. Larger tracking balls are appearing on portables and can effectively replace desktop pointing devices while providing increased portability. The smaller tracking balls also provide less resistance to movement due to their decreased mass and thus provide less precision than the larger tracking balls. When you are attempting to place the on-screen pointer on a small area, these inadequacies can be very frustrating.

One final thought on the subject of integrated trackballs...when considering a notebook purchase remember that, if the ball is located on the left, this may pose a problem for a right-handed person with little dexterity in their left hand. While manipulation of a full size trackball or mouse may be possible for that person, the smaller tracking balls and buttons provided on- portables may make this impossible. The same goes for left-handed persons and right-located trackballs. While you are unlikely to consider this a problem if you purchase the notebook, remember this if you intend to share the notebook with another person.

IBM's Trackpoint is an innovative and ergonomic alternative to most pointing devices.

If you are looking for the best solution to date, I recommend the IBM Trackpoint type pointing device. Currently available on a number of portables, the Trackpoint is a miniature stickshift that sticks up between the [g] and [h] keys of the computer. It operates much like the Portapoint by sensing the direction and pressure applied by either index finger and moving the on-screen cursor accordingly. It uses "strain-gauge" technology which means that the stick does not actually move but transmits the pressure and direction information to processors which move the pointer. The two mouse button are located on the bottom edge of the portable where they are accessible to either thumb. Since the Trackpoint is centrally located on the keyboard, the hands do not have to relocate to operate the mouse and, with practice, the operator can use the keyboard and mouse interchangeably for maximum efficiency. The Trackpoint provides good feedback to the operator and produces a very smooth on-screen movement. Precision is acceptable and, with minor practice, should equal the precision to be found in full size trackballs.

Batteries and AC Adapters come in different flavors.

Portables will operate on AC power or on battery power. Some "luggable" computers are designed to operate solely from an AC electrical outlet however, notebook and subnotebook class machines will all operate from internal, rechargeable batteries. The AC adapter/chargers included with portables are used for operating the portable on an electrical current and are also used to recharge the portable's battery. When shopping consider the following points. If you will be using the portable for international travel (not including Canada which uses 120 volt AC current) then confirm your intended purchase includes an auto-switching (or auto-sensing) 120v/220v AC adapter/charger. Such units tend to be larger than adapter/chargers designed solely for 120 volt U.S. usage. Because of this, some vendors now market portables with the smaller (and thus more portable) U.S.-only adapter/chargers. If the adapter/charger's size may be an issue, consider those portables sporting smaller adapter/chargers. Currently, Toshiba markets its portables with smaller adapter/chargers than many others. In actual use, the size difference is convenient for regular travel.

Which type of battery do I want...is Nickel Hydride worth the higher price?

Batteries are the godsend and the curse of portable computing. They last longer than previous generations but they never last long enough. Three popular technologies currently in use-are Nickel Cadmium (Ni-Cad or NiCd), Nickel Hydride (NiH) and Sealed Lead Acid. Other technologies such as Lithium Ion are currently under development for future use in mainstream notebooks. Sealed lead acid batteries, like the everyday batteries used in your flashlight and radio, may be found solely in subnotebook computers. Some such subnotebooks include other battery types (NiCd or NH) but may accept regular or alkaline battery substitutes as emergency replacements during travel. The IBM subnotebook incorporates the re-charging mechanism in its sealed lead acid batteries and does not require a separate adapter/charger. Such batteries are plugged directly into a wall socket for recharging. The disadvantage to sealed lead acid batteries is their low charging density which results in low battery life per charge. Nickel Cadmium (Ni-Cad) batteries are very popular for electrical appliances involving heavy usage and requiring frequent recharging. Camcorders and cellular telephones also rely upon Ni-Cad technology for portability. The advantage of Ni-Cad technology over sealed lead acid is double the charging density resulting in longer life per charge. Such batteries will also provide an equal number of recharges (measured in recharge cycles) to the sealed lead acid batteries. Ni-Cad's chief disadvantages are hysterisis and their poor environmental disposability. Hysterisis is the chemical process by which Ni-Cad batteries will fail to fully recharge, effectively reducing their subsequent life per charge over many recharge cycles. This effect is accelerated when the battery is not fully discharged prior to recharging and is known as the "memory effect" that afflicts Ni-Cad batteries. A Ni-Cad battery will also slowly discharge over time, regardless of use due, in part, to the chemical process that results in "memory". The time will vary on the condition of the battery and may vary from a few days to a few weeks time for a total discharge. Ni-Cads also possess toxic materials which impose additional disposal costs for manufacturers and environmental costs to the general public. Nickel Hydride batteries are the current battery of choice for portable computing. NH batteries possess a higher charging density than even Ni-Cad batteries providing longer battery life per pound. NH batteries are not subject to the "memory effect" of Ni-Cad's and so may be recharged to full capacity at any time without concern for lost performance. Finally, NH batteries do not pose an environmental threat. Their chief disadvantages are a shorter total life span than Ni-Cad batteries, thereby requiring sooner replacement, and greater manufacturing costs. The newer technologies mentioned above, will provide even greater charging density than current technologies however no release date is in sight for such products.

This is why you always want Nickel Hydride batteries!

When reviewing the battery options of comparable portables keep the following point in mind. While the battery is installed in your portable, it will be slowly discharging. If you then plug the computer into an electrical outlet, with the battery still installed, the charger will slowly re-charge the battery. This is no problem with the Nickel Hydride batteries which will re-charge to their normal capacity but it is a big, BIG problem with the Ni-Cad batteries. If you repeat this process enough times, your Ni-Cad batteries will permanently die. I know this because it happened to me. It happens like this. During the workday, the computer is plugged in and the charger charges the battery. At the end of the day, the computer is placed in sleep mode and the battery is slightly but perceptibly discharged over the course of the evening.

"Sleep mode", "rest mode" or "resume mode" is offered by many portable manufacturers. It enables the user to close the computer cover without exiting applications. When the cover is lifted (and/or a power button is hit) the computer resumes operations without needing to reload the software. In portables requiring many software programs to be loaded, this is a great productivity benefit and I highly recommend it.

The next day you go to work and plug the computer back in If the fully charged Ni-Cad is only slightly discharged before the computer is plugged in and recharged the next work day, its "memory" will only allow it to hold that slight charge. In less than a year, I killed my Ni-Cad batteries. The solution to this problem is to remove the battery at the start of each day and install the battery for overnight storage. A better solution to this problem is to purchase a portable using Nickel Hydride batteries.

This assumes that the computer will operate on AC power while the battery is removed. *Not all portables will apparently operate in this manner.* Of course, this is why I strongly recommend Nickel Hydride batteries for all portables.

Why doesn't my battery last as long as advertised?

Another point to consider when comparing intended purchases is the rated battery life of the portable. Battery lives, like everything else rated by their own manufacturers, are over-stated. Some manufactures provide more accurate ratings than others. The batteries actual life may vary from a few minutes to over an hour from the manufacturer's claims

---

Many word processor applications have an automatic save feature. When working on a document in such an application, the computer will regularly save the work to the hard disk. When this happens, the computer will access the hard disk and use battery power. Such features can be disabled but I don't recommend it. I regularly set up the automatic save features for colleagues...usually after they have lost a large document and complained to me.

A system's actual battery life will depend upon its workload and the number of mechanical devices it is called upon to operate during that work. The biggest power drains for portable computers are the backlit display, the mechanical hard disk, the mechanical floppy disk and finally the processor. If your work involves continuous transfers of information from the hard disk or floppy disks to memory or between the hard disk and floppy disk drives, the computer may operate for only 50% of the battery's rated life. Alternatively, if you are only inputting text into your word-processor, the computer will not have need to access the hard disk, floppy disks or memory and the computer may operate near its full rated life.

External accessories such as mice or trackballs will also draw power from the computer battery and internal devices, such as modems and fax/modems will draw power to maintain their configurations. If battery longevity is of paramount consideration, don't get a color display. While monochrome notebooks with modern power management features can attain battery lives of 4-6 hours or more between charges, color display notebooks generally average between 1.5 hours and 3 hours. Active-matrix displays, with their millions of processors, drain more power than passive matrix displays. This is another good reason besides prices to consider a good quality dual-scan passive matrix display.

Finally, keep in mind that portables with a higher rated battery life may attain that greater life by installing a heavier battery. This contributes to the total weight of the portable which you then must carry with you.

What else do I need to know about batteries?

The following are some final notes about portable battery features. Most portables will recharge their batteries in 1.5-3 hours with the computer off. Some portables will recharge batteries even with the computer operating, some won't. If you believe it is likely you will need to use the computer even while recharging the battery, make sure your intended purchase can recharge while being used. An alternative is to purchase an external battery cradle for recharging the batteries while you continue to use the computer. Another alternative is to purchase additional batteries for extended periods beyond the reach of an electrical outlet. If you opt for the charging cradle be sure that it doesn't require the use of your charger/adapter (which you may need to use your computer).

Also be aware that some portables capable of recharging during use will require 5, 6 or even 10 hours to recharge the battery, effectively reducing the benefit of this feature to zero. Batteries must also be installed and removed on a regular basis. Some vendors provide easier access to the battery. While most very poor designs have not survived the market, slight differences may make a difference to you and should be taken into consideration in your final purchase decision. The better designs will provide the ability to replace the battery without closing the cover or physically manipulating the portable. Toshiba provides a battery that slides to the front of the machine on railings and is released with the push of a button. The battery can be exchanged with minimal effort and is one example of an excellent design. Finally, vendors each manufacture their own batteries, at varying costs. When comparison shopping, take the cost of additional batteries into consideration when fixing your final cost.

What other features do I want on my portable computer?

There are other features that may be of interest or use to the portable shopper including dual display capability, flash BIOS, rest-resume and power management features. Dual display is the ability of the portable to output its display to an external monitor while maintaining the display on its own screen. The better portables will be capable of dual display and will further be capable of outputting their display to the external monitor in the higher resolutions such as 800 x 600 or 1,024 x 768. This feature can be useful for sales presentations or provide the ability to allow a colleague sitting across the desk to view your work from your desk monitor. Power management features will vary from computer to computer but most at least offer the basics...hard disk time-out, backlight time-out, standby timing and automatic rest mode. Others also offer the ability to resume computer operation with an incoming call to the modem or set the processor for fast speed or long battery life. See Figure 15-1.

Flash BIOS is the ability to update the computer's Basic Input/Output System (BIOS) by inserting a disk in the floppy drive and running an internal program. Most such updates are available from manufacturers on company electronic bulletin boards maintained by the portable manufacturers to provide useful utilities and updates to their customers. Why would you want an updated BIOS? The BIOS allows the computer to control and interact with its various components such as the floppy disk drive, hard disk and other such devices. Recent BIOS updates for my own computer have allowed the computer to use power management software that reduces power to the components when idle. Recent BIOS developments may allow computers to recognize and interact with newer PCMCIA devices.

What are "rest and resume", "sleep" and "hibernation" modes and how effective are they?

"Rest and resume" or "sleep" features are electronic bookmarks which keep the software and applications loaded in memory when the computer is closed. When the computer is opened again, it is not necessary for the computer to "re-boot", load the software applications or files again.

This feature makes the computer as convenient to use as a notepad. If you are working on a project for the week, you don't need to save the file at the end of each day, close the application and turn off the computer. Just close the lid (or hit the power button) and, when you open the lid tomorrow, you are back in place. This

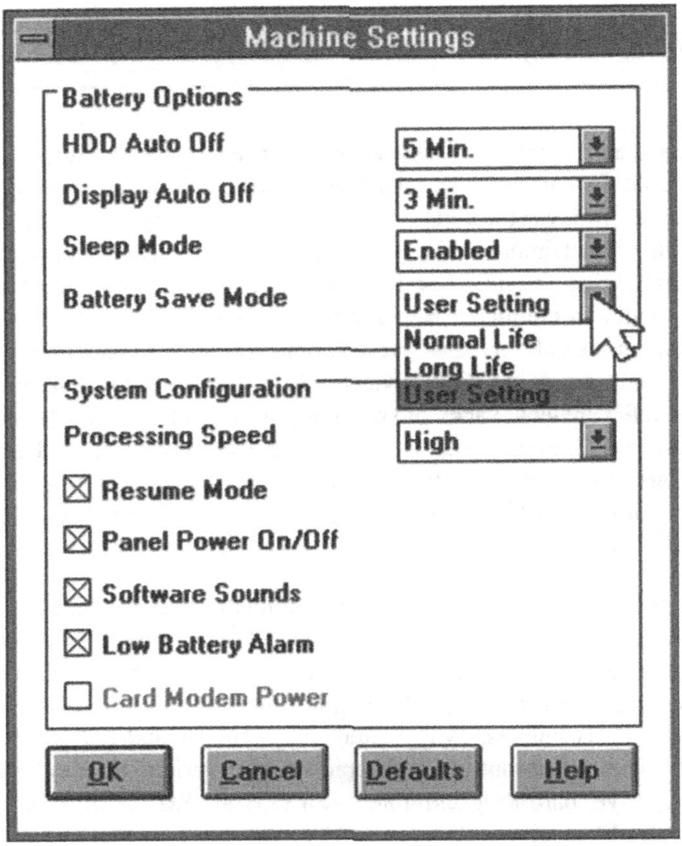

Figure 15-1 Toshiba's notebooks offer easily configurable power management options.

When a computer is first turned on, it performs self-diagnostic tests, loads configuration files and software files necessary to run the hardware (such as mouse drivers). It then loads certain software applications in memory such as the DOS operating system files and Microsoft Windows system files. Thereafter, the user can load other applications for their work. On my computer this can take a full minute.

---

feature is also useful throughout day to keep your place during those moments when you must leave your desk, attend to occasional interruptions or entertain a colleague or client in your office. The computer, which may be a source of distraction or contain sensitive material, can be shut and put aside until work can be resumed.

This last concern is not minor. While desktop systems provide "screen savers", software that blanks the screen during periods of inactivity, I find such software to be a waste of hard disk space. Moreover, most screen savers today are distracting. A better solution is the ability to suspend your work since no distracting screens are then present to interfere with the pending concern.

These sleep features are a trademark of the Intel SL line of processor chips which were designed exactly for this purpose. Portable manufacturers, however, include such capabilities on machines not containing the Intel SL chips. These machines may either use software to store the current status of the computer when it is suspended and restore the settings when it is resumed or used "SL Enhanced" processor chips which integrate the memory management features of the SL chips which allow memory contents to be saved. In practice, their is no practical difference

Some earlier machines were unable to properly suspend and store the portable's settings from within a Microsoft Windows environment. In most instances, these problems have been resolved..

It is always a good idea, however, to test your intended purchase for its ability to suspend and resume under a variety of "real world" conditions. If you have the opportunity try the following tests on a display model at your local computer store:

How to test a portable for its ability to use "rest" and "sleep" modes.

First, make sure the computer is set up with its rest and resume feature enabled, then

1. Suspend the machine while in Microsoft Windows and resume the machine. Check to see that applications will open and operate.

2. Suspend the machine with an external mouse attached and resume the machine. Test the mouse to assure that it operates. Perform this test both in a DOS program, such as WordPerfect 5.1 or 6.0, and in a Windows program (all such programs offer support to mouse input).

3. Suspend the machine with an external mouse attached, detach the mouse from the machine, wait 15-30 seconds, re-attach the mouse to the machine, resume the machine and test the mouse to assure that it operates. Also perform this test in both DOS and Windows.

4. Perform the same test as in test (3) but re-attach the mouse after you have resumed the machine.

5. While an application is open and the machine is on, pull the AC adapter plug from the machine (or remove the battery), wait 15-30 seconds and then re-attach the plug (or battery). Turn the machine on. The application should return to the screen.

Tests 1, 2 and 3 should work on a properly designed system using a PS/2 mouse. Test 4 may not work with the PS/2 mouse unless it is attached to a dedicated mouse port (see pg.?). If test 4 does work, the machine receives extra points. If you use a serial mouse the above tests may not be valid due to the potential operating differences between your serial port and your PS/2 port. In my case, the serial port cannot be disabled during nonuse. Because of this, once the mouse is attached, the machine cannot be placed in rest mode. The mouse must be detached from the machine before placing the machine in rest mode. For this reason, tests 2 through 5 will not work on a machine using a serial mouse. Test the machine by performing the same tests but detaching the mouse before entering rest mode. In a well designed machine, the machine should remember the mouse was attached and resume mouse operation when the mouse is re-attached and machine operation is then resumed.

"Rest" and "sleep" modes are effective features to protect your work when the battery dies.

Test 5 tests the ability of the machine to save your work and enter rest (sleep) mode if power to the machine is suddenly cut off. This is likely to happen if your battery suddenly dies or there is a power outage while you are connected to an AC outlet

---

> During a power outage, if your computer is connected to an electrical outlet it will lose power only if your battery is not installed. (For the reasons why your battery may not be installed, see Batteries, pg. ?) If your battery is installed when AC power is cut, the computer should not skip a beat in switching to battery power. In this respect, each portable includes its own built-in battery backup unit. This is a very handy feature in storm-prone environments like my own southern Florida.

This is one of the great advantages of a computer capable of rest and resume operation. While other portable users will need to keep a close watch on their battery status lights you can securely ignore yours. I regularly work on battery power even after the red glow of the low battery power light. When the battery finally expires, my machine saves my work and enters rest (sleep) mode. An internal lithium backup battery keeps the work intact while I change batteries. If a spare battery is not available, the lithium battery will save my work for several hours until I reach an AC outlet or recharge the main battery.

Actually, it is likely that the main battery has not been completely discharged at this point and provides sufficient power to maintain information in memory. You can test this for yourself by letting the computer sit idle for 5-10 minutes and then resuming operation. The computer will probably operate for a few minutes more before saving your work again and entering rest mode.

In all these instances, we are testing the real world efficiency of the machine's design. In actual operation, if rest and resume operation is used (and I've set forth several good reasons to use it), you will necessarily be attaching and detaching an external mouse (assuming the built-in mouse is not sufficient for everyday use). Well designed machines will allow re-attachment of the mouse. Other machines may not recognize the mouse after the machine is resumed. In this case, you must restart the machine to use the mouse. Not only is this very frustrating and unproductive, it actually reduces rest operation from an asset to a liability.

Warranty and Service policies are important considerations when shopping for a portable.

Another practical consideration when shopping for a portable is the vendor warranty and service policies. Currently, most manufacturers provide a one year parts and labor policy. In some instances, the manufacturer will extend warranties for a second or third year at additional cost. Compaq, IBM, NCR and NEC are some mainstream vendors providing standard three year warranties. In assessing warranty services, of greatest concern to the consumer are speed, reliability and convenience, not necessarily in that order. Speed is offered in a variety of ways. Certain vendors will provide next-day on-site service (also a convenience) while others will overnight ship a replacement machine for use during repairs. This replacement service should be highly considered when shopping for your primary business computer. Since time is money, the convenience and assurance that you will be without computing power for that one day period is to be cherished. Even if on-site service is advertised, there is no guarantee that repairs can be completed in that one day. The loan/replacement policies are better. Be careful when shopping however, since service policies will vary between product lines of the same manufacturer. Of course, the higher priced systems receive better support and service policies. Portable computers may also be subject to a different support and service policy than desktop systems from the same manufacturer. In such instances, the manufacturer may include on-site service for desktop systems (that are more difficult to ship than portables) but require portables to be returned to the manufacturer for service.

In some instances, the manufacturers on-site service may be available for its portable line of computers at an extra cost.

Many manufacturers also provide telephone support, FAX support and maintain electronic bulletin boards for updated software exclusive to its computers. The better such support provides 24 hour availability with toll-free calls. Be aware that free telephone support does not mean toll-free support. Another form of support that is increasingly available is remote diagnostic or call-back service. By including a modem and diagnostic software pre-installed in the computer, some manufacturers will initially attempt to service the computer or diagnose the problem by calling into and remotely operating the computer. One final note about service...manufacturers are continuously updating and improving their support services. At this point, AST, Compaq, Dell, IBM, Toshiba and Zeos (a mail order vendor) all provide consistently above-average service and are recommended purchases based on their service and support records. While service and support is not a flashy or visible feature, dependence upon your computer to operate your business requires that you consider the relative abilities and willingness of each vendor to repair its product with minimum delay and maximum convenience.

Some actual portable computer recommendations. These are the ones I would buy today.

Now that we have discussed the range of features available on portables, I will make some recommendations for actual products that meet many of the considerations I have set forth above. When considering the price of these or other products, remember that price is for a standard configuration that will not include the accessories you may need to outfit the computer to fit your needs. Such accessories may include additional RAM memory, fax/modem PCMCIA cards or internal fax/modem options, extra batteries and a carrying case. All of these additions are highly recommended. Other accessories such as an external display monitor, external mouse or trackball, network adapters or tape backup drives may also be necessary for your work. Always consider the cost of these accessories when deciding if the portable is within your budget.

Sub-notebook computer recommendations.

If you are in the market for a subnotebook, the offerings mentioned here will probably be superseded by publication with even more capable offerings. Gateway's 486 Handbook provides a very capable package, handicapped by its reduced keyboard and screen size. Its a secondary computer, at best, and is not, in any way, suitable for full-time use as a desktop replacement.

In all fairness, however, most subnotebooks will lose points on their display and keyboards when compared with full size notebooks. When shopping for a subnotebook, the reduced keyboard and display sizes should not discount the offering. If it really is a concern to you, then you should purchase a full size notebook. Many notebooks are available in trim 5.5 pound packages.

The Zeos Contenda 486SL provides a good package handicapped by a smaller hard disk than the Gateway and the lack of a PCMCIA slot for expansion. However, it does offer local bus video for faster video response. Hewlett-Packard's Omnibook utilizes some very advanced technology to produce an extremely portable and ergonomic package with a 486 processor but it lacks sufficient, affordable hard disk storage to replace your primary computer. The Omnibook also uses reflective screen technology rather than backlighting which handicaps even its portable use. Zenith and Packard Bell offer the identical Z-Lite and Diplomat subnotebooks. With two Type II PCMCIA slots, 170 MB hard drives, relatively large screens and even simultaneous video, I would highly recommend these products from a technological point of view. My experience with Zenith's service and product reliability has been abysmal, however, and I can't, in good conscience, recommend a product that's not well supported by its company. That's too bad since the few weeks I spent with the Z-Lite really impressed me. IBM produces the Thinkpad 500 series which is an excellent portable and desktop alternative. It provides a 200 MB hard disk, a very fast processor and sufficient RAM upgrades to qualify it as a potential primary computer. While it can be had with a color screen, the small size requires my recommendation that you use an external display while at the office. Finally, Toshiba produces the Portege series which is, perhaps, the best overall package (with the greatest strain on your budget). Available with everything from a monochrome screen to an active matrix color screen (of decent size), the Portege can be outfitted as your one and only computer. Hard disk sizes of 250 MB or larger, expandable RAM to 20 MB, local bus video, Trackpoint style integrated mouse and fast processors in a package less than 5 pounds makes this the business "toy" for the image-conscious executive. By the way, it also makes a very productive computer.

Notebook computer recommendations.

In the 5-8 pound full-size notebook category, my top choice for a reasonably priced, ergonomic and capable portable is your choice of any Toshiba 1900 series portable. At approximately $2,500.00 or less for a dual-scan passive matrix color notebook, the 1900 series includes most all of the features I've recommended in this chapter. It includes a true 486 processor, 200MB hard disk, 4 MB RAM memory standard (expandable to 20 MB), one PCMCIA Type III slot, an excellent keyboard layout and color display, rest and resume operation, nickel hydride battery, small adapter/charger and ergonomic clip-on trackball. Toshiba also rates very high in customer satisfaction, service and support.

The only drawbacks to this machine are the inconvenience of the clip-on trackball and the expensive memory upgrades. Toshiba computers use memory cards which are installed into a single memory slot on the right side of the machine. Since only one slot is available, the user must decide on a single memory upgrade of 4MB, 8MB or 16MB. If the user cannot presently afford the larger upgrade, she is left with the choice of purchasing the smaller upgrade and later investing in the larger upgrade which replaces the earlier memory card. The purchase price of the smaller memory card is not recouped.

The Toshiba and some Texas Instruments notebooks currently use a special version of the Microsoft Ballpoint Mouse trackball which directly connects to the right side of the portable through its "Quickport" connection. Although this connection eliminates the cord, the mouse is not permanently attached to the machine and must be disconnected for travel. Still, the trackball has a much better feel than many smaller trackballs built into other portables which offsets the convenience factor and provides an easier combination when actually working with the computer.

The machine is also an excellent choice without the color display for those on limited budgets. In my opinion, comparably priced offerings from AST, Compaq, IBM, Texas Instruments, Zeos or Zenith Data Systems compromise on one or more of the above features and fail to offer the well-rounded performance and ergonomics of the Toshiba.

High-end notebook computer recommendations.

For those persons on a higher budget, active matrix color portables are available with larger hard disks, faster processors and sophisticated video systems for increased performance. A few good choices would be the IBM Thinkpad 700 series computers, Texas Instruments 486 TravelMate Series and Toshiba 4000 series computers. The IBM portable sports an unsurpassed color screen and the Trackpoint II pointing device. Texas Instruments provides one of the most powerful processors available in a well-engineered package. Toshiba, while not boasting either the speed of the Texas Instruments portable or the breath-taking quality of the IBM's screen, provides excellent performance and ergonomics in a well-rounded package.

Chapter 16

Portable Accessories

As I stated earlier, portable computers have received greater widespread support from both consumers and manufacturers. Part of this support is in the form of increased compatibility with accessories and tools formerly available only on desktops. In this chapter, I will review such accessories as portable printers, tape backup units, CD-ROM drive units, external hard disks and scanning devices. Finally, I will review the available options to carry your portable and accessories.

Portable modems and fax/modems are also available however, these devices will be reviewed in Chapter 17.

Portable Printers lack the niceties of desktop units but provide a needed service to the frequent traveler.

Portable printers provide the means to print business reports and drafts while traveling. Such printers are a necessary evil for producing professional documents at minimal inconvenience. Even if your hotel provides a printing service, the service may not be available at all times or may not provide immediate service. Also, in the real world, "final drafts" are very rarely final drafts. A change here or there is almost always the case.

An alternative to the portable printer for those persons providing on-site consulting services may be to "borrow" an on-site printer. If this is your intention, your accessories should include a flat-ribbon printer cable to quickly and conveniently connect your portable to the on-site printer.

While there are approximately half a dozen such portable printers, they widely vary in size, weight and features. The most portable of these printers is the IBM Portable Printer model. This printer was first marketed as the Citizen PN48 Notebook Printer, measuring 2 x 12 x 3.5 and weighing 2.5 pounds and Citizen has improved its feature set and re-released it with color printing capability. On the upside, the Citizen model printer is small, light, produces very clear documents and can feed multiple sheets of paper without a feeder attachment, however it is slow and the cost per page can be high. Hewlett-Packard also produces a portable printer, the HP Deskjet Portable Printer. Measuring 2.5 x 12 x 6 and weighing in excess of 5 pounds, the HP is not as portable as the IBM (or Citizen) unit however, its estimated cost per page is significantly lower (3 cents per page) and it prints twice as fast as the other unit. The Olivetti portable printer is slightly smaller than the Hewlett-Packard model printer and shaves a pound or so off the traveling weight but doesn't offer color printing. What you do get is the ability to substitute store-bought alkaline batteries for the rechargeable batteries sold by Olivetti (a good option in an emergency), reasonable print speed, and a built-in paper feeder. Unless you have a habit of ending up with drained batteries at the worst times however, the Hewlett-Packard, at the same estimated price, and with a lower operating cost per page, is probably a more versatile choice. Either this or the Hewlett-Packard are the printers for a traveler needing (relatively) fast printing capability at the hotel or at the convention site. While other printers are available, these represent the mainstream offerings and are the most likely candidates to be offered by computer superstores or office supply depots at discount prices.

Parallel Port Tape Drives provide the convenience and safety of tape backups to portable owners.

Tape backup units have also become de rigeur for portables. These units are self-contained tape backup devices similar to external units offered for desktop computers. Since portables do not have the capability to accept an expansion board, however, external tape backup units sold for desktop systems are not compatible with portables The portable tape backup units however, will connect directly to the computer's parallel port with an included cable rather than connecting to an expansion board that must be installed inside the computer case. The portable tape backup units are also compatible with desktop systems and may be connected to the desktop's parallel port. This would be useful, for instance, to allow a business to perform backups on multiple desktop computers with one backup tape unit, thereby reducing equipment costs (but increasing time and productivity costs).

Since portable computers are shipping with 500 MB hard disks and 200 MB hard disks are offered as minimum configurations on many notebooks, tape backup units are almost a necessity to protect the data on those systems. There are drawbacks to using portable tape backup units however. Third-party software designed to recognize tape backup drives connected to parallel ports is limited (even Norton's backup software won't recognize parallel port drives) and the slower backup speed of the portables compared to the desktop systems makes them less desirable for frequent backup duty. There is nothing that can be done about the slower speed, which is a result of the limited capabilities of the parallel port. Enhanced parallel ports providing greater transmission speed and bi-directional communications will improve backup speeds in the future and, even today, new backup software has improved backup speeds through the greater use of software compression. Still, even with this handicap, tape units are preferable to backing up large amounts of data on floppy disks since the backup process can be completed without your attention once it is initiated.

While you can take a coffee break or lunch while the tape backup unit backs up your data, floppy disk backups will require your constant attention to exchange floppy disks every 30 seconds. If you are using a Windows tape backup application, you can even continue to work on the computer while the backup application performs its backup operations. This is one advantage to the Windows software in addition to its clear user interface.

When purchasing a parallel port tape backup unit, confirm that it includes software for your operating system. Some units include both DOS and Windows software. If you are using an advanced operating system such as OS/2 or Windows NT, the included software may not be fully compatible with that environment. In that case, the vendor may provide upgraded software for your operating system software or third-party software developers may offer backup software compatible with your operating system and the tape backup unit. Confirm these facts before making your intended purchase or you may be stuck with a white elephant.

Portable CD-ROM Drives allow even notebooks to access large databases on the road.

CD-ROM units may also connect to your portable through the parallel port. Actually, because of the potential need to transfer huge amounts of data in a given time, manufacturers also market portable CD-ROMs which attach to the portable through a SCSI to parallel port adapter or a SCSI to PCMCIA card.

Pronounced "scuzzy", and standing for "Small Computer System Interface", SCSI is an interface standard supporting high data transfer rates. It may be found in any setting where data needs to be shuttled from component to component in large amounts and at high rates. Large hard disks (1000 MB or larger), desktop scanners, tape drives and CD-ROM drives are all marketed with SCSI interfaces since these components are very often asked to handle large amounts of data in a short period of time.

At present, MicroSolutions, Toshiba and NEC (among others) produce CD-ROM drives specifically manufactured for portable use. Only the Toshiba is designed to operate on optional battery power while the others rely on AC power. While this limits their field use, these units are still a viable choice for the consultant relying on a portable drive for presentations or information access at a client's business site and for shared use within a small office.

Reduced performance in portable CD-ROM drives makes them less desirable for multi-media (video) presentations.

One drawback of these portable units is their increased access time. While newer CD-ROM drives utilize triple-spin or triple-speed technology (quadruple speed too) to triple or quadruple the transmission rate of information to the computer, portable units generally lag behind. NEC, of all the manufacturers, seems committed to maintaining parity between its desktop and portable units, and it is probably a good first choice when shopping for a portable unit. The slower speeds of the portable units and their reliance on the parallel port for their connection translates to slower data transfer rates to the computer's processor. While this may involve only a few more seconds (or micro-seconds) to access data, it substantially reduces the ability of these units to present professional and capable multimedia presentations since such presentations require a sustained transmission of video images to the computer for smooth video display. With slower transmission rates, the video image of your multimedia presentation may appear choppy and unprofessional. This aside, such units are fine for accessing large databases or information sources (such as customer infobases or encyclopedia information), only available or storable on CD-ROM disks.

If your portable's hard disk is full, try a portable hard disk drive. Using removable media, these storage units provide virtually unlimited storage capacity to the portable.

External hard disks ranging in size from 40 MB and up communicate through the portable's parallel port (possibly through a SCSI adapter) and provide additional storage capacity for large applications. Some of the more exotic (and sometimes expensive) disk systems allow the user to purchase one external disk machine capable of accepting removable and rewritable disks (called optical disks). In this manner, expandability is limited solely to the number of purchased disks. While such a system may be advantageous for continued storage of data (called archiving), it is an expensive proposition. Its advantage to tape backup units is the ready availability of the information on the disks without the necessity of finding and restoring the files to the portable's own hard disk. Such systems generally provide faster access to the information over comparable tape units. This difference in access speeds is due, in part, to the different manners in which information is stored on tape cartridges rather than rewritable optical disks.

Niscan's portable scanner provides medium resolution scanning to portables hampered by the lack of expansion capabilities.

Scanners provide the ability to input graphic images into your computer for insertion in reports, newsletters or presentations. The information that can be input may either be a picture or it may be text.

> If the image is a text image, it is still scanned into the computer like a picture. The image cannot be edited with a word-processing application unless it is thereafter converted to editable text using an OCR application. For more information on this manner of scanning see Chapter 20 and Chapter 22.

In this way, you may scan a logo, signature or other graphic image into the computer for later use.

I scanned my actual signature into my computer for later insertion on the signature line of correspondence. In this way, I "electronically" sign my letters before I fax them directly from the computer.

Sheet-fed scanners are a better bet than hand-held scanners.

Scanners are available either as flatbed scanners or as portable, handheld units. In addition, scanners are available with black and white (gray scale) and color capabilities. The latter scanners would be useful to any business needing to scan color images for publications while the gray scale scanners are sufficient for the vast majority of businesses needing the ability to scan text into the computer. Flatbed scanners operate much like a copy machine by reading the image of a page placed down on the scanner's glass bed. Flatbed scanners are costlier but provide the capability to scan an entire page in one pass. With a sheet-feeder, an option on many flat-bed scanners, the scanner can input an entire report or document without interruption. Hand-held scanners are small portable units which are guided across a page by the hand. The drawback to hand-held scanners is that the scanner face is smaller than a 8 ½" x 11" page and must be drawn down the page in two passes. The software included with the scanner must then "stitch" the two page halves together to produce a single page of text. In practice, it never equals the results of a flatbed scanner and, in some instances, can be very frustrating to use on large amounts of text or large graphic images.

The greatest limitation is the software. Although the software has been improved in recent years, the hand-held scanner places too much reliance on the software's ability to make up for the scanner's shortcomings. I think a better solution is offered in Chapter 22 on practical tips.

These scanners are better suited to scanning the text columns of magazines or newspapers and scanning smaller graphical images and pictures. In most instances, both flatbed and hand-held scanners require expansion cards that are placed in the open expansion slots of a desktop computer. One exception is Mustek Corporation's hand-held scanner that connects to the portable's parallel port. When it comes to portable offerings in the scanner market, nothing tops the Niscan or Logitech page scanners. These page scanners are portable desktop scanners. About the size of a carton of cigarettes, the Page Scanner feeds a full-size page through its body or, with its top removed, will glide across a larger image on its own wheels. The Page Scanner includes an internal battery pack so you can take it to the library for scanning text or graphics into your notebook. The advantage of such a portable system may not be its ability to scan so much as its ability to act as a fax machine while traveling. Combined with your computer's internal fax/modem, the scanner can scan in and fax a document not already available in the computer. While slower than a dedicated flat-bed scanner its versatility as a portable for sheet fed use or capable of hand-held use for bound books makes it an attractive choice.

Docking stations provide "desktop" expansion possibilities to your portable–but at a hefty price.

Docking stations or docking ports provide the person relying solely on their portable the means to attach accessories without resort to the parallel port or PCMCIA slots of the portable. Ranging from simple "replicators" designed to give quick connections to standard monitor, printer and keyboard connections on the back of the portable, to full-fledged computer cases which can contain hard disks, tape drives, CD-ROM drives and speakers, these docks are generally proprietary to the particular portable...and they can be expensive. The price will likely include only the docking station and not your accessories. The docking station, depending upon the manufacturer, may include drive bays, expansion slots and options for sound output jacks and controller circuitry for the various additions. By the time you are done outfitting it with your accessories, you could have bought another computer. In most instances, the need to access one or more of the components found in a docking station can be met through other means such as SCSI to parallel connectors or PCMCIA cards. If I were to need many of the accessories that generally dictate the perceived need for a docking station (for instance, I frequently used multimedia tools such as speakers and a CD-ROM drive) but still needed a portable computer, I would probably purchase a second desktop system and use a radio-frequency or infra-red file transfer system to automatically transfer files between the two computers. While initially more expensive than the docking station, when the portable is replaced, I wouldn't be left with a $800.00 (or more) proprietary docking station that I couldn't use with my next portable.

Taking it with you...picking the right computer case for your needs is important.

Finally, when you have your portable and all its accessories, you will need a carrying case. There are many available cases in a variety of materials designed specifically for computers. I highly recommend you purchase such a case. While portables are durable, manufacturers have not seen fit to include carrying handles and experience has shown a dropped portable is usually a dead portable. While you may transport your portable in a sturdy, hard-sided briefcase, such a case is not designed to offer the shock-resistance and protection of a padded computer case. For this same reason, you should avoid soft-sided leather, fabric or nylon cases designed as briefcase substitutes and not designed to hold a portable computer.

The one advantage to using a briefcase or soft-sided attaché is that observers will not know it contains a computer. If you must leave the case in your vehicle, it is less likely to be stolen than a case that obviously contains an expensive and easily pilfered portable.

It will carry the computer but not offer the protection you want if the case is dropped. Computer cases also include a shoulder strap for convenient transport and further provide special provisions for floppy disk storage not found on generic cases. Portable cases are available in many sizes to accommodate the different portable sizes and carrying loads. If you regularly transport your portable between office and your home but rarely travel with a portable printer, do not get the extra-large cases designed to accommodate bulky extras like printers and tape drives. Purchasing such a large case defeats the convenience of your portable computer. Companies such as Kensington and Targus market a line of medium size cases capable of transporting most portables with pockets and room for extra batteries, cables, disks, cords, and business papers. In most instances, these are the best choices. These cases are also more convenient for traveling since space is usually a premium on planes, trains and automobiles. It is unlikely that you will need your portable printer or tape unit on the plane. Rather than carrying these accessories on the plane when you travel, a better alternative is to pack them in your regular luggage.

SECTION V

Chapter 17

Modems, Faxes & Tele-Computing

Why be concerned with computer communications?

Throughout this book, I've discussed computer communications. I discussed using communications in the first chapter to increase your information base and communicate information, I discussed communications in the chapters concerning utilities and portable computers. I've told you that some companies (in fact, many companies) offer their own electronic bulletin boards from which you can receive free upgrades and "fixes" to their products. I've mentioned how you can access software applications to virtually meet your every business need and how on-line communications can provide contacts locally or on a national level. I've also mentioned that communications and portable computers are a powerful combination allowing you to stay in touch with the office or connect to a client's computer to provide services in an efficient manner. I haven't mentioned, but I will here, that communications will allow you access to many government bulletin board services for commerce and small business needs. Presently, and with greater latitude in the future, information on legislative bills and proposals is available through communication services and current financial updates, news, travel and weather are all available through particularized on-line services or comprehensive services such as Prodigy and CompuServe which provide all these services and more for monthly and hourly access fees. Any one of these benefits is a good reason to have a working familiarity with computer communications. I will not delve into the full range of communication equipment and software available today but merely provide some guidance to today's better alternatives.

What's a "modem" and what's a "fax/modem"?

Modems are "modulation-demodulation" hardware that convert the digital signals of a computer to analog signals capable of phone line transmission and then demodulate the signals to digital signals for receipt by another computer. Fax/modems improve upon the function of modems by providing these same electronic functions in a fax machine format. Fax/modems communicate with stand-alone facsimile machines or other fax/modems using Group 3 facsimile language. Although providing substantially improved communications options, fax/modems are only nominally higher in price (about $50.00) than modems. I will always recommend purchasing a fax/modem rather than a modem.

Do I want an external modem or internal modem and what's the difference to me?

Modems and fax/modems are available as external devices or internal devices. External models generally carry a higher price since the manufacturer must provide a case to hold the electronics and incur additional expense in its manufacture. Internal modems are "cards" containing electronics, which are placed in an open expansion slot of the computer. The obvious advantage of the internal modem is space. A less obvious advantage is that internal modems contain their own serial port connection. Since the serial port is the door through which all information must pass, the consumer will want a modern serial port containing modern communication capabilities. This is included with the internal modem but since the external modem is connected to the computer's internal serial port with a serial cable, the modem may have to rely on an older serial technology, thereby limiting its effective communication speed.

> I've seen serial port upgrades costing in excess of $200.00. Although not all upgrades are this expensive, this cost is not incurred in a capable internal modem including the updated technology.

The advantage of the external modem is the consumer's ability to connect the modem without delving into their computer's innards, the ability to reserve expansion slots for other devices such as tape drives or CD-ROM drives and the ability to easily move or transport the modem from computer to computer as necessary.

If I have a portable computer, what are my modem and fax/modem options?

Some portable computers are designed to contain an internal modem. In such cases, each portable manufacturer will provide internal modems specially designed to fit their portable computers. A few dedicated modem manufacturers also provide a range of modems designed to fit some of the more popular portable computers. Since some manufacturers may not provide modems or fax/modems with the range of functions available in today's leading edge products, you should consider your communication needs when shopping for a portable computer. Since each internal design is proprietary, you should review the options available from the portable manufacturer and third-party modem manufacturers before relying upon the portable to meet your communication needs.

Modems and fax/modems are also available on PCMCIA cards designed to fit in specially designed slots in portable computers. Since the cards are manufactured to an industry standard, any portable computer containing an industry-compliant PCMCIA Type II slot or greater can accept the cards. This increases the card's flexibility since one card can be used for multiple portable computers and purchasing a new portable does not require the purchase of a new proprietary modem. The PCMCIA cards are durable and have received good industry reports in their performance. Highly recommended for portables.

> While I'm on the subject of PCMCIA fax/modems, don't, DON'T get a 2400 baud modem. I don't care how much money you save, it isn't worth it. The minimum speed PCMCIA modem you should consider is the same as I recommend for desktops, 14,400 baud and nothing less.

How fast should my modem communicate?

If there is one thing about modem specifications, they are a confusing jumble of numbers and letters. The first specification, and the least confusing, is speed. Speed is rated at bits per second or a baud rate. Although not identical, both are substantially similar and are used interchangeably in most instances. When a modem is rated at 2400 baud or bps (bits per second), the modem is actually rated as capable of transferring 300 characters per second (cps). This is because computers communicate characters in 8 bit packages called bytes. 2400 bits divided by 8 bits per byte (or character) equals the 300 characters per second. This rated speed is usually never achieved however since telephone lines are not the ideal communication medium for digital signals. Telephone line noise and problems caused by atmospheric conditions or line maintenance reduce this effective transmission speed. Certain protocols will compress the transmission signals, however, and increase the effective speed of the modem.

2400 baud modems are available today for as little as $40.00 with comparable fax/modems costing as little as $75.00. Personally, I don't think they're worth it. With today's graphical environments and larger file sizes, this speed is downright inefficient. I know because my first modem was 2400 baud and took 30 minutes to transfer files that could be transferred in 5 minutes with the next generation of modems. This next generation of modems is rated at 9600 baud and was the practical minimum for business use...for about five minutes. Almost immediately, 14,400 baud modems came along and knocked the 9600 on its ear. Others have since come along but I will say, for those wanting to save a buck, the 14,400 baud modem is a minimum configuration. If you will use the modem on any regular or semi-regular basis whatsoever, for business or pleasure, the 14,400 baud modem is a must. Most such modems and fax/modems are available for as little as $160.00. The useful life of the 14,400 modem is also likely to remain viable for at least the foreseeable future. The 14,400 baud modem is unlikely to be as quickly supplanted as the 9600 baud modem for a few reasons. First, the irritating deficiencies of the slower speeds have been reduced to a tolerable level at 14,400 baud so that remote computing and communications are not the "coffee-break" events they once were. Additionally, although many local BBS systems will probably quickly upgrade to the V.FAST standard, others won't for the simple reason that their 14,400 modems are still new and are still viable vehicles for efficiently posting messages and downloading files. The larger on-line services, such as Prodigy and CompuServe, are notoriously slow to keep pace with communication upgrades (Prodigy is still at 9600) due to the large investment in equipment that is involved in upgrades.

The next generation of modems and fax/modems is the better value however. . If you can foresee calling long distance on any regular basis, go for the V.FAST standard modems. The modems at both ends of the connection must use the V.FAST protocol to take advantage of the savings since connection with a slower modem will leave you transmitting at the lower speed however, assuming your company transmits between long distance offices, an investment in two of these modems will quickly be recouped. The extra money saved on long distance billings will reduce the modem's higher initial cost. If you intend to keep your modem until it dies, invest $200.00 or more for these newer modems and fax/modems. Clearly, this is the upcoming standard and provides twice the 14,400 baud modem's speed for a nominally higher price. Many of these modems also offer programmable chips (using Flash technology) so that feature sets that were once "hard-coded" onto the modem's circuit board are now upgradable as new standards and features are released. Fax/modems will cost more than the above prices but, as I said earlier, they're worth it.

The idea that a modem or fax/modem could be upgraded by future releases is closely tied with the introduction of digital signal processors (DSP) into the mainstream market. A DSP is basically a chip, like your computer's 386,486, or Pentium processor chip. It relies upon software to tell it whether its a modem, fax, answering machine or even a sound board. Since it is a processor, it relieves the processing burden that would otherwise by borne by your main processor in handling the communication chores associated with modems, faxes and answering machines. Since it is dependent upon software, each function can be upgraded as new DSP compatible software is released. Finally, the ability to program the DSP chip to perform, not only modem and fax functions, but act as an answering machine, sound board or input device for voice recognition relieves the problem of expansion space and hardware configuration in already crowded systems. As time progresses, look towards DSP technology to integrate your communication and video tools on one multi-purpose board.

Modem protocols are the most confusing aspects of modems. Modulation, error control and data compression are all the subject of various protocols that indicate a modem's complexity and potential capability. MNP's, V.42, V.32, V.22bis, V.42bis and V.32bis (not to mention the newer V.17 fax and V.Fast modem protocols) are all protocols intended to tell the consumer how the modem will perform. The speed of a modem is defined by the following protocols. V.Fast has been left out of this chart because this protocol is still in the process of being standardized. Until it has been standardized, any modem including this protocol (and thus advertised as faster) can only claim to reliably attain this higher speed if connected to the same modem at the other end of the telephone line. At this time, I do not recommend spending a premium for this technology. In all these cases, remember these speeds are "rated" speeds and may be reduced by phone line conditions or increased through the use of compression protocols discussed next.

MODEM SPEED	MODEM PROTOCOL
2400 baud	V.22bis
9600 baud	V.32
14,400 baud	V.32bis

What about MNP 5 and V.42? What are they and do I need them?

Compression protocols allow the modems to compress and decompress files as they are communicated. This results in throughputs of twice to four times the rated modem speed but requires both modems (sending and receiving) to be capable of using a common protocol. This is usually not a problem since many of these protocols have been in use for some time and are industry standards on most modems sold today. These protocols include MNP 5 and V.42bis. While MNP 5 provides 2-to-1 compression in ideal situations, the preferred protocol V.42bis provides 4-to-1 compression. This results in a 100% increase in speed rather than the 60-80% speed increase available with MNP 5. Of course, V.42bis will add to the price of the modem and this is where you will start to see differences in product lines and prices in the slower 2400 baud modems. If you purchase a modem with V.42bis, it will also include MNP 5 for those instances when it connects with older (and cheaper) modems. Although some bargain 9600 baud modems may not include V.42bis, I know of no 14,400 baud modem that doesn't include both these compression protocols.

What other specifications do I need to know about?

If you want to use these compression protocols however, you must first establish an error-free connection with another modem using, you guessed it, another set of protocol standards. Included in this set are MNP 2-4 and V.42. While MNP 5 is a compression protocol, MNP 2, MNP 3 and MNP 4 are error protocols. Each protocol builds on the other and, in the event a modem cannot establish an error-free connection with MNP 4, it will attempt to "fall-back" to an older protocol such as MNP 3 or MNP 2. Similarly, V.42, the preferred error protocol attempts to establish a LAPM link (Link Access Procedure for Modems) as its preferred connection. If the conditions do not permit this type of connection, V.42 will attempt to "fall-back" first to MNP 4 and then MNP 3. Modems advertised with V.42 error control will always have MNP 2-4 as well. If you intend to use your portable computer modem and cellular connections to communicate, also consider a modem or fax/modem advertised as including MNP10. This protocol was recently developed to meet the specialized needs of cellular communications which are consistently worse than public telephone connections due to the nature of cellular service. With MNP10, the modem constantly monitors the connection status and adjusts transmission speed to those conditions. V.42 and MNP10 are also features that you won't find on the bargain brand 2400 baud modems, making such purchases short range solutions to your business needs.

Communication applications make the modem work?

Once you have a modem or fax/modem, you will need a software application to effectively operate it. Some modems come pre-packaged with communication and fax software however most such software does not compare with many of today's full featured applications. In addition to providing greater flexibility and customization, many retail packages present these features in a useful manner to even a novice communicator. I find the Windows applications to be the easiest to master however there are many DOS applications that have been upgraded to provide better guidance to communication new-comers.

What should modem software include?

The features any good communication program will offer are compatibility with your modem or fax/modem, multiple configuration settings, multiple phone directories and a good selection of transfer protocols always including at least Z-modem and CompuServe B transfer protocols. The software package will probably list the modems and modem manufacturers it is compatible with. Do not rely upon "Hayes-compatible" advertisements for either modems or their software. Although the basic Hayes commands are incorporated into many modems, slight differences in the advanced commands between modems and software render some software applications unable to use the modem's advanced features or maximize its potential. Applications programs will usually include a semi-automated set-up at which time either the application or the installer will select a modem from an installation list. In the best cases, the particular modem will be listed rather than relying upon a "generic" selection.

Multiple configuration settings are necessary to allow the modem's initialization for different uses. In some instances, you will know that another modem will not transmit above 2400 baud and so configure your modem (called initialization) for 2400 baud communications. In other instances, you will communicate at higher speeds or with error and compression protocols activated to boost transmission speed. These tasks are easier if your application provides for multiple configurations. Multiple telephone directories are helpful for networked communication applications. The ability to save and load different directories means each employee can load a personalized list of recipients rather than scrolling through a single company list. Finally, a good selection of protocols is necessary to allow modems to transmit information effectively. Once a connection is established, if files are to be transferred, each modem must have the ability to communicate in the same transfer protocol language. Two of the more popular protocols are Z-modem and CompuServe B. Other protocols may have such names as Kermit, X-modem, Y-modem, Y-modem batch and others. Some modem applications also support and provide proprietary protocol languages which improve upon the transfer speed of even the fastest public protocols. To use these proprietary protocols however, the application must be available at both the sending and receiving end, doubtful unless its communication between home and branch offices of the same company.

What's "Z-modem" and why do I want it in my communication software?

The simple reason I recommend Z-modem as a primary protocol is its speed and error-correction capabilities. With many other protocols such as X-modem, Y-modem and their derivatives, if a modem connection is lost during transmission of a file, the entire file must then be re-transmitted once the connection is re-established. Z-modem, however, can pick up where it left off and finish the transmission. The first time I lost a connection while transferring a 360K file using X-modem, I realized the advantages of Z-modem.

I was using the communication application included with Windows called "Terminal". Since it only provided X-modem as a transfer protocol I used that protocol for some time. Eventually, however, I got tired of having to re-transmit files and upgraded to an application providing Z-modem. Don't repeat my mistake...upgrade to an application including Z-modem and save yourself the inevitable aggravation.

If you regularly lose connections or experience file transfer failures, there may be causes beyond the occasional and inevitable phone line "glitches". Cheap serial cables may not contain the pins and wires for "hardware handshaking", a form of modem communication to make sure the transmitting modem is not sending information faster than the receiving end can process it. Other causes may include incompatible modem settings (like handshaking settings), lack of a high speed buffer (16550 UART serial port) or an old communications driver (MS Windows' COMM.DRV is a good example) that can't process information at high speeds.

One cause of repeated failures I've never noted in any books or computer journals is the use of compression software. If you are attempting to download a file to a directory on a compressed disk, the overhead incurred by the compression software (DoubleSpace or Stacker) algorithm in compressing the file for storage may interfere with the computer's ability to empty the communication buffer before it is "overloaded". The result is a "Data Overrun" error message. The solution, I've found, is to have your communications program default to storing downloaded files on the uncompressed portion of your hard disk.

In my instance, I experienced no problems with these errors while using Stacker 3 but I began to experience them with Stacker 4. I believe this is because Stacker 4 uses tighter compression which requires more processing power. If you are using compression software and try to increase your disk space by maximizing compression, be aware of this potential problem.

Three capable Windows applications (also available as DOS applications) are CrossTalk for Windows, ProComm Plus for Windows and HyperAccess for

Windows. Any of these three will meet the criteria above and most likely will be compatible with your modem.

There is also capable shareware communication software available at considerable savings over the commercial offerings listed above. What will you lose by going with a shareware package? First, don't expect any high-speed proprietary protocols. Second, don't expect the communications program to transmit and receive as quickly as some of the commercial offerings. Finally, the number of terminal emulations and download protocols may be limited depending upon the program. Still, the two listed below are capable products if modem communications aren't the lifeblood of your business.

UNICOM	Windows modem telecommunications program. Supports high speed communications and a wide variety of download protocols including Z-modem. Icons allow access to all necessary functions and multiple lists and directories can be stored and accessed. Works well during background file transfers and requires very limited hard disk space compared to many retail offering.
Registration:	DataGraphics P.O. Box 58517 Renton, WA 98058 Tel (206) 432-1201 Fax (206) 432-8673 $69.95 registration fee after 21 days.

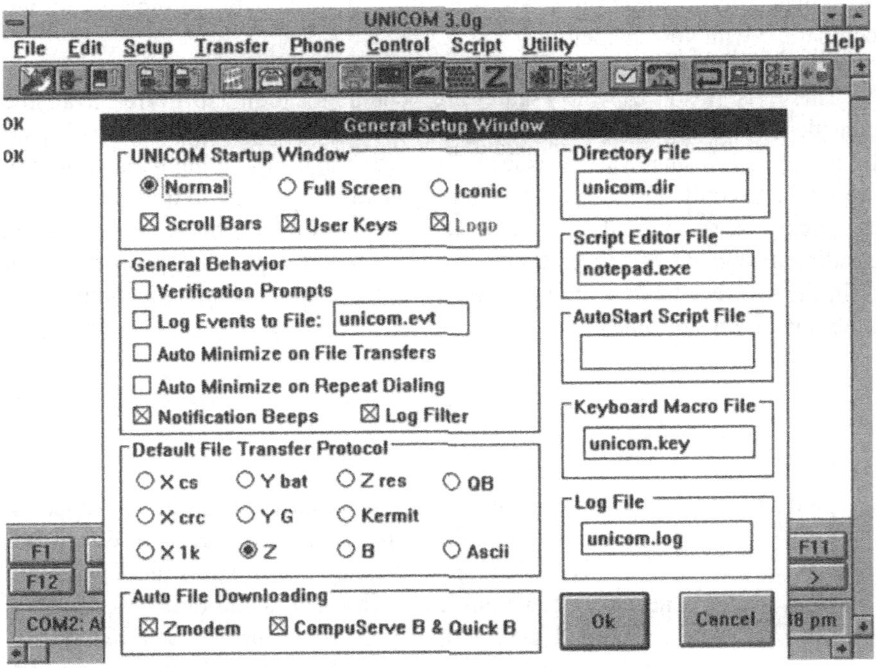

Figure 17-1 Unicom offers the features, if not the performance, of store-bought communication packages, including Z-modem and scripting capabilities.

MICROLINK — Windows Communication Software offering Z-Modem downloads, scripting language, script recording, internal modem status display and background operation in a compact 500K package at a very low price

Registration: $35.00 Registration Fee
MicroWerks
P.O. Box 768273
Roswell, GA 30076-8273

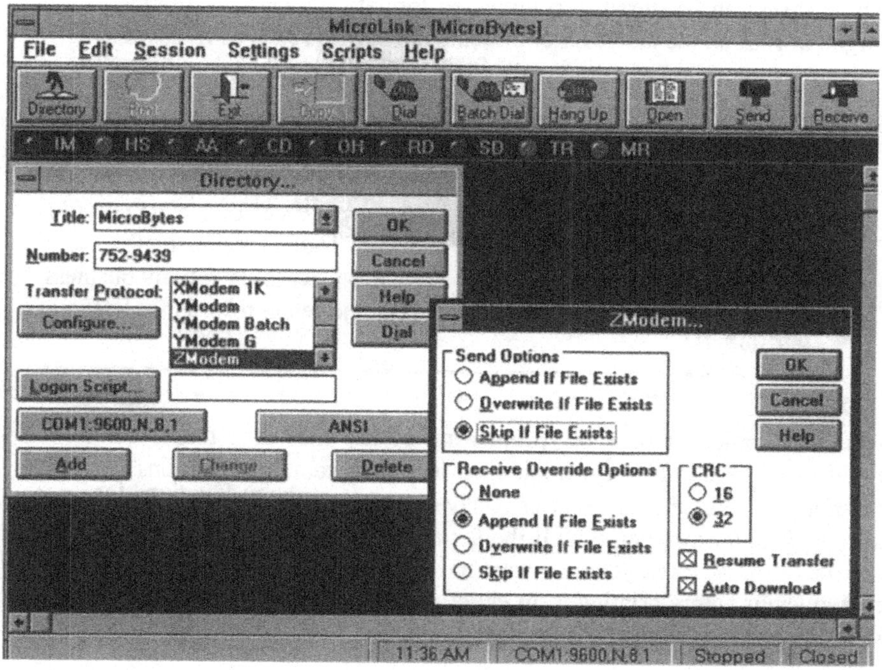

Figure 17-2 Microlink is inexpensive and provides all the important features. For local BBS mail and file services, its price and performance are sufficient and it won't crowd your hard disk like some other packages.

FAX software makes fax/modems act like the office fax machine.. but also offer so much more.

Like communication software, the fax software included with fax/modems is, at best, minimal, and, at worse, unusable. Again, the applications that provide features in a usable package are Windows applications. Within the past year, virtually every developer has upgraded their fax applications to include greater integration with word processors and other applications and improve the range of functions and operations to manipulate, store, access, edit and output information through the computer's fax/modem. In many instances, these applications provide merge functions to allow the same documents to be sent to multiple recipients, each with a unique and separate cover page. The applications also make good use of "drag and drop" to provide multiple recipients either once or as part of group lists for regular fax polling. Most allow both incoming and outgoing faxes to be stored with information for later retrieval by subject matter, date, keyword or other criteria.

These faxes can be stored in compressed formats allowing the storage of otherwise large fax files on the hard disk or on removable media such as floppy disks.

> Since fax files are graphic images like a picture, most such files are larger than comparable text files. As an example, a text file produced in a word processor may require 20K of storage space. That same text file stored as a fax file may require in excess of 150K. Obviously, the ability to compress these files for storage is a necessity for any business desiring to consistently use a fax/modem and retain records for later review.

Most applications also allow previewing of fax files in a thumbnail format (for multi-page faxes) and fax manipulation including zooming functions for review and rotation for faxes that are sent or received upside down or sideways. How can you send a fax sideways, you ask? If the fax is an image printed in landscape mode such as a large spreadsheet, you may want to review it before sending it or you may want to preview it before printing it. In either event, the page must be rotated sideways to view the image as desired.

Some applications even have sophisticated editing tools, beyond mere cutting and pasting, for adding notes, graphics and text to a received fax image before sending it on to the next party. These tools can be used to add comments to a fax while it is previewed on the recipient's computer and then faxed back to the original sender. These comments and edits can be saved as separate overlays from the original fax allowing further editing or removal of the comments before printing the fax. Many applications also provide smoothing features for smoothing the jagged edges of fax images and cleaning stray dots on the image resulting from transmission noise. Finally, many fax applications today are including Optical Character Recognition (OCR) applications as part of their package. OCR applications are used to recognize an image of a text document as characters and convert the image to editable text. Absent this function or separate OCR software, any text document sent as a fax is merely a picture which cannot be edited in a word processing application.

What's "remote computing" and will I use it?

If you are so inclined, a modem or fax/modem can also be used with remote control applications to connect to another computer over telephone lines and operate the computer from your own. This capability is included in some computer lines by manufacturers that found supplying modems and remote software enabled them to remotely diagnose computer problems and provide efficient warranty support at a considerable savings over "on-site" support. The feature also appeals to many consumers requiring immediate assistance without the inconvenience of shipping the computer or transporting it to a remote service center for service. Of course, remote computing also appeals to that segment of the population that performs their job outside the office but needs information or support only available on the office network. Finally, remote computing allows a person to reach and use the information, applications and data on their office computer whether they are at home or on the road. With remote applications, you can use remotely available applications and data, print documents to either the local or remote printers or transfer files to your local computer for continued use. Most of these applications provide multiple security levels to prevent unauthorized use or information access through computers available to remote sites and some remote computing applications also provide call-back services for long distance computing. This is particularly useful if you must call long distance from a client's office or, heaven forbid, your hotel room.

Multi-level security means individual user passwords and configuration setups, screen blanking and keyboard lockouts. The first two are to protect your office computer from "hackers" that try to gain access to the system. The program accomplishes this in two ways. First, it can require the entry of a password to enable access. Second, for greater security, the host (office) system can be configured to call back the remote site at a number supplied at the time of connection or at a pre-defined number. If the number does not match the application's records, access is denied. The second two security measures are to protect the system from interference at the host (office) site. Screen blanking prevents other employees or staff from viewing your computer activities without your knowledge (such as payroll information that may be accessed remotely) and the keyboard lock prevents host (office) site personnel from entering data or commands from the host site without your permission.

Most of these remote applications are sold in both separate host and remote packages and in packages containing both the host and remote modules. Obviously, if many employees will be equipped with portables and expected to call into the host computer from their remote sites, then only one host application is necessary while multiple remote applications will be necessary. This is the reason for selling these modules separately as well as a package. Remote applications will operate with virtually any operating system available today, including Windows. I have experimented with remote communication involving DOS applications at 2400 baud and have found the response slow but tolerable. However, due to the large amount of information necessary to process Windows applications and draw the information to the screen, remote computing with Windows requires modems communicating at 9600 baud or greater. Anything less will not be effective and will be more frustrating than productive. If, for some reason, you are stuck with a slow modem but critically need access to remote files, then the software can be used to remotely connect to your office computer and download the files for your local use.

If the idea of remote computing appeals to you, then strongly consider my prior caveats regarding bargain modems. Effective remote computing depends upon high speed communication. In this regard, investment in brand-name V.32bis modems will pay dividends. You should also consider the feature set of your intended remote computing application. The three major players in remote software are Norton-Lambert with Close-Up, Symantec Corporation with PC Anywhere and Triton Technologies with CO/Session. Any of these three are likely to be available through mail order, your local computer store or even your office supply warehouse. Close-Up uses compression and buffering technologies to offset the heavy information loads incurred by Windows users. By compressing the transmitted data and buffering screen images at the remote computer, information can be updated more efficiently and increase the productivity of the remote session.

For example, if all that is moved is the mouse pointer, perhaps 98% of the original screen does not need to be retransmitted to the remote computer for updating.

Another positive attribute of Close-Up is its ease of installation and, better yet, the courtesy it extends your system in not altering Windows configuration files. While this may not be a great concern for most users, those of us that experiment with software appreciate this courtesy tremendously. Finally, Close-Up provides multi-level security and password protection for the host system to prevent unauthorized system and file access. Triton Technology's CO/Session comes in two flavors, single user and network capable. With the network version, Novell and peer to peer networked systems can share modems. Both versions offer Windows compatibility although CO/Session, like Close-Up is a DOS application that can operate in Windows.

If you are new to computers and would be intimidated by the prospect of remotely connecting to your office computer, its Windows to the rescue, PcAnywhere for Windows, that is. The program is network compatible, enabling network systems to share communication resources (modems) and provides high-speed full screen and windowed communications. PcAnywhere uses compression like the other applications to increase transmission loads and reduce the lag formerly associated with remote Windows sessions. The program uses its Windows interface to simplify remote computing (such as dragging files to the remote screen for downloading to the remote or across the screen to the host directory tree for uploading. Multi-level security is also included. Perhaps the only drawback to the Windows application is that it will eat up two to three times the disk space of the DOS applications. Other than that, the program is a capable tool for your remote access needs.

Chapter 18

Computer On-Line Services

Using your computer to efficiently run your business means doing more with that computer than was done a few years ago. Along with book-keeping, mailings, inventory tracking and all the mundane tasks generally assigned to computers today, a whole new world is available for gathering information and news, tracking economic indicators and networking with others having similar personal and business interests. This world is the world of bulletin boards and on-line computer services.

What do on-line services have that I can't get from my local BBS?

The term "on-line service" is generally used to refer to the commercial services provided under the auspices of CompuServe, Prodigy, America On-line and Genie among others. "Bulletin boards", or BBS's, while providing some services shared by these commercial lines, are more limited in nature. While the commercial services provide the capability to shop, review dynamic publications and reviews, make travel reservations, review financial information and interact with a multitude of specialized information databases (Figure 18-1), most bulletin boards provide conferencing, file access and entertainment.

While both the commercial services and many bulletin boards are networked to other systems to increase membership diversity and contribution, the network of bulletin board systems is generally limited to those few activities I just mentioned. Alternatively, the commercial services may network with specialized business and professional databases, financial data systems (see Figure 18-2) and educational systems located throughout the country and thereby provide a wide range of electronic services under one roof. With the increased interest in commercial electronic services and the resulting increased competition, many services will occasionally complement their offerings with additional services and available databases.

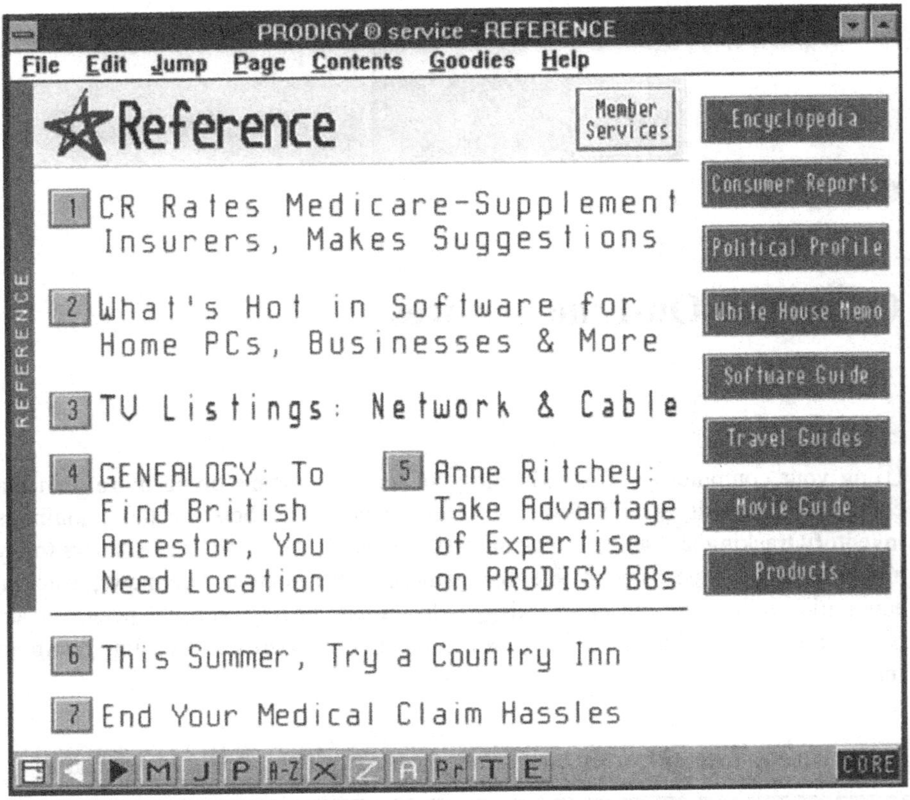

Figure 18-1 Prodigy offers a number of services for information, each easily accessible by clicking on your choice. Most of the commercial services provide an updated encyclopedia, news, consumer reports and shopping services like those available in Prodigy as part of their base subscription rates.

Every business can benefit from some use of on-line services. Whether you sell information and advice or need that information or advice to make better purchasing, hiring, or marketing decisions, it's available on-line. I use on-line services for many different tasks. Updated news and financial information is always available 24 hours a day.

Weather and travel information, reference and educational information, and general and home business tips are handy. I can also comparison shop products and review consumer information regarding intended purchases. Occasionally, I'll seek advice to specific questions in conferences and on boards that range from family issues to business issues to international issues and everything in between. Most of

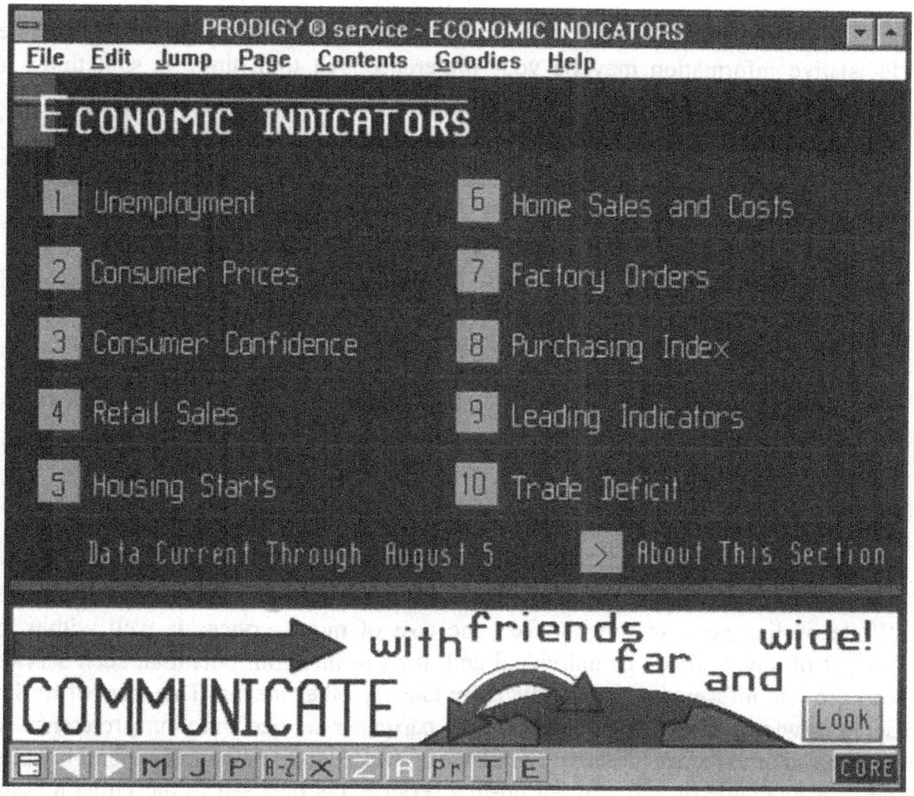

Figure 18-2 Immediate access to economic updates may alone be worth the price of the monthly subscription to your business.

the time, these conferences are a good source of information regarding vendors and new products that have been released. I certainly don't have first-hand experience with each new product and each vendor but, by perusing the boards and conferences, I have a good "feel" for the quality of vendors and their products.

How do you choose an on-line service?

What you will use on-line services for depends on how you schedule your day and the information you are looking for. The service or boards you want to subscribe to will also be dictated by the type of information you want since, as I've said earlier, each service and board has its specialties and strengths. One service may offer better manipulation of stock and financial information while another offers better support to a home-based business involving desktop publishing or marketing. Some government boards will offer exporters and trade businesses great opportunities but may not interest you one whit if you're a lawyer or accountant. Alternatively, if you are a lawyer or accountant, access to government boards providing updated legislative information may be your preference. All told, there is something for everyone.

Clipping services are businesses that provide copies of all articles contained in daily newspapers and daily subscriptions throughout a region or the entire United States pertaining to a particular subject. In some instances, large corporations use these services to locate all clippings pertaining to the corporation, its product or its competitors to keep abreast of developments in the business. Celebrities also use these services, among others, to gauge their popularity.

On-line service costs vary depending on your needs.

While on-line services are not free, the cost of most services is well within the budget of any business or individual and, used to their full potential, such services can provide information more efficiently than by other means. The costs of on-line services widely vary, depending upon the particular service and your preference for their basic or extended services. For instance, while world news and general business news is available on virtually all on-line services (as opposed to the bulletin board services), some services allow the user to custom tailor a "newspaper" solely towards the user's interests. While these "custom-tailored" news briefings cost extra, the effect is much like the "clipping" services provided to large corporations and executives...only now its available to small businesses and individuals at a reasonable cost. Electronic newspapers also provide the opportunity to download information for later review, retrieval or input in reports and memos. Since the information is already electronically stored, it can be distributed throughout a companies electronic mail network with little fuss or bother...and certainly less effort than copying and distributing hard copies throughout the company. Finally, electronic services allow, to a limited extent, the ability to conduct keyword searches for articles of interest, bypassing all the immaterial news in the process.

While this search capability to narrow topics of interest is presently limited in the arena of electronic news reporting (with the exception of specialized news services), this feature may be well integrated in other electronic information media. On-line monthly publications can often be downloaded from bulletin boards and on-line services and searched for keywords using virtually any word processor on the market. Some publications have been formatted especially to take advantage of linking. Linking or hypertext links is a means of jumping from one section of a file to another. Used often in Windows system help files and documentation to allow

When copying or manipulating downloaded information, whether an electronic publication or otherwise, be aware that copyrights still exist and may limit your ability to use the information as you might have desired. While copying and marking for personal use is unlikely to draw the ire of the publisher, any attempt to re-publish or use this information for commercial purposes, without the publisher's consent, may violate the copyright and land you in a legal stew. Too often, the ease with which electronic information or graphics can be "lifted" from one file and placed in a report or publication encourages copyright infringement however, publishers are taking greater note of these actions and now take steps to educate users to the illegality of these actions through increased prosecution and warning.

users to jump from one topic to a related but separate topic, hyperlinking is now used within a wide range of electronic documents including information files, electronic magazines, publications, and reference information such as electronic encyclopedias, indexes and menu systems. Hyperlinking and hypertext capabilities are even built into newer software applications to allow easy manipulation of cross-referenced materials. Hyperlinking is used to cross-reference the beginning of a chapter with its chapter reference in a Table of Contents or allow a referenced term to be linked with its glossary definition.

Using a word processor to view these publications, the user can mark portions for export to reports and memos, set electronic bookmarks for later review and add annotations for distribution. Clearly, the electronic publications allow for a wide diversity of business-related functions, allowing the user to manipulate and distribute this "information" in an easy and efficient manner.

Some business-specific services include financial and stock updates, databases, e-mail and fax services.

Other services that may cost extra include financial information updates to personal finance software on your computer, access to specialized conferences or information databases and the use of mail services to send or receive mail or faxes throughout the world. The cost of these services, in some instances, is built into monthly subscription fees or hourly access charges. In other instances, the charge may be on a per item or per access basis regardless of the time involved on-line. Despite the extra costs, many of these services provide electronic information not otherwise available to the user in an efficient and cost-effective manner and, as we've seen, may provide increased flexibility in the manner in which this information may be manipulated, incorporated into one's own work and distributed.

If you are only interested in local conferencing, networking and perhaps accessing shareware programs, my advice would be to access local bulletin boards as I discussed in chapter 8 when discussing shareware. In most instances, you will not be required to pay a fee or, at worst, a nominal fee, for the use of these local boards.

I've talked generally about specialized databases and financial services that can be accessed by some on-line services and I've said these may cost extra but they're probably worth it to some businesses. Let's take a look at some of these services.

Just a little about CompuServe, perhaps the most information-oriented service available.

CompuServe is a gigantic computer on-line service well known to the multitude of computerphiles out there. It provides every service discussed above and is an excellent source for business contacts, information and software applications. Interacting with CompuServe through a DOS menu or a Windows program makes navigating its many service areas easy and efficient. Help is instantly available and CompuServe is well staffed to provide on-line help from within any service area. If immediate help or advice is not available, messages can be sent to the system operators (sysops) for advice. CompuServe can be accessed through modems operating at speeds from 2400 baud to 14,400 baud (14.4K). Hourly access charges vary from $12.00 to $22.80 per hour depending upon the transmission speed of your modem. Additional charges are added for services networked to CompuServe such as Iquest, premium-based on-line databases. At the higher transmission rates, higher hourly fees are charged to offset the greater transmission of information.

This does not mean that if you have a 14, 400 baud modem however that you must always communicate with CompuServe at that higher transmission rate. In some instances, the higher transmission rate will provide greater service for the increased dollars but in others it won't. If you are reading messages or other materials while connected, it's a good bet that even 2400 baud transmissions can provide you with the reading material as fast as you can read it. In those instances, use the lower transmission speed. If you are downloading a file however, the higher transmission speed will substantially reduce the download time, give you the file quicker, tie up the phone line for less time and tie up less of your time. In that case, the higher access rate is worth it.

I find CompuServe to be an almost unlimited source for computer-related information (obviously of interest to me). All major computer hardware and software manufacturers maintain forums and boards accessible from CompuServe. Within these forums, users can post questions and comments regarding products, receive advice for troubleshooting problems and receive updated information and files pertaining to the sponsor company's products. Many shareware authors (see my discussion of shareware in chapter 8) also maintain mail addresses on CompuServe. Again, you have the ability to post questions and comments to these software authors and, in some instances, see your suggestion incorporated into an updated version of the shareware product. Now, that's service.

When I speak of "mail addresses" I am speaking of networked e-mail (electronic mail). Each account (member) can be directly addressed and the member is notified of any new mail or messages the next time they call the service. Mail can be read, saved, downloaded or deleted as necessary and responses can be posted as private or public. Whether the mail is private or public will depend on a number of factors including the nature of the forum, the message and the sender's preference. In most instances, public mail is encouraged for product and manufacturer forums which invite product inquiries and comments that would be of interest to other subscribers.

In addition to its extensive support for manufacturers and end-users of computer products, CompuServe is also useful to access databases, in excess of 900 and growing. If you want to access credit reports, archived newscopy or information on legal issues, IQuest and CompuServe can provide it. How about the Dun & Bradstreet profile of a prospective client or government publications dealing with the Americans with Disabilities Act. Just log onto CompuServe.

If you are into computers, Ziffnet is primarily a computer-oriented on-line service available separately or accessible through other on-line services like CompuServe and Prodigy.

In addition to CompuServe's own system services, CompuServe also hosts Ziff-Davis Publishing's Ziffnet On-line service, a computer-oriented service acting as an electronic complement to Ziff-Davis's monthly publications, PC Magazine and PC Computing. Accessible through CompuServe or through a separate subscription, Ziffnet maintains its own computer-oriented news services, product reviews and shareware libraries. In addition to computer-oriented news, forums shareware application files, and on-line conferences with selected hardware and software company spokespersons and executives, Ziffnet also provides on-line support services and advice on computer trouble-shooting, access to specialized databases through CompuServe and access to the electronic versions of Ziff-Davis computer publications, articles and reviews. Having subscribed to this service for a period of time, I can attest to the wide range of shareware files on hand and the range of other computer-oriented news services, shopping services and conferences, however, for the general businessperson, other services offer more services of general business and personal interest.

Prodigy On-line Service has the largest number of subscribers and offers a wide variety of business and family oriented possibilities.

Prodigy is another on-line service of great popularity. While not providing many of the specialized database services of CompuServe, Prodigy does contain a wide range of informational services, forums and conferences in a friendly and reasonably priced format. In addition, Prodigy supplements its own services through connections with other networks to provide products not carried by Prodigy. Having no library of shareware and public domain software applications, Prodigy offers connections with Ziffnet for an additional cost. It also provides a connection with the Internet service (as many other services do) for the exchange of mail in addition to providing its members with their own on-line mail system. Prodigy was conceived as more than just a business tools however and it offers a wide range of forums, bulletin boards and activities that cater to children and non-business interests. Prodigy can be accessed at 2400 baud or 9600 baud and supplies both DOS and Windows versions of its software. Unlike some other services, even the DOS software provides a mouse-driven graphical interface that makes it very easy to navigate through the different areas and requires no knowledge of DOS commands or on-line navigation commands. This makes the service a particularly useful tool for a group of people having diverse interests and comfort with computerized on-line services. Prodigy does not employ strict hourly access charges like CompuServe and costs will vary depending upon your preferences. While Prodigy first offered a single flat monthly rate, regardless of what "in-house" features you used, it then moved towards combination rates that bill on a flat fee for "core" services and allow various time limits on "plus" services before hourly access charges begin to accrue. Even so, the hourly access rates for "plus" services do not approach CompuServe's rates and still offer a great value.

Prodigy's "core" and "plus" services.

What are the "core" services and what are the "plus" services? Core services include the news highlights, shopping forums, topical news and articles posted in the various forums like computer news, financial news, and family or homelife news. Additional entertainment and educational materials (including an on-line encyclopedia) are also included in the core services and various consumer aids such as on-line reviews like consumer reports are also core services. Some "plus" services include stock quotes and updates, travel information and reservations and the Prodigy bulletin boards. The shareware files available through Ziffnet access are priced at an hourly access rate and are not included as part of the "core" or "plus" services since this is not an "in-house" service but a supplement to Prodigy's offerings. For those interested in accessing the Ziffnet files, Prodigy offers plans which include Ziffnet access in the monthly rate.

America On-line is another on-line service offering a balanced choice of business and entertainment options.

Also in the running for your on-line dollars is America On-line. Running third in the race in terms of subscribers (behind #1 Prodigy and #2 CompuServe), America On-line also sports a Windows interface a la supplied software designed for navigating its forums and services.

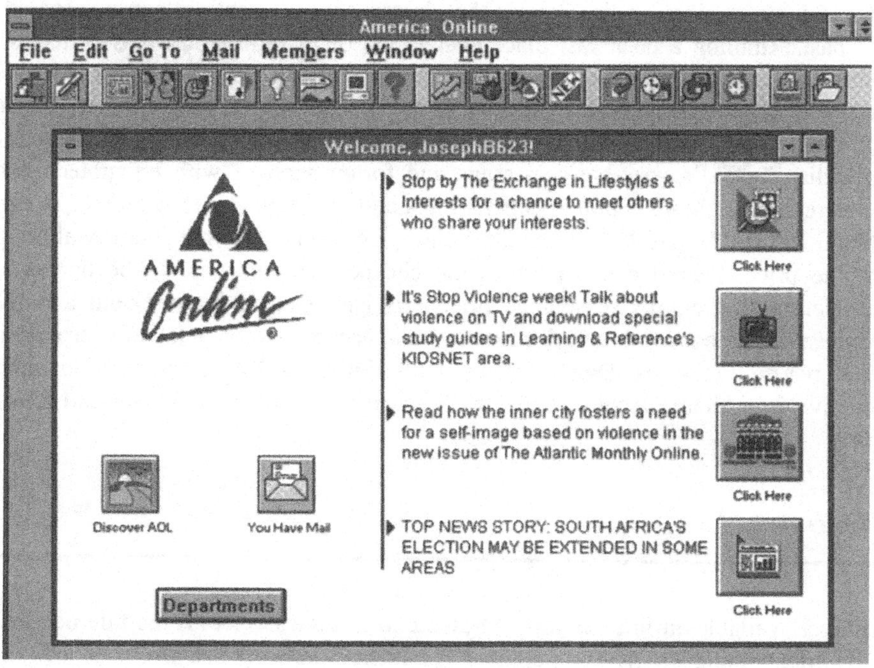

Figure 18-3 America On-line's opening screen provides you with a choice of topics to explore and lets you know of waiting mail. Like the other commercial services, the Windows interface makes it easy to navigate and save notes or research for later use.

America On-line may be of particular interest to those businesses with an entertainment or cable TV slant (although other services also have ties to entertainment forums and offer celebrity appearances) due to its cable television interaction conferences. Fans of Ricki Lake, Geraldo, CNN and the Sci-Fi cable network, among others, can consult schedules, request tickets, send e-mail and suggest program topics America On-line offers the same functionality of the other services such as e-mail, news, financial updates, general research facilities, file downloads and on-line games and interactive conferences. For business however, American On-line may be less useful than the data-intensive CompuServe. It lacks the full breadth of database information available on CompuServe and is oriented more with Prodigy's balance of general news and information on the one hand and entertainment or educational interaction on the other.

If you've never heard of the Delphi On-line Service, you will. Its perhaps the cheapest way onto the Internet.

Delphi is yet another on-line service that deserves more attention than it received in the past. Running a clear last place against the other on-line services in terms of subscribers, Delphi is poised for a change with its acquisition by Rupert Murdoch and its head start as a capable gateway to the increasingly popular Internet service. Murdoch, a major player in news and entertainment mediums, will hopefully embellish Delphi's very basic message and forum services with integrated global news retrieval, global communications links and interactive entertainment. In time, Delphi will also hopefully put a more friendly face on the Internet gateway although, for the price, Delphi offers perhaps the cheapest entrance fee to be had to the Internet. Still, Delphi's reasonable pricing is handicapped by weekend and after business hours access. Normal business hour access costs a relatively prohibitive $9.00 per hour to access Delphi through its SprintNet or Tymnet connections unless you live in a "home territory" of Delphi, currently limited to Boston and Kansas City.

The Internet...

Another available on-line network (I hesitate to call it a service) is the Internet. What is the Internet and why is it so popular? The Internet network is a global collection of separate and diverse educational, government and private computer systems. It is not a commercial information service like those I've previously discussed but it is open to all computers users (with some caveats) and may be a tremendous source of information to some businesses or entrepreneurs. If you're wondering why it took so long for this network to gain attention, it's most likely due to its academic nature. Until recent policy restrictions on commercial use of the Internet, the Internet had little prospect as a business tool. With attention now focused on means of improving information exchange throughout the United States by means of an "information superhighway", the Internet was the logical focus of renewed interest due to its established chain of computer networks. The Internet links universities, libraries, state and federal governmental institutions and numerous other private networks around the world and provides a common communication link for the transfer of educational, technological or personal information through electronic mail, document and file transfers and forum communications. The result of, first the United States Advanced Research Projects Agency, and then the National Science Foundation, Internet has gained wide popularity as an ever-increasing percentage of businesses and individuals became computer literate in the 1990's. If your business is technology-based, or even if such information may be important only for peripherally related concerns, the Internet may be a good source of recent global developments and secondary information sources. Market researchers may also find the wide use of the Internet and the opportunity to target international and domestic markets to be worthwhile for their needs.

The Internet may be a little daunting for computer novices.

Before you decide that the Internet, as the largest network of its kind, is the appropriate service for your needs, also consider that it is much harder to access and navigate the many informational sources available on the Internet. This is because the Internet is comprised of a diverse number of computer systems and operating systems all attempting to communicate using a common language. That common language is UNIX-based (an ugly term for those who have grown up on the civilized side of computing, i.e. DOS and Windows) and is called TCP/IP which stands for Transmission Control Protocol/Internet Protocol. This protocol (language) is but one of a related set of protocols such as Telnet, FTP, UDP and RDP; all of which allow people to communicate or perform functions on the Internet.

While there are some available software applications that allow people to communicate on the Internet through a Windows or DOS interface, most people do not directly connect with the Internet. While you can directly communicate with local bulletin boards and network systems from your PC, the Internet's members are primarily governmental and educational institutions. Connection by private individuals and small businesses is accomplished through gateways offered by Internet members. These Internet members may be freenet local bulletin board services or commercial access providers. In some instances, access may be through the provider's system, using the provider's menu or shell, or may be direct with the Internet, requiring your system to contain a version of TCP/IP for conversing in the Internet's "native" language. If you do decide to transverse the Internet and are looking for an access provider, be careful. When comparing access providers in your area, be certain that you will have full access to the e-mail services (usually), FTP (for file transfers), Telnet (for accessing programs and applications on the Internet system) and Usenet (for forums and conference services). While local networks and some commercial on-line services may provide certain access services such as access to Internet's e-mail system, access to forums and Telnet connections may not be available. Also closely review access costs since these may differ from the costs associated with the access provider's own similar services. The Internet does not track usage time nor does it charge an hourly access fee to its members. Accordingly, most reasonable access providers do not charge an additional hourly access rate for accessing the Internet but may charge a single monthly or annual access rate for unlimited access. You will still have to pay the access provider their own hourly access charge to use their service to access the Internet however. For this reason, if you want low cost access to the Internet, you may want to be careful how you choose an access provider.

The Internet proves you can sometimes have too much information for your own good.

Besides the language barrier, the Internet provides such a mind-boggling amount of accessible information that finding information can be an experience in frustration. To help its members access information, the Internet incorporates a collection of utilities. Telnet is a widely utilized application for accessing other computer systems. With Telnet, you can run programs on Internet computers around the globe (although this type of access is limited in some instances for security purposes). Telnet is also used to implement other Internet utilities for searching and retrieving information. Gopher is a menu utility that provides menu and submenu choices to guide you towards your desired goal...a particular document, file or forum. Since there are literally thousands of Gopher menus within the Internet, the Veronica utility is available to search gophers for selected text to help you narrow your search. Archie is another utility, more narrow in scope than Veronica, and is used to locate a particular file by name, directory or character string. These few utilities just begin to give you an understanding of what is involved in perusing the Internet. While the Internet was not conceived as a commercial venture or with commercial interests in mind, its global capacity in this age of dissolving economic borders may prove enticing to some of you venturers or entrepreneurs out there. At the very least, if you develop good skills at transversing the Internet, the chances are that any information you might want will be available somewhere in its labyrinth of networked computer systems.

If you're interested in learning more about the Internet or having on-line reference help regarding the Internet services, I've run across a freeware Windows help file called "InfoPop". Using the Windows Help system, this free file outlines Internet services, provides the names of documents for beginning and experienced Internet guidance and even gives the addresses (Internet locations) of potentially useful information like library catalogs, lists and university and college information services. See Figure 18-4. Since its free, and its always on-line for easy reference, if you are considering transversing the Internet, download "InfoPop" from your favorite BBS and read it.

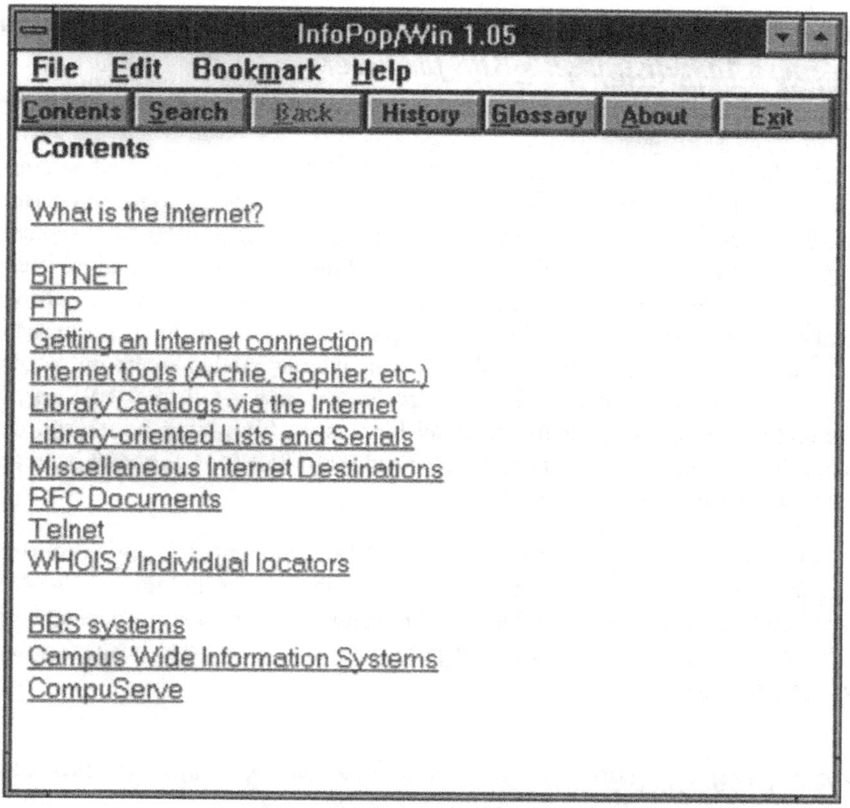

Figure 18-4 InfoPop is a hypertext freeware application serving as a guide to the Internet. Although it is not a comprehensive guide to the Internet, it does provide a number of lists for accessing educational institutions on the Internet, library catalogs on the Internet (including the Library of Congress) and documents containing information and FAQ (Frequently Asked Questions) of interest to first timers.

If you can't find a copy but are certain you can't live without it, contact the author (although a small processing fee is to be expected if he sends you the file on disk):

Author: Clyde W. Grotophorst
Email: wallyg@fen1.gmu.edu

BBS: (703) 993-2219
CIS: 70704,3376
Phone: (703) 993-2239
Fax: (703) 993-2229

There are other business-oriented services out there...try the Small Business Administration's BBS for Free!

What other on-line services and boards might a businessperson find interesting? How about the SBA BBS...that's short for Small Business Administration Bulletin Board Service. The Small Business Administration is a federally funded agency that promotes small business development through funds and assistance administered at the state and local level. In addition to providing advice through a network of volunteer professionals and businesspeople, it also provides information on accessing government business and accessing international markets not otherwise considered by many qualified small businesses. The toll-free BBS provides information on issues of interest to small businesses, SBA publications and census data. (800) 697-4636 for 9600 baud access and (800) 859-4636 for 2400 baud access cost you nothing, so give it a try.

Another government bulletin board is ALIX (Automated Library Information Exchange) at (202) 707-2885 for 14,400 baud or less access and (202) 707-4888 for 2400 baud access (here's where that fast modem saves you long-distance charges). Federally related articles, reports and publications of interest to businesses are all available for downloading.

Some specific business forums available on the commercial on-line services may be what your "networking" needs.

Each of the commercial on-line services also sports special forums or conferences of particular interest to small businesses and entrepreneurs. CompuServe members have The Business Wire, Entrepreneur's Forum and Information USA. The Business Wire is your source for company press releases, news articles and other business information available on-line or downloaded for later perusal. The Entrepreneur's Forum is where businesspeople go to discuss, argue, give advice and carefully take advice on an unlimited range of business topics. If you want business shareware, the Forum may be a good place to start. If you've grown stale for new marketing concepts, the Forum (or any other discussion-based service) may provide some ideas. Information USA provides access to government-grown information, access to more government services available on-line and an assortment of government publications. Before you spend your money on consultants and demographic analysis, log on-line and see what the government already provides for free.

America On-line subscribers have the Microsoft Small Business Center (Figure 18-5). Like CompuServe's Forum, the Business Center provides articles and discussions. Primarily an article infobase, the Business Center provides information from government agencies like the SBA, Chamber of Commerce, and National Federation of Independent Business.

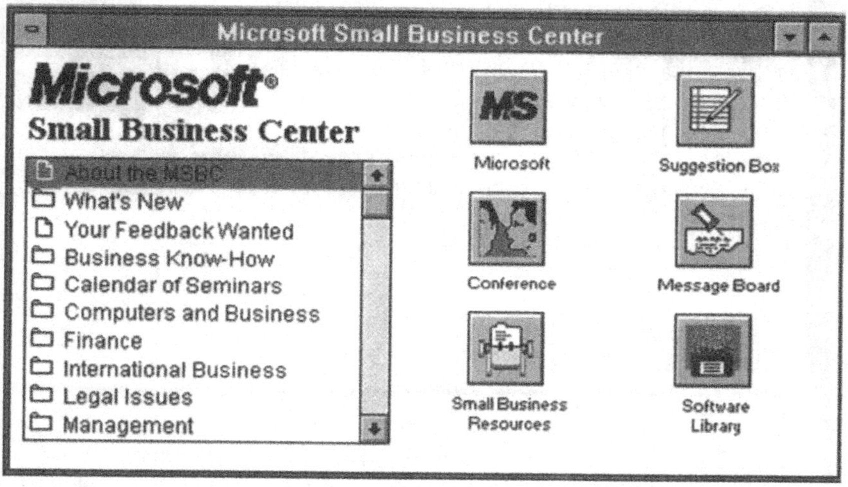

Figure 18-5 America Online's Small Business Center is pretty self-explanatory. In addition to information on specific issues, access to conferences, business software and mail services makes this a good networking tool for the right business.

Genie members have the Business Resource Directory and WorkPlace RoundTable. The Workplace RoundTable is much like CompuServe's Entrepreneur's Forum, providing a combination of business-oriented discussion and advice for the asking and business-oriented shareware available for downloading. The Business Resource Directory, however, is quite different from other offerings. Designed as a company database, you can list your own company service or product on the Directory and likewise use the Directory to locate a service or product you need. The Directory is a supplemental service and hourly access fees apply. If you are interested in perusing the Directory, my suggestion is to look during evening hours or weekends when the access fees are considerably less than during normal business hours.

Finally, Prodigy members have the Home Business Office. See Figure 18-7. In addition to an electronic bulletin board from which you can develop contacts, request advice and peruse topical discussions, the home business section of Prodigy also offers advice from Prodigy's home business authors and regularly posted articles and reviews (Figure 18-6).

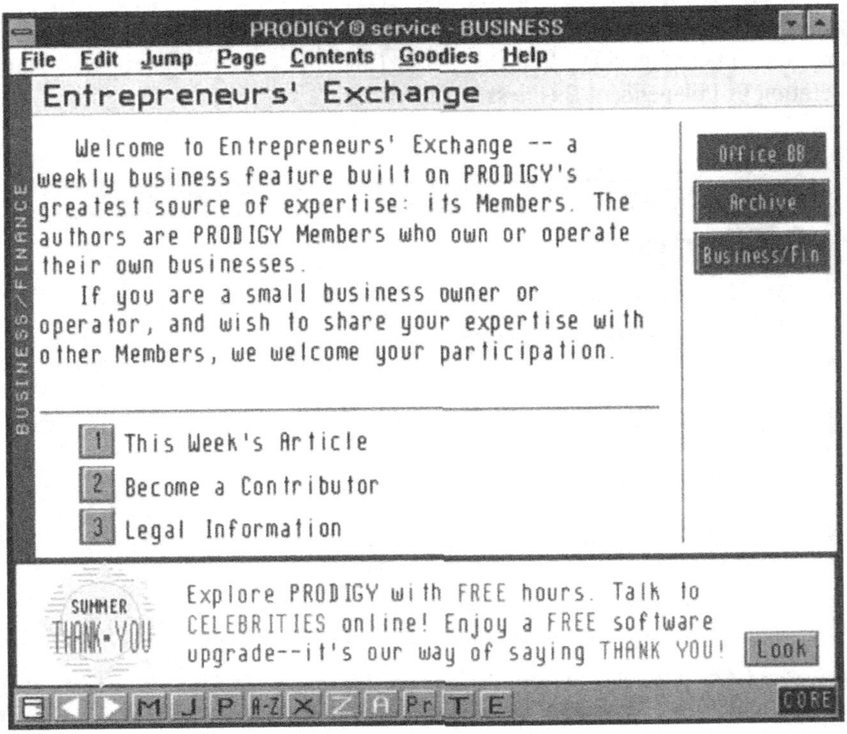

Figure 18-6 A Bulletin Board by the business owners and for the business owners is available on Prodigy. Like any other type of electronic bulletin board, topics and questions of interest to readers can generate a tremendous number of responses and information and contribution by way of articles or responses may prove a valuable networking tool for the budding consultant.

While on-line, you can review new trends in technology or the law that may affect your small or home-based business and download reviews or articles that may be useful at later dates. If an articles draws your attention and you have questions, the author is just a message away.

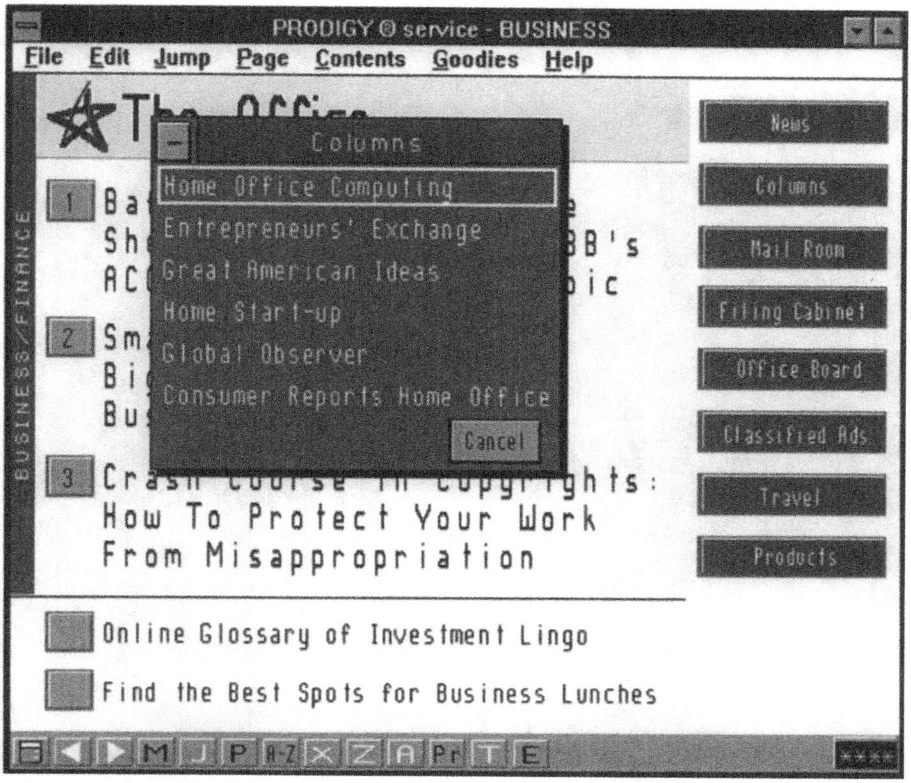

Figure 18-7 Small Business services through Prodigy include travel and product information, articles, mail and general business news. I'm willing to bet that you could make productive use of one or more of these services on a daily basis.

Prodigy also offers a number of other services of interest to the home or small business such as business articles, advertisements, mail, and consumer reports through its Office Center. See Figure 18-7.

While these business "centers" may not totally replace your current information sources or networking methods, they require very little investment for their potential return.

SECTION VI

Chapter 19

Mail Order, Discount & Computer Superstores

Once you know what software and hardware you need, how do you purchase it? Options include shopping at discount and office supply houses, local computer stores, computer superstores and mail order purchases. Let's look at each of these in turn and consider their advantages.

Discount and office supply houses have the price but not the selection to choose from.

Discount and office supply houses are generally not the best choice for computer products since the wide diversity of today's products cannot be carried by general merchandisers. While the office supply houses will usually provide a better selection than general merchandise discount houses, these outlets are still limited in their hardware and software choices. Companies such as Sears Roebuck carry IBM computers and perhaps one or two other brands. The few choices are sold off the shelf in one or two basic configurations and additional accessories and upgrades are not generally available at the store or through an on-site technicians center. More importantly, most salespersons in discount retail outlets such as Sears do not have the expertise to properly advise a computer customer and do not have sufficient knowledge of their products beyond that gleaned from a cursory review of the box or instruction manual.

Stop and think of the types of questions you want answered after reading the first half of this book. You may want to know how the computer is designed to accept additional RAM memory, the size of the hard disk and processor caches, the number and types of expansion slots, the availability of internal and external bays for the computer to accept tape drives and CD-ROM drives, the ability of the monitor to avoid flicker at higher resolutions, the type of video card installed in the system, the type of UART chip used in the serial port and maybe even the availability of upgradable processor chips. Getting a correct answer from your average K-Mart or Sears salesperson for each of these questions is unlikely. Even if you do get an answer, I would be concerned that the answer may be incorrect. Unless the salesperson has a personal interest in computers and computer products, I would doubt they have the particularized knowledge to answer your questions. If you read through this book you are probably better qualified to answer your own questions than they are. I think it's unlikely that Sears or K-Mart would specially train that person to field such questions. In fairness to K-Mart and Sears however, they do not anticipate receiving these questions and carry these products for people that, quite honestly, are not as concerned as you are about a computer purchase.

Office warehouse superstores have a better selection but don't offer customized or upgraded configurations.

While I have lumped office supply houses into the prior category, I do not intend to include the office warehouse superstores such as Office Depot and Office Max. Most such stores have, in my experience, a much greater selection of hardware and software. The salespeople at these office supply houses are generally knowledgeable about their products and, from my conversations with them, many have a genuine interest in computer products, even having considerable knowledge regarding products not carried by the office supply house. Still, while their selection is greater, this selection is comprised of more configurations offered from three or four manufacturers. If you have already decided that you want a 486/66, you may be relegated to one or two such choices at the office superstore. If you want that configuration upgraded with more RAM memory or a larger monitor in place of the standard 14" monitor, then you are generally out of luck. Finally, such stores will not usually carry higher capacity, upgraded configurations of manufacturer computer lines preferring more value-based product lines. As a result, those of you desiring more complete systems, and I assume that is why you are reading this book, will have to look elsewhere.

> As one example, most office supply superstores carry notebook computers with the smaller hard disk capacities. Although you may find that 486 color notebook you always wanted, be prepared to settle for the 120 MB hard disk version rather than the 200 MB (or larger) version if you purchase it at such an outlet.

The higher price but greater personal attention and service at local computer stores may be a good tradeoff for the novice.

Local computer stores and computer superstores each have their positive points. The local store's great advantage is the time and attention that you can receive from the manager or salesperson, the knowledge that most such stores can offer regarding new technology and the willingness to configure a system particularly for your needs. This last point is perhaps the greatest advantage of a local computer establishment. Many such stores have technicians that build computers on-site and will configure a computer system with the components and subcomponents that you want or need.

> Custom built systems by local computer stores are generally of high quality however care must be used to ensure that the system components that are used by the store are not older components supplanted by newer, more capable versions of the same product. Since many such stores receive a supply of components, and since standards may change in less than six months, the consumer should be aware that the system may utilize a superseded board or component developed six months prior.

The store's technician is also capable of answering even the most obscure question regarding the computer's components. For those knowing exactly what they want, this option may be the most cost-effective option in terms of time and money. It's no secret in the computer industry that some machines are better suited for running DOS programs or Windows programs (or OS/2 programs). These machines are better suited to one environment rather than another because some individual components, such as graphics boards, operate better in one environment rather than the other. If you are unable to find the correct mix of processor and graphics performance for your intended use, then a custom built system may be a better option than purchasing a base system and then investing more money in an additional graphics board to get the performance you were shopping for in the first place.

Finally, a local store is convenient in the event you need service or support. If you purchased a custom system, the technician will be better able to provide instant and knowledgeable service and the "downtime" of shipping and dealing with service via mail or telephone is eliminated.

My first computer was purchased at a local outlet store and it's a good thing it was. I really needed the advice and technical support the local store's salespeople offered. When I had problems installing software, they were available and willing to help me install the software. When I thought the computer had memory problems (it didn't), I brought the computer back to the store and, in less than fifteen minutes, it was checked for defects. All in all, I probably brought that computer back two or three times for problems caused by my inexperience with the equipment. In such an instance, locality counts for more than a few dollars in price or a few MB of hard disk space in features.

Computer superstores pick up where the local, smaller operation leaves off. Stores such as Computer City and CompUSA, two local computer superstores in my region, offer a wider variety of hardware and software options. Their salespeople are generally well informed and many such stores have on-site technician centers for repairs, warranty work and upgrades to newly purchased equipment or even existing computer equipment.

What types of work will the tech center do for you? If you bought a larger hard disk for your existing computer, the technicians can install it for you. If you purchase RAM memory, an upgraded video card or a fax/modem for your existing system, the technicians can install it. Besides the convenience of having your new purchase installed on-site, you can be assured that any installation problems or product defects will stand a greater chance of being corrected and not blamed on any "incorrect" installation or product handling by the customer.

The superstores also provide displays of most desktop systems, portables, printers and peripherals for on-site review. As I mentioned in Chapter 15 on portable computers, gaining some on-hands experience with your intended purchase can be very important. The ability to perceive the relative performance of different configurations using similar software is a tremendous help. In this manner, the consumer can determine if a 486/66 is really that much more necessary than a 486/25 on sale at the time. Similarly, comparing 14", 15" and 17" monitors side by side, displaying the same image, can also help the consumer understand the practical differences between monitors costing $300.00 and those costing $1000.00 or more.

Superstores may seem to offer everything...but they don't.

While superstores carry a wider variety of computer products than others, this variety is still limited. There are a tremendous number of manufacturers and products available today and computer superstores carry a small percentage of these products. The two superstores I mentioned earlier, Computer City and CompUSA carry perhaps 10 different computer system manufacturers. While this is a tremendous increase over the two or three brands carried by office supply superstores or smaller computer stores, it does not take into consideration the great number of manufacturers that market their products solely through mail-order or direct sales. In some instances, manufacturers, having an established distributorship chain and/or direct sale division, will limit the configurations they make available through superstores. While the superstore will carry certain configurations, the consumer may be better served to consider additional configurations available solely through the dealers or available through direct sales.

Mail order or direct sales is the fastest growing segment of the computer sales market. It's also the newest environment for today's shoppers. Consumers should know that mail order shopping is different in nature than traditional retail shopping and consumers have different rights than those afforded in face-to-face sales.

Mail order purchasing offers a great combination of selection, price and delivery.

For the educated consumer, mail order purchasing has many advantages over traditional sales methods. Convenience and time savings are perhaps the two best selling points for mail order shopping. Any businessperson today does not have an abundance of time and an afternoon saved in traveling from one store to another or arranging delivery of the product can be a godsend. The time savings of mail order is generally recognized only after the consumer has decided on a computer configuration or product. In that instance, the consumer can comparison shop products, via telephone, with knowledgeable salespeople and get product information and pricing in a relatively short period of time. Although time would appear to favor the local store, overnight shipping is almost universally available (at extra cost) and minimizes the time difference of on-site purchases.

If the sales department can't answer your questions, the tech department is standing by.

Getting accurate information to obscure questions regarding a computer product is always an "iffy" proposition in my opinion since many salespeople, even those familiar with the product, do not necessarily work with the product on a daily basis. If you are shopping by telephone however, I have found that most mail-order salespeople will transfer you to extremely knowledgeable technical service people for answers to your questions if they are unsure of the answer themselves. This is a great opportunity to find out very technical information regarding a product and such help is generally not available at computer superstores or other such outlets.

Mail order shopping means price savings but watch out for the conditions of sale.

Product availability is also an advantage to mail-order shopping. If the mail-order house you called does not have the product, alternative mail-order companies will generally have stock. In most instances, absent special circumstances, price matching will guarantee that availability is at the lowest advertised price.

> There is one caveat to be noted here. Although alternative mail-order companies may provide price-matching, other terms of sale will not necessarily be matched. As I will discuss later, re-stocking fees, return policies, credit card surcharges, guarantees and service will differ from company to company and should always be a consideration in the final decision of your purchase.

Price, of course, is always a consideration in small business purchases and mail-order purchases are noteworthy for their low prices. Absent overhead customarily required for retail businesses, most mail-order companies provide savings averaging 10% of the product's price. When comparing prices, consider the following:

Ask if a company collects sales tax on mail-order purchases. Under the law, sales tax on a purchase may be collected by the vendor or may be payable as a use tax by the purchaser to its home state. Whether the vendor is required to collect sales tax may depend on the location of its corporate offices and whether it is registered to do business in the purchaser's home state;

Ask what shipping charges will be billed for the entire purchase. In some instances, purchasers have been unpleasantly surprised by ridiculously high shipping charges;

Ask about handling charges. Like shipping charges, these charges may exceed what the purchaser assumed to be a reasonable sum;

Ask about any other charges the vendor may take such as a credit card surcharge. Although such surcharges are becoming the exception rather than the rule (due to the competitiveness of the mail-order business and increased consumer awareness and sophistication) some such charges still exist at some companies;

Finally, consider the vendor's return policies. While most vendors will reasonably require a return authorization number be procured through their sales or customer service departments, other return polices widely differ.

- Some vendors provide toll-free support, others don't.

- Some vendors provide overnight replacement shipping and longer money-back guarantees than others.

- Most importantly, some vendors charge a "restocking fee" on returned merchandise. This "restocking fee" is a charge or penalty, calculated on the total purchase, for returns. Although I have never experienced such a fee (since I won't do business with vendors that charge these fees), there is nothing to prevent a vendor from charging these fees...even on merchandise that is returned due to defects or returned pursuant to money-back guarantee policies. These "restocking" fees vary and, in some cases, constitute a 20% penalty for returns. My advice is to avoid them like the plague. Any purchase, even as nominal as the purchase of memory chips, is available through vendors with competitive credit-card pricing, without restocking fees.

- With respect to credit cards, this is the preferred payment method for **all** purchases, and, as with "restocking fees" credit-card surcharges are also passé with most reputable and desirable vendors. The surcharge, to cover the fees paid to credit companies for guaranteeing payment on the credit card, should be built into any advertised price. Again, I won't deal with any vendor that doesn't advertise "No surcharge for credit cards".

- Money-back guarantees for, let's say 30 days, should begin on the date of receipt. I've heard of one case though, when the manufacturer delivered the product on the 22nd day and counted the order date as the first day of the guarantee. A very poor practice indeed. Be aware of this and, although I expect that case to be the exception, confirm guarantees and policies before the purchase.

PAY BY CREDIT CARD !!

Once you've made the decision to purchase your computer system and accessories through mail-order, and being aware of the preceding concerns, what do you look for and what do you avoid? Although it won't guarantee a problem-free relationship with the vendor, I use the following practices:

- I will only pay by credit card. Not by check, certified or personal, and certainly not by cash or money order. I put this first for a reason. It is the most sacrosanct rule of consumer mail order purchasing...use a credit card. Why? Paying by credit card gives you recourse in the event of a problem. While failure to receive the product may be one problem most people consider, other problems may arise including service related problems, warranty problems, and misrepresentations by salespersons resulting in receipt of inadequate merchandise. Disputing payment under the Fair Credit Collection Act gives the consumer much greater leverage to resolve the dispute than if payment were rendered by check or money order. Payment by most credit cards today will also effectively double the one-year warranties offered with most systems. If the salesperson is reluctant to accept credit card orders or offers a "special" deal only with cash or check payments, be wary. In some instances, this is an indication that the manufacturer is using customers' money to pay manufacturing and business costs and may be under-capitalized (a term meaning the company has less cash than it really needs to carry on its business). In extreme cases, this is an indication the company may be close to bankrupt or may be involved in marginally illegal or fraudulent activities. Resist the temptation to save a few dollars by paying cash. More than a few people out there wish they did.

Check the advertisements carefully.

I look at written advertisements for complete terms of sale. This includes statements of guaranteed replacement, no restocking fees and no credit card surcharges. I also look for overnight replacement on critical components. Why the written advertisement? Because, unlike the telephone salesperson's verbal statements, the advertisement can be carried into court as proof of your contract terms, if necessary. One caveat offered by some consumer advocacy groups is look for a company address in the advertisement and note whether the address is a street address or post office box. Most recommend avoiding businesses operating out of post office boxes. In my opinion, however, the distinction is minor since any business that can abandon a box can also abandon a street address. Moreover, some boxes are located at private mail facilities and are provided addresses that appear to be street addresses. Others recommend looking for representations that the company has been in business "since 19--". Again, some businesses take editorial liberty with their advertisements and such claims may not be entirely accurate. A better precaution may be to contact the state and county consumer protection agencies (usually operated by the State Attorney General's office) or the Better Business Bureau of the locality. Also consider checking with the Direct Marketing Association (212-768-7277), Federal Trade Commission (202-326-2222) or the Electronics Industries Association (202-457-4900) I usually just pay by credit card and don't worry about it.

- I also look on the advertisement for toll-free service and support numbers. While many companies provide toll-free sales numbers, the free ride stops there. If you are considering the purchase of equipment you are not familiar with, the few dollars saved by mail order can quickly disappear when sitting on a vendors toll support line waiting for a representative to solve your problems. Better vendors provide toll-free technical support. If you are considering the purchase of an entire system, also consider when support is available. 24 hour, 7 day support for those working in evenings and on weekends is worth the increased productivity of getting answers today and not Monday. Finally, ask about remote diagnostic software services and BBS services to download updated drivers and software for your system.

- If I rely upon answers from telephone salespersons regarding shipping dates, quotes for shipping charges and other terms that can't be disclosed in an advertisement, I insist on the salesperson's full name (first and last) and note the name, date and time on the advertisement. In the law, this may be considered a contemporaneous statement admissible as evidence of the contents of your conversation. It also helps when the next technician or manager wants to know who gave you the "erroneous" information. Having that information as well as the date and time of the conversation is usually enough to convince the person on the other end that you are an organized and knowledgeable individual unwilling to accept sub-standard service.

- Before the sale is completed by telephone I will request a total product cost, separate shipping cost and a total cost to be applied against my credit card. This avoids unpleasant surprises regarding shipping or handling costs that may be tacked on by some vendors. I also request their internal order number, ask that the salesperson confirm that the product is in stock and further request a shipping date based on product availability and the time of day the order was placed. This is also a good time to get the full name of the salesperson and note the name, date and time on the advertisement along with the order number and shipping date.

Verify shipping or you may be waiting for a computer that never left the shipping dock.

A reasonable time after the sale is completed, I will call to verify my order's status. This avoids miscommunications or delays that will frustrate you and potentially damage your business. If the order is shipped overnight, you obviously don't want to call before the 24 hours has passed and you haven't received delivery. If the order is shipped U.P.S. Ground, wait two days and then call. If you were told it would be received in five days but hasn't been shipped after two days, you have the opportunity to make other arrangements so that you receive the product as expected. In appropriate instances, demanding priority or overnight delivery of critical purchases when shipment is delayed is your perogative (in my opinion). Alternatively, if the product is not in stock, despite being told otherwise when you placed the order, you then have the opportunity to cancel the order and place it with another vendor. In either event, following up is to your advantage. If the company representative can't tell you if it shipped (such as when their computers are "down"), get the name of the shipping company they use (U.P.S., Airborne Express, Federal

Express, G.P.S., etc.) and call the shipping company's local office. Sometimes this is a quicker and more accurate method of confirming shipment and an expected delivery date.

- When I first receive a package, I check the condition of the box before signing for its receipt, inspect the packing slip for accuracy of product and price and, only then, open the package.

- If I encounter any problems that remain unsolved after speaking with service representatives, I ask to speak to the customer service manager. The manager has the discretion to prioritize customer requests and to grant customer compensation not in keeping with normal company policies. If a product is faulty and you want it replaced with overnight delivery, the manager may be the person to speak with. If the product was misrepresented, albeit unintentionally, the manager can expedite resolution to keep your business. If you have properly documented your transaction and it is clear that you are familiar with your rights, most managers will treat you professionally and with respect. Those that don't are another reason to pay by credit card.

Consumer rights for mail order purchases.

If all the prior precautions still leave you with a bad taste in your mouth after dealing with a mail order vendor, what are your rights? By law, purchases must be shipped within 30 days. If the order will not be shipped within the 30 days, the vendor must notify you by mail, in advance, and provide a new shipping date. Absent your agreement to a delay, the vendor must ship the product within the original 30 day period or may cancel the order. Vendors are also subject to the provisions of the Uniform Commercial Code governing sales, warranties and remedies. While the Code provisions may vary slightly from state to state, the merchant is generally required to provide products in merchantable condition. That is, the product must be fit for the ordinary purposes for which such goods are used and conform to the promises, representations and qualifications set forth on the package. While this is a limited description, it is clear that products "dead on arrival" or soon thereafter do not qualify as merchantable. In such instances, the purchaser should presumably be capable of "rejecting" the goods and returning them to the vendor, with or without a money-back guarantee. Most reputable vendors have no problem with these terms and will accept such goods for replacement rather than repair.

Avoiding problems with mail order companies through a little "homework".

Having considered all of the above, isn't there some simply way to shop the hundreds of mail-order houses all over the country and be fairly certain that I will avoid problems. To those that ask this question, I have three suggestions. First, pick up a copy of the "Computer Shopper". This over-sized soft-bound monthly publication is the mail-order shopper's Bible. Not only does it have hundreds of mail order vendors to pick from, it indexes vendors by product, provides a summary of vendor policies and will even intervene if problems arise between a consumer and a vendor advertising in Computer Shopper. Second, go to the library and ask for PC Computing Magazine. Somewhere in the year's issues will be a review of direct market vendors. PC World Magazine also devotes space to solving consumer problems and may be a good source for information on various vendors. Finally, if you or a friend subscribe to any on-line service, or even a local BBS, get on-line, review comments regarding vendors and products and even post your own questions asking other subscribers for their input on a vendor or product. Even a family-oriented service such as Prodigy has an extensive computer-oriented bulletin board and comments are posted daily on vendors and their products. Most responses are quick and, most importantly, brutally honest.

SECTION VII

Chapter 20

Computerizing Your Service Business

Any service business today that doesn't use a computer to manage itself is giving up a tremendous competitive and strategic advantage to its opposition. Service businesses, while generally including attorneys, accountants, architects, doctors and other professionals, also includes consultants, public relations and advertising firms and any other business that "sells" its time and expertise. In addition to the regularly cited uses service businesses have for computers: word processing, time-keeping and billing and calendaring events, there are a great number of other uses that are passed by. In this chapter I am going to discuss three types of products: (1) the usual products of use to service businesses such as word processing packages and the others described above, (2) features in the above products that are sometimes over-looked by people but really shouldn't be; and (3) other products and services that may provide that competitive edge you've been looking for.

Many businesses live and breath on word processors.

First and foremost, virtually any service-related business will get great mileage from word processing software. For years, WordPerfect 5.1 (for DOS) has been the mainstream word processing package for lawyers and other professionals. Its virtually universal acceptance has resulted in word processing seminars on using WordPerfect, books and training systems (video and tape) on using WordPerfect in a variety of business settings and add-on packages to complement its capabilities. These additional software applications vary from simple legal and medical dictionaries to packages that merge data with specialized forms.

What's "document assembly" software and is it worth the money?

Document assembly software uses fill-in menu systems to combine client data with company forms and output a professional, custom-tailored form for filing or other use. The better packages will also allow the business to add customized forms from its own library and set up customized menus to suit its unique needs. Finally, these packages can merge client data into any number of forms at one time to produce a complete package for real estate closings, bankruptcy filings, stock sales and transfers, incorporations or any other action involving multiple forms and statements.

When I used WordPerfect with an add-on form package, I setup packages of forms to complete incorporations, probate administration and simplified litigation filings with the input of client information only once. It is a very efficient manner of managing any service-oriented business.

I'm not going to bother trying to review all the packages available to lawyers or other professionals that provide document merging and customizing. Most such packages can be found advertised in your professional association's magazine. For lawyers, this would be your state Bar Magazine and for accountants, CPA Today has advertisements for these products. Most of the companies that offer these packages will send sample program diskettes and promotional materials that will tell you if the program meets your needs. I can offer a few caveats however.

1. Look for a program that will allow long descriptive names of the forms within its database. With over 2500 forms on my own computer, if I didn't have descriptive names, I'd be sunk.

2. Look for a program that will allow you to add your own forms to its form database and will alter those forms to accept menu-input client and case information identical to its included forms.

3. The program should allow you to group forms by their nature or content so that real estate forms are not listed with your litigation forms.

4. Finally, the program should not unduly limit the length of input data and should retain any formatting you apply to the input data.

By way of example, those of you that practice civil litigation will recognize that five or more forms are necessary to process a default when a Defendant does not answer within the response period. In addition to the default motion, a motion for final default judgment, the client's affidavit in proof of claim, your affidavit for fees, your affidavit for costs reimbursement, another attorney's affidavit in support of your fee application and the final judgment all need to be processed. Set up as a set of forms, all the information can be input through menu prompts and then all the forms "spit" out of the printer at once. As I said, a great time saver.

The transition to a Windows word processor does not necessarily have to be "rocky."

Other word processors, although not as widely entrenched as WordPerfect, also provide the wealth of word processing tools necessary to streamline document production, the mainstay of any service business. The features of these word processors are discussed in greater detail in Chapter 9 which is devoted to word processors however, having some experience which each, I can say that each is a very capable performer.

One concern that you shouldn't have, and I'll repeat it here even though I've said this in Chapter 9, is the feature set of your intended purchase. If you are intending to switch brands because another product has one or two killer features that you want, my advice is to wait. In many instances, the software vendors look at their competitor's newest releases and incorporate the newest "killer" features and innovative revisions into their next product upgrade. As a result, "editor's choice" awards in computer magazines are often awarded to the newer product. Once a competitor releases an upgrade, that product becomes #1 until the next released upgrade. As a result, feature shopping is usually not worth the hassle of changing formats.

I suspect, however, that your choice may depend more on non-computer issues than anything else. If you are considering a transition to Microsoft Windows in your office or you are considering changing word processors within the office, you are probably wondering how it will affect your practice. If so, you are probably concerned about three things, hardware compatibility, document conversion to new formats and personnel training. What's the problem with hardware compatibility? If your office has older computers using WordPerfect 5.1, will it stand the upgrade to WordPerfect 6 for DOS or a Windows word processor? An emphatic NO is the answer.

I don't care what reviewers say, I think WordPerfect 6 for DOS is a "dog" on 286 and 386 computers. In its graphical mode it is much too slow, even on a 386 computer and, if you are going to use it in its text mode, why both to upgrade from WordPerfect 5.1?

WordPerfect 6 for DOS is too much for a 286 computer and the Windows processors require at least a 386 computer to operate properly. If you have a great number of computers to upgrade, and many offices still rely upon 286 computers for their output, factor in the cost of the newer hardware (computers, additional memory and color monitors) before you consider a word processor upgrade. As you will see later, if upgrading is not a viable option, now may be the time to invest some thought in using the advanced features of your current processor to streamline and automate your work.

Handling document conversion when switching word processing platforms just requires some forethought.

If this first hurdle has been leaped and you are not concerned about hardware capabilities, what about document conversion. While word processors are advertised as capable of accepting many different document formats, most will not make the transition seamless. This is true whether you are merely changing brands of DOS or Windows products or you are considering migrating from DOS to a Windows word processor. Part of this problem is due to the different means each vendor has of encoding formatting within their documents. While WordPerfect places codes at the formatted text, Microsoft does not use this method. The result is a conversion program that imports all the text but does not convert the formatting as expected. And the reverse holds true as well...importing a Microsoft or Lotus product into WordPerfect is likely to yield imperfect results. Consequently, if you have an investment in hundreds or thousands of forms...what do you do?

WordPerfect for Windows may be a good choice for those offices already using WordPerfect for DOS.

If your interest is in migrating to a Windows or OS/2 operating system and software, retain the same brand of word processor. WordPerfect is available as a DOS and as a Windows product and file compatibility is one of the strongest selling features for making this transition. Do you want an even stronger selling point? If you will be making the transition slowly, perhaps upgrading five or ten machines in your business while retaining some older machines, maintaining the same brand name will allow all your people to use the same files. For instance, a small office consisting of ten computers could make a modest investment in two 486 computers and a couple of WordPerfect for Windows software packages while retaining WordPerfect 5.1 on the older 286 machines. The Windows word processors could be delegated to the neophytes unaccustomed to working on a computer (since Windows ostensibly makes it easier to use the computer) and the secretaries, well versed in using the computer, could remain on WordPerfect 5.1. By saving all files in the DOS format, the files could be accessed by any machine in the office, Windows or DOS. As the office upgrades its older computers over time, it could phase out the DOS product and migrate to the Windows product with no file incompatibility problems. The same holds true for those offices using Microsoft Word for DOS...upgrade to Microsoft Word for Windows slowly, if necessary, to gain comfort with the newer systems while retaining file compatibility between platforms (DOS and Windows or DOS and OS/2).

The training needs of your employees are probably met by features built into today's word processors.

Finally, personnel training may be a concern. What is the downtime in retraining office personnel if you upgrade to a different brand name processor or to a Windows product. I won't lie to you...there is some downtime in either event but it doesn't have to be considerable. Moving from one brand to another or from a DOS to Windows product does not require an investment in classroom courses or computer consultant training. Manufacturers are hungry for the huge installed base of word processors out there. As a result, manufacturers have strived to reduce the anxiety and flatten the learning curve for transitions to their products. I've discussed tutorials, coaches and wizards in Chapter 9 on word processors but, simply speaking, most applications now install a series of lessons to guide the user through the application's features. Taking an hour or so to complete, these tutorials are a fair introduction to the product although they don't begin to touch upon the more advanced features of the newer word processors. "Coaches" and "Wizards" are always available as on-screen guides to completing some of the more common and advanced features of the application such as charting data or formatting a document to a specific style. These coaches have progressed to the point where they will guide the user through the steps, using the actual document rather than sample data and, in some instances, will anticipate likely choices from a historical review of prior choices, in effect, guessing how you work. Windows also provides tremendous on-line help, almost to the point of replacing written manuals. In some instances, the on-line help contains information not contained within the written manual and may be the only source for assistance. While discussed in greater detail in Chapter 9, on-line help is often context-sensitive and provides the user with a choice of help topics based on where the user is in the document. For instance, if the user is attempting to format a paragraph, invoking help will produce a window containing explanations of paragraph formatting choices. Finally, some manufacturers, most notably Microsoft, recognize that their main competition is from WordPerfect. As a result, they have incorporated options into their products that allow the user to work as if in WordPerfect, providing help screens specifically geared to assisting in a transition from WordPerfect to Word and helping the user to learn Word key assignments equivalent to their WordPerfect counterparts. I made the transition from WordPerfect for DOS to Word for Windows and I cannot recall any serious problems or downtime in making the transition...and that was before coaches and wizards were available.

Timekeeping and Billing software is "key" for lawyers and other service-oriented (and money-oriented) people.

Time-keeping and calendaring programs are probably second in any service businesses repertoire of computer software. An attorney's or accountant's commodity is time and, consequently, time-keeping is essential to their livelihood. Even attorneys that accept matters solely on a contingency basis should track their time. Some courts will award fees in actions, but only if proper time records are kept. If these records are not available, imagine having to explain to your client that you will be taking that one-third contingency fee even though the court could have awarded your fees to be paid by the opposition. Think of time-tracking in the service industry as the equivalent of retailers tracking their inventory. Without knowing how the time is spent, the business loses the capability to adjust work habits to increase revenues or explain billings to clients on a periodic basis.

Computerized timeslips provide interim reporting and reduce book-keeping chores.

Why should time-keeping be kept on the computer? At my old office, everyone prepared written timeslips which were then collected and input by book-keeping personnel. Without a network of computers throughout the office, this probably made the most sense to them, but what a waste of time. A better solution for today's office is to set up a peer to peer network system, allowing computers throughout the office to share information.

> This isn't the only reason for simple networking in the office. With some thought, and as we'll see later, networking can provide many other productive benefits...electronic mail and messaging, shared file access, work delegation and distribution and scheduling are a few of the reasons to consider the small but reasonable cost of establishing a peer to peer network in your office.

While I won't delve into an in-depth discussion of networking here, let it suffice to say that peer to peer networking is not much more involved than attaching cables between all the computers in your office and installing software in the computers that allows them to manage the "incoming requests" from other computers on the network and send "out-going" requests to others on the network. These requests are usually for files, and less usually for applications, on other computers. Each computer is a complete work-station unto itself and does not depend on others for its applications, files and processing. Peer to peer networking is becoming so popular for small offices that Microsoft and others incorporate its capabilities into their operating systems. What are the advantages? All time-keeping can be input once, from any machine, and "sent" to a time file on the accounting department's machine. Duplicative work is eliminated and, minute by minute status is available to the supervisor for each client and matter. While this may seem inconsequential in those instances when a client is handled by one person in the office, more often, even in small businesses, more than one person may be involved in a matter and accountable to the client for an updated status. With a peer to peer network, the left hand can know what the right hand has done.

> One of the quickest ways to review actions and developments on a matter is to review detailed timeslips. Properly input, a timeslip should provide a description of whatever the person spent time on. As a result, the supervisor should not even have to "track" their associate down for a status update on the matter and, if the client calls, the supervisor can access the records and provide a simple status report.

Timeslips Corporation's Timeslips is a popular, reasonably priced time and billing application.

While there are a good number of time-keeping programs available to service professionals, a very few have gained wide-spread acceptance. At the top of the list is Timeslips Corporation's Timeslips. See Figure 20-1. This program, available in either a DOS or Windows version, is compatible with all operating systems and provides the flexibility to manage more matters and clients than any one person is likely to handle at once.

The application, in its simplest configuration can handle even a medium sized office and I doubt anyone reading this book would require the upgraded network version necessary to manipulate enormous numbers of clients and matters generally not encountered within small or medium sized service businesses. The program retains flexible formatting and updates account balances based upon client payments, credits and adjustments. Time can be selectively billed or merely reported and costs can be categorized and billed separate from time. The program will handle multiple matters for the same client on separate bills and provides flexible billing options for each professional, client, matter and category. Finally, the price won't kill anyone. At around $200.00 discounted, this program will produce reports, billings and account summaries for more clients and more matters, in more formats, than you will ever need. In an area where billing programs can exceed $1000.00, Timeslips is a bargain. I recommend it.

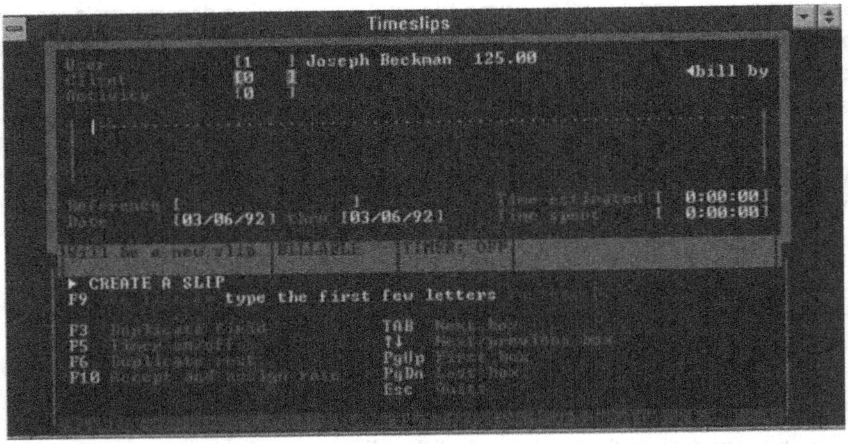

Figure 20-1 The Timeslip screen records events one at a time. All User, Client, Activity and Reference categories have "pull-down" lists to facilitate data entry.

There are a number of other time-keeping systems out there designed for service businesses, many of which cost considerably more than Timeslips and do not provide additional needed functionality for the increased cost. The one justification for some of these packages is that many include, in addition to time-keeping functions, ledger and payroll services and some check-writing functions. Others combine time-keeping with calendaring functions. A partial list of products is as follows:

Timeslips	Timeslips Corporation 1-800-285-0999
PCLAWjr.	Alumni Computer Group 1-800-387-9785
Juris	Juris, Inc. 1-615-242-2870
TABS III	Software Technology 1-402-423-1440

There are calendaring software applications that do more than your average PIM.

Calendaring software is also a necessity in the hectic world of business. In addition to providing yourself with an easily updated schedule, calendaring software also provides your secretary and colleagues with an updated account of your whereabouts and, on a peer network, provides the opportunity to schedule group conferences with minimum effort and frustration. All of the above is available from many general utility computer calendars and PIMs (Personal Information Managers--see Chapter 13)

Lawyers most certainly benefit from calendaring software however, for a law practice, my recommendation is not to rely on a generic PIM. While its possible to use the built-in calendaring programs provided with WordPerfect Office, Microsoft Windows or any other number of desktop shells and shareware products, specialized lawyer calendaring applications will automatically calculate the appropriate responsive periods for pleadings, calendar limitations periods and, generally, reduce your malpractice rates and your blood pressure. The specialized packages will link the key date to other relative dates and update the linked data when key data is changed. As a result, if a trial date is rescheduled, the calendar program will automatically update disclosure deadlines and similarly related trial deadlines. In the long run, such a specialized package reduces potential errors and headaches. One of the better known calendaring packages is from Abacus Data Systems (800-726-3339). Abacus Calendar provides general calendar functions, a to-do list that "rolls" from day to day until completion and the specialized docket calendaring I've discussed. In addition to providing software compatible with your own state court's rules and deadlines, Abacus can also be customized to provide calendaring and docketing based upon custom rules and entries. Juris, Inc., in addition to providing time-billing software, also provides a calendaring system that incorporates many of these features.

When deciding upon the appropriate application for your business needs, again, keep the following three points in mind:

1. Budget
2. Needs
3. Adaptability

Some thoughts on keeping your purchases in perspective...don't overbuy.

These are the same three points I raised at the beginning of Chapter 2 of this book when deciding upon hardware needs for your business and they are just as applicable here as there. First, some of these time-keeping and calendaring packages cost thousands of dollars as compared to hundreds for others. If you have a small or medium sized business, and I believe 75% of America falls into this category, you don't necessarily need one of the larger packages. If your firm handles 200 clients and has 10 people on staff, even a package like Timeslips could accommodate you. If you are a sole proprietor or very small firm of two or three people, don't let some consulting expert "sell" you on a custom package that will work no better than a reasonably priced commercial package.

In some instances, consultants can provide customized applications necessary for business needs. Many professions are so populous and visible however, that most software needs are provided by commercial vendors. As a result, there is very little need to resort to independent contractors for time-keeping, calendaring or other mainstream applications. The benefit of this is that product support is not tied to one consultant and commercial vendors, forever in competition, will strive to upgrade their products at no cost to you (unless you buy the upgrade).

Similarly, don't let anyone sell you an expensive package with the idea that you'll grow into it or add to its many other capabilities at later dates. To me, this is almost like blind investment and, unlike hardware upgrades, there is no certainty that the untapped power of the application will ever be needed or used. These comments, of course, bring us to point two.

Your business needs, now and for the foreseeable future, are your primary investment criteria.

This is as true for software as it is for any business investment of a depreciable nature. Again, don't overbuy. When considering your needs, also consider who will actually use the program. Of course, any time and billing program is going to be used by the professionals to input their time, but also consider support staff that will input time and expenses. Consider whether the program allows easy time input and can be adjusted to meet individual needs, codes and billing rates. Also consider whether the application should integrate with your companies Equitrac or other expense-tracking systems to facilitate and automate expense tracking from the telephone and photocopier directly to the client's bill. Some programs won't do this...others will. Perhaps most importantly, once all the time is on there, consider whether the program is compatible with the people that will actually output the billings. If that's your book-keeping staff, get their input. Ultimately, any attempt to computerize the business can be thwarted by people that are uncomfortable with the product, so avoid this problem. If possible, get hands-on experience or a demonstration of the application before diving into the water. While this may not be possible with a small commercial package like Timeslips, other applications costing two thousand dollars or more should at least come with a demonstration. Again, the point is to get your staff involved in the decision-making process to help you purchase a product that will improve, not hurt, job conditions and hence productivity.

I consider macros an indispensable tool for automating your computer applications.

Now that we have discussed some of the computerized "tools of the trade", let's discuss what these tools can and should be doing for you to make your life easier. WordPerfect has gained wide acceptance within the business community because it is a powerful and flexible program and, with each upgrade, it only becomes more powerful. One of the features of WordPerfect (and virtually all other word processors) that makes it such a great tool is its macro language. Macros are small "programs" that are launched within applications. Generally, macros use the application's built-in command language, to perform a group of functions automatically. Many of the functions that you invoke through menu commands may be functions that are a part of the application's command, or macro, language. For instance, when a document is finished, you may spell-check the document and then print it using a fairly standard printing setting. Invoking these two commands (the spell-checker and the printer command) could be accomplished by writing a macro that invokes both commands. The macro could then be saved, it could be assigned a hot-key, and invoked with the press of one or two keys. Most software vendors will build in some hot-keys to their applications. Most will also include some macros that can be used to perform common tasks with the application such as preparing a fax cover sheet or preparing a glossary of terms or table of contents from chapter headings. WordPerfect, having such universal acceptance is a prime candidate for using macros. Why? Because even if you don't want to take the time to write your own macros (and I can understand why most people don't have the time to bother with this), so many millions of other people use WordPerfect and have developed macros and mini-applications composed of macro commands compatible with WordPerfect that, for a nominal sum, or even nothing, you can use these pre-written macros to automate your business with virtually no effort at all. In addition to the add-in packages I discussed earlier, hundreds of macros are available in shareware packages through the mail or, as is my preference, on local and nation-wide computer bulletin boards. While perusing local bulletin boards in my area, I've seen WordPerfect macros that will design custom letterhead, print out Federal Express Airbills, address envelopes, maintain a log of contacts, make calendars, catalog files by long names, prepare custom invoices, or out-put customized forms. If you don't want to take the time to peruse bulletin boards, many companies specializing in mail-order shareware (Reasonable Solutions, for one, 1-800-876-3475) will send you full-color catalogs which include WordPerfect add-ins and macros.

Fields are another useful word processing feature too often ignored.

Another useful feature too often ignored in word processors is the "field" feature. "Fields" are codes that instruct the application to insert information. In the simplest cases, fields are used by applications to insert dates, page numbers and symbols.

> I say "simple" because the information is input only one form at a time as opposed to inputting information in many forms at once. This second action is possible but requires more time and effort to set up.

Most applications however, have a wide variety of field functions that allow automatic insertion of names, blocks of text or other information input at a prompt. This last option, inserting information at a prompt, is the easiest and most flexible option to introduce simple form automation. Many fields can also be instructed to input information in a particular format. For instance, the date field, found in word processors everywhere, can be formatted as January 1, 1994, 1 January 1994, 1/1/94 or 1-Jan-94. How it is input can be predetermined with a field "instruction". Fields, when combined with the macro capabilities of the word processor, can automate form production almost to the level of the packages that merge data with forms. In fact, most such packages use fields to input client data into the forms. Of course, buying a package is easier (and for most businesses, more cost effective) but, if the forms you use in your business are not available in any package or cannot be integrated with any package, designing your own package using fields may be worthwhile in the long run. For those young business-people out there (of which I was one), with more time than money on their hands, those idle moments not spent learning the business or networking can be used to set up forms for later use.

Glossaries can contain "boilerplate" text or other commonly used terms for easy insertion into documents.

A third feature very often ignored is the "glossary" function of word processors. "Glossaries" are text blocks given simple names or abbreviations. The text block is then inserted in the document by typing the abbreviation and pressing the glossary function key. With glossaries, entire blocks of text can be inserted within documents to compose a customized document or form. For example, stockholders agreements generally include provisions relating to the sale terms of stock, redemption rights, voting rights, future subscription rights and other standard terms. Some stockholder's agreements, however, may also include non-competition clauses, restrictive sales provisions, voting trust restrictions or specialized buy-out provisions depending upon the stockholders' relationships and the nature of the business. If each of these custom and alternative clauses is saved as a block of text under glossary names such as "stock 1", "stock 2" or similar terminology, custom agreements can be quickly and efficiently reproduced without resorting to inefficient methods commonly employed at many offices. What inefficient methods am I talking about? Many times, customizing is accomplished by opening second and third documents containing the desired language, copying the blocks of text and then pasting them into the current document. Instead of this inefficient method, the glossary abbreviations can be input into the document, highlighted and then updated all at once with the glossary function key.

Multiple glossary entries can be cataloged and available on a list, either on-screen or on a printed sheet, for quick reference. Macros can even be designed to call up a list of glossary entries each time it is needed for quick review.

Finally, combining glossaries with fields enables enterprising offices to quickly produce custom forms using prompts and glossary entries to keep scrolling and key input to a minimum. Yes, it requires a little bit of thought to set up and train a person to use these features, but it is available on your word processor, free for the asking.

A practical example of what we have discussed so far.

What is a practical example of what I have discussed? While my word processor has a built in envelope addresser that allows me to type an address in a box or pulls the address from a letter, very often I need to send documents to clients, or others on a regular basis that don't include pre-printed addresses. Over time, it became a bother to hand-type the client's address into the box to print an envelope. Sure, I could have separate files, each with a different addressed envelope or I could use the print-merge feature of my word processor to pick the one or two addressees from a database, but neither solution is the best solution. The first requires storage of many, repetitive files, cluttering up the hard disk and taking more disk space than necessary. Moreover, each envelope file must be opened and printed separately. When I send out billings, I may need 30 or 40 envelopes printed. The second solution requires more input from me than necessary. Most print-merge features do not allow hand-picking of names at random. Rather, print-merging will generally allow specified ranges to be selected within a database. The range can be a range of numbers, a range of names selected alphabetically (all the last names beginning with "A", for instance) or a range of states or zip codes. It is an inefficient method of selecting a discontinuous range of names.

So, what's my solution? I set up a numbered database comprised of names and addresses and saved it as a file (we'll call it "client.doc"). I then set up a preview file consisting of a list of numbered names but no addresses (we'll call this "prevlst.doc"). Next, I set up a third document, formatted it as an envelope, and inserted fields for the name and address of the recipient ("envelope.doc"). I then wrote a macro that opens envelope.doc, opens prevlst.doc and then prompts me to enter the numbers corresponding to my intended recipients. The entry screen appears in Figure 20-2:

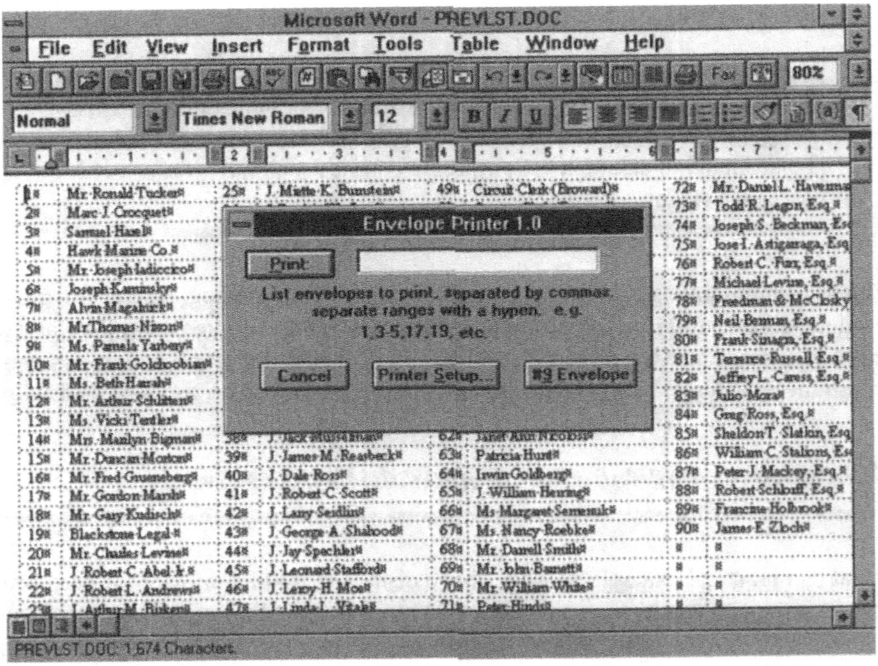

Figure 20-2 "Envelope Printer" uses very simple WordBasic commands to automate and streamline everyday business tasks.

I can enter as few or as many numbers as I want, separated by commas. I can even temporarily reformat the envelope as a #9 envelope (for return mail) or change printer setups. It then takes these numbers, pulls the corresponding data from client.doc and inserts each name and address into envelopes which are then automatically printed. When it has printed all the envelopes, it closes all the files and I am back where I started. This makes good use of the macro, field and prompt features of my word processor. I could just as easily have used glossary entries in lieu of a database and achieved the same result.

Another macro I wrote uses Microsoft Word's FileFind feature to look for files in specific form categories or any other directory on my hard disk. The macro can limit its search for files by text or keyword and can be selectively told to search subdirectories. Its advantage over Microsoft's version is that the menu first displays itself to receive input. Microsoft's version first conducts a time-consuming search based on the last search criteria entered before allowing the user to input a new "search pattern". Figure 20-3 is the resulting input screen:

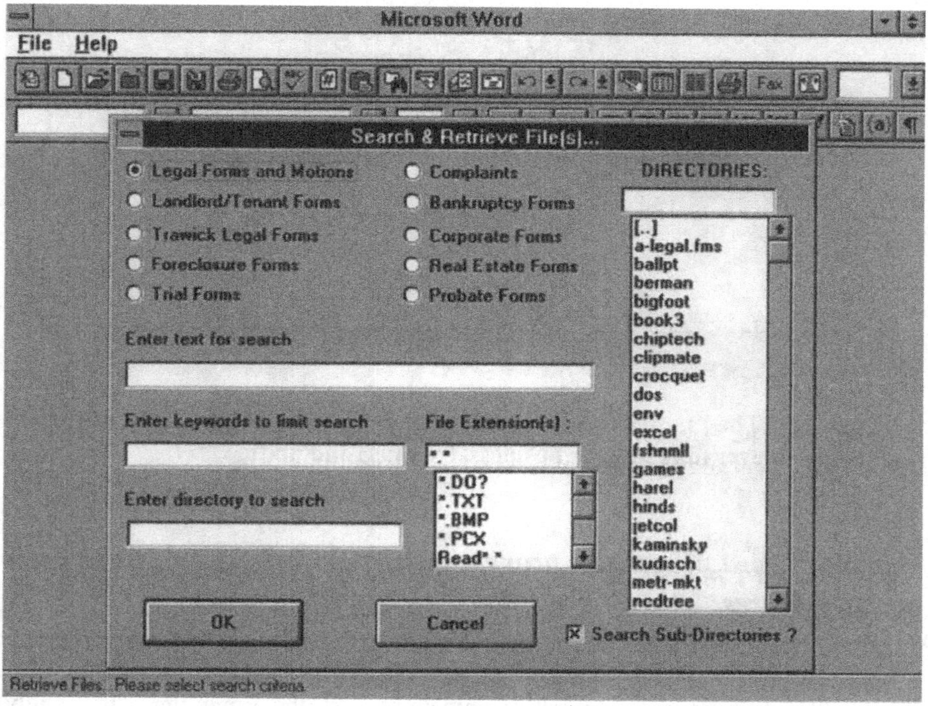

Figure 20-3 If your business has collections of forms, a macro like "Retrieve Files" can simplify the search process.

Other macros let me quickly choose letter templates that reflect different headings for mailing, faxing or service by both methods. See Figure 20-4.

The lesson of these examples is that, with some thought, there are a number of mundane, everyday tasks that can be automated to your benefit.

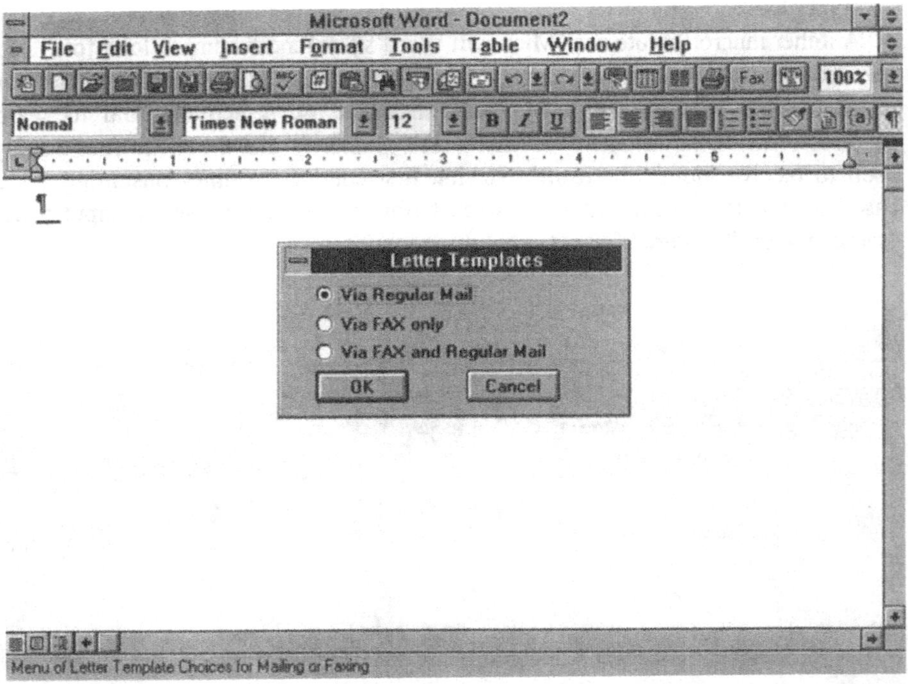

Figure 20-4 The "Letter Choice" macro can be used to present a list of form letters used everyday in your business. No muss and no fuss.

Windows word processors provide some help in implementing their macro features.

If these features interest you but intimidate you at the same time, I strongly recommend looking into one of the mainstream Windows word processors on the market. Each of the Windows word processors contains a powerful macro language. Each product also includes a "macro recorder". How is this helpful, you ask? In one of the previous examples where I suggested that spell-checking and printing a document may be one task you do quite often, I said you could write a macro to automate the task. Macro recorders allow you to press the keys necessary to perform the functions and record those actions in the macro language. When you are finished recording the actions, you turn off the recorder and it prompts you for a macro name ("Spell-Print", for instance) and gives you the option of assigning a hot-key combination to the macro ("Ctrl-P", for instance). Macro recorders simplify the task of automating your work. You don't even have to know the macro language.

Although you can record macros using key input (and in some cases, mouse input), more complex macros, such as my envelope addresser, require some knowledge of your word processor's macro language.

Other features and utilities that are quite helpful include clipboard utilities and the built-in outline features of many Windows word processors. When composing documents, very often attorneys (and others) want to re-organize the document sections in a new, more logical manner. A point that seemed only secondary while the document was under construction now takes on new importance and deserves greater emphasis at the beginning of the document. In other instances, the reconstruction may take the form of a complete reorganization of many small sections, paragraphs or entire chapters within a book or report. The one drawback is that the Windows Clipboard, the utility provided by Microsoft for cutting and pasting materials, using the edit functions of Windows applications, is capable of holding only one item at a time. Accordingly, major reconstruction can require cutting and pasting first one item and then another, checking your results and then cutting and pasting some more. The outline function of the word processor eliminates this inefficiency. By using pre-defined headings and sub-headings when organizing the document, the composer is capable of viewing the document in outline view and selectively seeing only the headings, headings and subheadings or the entire text. When the document is reduced to headings, entire portions of the document can be repositioned solely by dragging the heading. The text below the heading is automatically repositioned with the heading. Similarly, if ten or twenty pages of a document are considered surplusage and need to be deleted or you need to copy those pages to another document, outlining can reduce the time involved. By designating that text under a single heading and then switching to outline view, the entire ten or twenty pages can be deleted or copied in one second by deleting or copying the heading. While this feature requires a little forethought in document design before you can gain its benefits, the feature is worthwhile to anyone regularly recomposing medium to large documents on a regular basis.

A solution for those recomposing small to medium documents involving the movement of smaller blocks of text is to use clipboard utility applications. These utilities allow you to permanently or temporarily store copies of everything that is copied or cut to the Windows Clipboard. This includes both text and graphics and the items that are stored by these utilities can then be copied back to the Clipboard one at a time or in a group for insertion in any Windows application. In this way, text blocks that are regularly utilized by the office (such as signature blocks) can be stored and retrieved at will. If the user is so inclined, these utilities can replace the glossary function of their word processor and store hundreds of text blocks, each containing boilerplate text regularly used by the business in contracts or other documents. Perhaps this could be thought of as the poor man's document assembly alternative. Similarly, if a document is to undergo considerable rearrangement, using these utilities would enable the person to store all the text blocks and rearrange them with the utility before pasting the finished product into the word processor.

I've experimented with two such utilities, one shareware and the other freeware. Each has its own benefits and detriments and I highly recommend that you review each of these if this type of utility appeals to you. The shareware product is ClipMate for Windows (see Figure 20-5).

Figure 20-5 ClipMate's screen is icon-driven for quick but powerful text arrangement.

In addition to providing thumbnail sketches of each stored piece of text or graphic in a grid of thumbnail-sized boxes, ClipMate offers a very easy utility, shown in Figure 20-6, to attach and group or regroup the stored items before pasting the result onto the Clipboard and into the application.

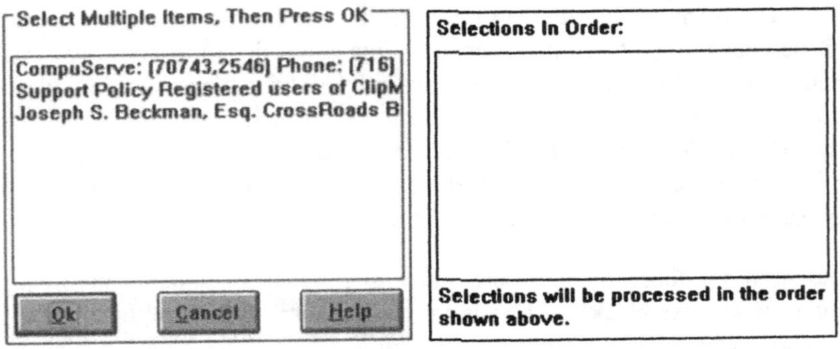

Figure 20-6 Each text selection in the left column of this ClipMate screen is reorganized in the order shown in the right column. Quick and easy, just the way it should be.

Commonly used items can be stored in the safe list to prevent accidental deletion and items can be pasted in reverse order to their position on the ClipMate list just by clicking on the power icon (at the far left). While ClipMate is not free, its can be a great time-saver and, after all, time is money. Even if your word processor has a glossary function, consider whether ClipMate, or its freeware alternative, could be put to good use with any other Windows application you may use. If you're interested and can't find it on a BBS or in a catalog, contact the author at:

CompuServe:	(70743,2546)
Phone:	(716) 227-6505
FAX (24 hrs):	(716) 227-1145.
Mail:	Thornton Software Solutions Attn: Customer Service PO Box 26263 Rochester, NY 14626

The freeware (absolutely free!) Clipboard utility is called UltraClip. See Figure 20-7. While it has the same functionality of ClipMate, it does not offer the same easy grouping function provided by ClipMate. Consequently, multiple items can't be regrouped using the utility before pasting the result into your document. In the end, you have to decide if price is a stronger motivation than receiving this one function.

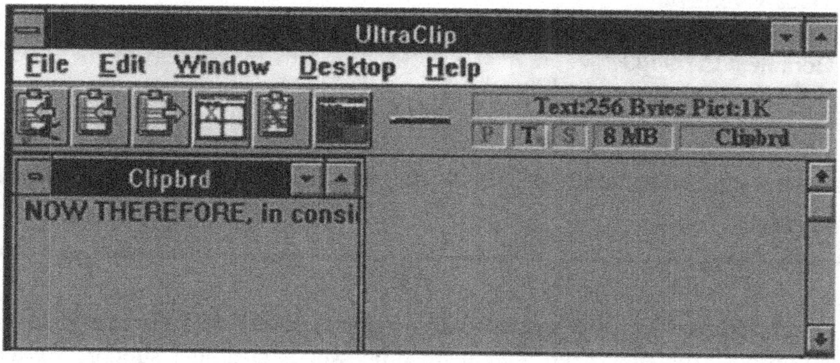

Figure 20-7 Not as compact as ClipMate, UltraClip still provides great functionality and its free. In this case, you get more than you pay for.

UltraClip does provide many other functions and capabilities however, including the following:

* create mini-clipboards that store snapshots of the Windows clipboard

* create OLE objects with embedded or linked data

* view graphical thumbnails for quick retrieval

* track the contents of the Windows clipboard in an iconic window

* print proof sheets of the thumbnails or graphics from a disk file

* save and retrieve the mini-clipboard objects as .CLP files

* directly create mini-clips from .BMP, .PCX, .GIF and .WMF (Aldus) images stored on disk

* save and restore the current UltraClip desktop and all its objects

* edit and manipulate mini-clips with text objects < 55K

* edit OLE objects by double-clicking

(Excerpts taken from UltraClip's Help file)

Finally, UltraClip uses "drag and drop" to allow a person to drag text or graphic objects onto the icons to perform functions and it uses the right mouse button to change the utility configuration, manipulate objects and to invoke text editing. If you're interested in UltraClip and can't find a copy on any BBS, write its author:

Doug Overmyer
1817 San Pedro Avenue
Berkeley, CA 94707
USA

Customer support can help even if your word processor is working properly.

The final feature I'll discuss that many offices don't take advantage of when wringing out efficiency from their word processor is customer support. "What can customer support do for me if I don't have a problem with my processor?," you say. Plenty, I say. If you are an attorney, you should know that the word processor manufacturers provide supplements for their products directed just towards attorneys. Even if you aren't an attorney, I can tell you these materials are still a very useful guide to the efficiency enhancements built into today's word processors. In some instances, the sole support may consist of written materials highlighting functions already built into the product but useful to lawyers such as redlining, annotation features or comparison and revision features. Microsoft, however, supplements its Word for Windows product with macros that create legal indexes, format briefs and pleadings and allow the word processor to be used with legal on-line services such as Westlaw and Lexis. Lotus Development Corporation, not to be outdone, also provides support for its Ami Pro processor. Best of all, these supplements are free for the asking...so ask.

Much of the information that I've discussed regarding the choice of a word processor is equally applicable to accountants or others looking for a good accounting or spreadsheet application. Again, many everyday tasks and repetitive functions can be simplified by taking advantage of the built-in programming language (macro language) of these applications. Every Lotus 1-2-3 user I have ever met had at least one macro they depended on every day to automate and simplify their work. Picking a mainstream application like Lotus 1-2-3 or Microsoft Excel means that, many times, you won't have to write your own macros. You can just purchase a collection of ready-made macros for these applications either through shareware channels (on-line boards or catalogs) or commercial channels (mini-applications or add-ins). In some instances, the more sophisticated add-ins (also more expensive than shareware macros) may lend presentation capabilities to your spreadsheet and extend its usefulness in this regard. Finally, while I've covered spreadsheets in Chapter 10, I will remind you that some very useful functions are ignored by many people using these powerful and feature-laden software packages. E-mail routing, revision tracking, outlining (if you have Microsoft Excel), and scenario managers are all very productive features that I've noticed many people do not use to their advantage. Instead, spreadsheet proposals are passed by hard copy or by "sneakernet" (the passing of files on floppy disks from one person to another...not considered very safe computing and *very* despised by security-minded network administrators).

There are many other computer products available today that shouldn't be ignored by businesses. Some are geared exclusively towards particular markets such as on-line legal networks, on-line legal research services and CD-ROM legal publications for attorneys but others are available, using these same outlets, that are of great interest to marketing or consulting businesses. Other products, although not directed towards any particular market, can increase your efficiency and productivity. First, let's take a look at some of the specialized products available today.

On-line networks for attorneys and other professionals have made great in-roads as the business community becomes acclimated to the benefits of computer technologies. These networks may be narrow in scope, offering research tools but little else, or they may include a wide range of reference materials, forums and work product materials.

On-line services for attorneys provide peer support and legal updates.

One such network, the National Network of Estate Planning Attorneys (800-638-8681) offers "the benefits and security of a large firm" with the concurrent benefits of a small or solo practice. The network stresses joint cooperation in marketing, training and practice development between members linked through a nationwide bulletin board system. Once on the network, an attorney has access to electronic publications, legal forms and conferences for discussions centering on, you guessed it, estate planning. In effect, this network offers many of the services marketed through other mainstream on-line services such as CompuServe and Delphi but targets a select business group, attorneys specializing in estate planning. It goes beyond the mere mailbox and conference forums however, by also offering non-electronic network training and support. According to its promotional materials, legal developments are monitored by the network's technical staff and changes in the law or drafting requirements are communicated to network members.

Another lawyer-oriented service currently available in Florida, is called LAW/net (800-940-1402). This on-line service uses the Windows and Macintosh computer graphical interfaces to bring a wide variety of legal services to attorneys. In addition to the usual electronic mail and conference forums, the service also includes access to state statutes, state and federal caselaw including newly issued slip opinions and Bar resource materials. While this service has not been fully implemented, its advertised scope is undeniable. With full support of the state Bar and the state courts, such a network could provide the networked cooperation advertising by the estate planning network and also provide on-line research and communication between members and the Bar and its members. If such a proposition interests you, a call to your state Bar association will tell if such a system is implemented or will be implemented in your own state.

CD-ROM products are increasingly useful to businesses.

CD-ROM products are also an ever-increasing presence in the business sector. A wide variety of CD-ROM products provide research and reference materials and now that CD-ROM drives are regularly included in many computer systems, more CD-ROM products than ever, at increasingly cost-effective prices, are becoming available. This increase in CD-ROM availability can be attributed to at least two factors. First, the cost of CD-ROM recorders has dropped to the point that even a small to medium sized business could purchase one and produce their own CD-ROM product. Second, CD-ROM drives have improved to the point that searching and retrieving information is not an exercise in frustration. The CD-ROM, while a great tool for storing humongous amounts of data (600 MB per disk) is not an ideal substitute for your computer's hard disk. This is because, while hard disks can access a particular piece of data in 16 ms. (milliseconds) or less, CD-ROMs sport access rates of 150 ms or greater. While access rates are continuously upgraded as newer CD-ROM drives are released, it's still quite off the mark from other storage solutions. Nevertheless, since the advent of double-speed CD-ROM drives, access speeds have been adequate for most business purposes and, as speeds increase and access improves, the market will only get better.

With the wide range of products, however, people have to be careful that they understand what they are receiving and the limitations of each product. Like software, CD-ROM products are not all created equal. In some instances, interface designs may make a difference to you. In others, these differences may not be so notable. While I have the greatest experience shopping for attorney-related CD-ROM products, and I'll discuss those products below, much of what I discuss is equally relevant to any CD-ROM product advertised as a research substitute. It really doesn't matter whether you are considering the purchase of a CD-ROM containing state statutes, legal cases or the entire Internal Revenue Code and Regulations. In all instances, each company that markets a CD-ROM product may provide different search software, different information layouts, different physical and computer hardware requirements and different features to augment their product. Finally, like any electronic or written informational product, copyright, licensing and upgrade limitations may affect your interest in the product. While I discuss the particular CD-ROM products below, keep all these matters in mind when considering your own CD-ROM interests.

There are a number of CD-ROM products that provide statutes, codes and caselaw to attorneys and other professionals.

Today, state and federal statutes, state and federal appeals and supreme court caselaw, and administrative decisions of federal agencies are all available on CD-ROM. In addition, particular administrative codes and databases of specialized decisions, such as bankruptcy decisions, are available on CD-ROM. The larger legal publishing companies, West Publishing and Thomson Electronic Publishing (a division of Lawyers Co-Operative Publishing) are head-to-head competitors in this field and offer enough differences in their products to warrant a look at each. In comparing the state caselaw databases offered by each, two major differences quickly rise to the surface and will account for the majority of product choices by reviewers. First, the software used by each to perform searches and manipulate the data contained on the CD-ROM's is different. West uses PREMISE software similar in operation to its older interactive software used on the Westlaw systems. I say "older" because West has since moved to a much more powerful software application for its on-line Westlaw services that extracts keywords from "plain english" information requests in lieu of the boolean and logic structured search phrases of its earlier system. West has not incorporated this "plain english" software into its CD-ROM products and I suspect this may be because this software, being more complex, requires tremendous disk space and processing power to operate. Of course, West can supply this space and power on its on-line service but can't require every purchaser of a CD-ROM product to upgrade their equipment just to use West's product. Thomson Publishing uses a newer data retrieval software called Folioviews. Folioviews is available, through its parent company, as separate software, for use with other company's information and, as a result of this, it is a widely supported search and retrieval engine. The software is both efficient and does not require tremendous disk storage for its use. As a result, the search engine is placed directly on Thomson's CD-ROM disks obviating the need to keep the software loaded on a computer. West, on the other hand, requires 5 MB of hard disk space to store its search engine. For the business that may desire to access this information both at the office and at home (or on a client's machine), the convenience of always having the search software with the disks places Thomson in the lead in this respect.

In most attorney's eyes however, West more than makes up for this technological disadvantage (and others I will discuss later) through the use of its proprietary West key numbers and parallel page cites to the bound series of state and federal West Reporters and West Supplements. For those attorneys that use the West key numbers and find them useful to cross-reference research efforts, West's exclusive right to include these key numbers in the CD-ROM versions of its products is a strong selling point. Even stronger, West has exclusive use of its headnotes. Those little summaries at the beginning of each case contained in a West Reporter or Supplement are very handy items and I know of no attorney that doesn't use the headnotes as reminders or quick references of case content. Finally, West has disputed, exclusive right to use West's bound version's volume and page numbers for each case on CD-ROM. What this means is that a case displayed or printed through West's CD-ROM products will contain volume and page numbers corresponding to West's written version of the Reporter or Supplement. Other companies, most notably Thomson Electronic Publishing, have to use electronic cites. These cites are ostensibly recognized and sanctioned by various court systems however I don't ever recall anyone citing a case in court using the electronic cite. If you stop and think about this, imagine the disadvantage you may be placing yourself in if you conduct all your research on a CD-ROM product but you have no idea what cite to communicate to the lower court judge sitting before you. If, as is sometimes the case, the judge wants to see the case on his own library, the electronic cite may not be to his liking. And with state and local budgets being what they are, you certainly can't be certain the judge will be familiar with the electronic version of the court reporters. Add to this disadvantage the fact that any case you print out won't contain key numbers and headnotes, two sights that have become traditional on copies of cases passed from counsel to judge, and the judge (and opposing counsel) may think twice about the "case" you've been arguing. At the very least, an untraditional approach may distract the judge from the real issues you are trying to present (which, at times, may be desirable). In either event, the result, in my experience, is that many attorneys opt for the traditional West product, irrespective of its many short-comings.

There are some pros and cons to each of the CD-ROM products, so shop carefully.

What other facets of CD-ROM products do you want to consider? The West set of court reporters for my home state of Florida includes three disks. As a result, if a case is not on the disk that is currently loaded, you are prompted to insert the correct disk.

CD-ROM drives generally use a SCSI (Small Computer System Interface--pronounced "scuzzy") connection. The advantage to SCSI interfaces is that such devices can be "daisy-chained" one after another and provide data transfer rates significantly greater than other computer interfaces used in computers.

While this may be a minor inconvenience for a sole practitioner with the disks and computer next to each other, I suspect more and more law offices will integrate this technology with their networks. In that instance, in addition to the network license (which won't be cheap) also factor in the cost of a jukebox CD-ROM player or, at the least, three separate inter-connected drives. Thomson Publishing uses one disk for the entire set of cases. There are different reasons given for this, depending upon who you talk to. West says its because the headnotes and key numbered items add significantly to the stored data. Others say its because the PREMISE software is not as efficient as others. My belief is that it is a combination of the two reasons. The data necessary to format the electronically stored versions to display and print identical to their written counterparts most certainly adds some overhead to the West product.

Another difference, important to some, is the licensing agreements. While agreements can certainly change over time, I've reviewed two licensing agreements for these products. While one agreement provides that the attorney has purchased and now owns the disks, another provides that the price covers a license to use the disks for so long as the customer pays for periodic updates. Ostensibly, once the attorney decides not to continue paying for quarterly updates to the caselaw, the company could enforce the product's return, leaving the attorney with nothing to show for thousands of invested dollars. In other respects, the licensing agreements are substantially identical. The purchase of one set of disks on an individual license allows for single use, not network use, and the disks cannot be sub-leased, transferred or used for commercial sale of their information (through the use of your own on-line research network, for instance). Although I don't usually provide legal advice to other attorneys, I will say that you should insist upon a copy of any licensing agreement or contracts that you will be bound by before subscribing to any such service.. In some instances, you may have to be very insistent, as I was, before the company will provide you with a preview copy of its licensing agreement. This alone, should be reason enough to be concerned.

The other differences between these products may include a combination of the following:

1. The ability to integrate with particular word processors (both DOS and Windows). Some products will automatically provide a legal cite for material that is copied into your documents...a very useful feature;

2. The ability to display separate and multiple windows for different cases or statutes;

3. Integration with state or federal statutes on the same disks to provide cross-references and annotated statutes. While this may be provided as a separate product by some manufacturers, integrating it with the caselaw provides a more comprehensive product in my opinion.

You want a real demonstration of the product's research capabilities, not a "canned" presentation.

Finally, after you have considered all the above, ask for a demonstration. Before the demonstration, have some research questions for the session and insist on using the product yourself at the end of the demonstration to search out answers to one or two questions. The demonstrator will have used canned demonstrations that show the product at its best, with all the "bugs" worked out of the demonstration. Using the product for an unprepared session will often point out product limitations that you can expect when you invoke your own research methods. Ask to see actual printed output through your own word processing application and determine if that output is something you are willing to share with a client or judge.

There are also a generous supply of CD-ROM products available today that may be of great interest and help to any service business. CD-ROM disks are available for providing extensive help in computer software trouble-shooting for consultants and others involved in computer service. Other CD-ROM products provide detailed and comprehensive lists of manufacturers and one even provides a comprehensive list of residential or business addresses and telephone numbers on CD-ROM (PhoneDisc 800-284-8353) for less than $80.00. For those of you involved in sales, the ability to access millions of residential or business addresses, automatically dial numbers or send out advertisements, all for a measly $80.00, CD-ROMs are the best thing since sliced bread. If you're more the "James Bond" type, PhoneDisc even offers a "reverse" directory that will provide you with the phone number for an address or the address from a phone number (for less than $250.00). For lawyers, real estate salespeople or investigators, this is a real bargain. Before you discount the business opportunities to be found through the power of CD-ROM, you may also want to contact the United States Government Printing Office. Their catalog of information, records, reports and law available on CD-ROM is actually quite impressive. For example, while an annotated copy of the United States Code would cost hundreds to purchase from a legal publisher, I picked up an unannotated copy of the entire Code for $34.00 (and this included the software to run the program from DOS and Windows). What a deal! Federal tax forms, HCFA laws, regulations and manuals (Medicare/Medicaid), health surveys, genetic research and databank information, OSHA regulations and documents and State Department documentation on foreign affairs are all available in the last catalog I received.

Scanners, document storage and management and OCR are other tools that are helpful to any business managing large numbers of text documents.

There are also other hardware products that may be of interest to any service-oriented business. Many of these products allow more efficient use of time and eliminate the need to devote your own time or the time of an assistant to many mundane but necessary tasks. Computer scanners are one such item. A scanner, available either as a hand-held unit or a flatbed unit, is very useful for entering graphic images into the computer. Once an image is "scanned" into the computer, the image can be manipulated, changed, enhanced and, perhaps most importantly, stored, transmitted and retrieved in its electronic format. There is a great advantage to storing documents electronically. The documents can be easily transmitted, retrieved by using your computer's search features, copies can be stored off-site for security and back-up purposes (are you listening hurricane-prone Florida, earthquake-prone California and flood-prone Midwest?) and, when the file is finally closed and ready for archiving, electronic archiving of all but important original documents can substantially reduce archiving and storage costs. If your business regularly employs a printing house to input color graphics into your company newsletters or proposals, you may want to consider the purchase of a 24 bit color flatbed scanner. Available for less than $1000.00, the best of these scanners can put color or black and white photographs, news-clippings and graphic art into your computer. From there, the graphic software included with most of these scanners can adjust colors, hues, contrasts and a million other features to give you color images that you can include in advertising proposals, company brochures and even in your everyday correspondence. If your originals are small enough to fit on a flatbed scanner and you have a color inkjet printer for outputting color images, a color scanner can provide a wealth of possibilities for your sales and advertising departments. While not matching the output of the professional printing houses, 24 bit color images are perfectly appropriate for most business needs and the costs are certainly reasonable. When you add in the low (reasonable) cost of the scanner, the included software, and the convenience of experimenting with different layouts, in color, you just may find the scanner to be indispensable.

> Electronic storage is a very practical and necessary solution for even a small business. I know of one sole proprietor who has "devoted" an entire wall of his garage and one wall of his assistant's office to storing files. At this point, converting all those files to electronic format is a formidable job, at best. If he were to begin storing new files electronically however, future storage needs could be eliminated. Best of all, the time he occasionally takes to search old files for forms or documents of interest would be reduced or, at the least, would not be a back-breaking ordeal.

Scanners are graphical devices, not text based devices.

Scanners do have limitations however. Scanners deal only in graphical images, and this is the greatest misunderstanding among those involved in text-intensive tasks such as lawyers and other business professionals. Scanners do not, in and of themselves, allow the user to input a document into the computer and then edit the text to their liking. A text-based document is input as a graphical image. The computer, and your word processor, won't recognize the existence of any words in the file. To the computer and its programs, the file is nothing more than a picture. As a picture, it can be rotated, sized, colors can be altered and portions can be cropped from the "picture" and placed elsewhere...but it cannot be edited like your WordPerfect documents (or your Word documents). The solution to this problem is in software that is available, both bundled with most scanners and as separate program applications. The solution is OCR, meaning "Optical Character Recognition". OCR software "reads" the image scanned into the computer, and recognizes a picture of an "a" as an "a", a "b" as a "b" and so on. It converts each "picture" into letters, numbers and ultimately, back into words. As the application converts each character, it turns the "picture" back into a textual document, capable of being edited on your word processor.

OCR is capable but not perfect technology.

The process of optical character recognition is not perfect, however. Most of the more capable OCR applications boast of a 95-99% accuracy rate. These quoted rates however, are based upon very clear, straight laser-printed text of 10 points size or greater. If the originally scanned document is a copy, contains very small or very large text, sports unusually complex formatting or is of otherwise bad quality (creased, stained, bad contrast), the quality and accuracy of the OCR conversion subsequently suffers. OCR applications also vary in their capabilities to maintain document formatting (so that you don't have to reformat the text into paragraphs or columns like the original), allow correction verification and spell-checking and otherwise manipulate and save the documents and files in your preferred formats. If a scanned document contains portions of text you don't need or want copied, most OCR programs allow you to pick "zones", or multiple portions of the document page for conversion while ignoring others. Most of these applications also allow you to pick conversion of text or conversion of text and graphic images (portions not otherwise recognizable as text) for input in the final document. Finally, the more advanced applications have various means to allow user verification of the conversion process, correcting any unidentified words or letters, and automatic file creation in the word processing format of your choice.

While many scanners include OCR applications with their purchase, most such applications are inadequate or "scaled" versions of full packages. Many lack the ability to define multiple zones on the same page, save formatting or re-format documents to your office standards, and fail to allow easy correction or interfacing with word processors like the full-featured packages. In some instances, the conversion "engine", the algorithm or formula these packages use for identifying and converting text characters, may be older technology or even unoptimized newer technology. The result, in the field of OCR, is a product that doesn't work well enough to justify its use. If there are too many errors, or you have to spend too much time re-formatting the document, you can be better served re-typing the document from scratch. The stand-alone packages however, generally avoid these pitfalls and I've found them to be truly useful. Using OCR technology, I have scanned hundreds of forms onto my computer's disk for later editing and use and saved copies of contracts and exhibits for later retrieval or review. In some instances, when collaborating with others, I've received draft copies through my computer's fax and converted the fax to an editable text document using these OCR applications.

I discuss using your office fax machine as an inexpensive scanner if you have an office computer with a fax/modem installed in Chapter 22, Tips and Tricks. There are two drawbacks to this method other than tying up your office fax machine while the documents are faxed to your computer. First, fax machines, even operated in fine mode, transmit information at 100 x 200 dpi (dots per inch). Scanners however, transmit information at a much finer 400 dpi (or even finer resolution). Since the OCR program is trying to identify an image as an alphabet character, the better the image, the quicker and the more accurate the result. Second, fax machines do not have the adjustments found in scanners for managing document contrast and other scanning conditions. As a result, some documents capable of scanner input (such as those on colored paper) may not transmit very well as a fax. Consequently, the results suffer.

While there are many companies marketing OCR software applications, two such companies stand out from the crowd. Calera Recognition Systems, Inc. (408-720-8300) markets Wordscan and Wordscan Plus. See Figure 20-8. I use Wordscan Plus and find it to be a very capable product.

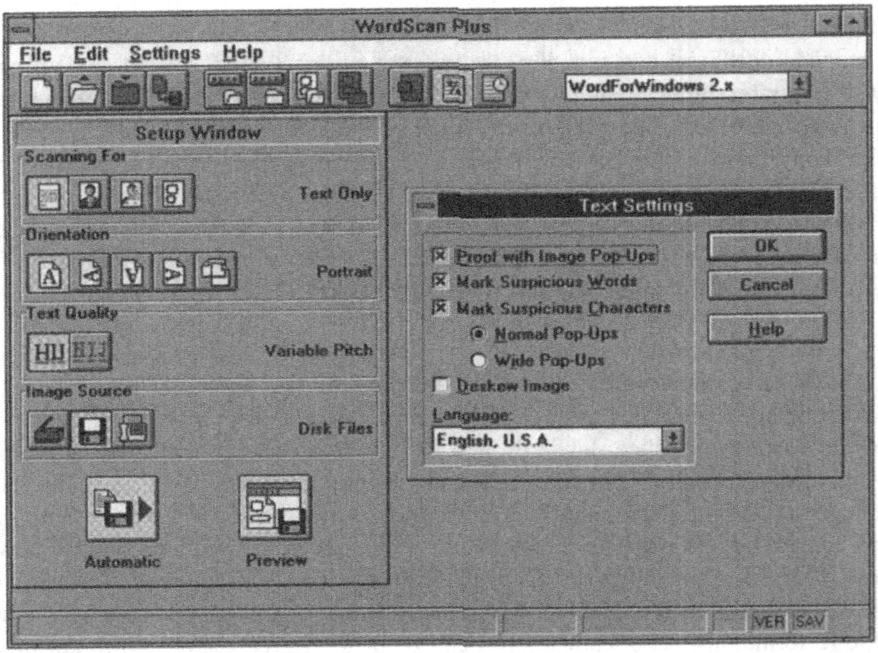

Figure 20-8 Like everything else, Wordscan is increasingly icon-driven, which speeds up selections once you know what the icons represent. To help you, Wordscan has "Hoverhelp" which gives an explanation of the icon in the status bar at the bottom of the screen when the mouse pointer "hovers" over an icon.

Making good use of the Windows interface, Wordscan offers conversion from on-disk files, fax files or directly from a scanner. It integrates with my word processor so that I can invoke it directly from a document and insert the scanned text all in one step and it integrates with Winfax Pro to identify and convert fax files (great if you use the fax machine as a scanner, see Chapter 22, Tips and Tricks). Wordscan Plus allows as many as 100 text and graphic zones to be identified and conversion order to be set for each zone on the page. See Figure 20-9. In this way, complex pages or multi-column pages that would cause confusion can be manually re-ordered for single column output or specific text regions can be converted while other regions are left alone.

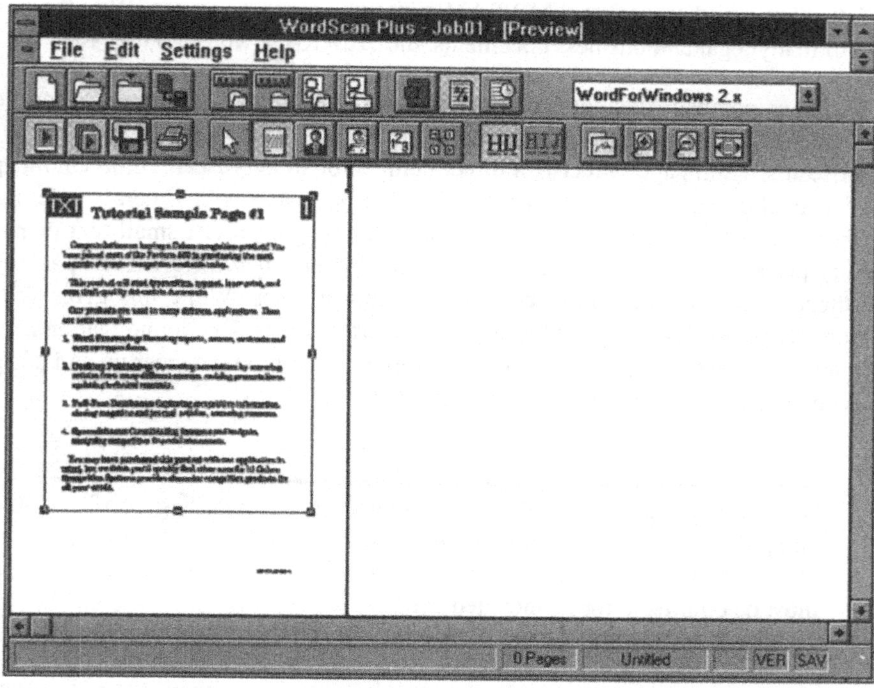

Figure 20-9 The document has been scanned into the computer and is now ready to be "recognized". The text can be recognized in a different order than on the original or some text regions can even be omitted if they are not needed.

The program will default to automatically invoking a verifier feature to confirm the accuracy of the scan and then prompt for a filename before automatically saving the resulting file in my word processor's native format. Finally, the accuracy of character conversions is greatly improved over prior versions of Wordscan and over current offerings from other vendors. Unlike other programs that failed to adequately convert poor quality originals, Wordscan de-skewed and converted even faint and broken letters I had difficulty deciphering. While I purchased the product through an upgrade offer, the price is reasonable for the resulting accuracy and feature set. Like any other powerful and capable Windows program however, you need the equipment to support it. The speed is adequate on a 386 computer but visibly improved on a 486 computer. This is due to the processor intensive work OCR entails. Also, and despite any recommendations to the contrary, Wordscan requires 8 MB of RAM to work properly. Less than this and you may experience out of memory messages halfway through a document conversion. If this happens and you can't save the work completed thus far, be prepared to start all over. As a result, don't consider any substantial OCR work unless you upgrade your machines (386,

486 Pentium or otherwise) to 8 MB RAM minimum, more if you can. With the large size of many legal and business documents, the extra RAM won't go to waste.

Another company heavily involved in OCR conversion is Caere Corporation (800-535-SCAN). Omnipage, Caere's OCR product, is available in two flavors, as is Wordscan's. Omnipage Direct is a direct competitor to Wordscan while Omnipage Professional competes with Wordscan Plus. Keeping step with Calera's offerings, Caere offers improved recognition algorithms to recognize even small text or poor quality print. Caere's OCR engine is also included in a few different fax packages for those that deal primarily in converting received faxes. While this gives you a reasonably priced and integrated means of converting faxes, I've found that, in many instances, this technology, like any other, requires substantial engineering and design effort before exceptional results can be expected.

Just as using the latest micro-processors will not necessarily give a computer better performance without proper engineering and design to implement the newest features, so it is with software. The software must be optimized for its intended use.

A fax software package that includes OCR conversion may be a good choice for those that want OCR capabilities to convert faxes or that may want to take my suggestion outlined in Tricks and Tips and use the office fax machine as an inexpensive scanner. The "upside" to this is that you get reasonable OCR capabilities from a fax software package costing hundreds less than dedicated OCR software applications but the "downside" is that you do not get the wealth of features for controlling and formatting your converted documents from within the OCR application. Winfax Pro includes Caere's AnyFax OCR conversion capabilities but, in my experience, results were less than ideal. As I outline in Tips and Tricks, I've found Calera's products to be of uniformly high standards and to give good results (excellent results with the newest version). While this may be attributable to differences in the recognition algorithms, I suspect it is more likely that Delrina, manufacturer of Winfax, could not optimize the OCR software as well as could be expected of Caere, its developer. As a result of this, even though I use my fax machine in lieu of a scanner, I also use Calera's Wordscan Plus separate from my fax software and I do not depend upon any OCR software included with my fax software.

By the way, many fax software applications that include integrated OCR capabilities are good for more than converting faxes. Many of these applications also have the capability to receive input from a scanner attached to the computer. From the software's point of view, it shouldn't care whether it receives input from a fax or a scanner. In the past, the wide range of scanner drivers necessary to allow scanners to communicate with software prevented this integration. With Windows applications however, a new scanner interface standard was developed, called TWAIN. With only one standard interface, it then became very easy for software vendors to include compatibility with scanners by making the application "TWAIN-Compliant".

Business card scanners can be helpful and the software can be used with your existing scanner.

One of my regular networking practices is to send follow-up letters to prospective clients with whom I've exchanged business cards. Inputting the information in a mail merge program is not difficult for 2 or 3 prospective clients but even 5 or 10 can take too much time. Added to the input time is the lack of organization in tracking these networking opportunities and, in the future, recalling information without access to a business card "stuck" in a drawer or card file.

Consequently, another tool of some value to those "rain-makers" out there is business card scanners. Available as hardware/software combinations or as separate software for use with your own scanner, these tools allow the busy, networking professional to input most important information regarding new prospects into a computer database for numerous later uses. The ubiquitous business card is the trademark of every business, and everyone exchanges and collects them to some degree but, be honest, how many of the business cards you've collected in the past year or two years are still around or, more importantly, instantly available for reference. With the scanner and software, information from cards is automatically entered into a database application, a copy of the actual card is projected on-screen with the information and additional contact information can be retained with the card and client data. The database can be used for contact management, client follow-up and active networking at minimum inconvenience. Even better, with a number of people in the office inputting cards into a centrally available database, true networking between clients and database searches for complementary business associations can be accomplished without any serious effort. For example, consider how many times a client may ask for a business referral or how many times you want a referral from another firm member for a service you need. With information and a copy of the business card centrally available, a search based upon occupation, address or any custom assigned fields can yield immediate results. Need an accountant? "There are five accountants cards inputted in the computer, two near the client's place of business and, from a review of the contact information, at least one is used by a firm member." How much easier can you get?

If you are interested in such a product contact the following companies for a review of their latest offerings:

Microtek Lab Inc.
680 Knox Street
Torrance, CA 90502
(800-654-4160)

CypherTech Inc.
250 Carribean Drive
Sunnydale, CA 94089
(800-294-7226)

Cognitive Technology
100 Larkspur Landing Circle #106
Larkspur, CA 94939
(415-925-0707)

Finding a needle in a haystack is the job of indexing and document management software.

Another tool, indispensable for some offices, is indexing and search software. As files accumulate on your computer over time, it invariably becomes more difficult to locate a particular file or files. While good disk management can reduce the chaos of storing thousands of data files, forms, reports, and documents, it can only do so much good. Eventually, even good disk management is going to leave a business of any appreciable size with directories containing hundreds of files. If your office has taken document storage to its extreme and now has all files, past and present stored on disk or contained on removable media such as optical disks, floppy disks, or tape, your search needs are well beyond the basic features of the search functions incorporated in many word processors and workplace shells. Even though word processors provide search functions to locate files based on name, keywords, subject matter or textual content, none offer the speed or flexibility of dedicated index and search software. Even WordPerfect's capable search function fails to allow the speed and flexibility that dedicated programs offer.

How do dedicated search applications prevent "coffee breaks" while you search a disk for that one indispensable file? These applications provide quick response times by building an index of words from all the files on your disk. As a result, the application has already spent its time searching files by word and now only has to review the index for filenames. The advantage to this method is speedy file retrieval but there are some disadvantages. First, indexes take time to build and, if files are routinely added to the system, an out-of-date index can provide inaccurate results, making the application more a frustration than a savior. Second, indexes take up valuable hard disk space. Cataloguing thousands of files using an index of words contained in those files can eat up a lot of space. If your system is at its limits in terms of disk space, that index can seem a poor use of resources. Finally, nontext items must be manually indexed, something most offices just don't have time to do on a large-scale basis. Moreover, indexing faxes (stored as images) or other nontext-based files means that search results are dependent upon your ability to recall the method (and madness) of assigning keywords to files. If you are interested in text retrieval applications, contact:

Phoenix Technologies
846 University Ave.
Norwood, MA 02062
(800-452-0120)

ZyLab
(800) 544-6339

Caere Corporation
100 Cooper Street
Los Gatos, CA 95030
(800) 535-7226

askSam Systems
P.O. Box 1428
119 South Washington Street
Perry, FL 32347
(800) 800-1997

Some document management software can also store and index graphical images.

If the idea of a document management and index system appeals to you but you balk at the limitations of a text-based storage and retrieval system, there are other, more sophisticated solutions. Caere Corporation, well known for its OCR software, markets PageKeeper, a document storage and retrieval application. PageKeeper, and others like it, take document management to a new level...as evidenced by its substantially higher price and system requirements than the simpler index systems I've already discussed. PageKeeper inputs both text and graphic images and then uses Caere's OCR technology to selectively convert text-based documents for indexed storage and retrieval. Copies of converted text images are also stored for retrieval and reference and graphic images are catalogued for retrieval. The flexibility of inputting faxed or scanned documents for conversion and storage in addition to document files already stored on-disk automates the storage of client files for archive purposes and the indexing of faxed documents for easy search and retrieval. Retrieval is based upon three methods: Boolean, document agent or weighted word. For the price however, PageKeeper should tell you which documents are your more likely choices and it does just that. Color-coded retrievals tell the user which retrieved files are more likely to be relevant based upon the search criteria. Once files are retrieved, they can be forwarded through the office network using PageKeeper's e-mail system. Drawbacks to PageKeeper include those already mentioned. Indexing takes time, eats disk space and requires diligence in assuring that the document you want was not added after the last index update. For a comprehensive storage application however, PageKeeper and its ilk may be the choice of small to medium businesses.

Free-form database software is useful for adapting the computer to store unconventional information.

Finally, there are a great number of other tools that can assist you in your work. The key to using computers is to be creative in adapting mainstream tools to the job at hand. While I've mentioned Personal Information Managers (PIMs) in chapter 13 and calendaring and contact software in this chapter, don't dismiss the use of free-form database applications to store and retrieve client and project information according to your own needs. While most PIMs and contact managers come with a number of pre-defined fields and offer some customization of the database to suit personal preferences, free-form databases can be tailored from scratch to provide fields for information necessary to your business. A personal injury attorney I know uses a free-form database in lieu of contact management to maintain information necessary to his practice. Rather than search for information by client name, he may want to search for information by insurance adjuster, doctor or opposing counsel. His database allows him to record information relating to these subjects and retrieve the information without jumping through the pre-set "hoops" of a standard information manager more appropriate, perhaps, for a salesperson or managing supervisor.

The upside to using free-form databases is their customization and the freedom of pre-determined starting points for searches. The drawback is that many people do not want to take the time or effort to design their own PIM and willingly use products not perfectly suited for their needs. If you haven't found what you are looking for or you are dissatisfied with your current product, consider products incorporating free-form capabilities. This alternative to other pre-designed database programs at least gives you a starting point you can fall back on. If you decide you don't won't to or can't design your own database, you can defer to the program's own feature set or call in a consultant to customize it to meet your needs.

If you do call in a consultant to customize a PIM or information manager for your needs, they will most likely use a free-form database as their starting point. Sometimes, tremendous flexibility can be both a curse and a blessing and, in the case of free-form databases, this especially seems to hold true.

People can also use sound to enhance their productivity around the office.

Other tools that may prove useful to the forward-thinking business are sound boards and microphones. While dictating a document to your computer is still years in the future, adding moderate quality sound boards to the office computers would allow people to input their comments and suggestions directly into documents or project files and distribute these files through the office network (or even by floppy). Since most people can talk quicker than they can write, comments regarding proposed revisions or responses can be inserted quickly and efficiently. Assistants will have no difficulty deciphering scribbled writing and suggestions, as opposed to revisions, can be complete and without the hesitation introduced by the need to write thoughts on paper. Perhaps the sole downside to this method is that inserting long-winded voice annotations into a document results in a tremendous increase in file size. As a result, diligence should be employed to delete these "messages" from the file once they have served their purpose.

The low-tech alternative to this is the use of hidden text and annotations within documents. Most word processors allow annotations and text to be added and then selectively displayed or printed along with the main textual content. The downside to this method is that most people would be dissuaded from introducing extensive comments that had to be typed and then formatted as hidden text. The advantage to this method is that annotated or hidden text requires much less disk space than voice annotations.

Some software applications provide password security to protect confidential information.

One final note for attorneys and other security-minded businesspeople. When shopping for computers and software, consider the security features offered by various hardware and software applications. Many computers, particularly portable computers, and most software applications offer varying levels of security or password capabilities. If you operate a sole proprietorship, perhaps only one level of security is necessary to prevent unwanted scrutiny into your client files and financial databases by office personnel or others having access to your computer. If you manage a small or medium office, you may want multiple levels of security access. At the network or supervisor level, management or supervising personnel would have access to financial and payroll records while the staff would not be granted access. Similarly, access to time records could be limited as appropriate and, of course, e-mail should be subject to a hierarchy of security measures, granting substantial privacy while preserving a professional and confidential work environment.

Using portable computers in public requires some consideration of etiquette.

Other factors to consider when you are shopping for hardware and software is the ability to use the product in your working environment. In the case of portable computers intended to be used both in your office and in public, you have to consider how the computer will operate in both environments. For an attorney, this may involve a consideration of how the computer operates during a trial and for another businessperson, this may involve considering how the computer operates in a restaurant or on an airplane. Quiet keyboards, long battery lives, password-security features and the ability to turn off warning beeps are some features to keep in mind. If the computer draws attention to itself, your public presentation may not be appreciated by your client, supervisor or the presiding judge. Some computers also insist on warning you with loud chirps if an error is encountered or the battery is running low. The better portables allow this feature to be disabled. Remember, a portable can have a wonderfully fast processor, enormous disk space and a beautiful color screen, but if it produces loud obnoxious chirps every time you do something with it, the people around you will feed it to you for lunch.

What about hardware compatibility?

Some businesses also have special needs which must be met by carefully considering the limitations of their computer equipment. In some instances, your work may place demands on equipment that require extra attention to your equipment choices. For instance, I have one friend that complains his accounting charts cause "out of memory" messages on his laser printer. How does the printer handle this? It spits out his charts, divided on two pages...this doesn't make him happy. The problem is his printer, of course. He uses a laser printer with 512K of memory, the standard memory configuration for older, base configuration laser printers. In most instances, today's laser printers, even the low-cost personal lasers, will have 1 MB (1024K) of memory and some even come with 2 MB. So, does that mean you won't encounter the same problem? Probably not...if you output your graphics at 300 dpi.

To give you an idea of how much work can be involved, a standard 8 ½" x 11" page contains 33,660,000 dots at 600x600 resolution while that same page contains only 8,415,000 dots at 300x300 resolution.

Today, however, 600 dpi is the graphics standard. This means that the printer has to collect four times as much information before it can process the page. You can already see that doubling the memory while quadrupling the information load is not going to be a good combination. Some printer manufacturers, like Hewlett-Packard, offset this information overload by incorporating memory compression within their printers. Theoretically, this evens the odds that your graphics will print, even at 600 dpi. If you do a lot of charting or graphics work either as a result of accounting or as a result of sales or presentation needs, take this into consideration when shopping for a printer. If necessary, factor the purchase price of additional printer RAM into the total price. A printer with too little RAM is just as frustrating as a computer with too little RAM and it puts a real crimp in your productivity.

If there's a dot matrix printer in your future, there is more to consider than just 9 pin or 24 pin.

Another business concern may be the capability of printing large spreadsheets or other graphics. If this is your concern, then a wide-carriage impact printer (dot matrix) may be a cost-effective solution for you. While laser printers capable of printing on stock larger than legal size are available, the cost easily exceeds a few thousand dollars, perhaps beyond the reach of most small or starting businesses. Even so, most such lasers will reach their limit on B-sized stock of 11" x 17" while wide-carriage impact printers can handle paper as wide as 17" and as long as you care to print. While most of the printer market's attention has been focused on laser and ink-jet printers, impact printers still undergo development and there are some features that can extend your printer's versatility. If you decide you need an impact printer, look for multiple paper paths and paper parking to easily switch between paper sources. This way you can load both letter size and continuous feed or bar-line paper and switch between these formats as necessary.

Impact printers, like laser printers, use printer drivers to communicate with the software application that is printing. These printer drivers can vary in their capabilities, particularly when it comes to color printing. Before you purchase a color printer with the intent to print out color coded spreadsheets or graphs, make sure that the printer driver currently provided by the printer manufacturer will communicate with your accounting software or applications and that your accounting software can be configured to print in color. If in doubt, and I would not trust a salesperson to advise you on this point, call the printer manufacturer. After that, a call to your software's manufacturer is in order if you are unsure of its color capabilities.

If you think you may print graphics now or later or you want to color-code spreadsheet figures, factor in the printer's ability to print color. Even some wide-carriage printers include color as an option. Finally, look at the resolution provided by the printer. While some impact printers provide 360x360 resolution, on par with lasers and ink-jets, other impact printers may only be capable of 240 x 216 or 240 x 144 resolution, well below professional output standards.

As you can see, there area tremendous number of products and devices on the market to increase your business efficiency. While most businesses probably won't have a need for all of these products, virtually any business can find one product in these pages that would be helpful in managing or disseminating information...and increasing their profit margin in the process.

Chapter 21

Computers for Home Business

Home based business or consulting just may be a factor in your future.

Home-based businesses have been a fast growing sector of our economy and this is likely to continue for some time. Even if you are not presently considering operating your own home-based business, don't be surprised if you or your spouse eventually work at home. In addition to home-based businesses, there are millions of tele-commuters in this country that utilize the same tools and resources as the home business, and there are going to be a lot more in the coming years. The Clean Air Act, which mandates incorporation of "average vehicle occupancy" rules has served as a partial impetus for increasing interest in the role of tele-commuters in the future work force. Consequently, the number of people working at home, either for themselves or their company, will dramatically increase as the last vestiges of prejudice directed towards home-based work disappear and the advantages of this work style are more readily recognized by the management population.

If you operate a home business, you need the same equipment as your office counterparts.

What equipment considerations should concern a home-based business owner or tele-commuter? The same considerations as any business owner...price and performance. The acronym "SOHO", meaning "Small Office, Home Office" has been widely disseminated throughout the media as a means of describing an office environment requiring special consideration separate from the needs and requirements of other small businesses. In fact, many large computer companies, most notably IBM, have marketed products blatantly directed towards a home market. Less blatant is the implicit marketing that these home products are also eminently suitable for home-based businesses concerned with remaining within budget. This marketing is a disservice to home businesses. In fact, with few exceptions, the products recommended to small or medium businesses are the same products that should be considered by any home business or entrepreneur. The specialized "SOHO" market is, in my opinion, a farce. Those persons needing a computer for home use really require the same computers purchased by small and medium businesses.

Why the same computers? For the same reasons I cautioned earlier in this book; hardware needs are dictated by the software applications you intend to use in your business. Consequently, the home business, using the same software as any business operated out of an office building, requires hardware capable of smoothly operating Windows (or OS/2), word processing applications, accounting packages and presentation applications used in their business. Settling for less powerful, less expandable hardware will only speed up the cycle of obsolescence and provide a short return on what should be a medium range investment.

> I hesitate to call any computer-based investment a long-range investment (I don't care what ridiculously long depreciation life the IRS gives this equipment) since the technology that used to take years to double in capability now takes mere months. With increased competition from micro-processor manufacturers like Cyrix, AMD, IBM, Apple and Texas Instruments, you can expect the number of months to continue to dwindle between substantial processor improvements. The same holds true for software. Upgrades that used to take years now take months.

What's wrong with "home computers"?

Many of these "home" products are all-in-one packages that include everything...but not enough of everything to make the purchase worthwhile for a home business. That is, the computers directed to home sales will include accessories such as fax/modems which, while operating at a business-standard 9600bps for faxing, will probably be relegated to 2400 baud or 9600 baud modem operation in an age when business communication is now approaching 28,800 baud.. Monitors will typically be 14" VGA or SVGA monitors of acceptable but not superior quality and video graphics cards will similarly be of adequate but not superior quality. Hard disks will be available in moderate sizes and the included RAM will generally not exceed 4 MB (although you will have the ability to upgrade the RAM). Perhaps the greatest limitation of such machines is in the design compromises that are inherent in these "value-line" systems. Memory and hard disk caches will be minimum configurations not capable of maintaining top performance in the event of a processor upgrade (if that is even possible), the serial port will probably not include the high speed buffering available with a 16550A UART COM port chip and the limited room may prevent installation of tape backup drives or a second, larger hard disk when necessary. For all this "value", you can hope to save less than $1000.00 and, when newer software won't run smoothly on the system, it will become a business liability.

Also consider whether you or your family will be using your "business" computer for entertainment or education during the evening hours. Many of today's multimedia games and educational tools require real power...and bargain systems don't provide it.

What about "Works", that all-in-one package that came with my computer?

All the above assumes that you, like me, will not decide to use the "all-in-one" software bundles that are generally included in these home and small business targeted computer systems. Microsoft Work's, the entry-level office package by Microsoft Corporation (or Claris Works or WordPerfect Works), while capable, imposes flexibility limitations that aren't tolerated by any small or medium business I know of. If you are going to be operating your business solo, as I do, I would expect that you would find these limitations just as frustrating and damaging to your business. What are some of these limitations. Some of these software packages do not provide the on-line help, automated "wizards" and "coaches" of full-featured packages to help you and your employees design the best presentations, graphic-based financial reports and business correspondence that mainstream applications offer. Quite simply, the "intelligence" built into mainstream applications, which is reflected in the price and the amount of hard disk space the applications require, is a feature some will use (need) and others won't want. For simple business letters, maybe you won't want the overhead...but for more complex documents, books, manuscripts, or business proposals, the automatic formatting, corrections and flexible document manipulation of mainstream applications will be a necessary ingredient for your business. Also consider whether you can do without context-sensitive help while doing mail merges, indexing or cross-referencing or use graphics in your presentations and reports. In these instances, skimping on a software purchase, especially in this, the decade of consumer-ware, is not good business sense.

"Consumer-ware" is my term for the trend of discounted software prices designed to entice new users and encourage conversion of competitor's existing customer bases. Software that would be sold for hundreds of dollars before the 1990's is now sold through upgrades to existing customers and through competitive upgrades to new customers for around $100.00. While some think this will end, increased competition and consumer sophistication is likely to keep consumer-ware going for a long time.

While these integrated, low-cost, packages do provide many of the basic input and formatting functions of the mainstream word processor, spreadsheet and database applications, they do not include some features you may consider "deal-killers". A major, continuing limitation with Microsoft's family of Works integrated applications is its flat-file database. Very simply, a flat-file database will not allow the current database to access information stored in a second database file. This impedes the flexibility and efficiency advantages of implementing databases to manage your business. For instance, database reports and forms are constructed of information culled from database files. By allowing the database to construct reports and forms from more than one database, you can manage separate customer, supplier and inventory databases rather than storing all information within one large file. Database management then becomes more organized and flexible. The database also lacks sophisticated updating capabilities for maintaining database records in multiple tables and lacks charting capabilities. Works word processor provides a number of basic and intermediate functions, including mail-merge capabilities, but it lacks multiple undo levels (a feature I've found extremely useful in everyday use), collapsible outlining (as I discussed in Chapter 9) and automatic indexing and tables of contents. The spreadsheet module, while capable, lacks the query functions and cross-tabulation found in mainstream spreadsheet applications (such as Excel's PivotTable, see Chapter 10). Works, like the other integrated packages also offers no integrated macro language to help you automate your work. Considering that most of the mainstream applications are offered at substantially reduced prices in the competitive software market, the one or two hundred dollars saved just doesn't seem worth it.

Most "add-ins" are offered only for the popular mainstream software applications.

Finally, consider all the add-in packages that are offered for mainstream applications while entry -level packages are ignored. If you think you may want to automate your applications by writing macros or taking advantage of the integration offered by your fax software, database application or e-mail application, consider that these applications probably have macros or design features to integrate with mainstream applications like WordPerfect or Word but not for entry-level applications. If you like the idea of perusing electronic bulletin boards for shareware macros already written for a word processor, you will find them for WordPerfect and Word but not for Works. In the end, the two or three hundred dollars that you save just isn't worth it.

Now that I have said my peace about integrated software packages, let me say this...in all fairness to these integrated entry-level packages, I have been quite impressed with some of the features that are included for the price. Object Linking and Embedding (OLE), customizable tool bars, some wizards and coaches and "cue cards", a summarized presentation of context-sensitive help and decent drawing packages to complement their word processors. For those persons using 386 notebooks with limited hard disk space, as a second traveling computer, these applications may make a good complement to the full-featured applications on the office computer. You then gain the ability to work with applications requiring less overhead (quicker response time on slower computers) while retaining the familiar atmosphere of your office applications and the ability to transfer documents between machines without file conversion limitations.

What about software suites?

If the above discussion has convinced you that you need a full-featured software set, perhaps you are thinking that the bundled full-feature software packages marketed by Lotus, Microsoft and Borland/WordPerfect are a great deal for you. My opinion is they are a great deal...for the right person. Microsoft markets its full-featured Word, Excel and Powerpoint packages as Microsoft Office. Lotus sells its similar Ami Pro, 1-2-3 and Freelance as Lotus SmartSuite. Borland, not having an award-winning word processor of its own, teamed up with WordPerfect Corporation to market WordPerfect, Quattro Pro and Paradox as Borland Office. For the business needing a full-featured word processor, full-featured spreadsheet and full-featured presentation or database application, these "offices" are a tremendous value. This is particularly so if you have a prior version of any one component and can upgrade to the bundled package for a couple hundred dollars.

If you don't use 2/3 of the suite package, don't pay for it.

The problem is that some people use many of the advanced features of their word processor but almost never use a spreadsheet or presentation package. In fact, I know people that use the capabilities of their word processor's built-in table and charting functions when they need simple spreadsheets or graphs in their documents. When they need overheads or require "presentation-type" documents, again their word processor has the functions and templates to meet this need. In some instances, having used their word processor every day and haven taken the time to explore its features, they find it easier and more productive to use this one program rather than keep installed versions of full-featured spreadsheet or presentation packages on their computer. Is this a sell-out of what I said earlier about investing in full-featured applications rather than get three or four entry-level packages for the same price. I don't think so. I've argued that you will use the advanced features of the mainstream applications and this is exactly what they do. I mention this because some people may not find it worthwhile to spend the extra money for the entire "office" when upgrading their software. Receiving spreadsheet and presentation applications for approximately $160.00 more than upgrading only the word processor is only money well spent if the applications will find some use on your computer. If you don't use these applications, the $160.00 would be money better spent elsewhere.

When is it well spent? If you use any two of the offered applications on a regular or semi-regular basis, then purchasing these "office" packages is worth the money. If not, the extra money may be better spent on additional RAM memory, a full-featured fax or communication package or even a tape backup system (yes, you can get one for about $160.00 with careful shopping).

Hardware recommendations are as follows...

Now that I've given you my opinion of entry-level hardware and software, what are my specific recommendations? Very simple, a 486/66 with 8 MB RAM, 250 MB hard disk and video graphics card with 1 MB RAM, **minimum**. Hardware accessories for the above system should include a 14,400 baud fax/modem and mouse, **minimum**. The included 3.5" floppy drive can be used for backups, if necessary, and a 14" VGA monitor will suffice if your budget can't stand more. With laser printers now under $500.00, there is no excuse for anything less...unless you really need color or use multi-part forms. For color, ink-jet printers are capable, if slow performers and multi-part forms require a dot-matrix (also called "impact")printer.

If you do use multi-part forms (for instance, you regularly ship using Federal Express airbills or provide multi-part lading or invoicing sheets, my advice is to purchase a low cost laser printer and the dot-matrix printer. With dot-matrix printers available new for under $150.00 (and I've seen good, used Panasonic printers advertised for $50.00), there really is no excuse to allow your other business correspondence to look less professional than laser-copy. Businesses today expect laser output (or its equivalent) and dot-matrix correspondence just won't project the business image you want.

If you plan to use a dot matrix printer for airbills or other business forms, you may want to consider an alternative. I've seen most such business forms available on bulletin boards for LaserJet and LaserJet compatible laser printers. Another alternative is form software, applications that specialize in drafting business forms (also compatible with laser printers). The only drawback to this method is the lack of multiple copies with one pass.

I don't use mailing labels and I don't think you should either.

If your business involves a lot of mass mailings, you may be considering a dot matrix printer for printing labels or perhaps a dedicated label printer. Label printers are dedicated desktop printers that print on a roll of single-column labels. Costing less than $200.00, these printers use software applications designed especially for the label printer and simplify the process of label-making. Personally, I think that most businesses are better off without labels. A more professional solution is to mail-merge a database of addresses with an envelope template and run a stack of envelopes through your laser printer. The advantages to this are many. First, it appears more professional. Second, it allows greater flexibility in selecting font types and type sizes. Third, it allows the printing of a graphic or logo on the envelope to communicate your message and "grab" the addressee's attention. Finally, the one drawback, cost, is minimal. While single column labels are available at ridiculously low prices, packages of plain, white envelopes are available at office warehouses at prices low enough not to compromise your professionalism. It really begins to make sense if you've been sticking labels on pre-printed company envelopes you paid a printer dearly for. Why pay for a label and an envelope? While I use an envelope feeder on my laser printer, even a printer with a letter size tray can be quickly converted for those large mailing jobs.

Choosing your software is harder than choosing your hardware.

Software configurations are harder to generalize. Its easier to give hardware recommendations because newer software applications today require similar resources. While few programs will require a mouse, most of today's applications recommend a mouse and make good use of one. Similarly, the RAM requirements may vary between 4 MB and 8 MB of RAM for various Windows applications but the writing is on the wall. If your current application requires 4 MB today, the upgrade will probably require 6 MB. The same holds true for hard disk space and processing power. Software, however, must be purchased to meet your business needs. In some instances, spreadsheet or presentation programs are a necessity...in others they are not. Some businesses require sophisticated desktop publishing packages that are tailored to give writing and publishing control exceeding even the full-featured word processors I've previously discussed. Other businesses will require programmable databases for custom application designing and still others will depend upon a strong but diverse communication network with clients. I can offer a few suggestions however.

Some thoughts on choosing your "key" software application.

A successful business requires good communication. On one end, your business will communicate with your subcontractors, suppliers and colleagues. At the other end, your business will communicate with customers and clients. Your primary type of communication will dictate the type of key purchase you must consider. If you are in retail sales, your primary communications will be with wholesalers and with customers. In each instance, two common themes emerge...inventory and money. The application you want to purchase then will provide you with the flexibility of tracking and updating your inventory and sales. Your primary concern in shopping for the software application is not the ability to compose large manuscripts or documents. Features that will get some use, however, may be integration with compatible accounting, inventory and database applications (if these are not built into the package already), the ability to perform mail-merges and perhaps produce simple promotional materials for sales and marketing.

What works in this instance? One solution, although not necessarily the best for you, is a combination of complementary products. I can envision using two separate, but complementary, accounting and database packages, to automatically update and maintain inventory, accounts payable and accounts receivable files. Sales are recorded, invoices are printed and receivables and inventory are updated. "Flags" could be programmed to notify you if receivables become stale or inventory drops below a pre-set level (another flag could be used to caution you regarding stale inventory sales). While not necessarily the easiest combination to set up for the beginner, this automates many of the functions that are critical to your retail business. Simpler solutions could incorporate many of these functions solely within an accounting package and may be the better solution for businesses that are just getting started. I've even seen shareware packages targeted towards retail businesses, restaurants, beauty shops and other specific businesses that are tailored to track their inventory and provide receivables information. These programs, available through many bulletin boards, are just database and accounting programs which have already been customized with fields appropriate for the type of product being tracked.

Some Windows database applications can also store graphic images for easy reference. While businesses have survived without these "luxuries", the purpose of this book is to provoke improvements in the productivity and efficiency of your business. If the additional flexibility of a separate database will help you, even with the added setup and training costs, you should consider its long-range benefit.

Why do I recommend the separate database application if the accounting package would suffice? Because database applications will allow you to manage separate databases of inventory, wholesalers, and customer names while importing selected information into customized reports that can draw from these disparate and separate database fields. The result is increased flexibility. Added to this is the ability to use these databases with other applications for mail-merged marketing, contact follow-up and presentations. The amount of information that can be input and altered, if necessary, while maintaining your accounting package's integrity, grows tremendously with the addition of a database application specializing in sorting and organizing databases of information.

Service-oriented businesses have to keep track of clients, not inventory.

Other businesses may not track receivables by inventory but by client. A law or accounting practice is one example but this probably will hold true with any service-oriented business. In most instances, the primary software application for the service-oriented business will be the application that enables the service to be provided most efficiently. For lawyers, its the word processor. For accountants, it may be the spreadsheet. For promoters or designers, graphics programs like PageMaker, CorelDraw or similar applications may be the key application. For business consultants, its probably going to be the programmable database. Notice that, in all these instances, I've placed the emphasis upon applications that help you serve the client.

I've said accountants may primarily rely upon the spreadsheet because I think accountants have other services that could be offered by an enterprising individual that involve other key applications.

I've always thought that a young accountant, looking for their niche in the field, could offer finance management assistance (not financial investment advice) to busy professionals and senior citizens uncomfortable with their own book-keeping skills. Armed with a portable computer and a simple financial package like Quicken, the accountant could provide updated book-keeping and checking services for these individuals. I know that, in my home state of Florida, a tremendous number of senior citizens rely upon their hired help to pay their bills and do their account reconciliation. I know about these services because it makes news when these same individuals embezzle thousands of dollars from these trusting souls. Accordingly, in my opinion, a licensed accountant could really "clean up" offering these services. Want more? Okay, come tax time the accountant could use a tax application to import all the financial data already on his computer to efficiently prepare tax returns for these same individuals.

Some key points to consider when shopping for business software.

When first considering the purchase of this key application, consider some of the following points:

1. If I exchange data with clients, will my application support different data formats;
2. Is the application network capable;
3. Can missing features be complemented by other applications; and
4. Is the application still actively supported by the software company and likely to be upgraded and supported in the future;

The first three points are self-explanatory. The fourth however, probably doesn't occur to most people. It occurs to me because, with the advent of Windows and the large push towards graphical environments, some DOS products are not as fully supported by their manufacturers as the Windows versions. In some instances, even with major manufacturers, some products are discontinued or become industry orphans, even good products. Two good examples of such products come from Lotus Corporation. Lotus marketed Agenda, a free-form database and Magellan, a file index and retrieval application. Both were excellent products, both powerful and flexible, and are still in use on a number of machines, but they are discontinued. The last thing you want is a substantial investment in time and data in a software application that isn't going to get any better.

Avoiding "dead-end" software is a must.

While I can't offer any concrete advice on avoiding "dead-end" software, I will suggest that any intended purchase should ideally store its data in industry-standard file formats or be capable of exporting that data in industry standard formats. For database files this means "dbf" format, for word-processing files it means "rtf" or "ascii" format and for spreadsheets it means "xls" or "wk" formats. If the application is a DOS application, be aware that its capability to "communicate" with your monitor and printer depends upon its device drivers, supplied by the software manufacturer. Most actively supported applications will have device drivers updated to work with the newer graphics and video cards and the newer printers. If the application does not include device drivers for newer video cards and printers and a call to the manufacturer reveals there are no plans to provide new device drivers, the applications lifetime is limited. For instance, while software applications all include drivers to communicate with Hewlett-Packard LaserJet II printers, if the manufacturer has not yet released a printer driver to allow the application to be printed on the LaserJet IV, then you should be concerned. Likewise, if the application cannot be displayed in 600 x 800 resolution, this means the manufacturer does not place a high enough value on the continued support of the product to supply new drivers for today's equipment. Again, the application's life is limited. This limitation, while not likely to be incurred with mainstream applications by major vendors, may occur with smaller applications and shareware applications that are targeted towards niche markets.

Some thoughts on support software for your business.

Once you've selected your key application, you can then consider supporting software. In a service-oriented business, time and expense tracking is important. Scheduling and payroll tracking are also important. Inventory tracking in this instance may not be of great importance to professionals that incur few product-oriented expenses but may be of great importance to services, like general contracting, that involve a greater proportion of product sales with the service. Timeslips, a time tracking and billing application I discussed in Chapter 20, is an excellent general application for these purposes. For those small businesses on a budget or not requiring the reporting options and flexibility of a commercial application like Timeslips, there are budget-priced time and billing programs written for Windows. Scheduling and employee management applications are also available in commercial and shareware versions for managing individual and group schedules. When comparing this type of software, keep these points in mind:

Q: Is the software network capable?

Although you may not use the software for anyone else when you first launch your business, consider what will happen a year or two down the road. If you've settled on an application that otherwise meets your needs and with which you've grown comfortable, wouldn't it be a shame to have to "deep-six" it in favor of a network compatible scheduler so that you can effectively schedule matters and communicate with your employees and support staff on the new office network?

Q: Does the software work the way you expect it to work?

Scheduling software is like Personal Information Managers (see chapter 13, PIMs). It should be designed to make your life easier, not harder. In some instances, the functions you want may be buried too deep in the menu hierarchy to be of efficient use. In other instances, the application may provide more information on-screen than you want (or less, although this is not often a problem). The scheduling software should be capable of individual configuration (even on a network) so that each person receives on-screen information in their preferred manner.

Q: Does the software provide basic but necessary features?

Some features that should be included are automatic conflict notices, automated group scheduling, e-mail capabilities (preferably across multiple mail platforms), and configurable advance notice capability. Cross-project allocation is also useful for companies that will manage multiple projects with a single pool of resources (manpower) and material (inventory or supplies). The application should be flexible enough to lock manpower allocation by project while still re-allocating time resources between projects. Drag-and-drop reorganizing is very handy as is automatic re-scheduling and flexible rescheduling based upon dates, project times and budgets. It should be a simple task to reorganize employees or projects solely by extending timebars (on a Gantt chart) and to display information in multiple formats (for those people that find Gantt charts disconcerting). Applications that provide sample "scenarios" can help project managers analyze scheduling alternatives and a strong collection of specialized tools can help analyze conflicts, overruns and schedule "float" tasks (non-critical tasks from the perspective of other tasks or available resources).

Project Scheduling software may be helpful in your business.

Project scheduling and management applications may also be useful to beginning businesses. While many people think such applications are useful solely to manage groups of people, these applications are very helpful in tracking project expenses, measured in man-hours and material costs. If you are planning to operate or provide consulting to manufacturing, engineering or construction-based businesses, consider adding the application to your list of tools and project analysis to your list of services. Tracking project time and expenses by stage is also useful to help the business provide more accurate bidding for later work and justify costs over-runs under contract. If, at one point, current project resources substantially differ from initial projections, the business then learns a valuable lesson on correctly allocating resources or controlling costs.

> How can the application justify cost overruns? Many times it is alleged that the company (you) intentionally underbid the job to get the contract. If an initial project analysis is computed based on information disclosed by the contracting party, and subsequent project updates are kept, you then have the evidence to show a bid based on prior project analysis and further evidence to show that the project was managed as efficiently as time and resources permitted.

Better yet, periodic referrals to the project schedule during the on-going project can reveal potential conflicts with current resource and budget constraints before progress is halted and alternative allocations can then be implemented. The result is saved time and money.

Let's discuss some practical uses for project scheduling software. Manufacturers or designers can use the software to schedule and manage the research and development, design, raw materials procurement, assembly, distribution and marketing of a product. If you are a consultant or contractor, the software could be used to produce graphically based presentations and bids to prospective clients concerned with project costs. As I said earlier, this information not only gives you a good foundation for fixing the contract price, it may also impress your client with the management skills and foresight you will bring to the project. If your business is marketing, project management may include careful allocation of advertising resources to meet advertising deadlines and coincide with product releases.

> Be aware however that non-traditional uses of project scheduling software may be better served with applications geared towards those purposes. Although an attorney could track cases on a project scheduler, there are specific calendaring applications for these purposes. Still, an office where attorneys collaborate among multiple cases could benefit from a project manager that provides cross-project allocation to track deadlines and case preparation against available resources on a firm scale. Its just a thought.

Non-traditional uses for this software may include case management for attorneys and other case-oriented professionals and inventory allocations for distributors. Any time your business depends on an allocation of time and money, project schedulers of some size may be appropriate tools.

What about presentation and graphics applications?

While no substitute for an experienced and persuasive speaker, presentation and graphics applications have a firm foothold on corporate America. Presentation programs like Lotus Freelance, Microsoft Powerpoint and Harvard Graphics all perform the same basic functions...convert text to bulleted lists and organizational charts, chart data and provide special effects, backgrounds and transitions to keep your audience awake between slides or overhead projections. High performance packages such as Aldus Persuasion and Charisma are targeted more towards professional designers and presenters, fine if that's what your business is, but may be too much , in terms of features and price, for the average manager or businessperson using the product "in-house".

> People still remain unpersuaded and still fall asleep during graphics presentations for a very basic reason. All the bells and whistles won't make up for inadequate speaking ability. You don't have to take my word for it...consult any number of management gurus and they'll agree that good speaking abilities, posture, resonance, projection and materials are all necessary ingredients for the well-heeled manager and leader. If you lack in these areas, don't use your computer as a "crutch", get experience and help. One group, Toastmasters International, provides good advice and experience for improving your speaking skills. Enough said.

The mainstream presentation packages all offer templates to simplify choices and maintain consistency throughout your presentation. Wizards abound throughout these applications to assist in designing the appropriate presentation and, in some instances, even offer advice on textual content. Linking with word processors and spreadsheet applications is included to import data and reports for conversion into a presentation format. If this last feature is something you will use often then you will want to consider a presentation application from the same vendor as your spreadsheet or word processor. Many vendors provide "special" support in their spreadsheet and word applications for exporting materials to their presentation applications. Microsoft Word, for instance, uses a macro that converts its documents to Powerpoint slide shows. Other manufacturers provide similar support for their presentation applications.

Getting the most from your presentation application means being honest with yourself regarding realistic output choices.

While presentations spiffed up with neat transitional special effects and moving graphics all look wonderful on your computer screen and play smoothly with your computer keyboard and mouse in front of you, consider how the application will be used under real world conditions. If your business will primarily give presentations using overhead transparencies or slides, don't buy an application because it provides great special effects. If you don't have a color printer and you are not willing to have a service bureau print your slides or transparencies in color, look for application features that will enhance black and white presentations such as shadowing and textual special effects that aren't lost in the transition from color to monochrome. Some applications, like Microsoft Powerpoint, will provide guidance in picking a presentation template based on the projected output. By asking you if the output will be slides, overheads or printed materials, the computer really helps you communicate most effectively. If your presentations are likely to be run on other systems (in the office or on a client's computer) consider the application's ability to be operated across platforms (PC, Macintosh). Microsoft's Powerpoint includes a viewer utility that allows another person to view presentations even without the Powerpoint application installed. Finally, if the presentation may be subject to interruptions or questions that dictate a shift in focus to another portion of the presentation (like if your boss or a client wants information on next year's projected budget now), hot-links (also called "hyperlinks") are imperative for "on-the-fly" control of computer-generated presentations. With hyperlinks, if an audience member shifts the presentation's focus with a question, you can immediately shift the computer presentation to those slides responsive to the question. Obviously, if your presentations involve overhead projections or slide shows then hyperlinks may be less important to you.

What about video and sound, the "multimedia" element of presentations.

The final consideration when shopping for presentation applications is your intention and capability to integrate sound and motion into your presentations using new "multimedia" tools and support. While multi-media is widely advertised as a great means of incorporating video and sound into computer presentations for increased persuasion and appeal, you must consider a few facts before you decide "multimedia" is for you.

First, multi-media presentations are computer-generated presentations, not slide shows, overhead projections or printed materials. If your needs are met by these presentation methods, then investing time in multi-media presentations is perhaps more wishful thinking than anything else.

If you are presenting "in-house" financial reports to your department head, they may be less impressed with the multi-media presentation than with the financial results. If the results aren't good, maybe they will wonder if the time and expense of preparing fancy multi-media presentations is the reason why. Not everyone waits with baited breath for the newest and coolest computer "toys". Just a thought.

Does MPC compliance mean the product is multimedia capable, yes...but

Alternatively, if you've been depending upon computer-generated presentations and your product will benefit from motion or sound to enhance its appeal, then you're ready to consider "multi-media" as a useful business tool. If so, I have two questions...do you have the hardware to run these presentations smoothly and, if you'll be using your client's hardware, do they? Full motion video and sound require specialized video and sound cards in addition to fast processors and lots of hard disk storage. MPC was the first standard to be developed (by a consortium of vendors) and called for a 386SX processor, VGA video, 8 bit sound card and 150 kbyte/second CD-ROM drive system. It was hopelessly outdated before the print was dry. Consequently, enter MPC-II which defines a 486 processor with 8 MB of RAM, 16 bit sound card and 300 kbytes/second CD-ROM drive as the multimedia entrance fee. While useful as a standard, and a starting point, multimedia technology will only get more demanding. The resultant lesson is...only use these performance figures as a base guideline. While these standards have been introduced to increase consumer confidence in products meeting these specifications, in reality, these minimum specifications will rarely produce professional results. Jerky motion, missed video clips and inaccurate sound reproduction or, worse, sound unsynchronized with the video portion, is the result of inadequate hardware. Consequently, such presentations yield an air of "amateurism" in a field that may be only large enough for "professionals". If your business requires multi-media to remain competitive or, perhaps you see multi-media as your distinguishing product, invest in equipment capable of meeting its demands.

In practical terms, real time video requires approximately 1800 frames per minute (at 30 frames/second). Add quality sound (16 bit vs. lower quality 8 bit) to the presentation and you may be looking at 20 MB of data, not including the presentation application itself. In addition to the processing power used by your main processor, also consider the ever-important video subsystem's capability to keep time with video data, the necessary hard disk space to hold the data and the cost of a monitor that will do your presentation justice (remember, 19" or greater size monitors cost thousands of dollars, not hundreds). If you have a base system with a high-end 486 processor, a VESA VL-Bus or PCI Bus with a graphics accelerator card (containing on-board VRAM), a large hard disk and at least 8 MB of RAM, then you have to consider the specifications of the sound board and speakers you will need for your system. What should you look for? Sound cards that reproduce the actual recorded sounds rather than digitized renderings will be better choices in those instances when a human voice might accompany a sales presentation or offer training via interactive computer video. Specifications that you may have memorized when shopping for a stereo system will also abound when comparing sound boards. A comparison of Total Harmonic Distortion (THD), Signal-to-Noise Ratio (S/N) and Frequency Responses between competing sound cards is in order. I won't bother to quote currently competitive specifications since these are likely to be hopelessly outdated by the time you read this however THD should fall below .1%, S/N should fall above 65 decibels and frequency response should cover from 20 Hz to 20 kHz...at the least.

The access and transfer rates of the CD-ROM drive included in many multimedia systems may not be of great concern to you if you custom design your own presentations. While CD-ROM recorders are a viable purchase for specialized business needs, in most instances I would expect presentations to be designed and run from data stored on your system's hard disk. The CD-ROM unit is a staple of multimedia systems that run pre-fabricated multimedia presentations and software, access reference materials or provide interactive entertainment and training media. Once you have finished a training or sales presentation that requires portability between systems or that will be run, unaltered, for a time, then you can have the information recorded onto a Compact Disk and then you can worry about the access and transfer rates of your CD-ROM drive. By the way, while slow processing can account for jerky video, just as likely is the inability of the CD-ROM drive to find and transfer all the necessary information into your system's memory fast enough to maintain 30 frames a second video.

Video cards, however are something to worry about. They are a vital component of video presentations and anyone purchasing a system with an eye towards multimedia presentations has to give the video card the same attention and priority as they lavished on purchasing a fast processor and large hard disk.. I say this because, very often, processor specifications, RAM specifications and hard disk sizes are sufficiently advertised to make consumers aware of system differences but very little may be said of the video capabilities of the computer system. If you purchase your system from a vendor that custom designs systems and offers upgrades to the processor, hard disk and RAM, also discuss the video card. For more information, see chapter 3, Video Cards.

Once you've purchased the hardware to run multimedia, what do you do next? Buy software, of course. While presentation applications like Lotus Freelance, Microsoft Powerpoint and Harvard Graphics all offer some multi-media support, there will be differences in the level of integration and support each application offers. Primarily, look to built-in video and sound support rather than support through linking with external modules or applications. In most instances, however, these applications, which are bested used for slide or hard copy output, must depend on a number of external modules for their multimedia support. Microsoft's Media Player is perhaps the universal key to unlocking the multimedia capabilities of these applications. Using OLE to embed a multimedia event (such as sound or a video sequence) within a slide is the most popular "trick" for spicing up these traditional applications.

Software applications designed primarily with multimedia in mind.

There are other presentation applications which are designed primarily with multimedia in mind and include the tools necessary to make multimedia the thrust of your presentation rather than an accessory or diversion as is sometimes the case with the prior products. Compel and Action! are two such applications. Be aware however, that these packages favor multimedia presentations and lack some of the traditional tools found in the prior applications which, of course, are currently better suited for slide shows and hard copy presentations. Compel takes advantage of multimedia animation by allowing graphics and text to move within a presentation, all without serious programming or formatting effort on the part of the author. Compel also provides links to video files for runtime presentations and advances the presentation through "triggers" activated by automatically or manually acting upon objects within the presentation. Macromedia's Action! is a pro at pulling various multimedia tools together into a synchronized package. Action! uses a timeline to place objects such as sound and video in place. After objects are placed in order, Action! provides a Scene Sort, the equivalent of a slide sorter, to view the presentation's flow and a Content List to present elements by scene (slide). Animations are also simplified and integrated spreadsheet and charting functions support the program's primary function, multimedia presentation, with animated data charts.

If multimedia is to be the staple of your business (or you think it might make a good venture) you will probably have to take a couple of steps up the evolutionary ladder and invest (thousands of dollars) in a multimedia authoring application. I have no experience with these applications however, from what I have read of them, multimedia authors provide increased flexibility in the runtime presentations that is particularly suited for wide variations in user input, as might be expected in computer based training programs (CBT) or sophisticated trade show exhibits. Two such applications, Macromedia's Authorware Professional for Windows (800) 945-

4061 and AimTech Corporation's IconAuthor for Windows (800) 289-2884 are good starting points for that computer-based venture or multimedia art department you may be considering.

What is "MPEG" and do I need it?

What else should you know about multimedia. While I can't give you all the answers here, I will introduce a couple of terms you may come across in your trials and tribulations. The first term is MPEG (Motion Picture Experts Group). This is a compression standard used in the production of CD-ROM movies and, ideally, any video board and multimedia-specific application you purchase should be MPEG compatible. MSACM stands for Microsoft Audio Compression Manager and is the audio equivalent of MPEG.

Shareware software for the home or consulting business.

For those of you on a budget, you may be saying "surely you can suggest some software that doesn't cost an arm and a leg to help me manage my business". Alternatively, you may be saying "I'm not into computers and I don't want all the bells and whistles the commercial programs come with". Actually, there are a great number of software applications out there that may be just perfect for your home-based business that are simple but effective and don't require a lot of money. Finally, they can be evaluated before you buy. Of course, if you've read this book from the beginning, you already know that I'm talking about shareware.

> For a discussion of the "rules and regulations" pertaining to shareware, see chapter 8. In that chapter, I primarily reviewed shareware applications that helped maintain or organize your computer and your life. I also reviewed a few games since everyone needs to take a break at some time or other.

Before I review some business-oriented (vs. computer-oriented) shareware applications, let me present some caveats:

- Most shareware applications make great support packages but don't rely on a shareware application for your key business application.

With no apologies to shareware authors (who I think market great products), you shouldn't rely on a shareware publishing package for your market or advertising proposals. If you're just getting started in business, you may be amazed at the output of some shareware applications but, others that have seen what full-featured applications can do, will probably be less impressed.

- Shareware applications can be limited in their capacities and flexibility.

While a shareware database may not necessarily be too limited in its capacity, confirm this before you develop a dependency upon that program to store all your records. If a year later, you reach the end of its capacity, you will regret the lost time involved in re-training on another application that can grow with your business. Also be aware of the relational or non-relational nature of the database and its capability to accept lengthy data input within each field.

- Your chosen shareware application should produce records or documents in a universally recognized format.

Even if capacity does not appear to present a problem, consider format compatibility. While most document applications will advertise universal conversion in ASCII or text formats, be aware that saving a document in ASCII or text formats, as opposed to proprietary application formats such as WordPerfect formats (.doc), Microsoft Word formats (.rtf or .doc) and Ami Pro formats (.sam), means that the document loses its formatting and special text attributes such as bold, italic or underlining. While such conversions are utilitarian, they may do little to communicate and persuade with the effectiveness of a formatted document.

This, in a nutshell, is why e-mail has not quickly overtaken the fax machine as a viable business communication tool for mainstream business. E-mail does not provide the opportunity to impart emotion and visual persuasion in the manner of a formatted document or presentation. Selling your service or your product then, becomes less desirable by e-mail, which remains a viable communication package for transmitting raw data.

If your business entails sharing documents or presentations with clients among different platforms such as DOS, Windows, or Macintosh operating systems, consider your ability to do without an application that is supported across these platforms.

If this cross-platform compatibility issue means that you may invest in more than one operating system, and you need a well supported word processing application, then seriously consider WordPerfect. WordPerfect Corporation supports many different operating systems and its license is extremely liberal in granting upgrades and conversions among platforms. If you currently use an IBM compatible PC but then convert to the Apple Macintosh system, WordPerfect will provide the disks (and manuals) to licensed users for a reasonable fee.

This same advice holds true for other applications including spreadsheets, databases, graphics files and communication protocols. While much of the computer industry depends upon compatibility and standardization, it is surprising to note how many pseudo-standards are out there.

- Shareware applications still cost money and, depending upon the scope of the application and its features, this cost could approach that of a commercially available application.

Some of the more capable shareware applications can actually cost close to the discounted price of applications available in your local computer store. While this is no reason to immediately discount these shareware applications, consider that the commercial applications may provide immediate telephone support with a software technician (as opposed to the written and e-mail support provided by shareware authors) and company operated BBS systems for application patches and upgrades (as opposed to the necessity of awaiting an upgrade from the shareware author). The commercial applications will also include written manuals while shareware authors provide these manuals at extra cost. If your past experience with computers convinces you that you will use technical support or that you will refer to written materials for help, then shareware may not be competitive with closely priced commercial applications.

Shareware authors have their own little "perks" to entice you. Shareware registration policies vary however, some authors will provide unlimited free upgrades to registered users or limited, free upgrades for a period of time (for instance, one year). Others provide registrants with other shareware programs for review, hoping to entice further registrations from a proven customer. Neither of these "perks" is offered by the commercial vendors.

- Shareware applications will not garner the widespread support of "hackers", programmers and other people that may design add-ons, utilities, macros or scripts to increase an application's productivity.

I've mentioned this facet of software support before in a prior discussion on choosing a word processor. In that discussion I said that the advantage of choosing a popular word processing application is that many utilities and macros have already been written for these applications. As an example, WordPerfect has such a large following that many thousands of macros have been written in WordPerfect's macro language to do such things as produce letterhead stationery, print fax cover pages and address envelopes. There are also hundreds of add-on utilities (many shareware, some commercial) that interact with WordPerfect to provide integrated address books and contact managers, publishing or spreadsheet functions or file cataloguing. If you depend on another, less popular word processor, you will be giving up the opportunity to acquire some of these products and enhance your word processor's utility.

If you will use a communication program to connect to commercial on-line services, most popular communication applications, such as ProComm, already have scripts that automate connection, navigation and e-mail functions with these services. By the way, some shareware communication applications with a devoted following, such as Telix and Q-Modem, also have a ready supply of macros and scripts for automating tasks. If you use the communication modules that come with Windows or PC Tools however, don't expect a wide range of people to be offering utilities to enhance their use.

Spreadsheet and accounting applications are another area where less popular programs lose ground to the informal support offered by a large base of established customers. Perhaps the best example is Lotus 1-2-3. With 1-2-3, a person can format, calculate, project and analyze a great number of business and financial scenarios. Templates for annual budgets, projections, amortization schedules and financial analysis reports can be prepared and saved for future use. Although Lotus provides some template guidance, the tremendous existing customer base provides hundreds of templates, macros and use tips, all available for downloading (many for free). Somewhere out there, someone has already prepared an amortization template for real estate brokers, a sales report template or inventory tracking template for retail sales and a database template for human resource management, all in 1-2-3 format. While you save some money with a shareware spreadsheet, you just may invest more time than you want in learning and customizing the application for your needs.

Now, with these caveats in mind, let's review some shareware applications that may provide sufficient, secondary support for your business. All of these applications can be downloaded from a BBS or purchased through mail order catalogs for evaluation however I also include the company and telephone number of the shareware author for those of you without the inclination or time to consider these other options.

Early in the planning stages of your business, particularly a retail or product oriented business, you will need a business plan to attract financing and partner interest. Later in the business, the plan can be updated to reflect new concerns or developments in your original plan. A few shareware applications can help you prepare these plans. MoonLite is a shareware brainstormer. Like a good teacher, MoonLite will prod you for goals and available assets for reaching those goals. It provides analysis based on these criteria and even throws in its own ideas, hence the brainstorming. If you work solo or consider brainstorming to be the creative kettle for your entrepreneurial spirit, try MoonLite. The registration fee is $30.00 and is available from CCI Limited, P.O. Box 286,6800 AG Arnhem-NL, Holland.

Another start-up guide is the Small Business Advisor. Rather than approaching business start-up from the view of numbers, Small Business Advisor assumes, correctly, that you will have some basic questions regarding marketing, taxes or employee regulations. Small Business Advisor references Federal regulations that may be of interest to small businesses and is updated regularly to keep pace with changes in the law. Registration varies depending upon the feature set desired and it can be purchased from Ronin Software (206) 391-4036.

Databases are one of those tools that every business can benefit from using but not all people are comfortable with them. In some instances, spreadsheet programs are implemented to replace the functions of a database, with varying degrees of success. If you have been using your spreadsheet but have run across limitations or you just want to explore database functions without investing in a full-featured application that will set you back hundreds of dollars and 5-10 MB of disk space, consider the following:

WAMPUM is a very popular shareware database application that uses the universally accepted dBASE file format. WAMPUM is a relational database which can display PCX graphic files (like the big boys) so that, if you catalog your inventory, you can attach visual cues for you, your staff or your customers. The registration fee is $50.00 and its available from Mundy Software (404) 237-9420.

If your a Windows fan (as I am, if you couldn't guess), then try ButtonFile. Already included are personnel records and rolodex templates and a slew of report forms for accessing information in a meaningful manner. Like any Windows program worth its salt, ButtonFile depends on icon buttons to perform many functions and is very easy to learn. Its available from ButtonWare for $70.00 (206) 454-0479.

Financial applications with an emphasis on business can sometimes replace that ever-present spreadsheet for simple but necessary tasks. Two such programs are Financial Analysis for Windows and Hi ! Finance. Financial Analysis has 16 mini-analysis modules for calculating auto leases, interest payments, return rates and the like. Registration is $39.00 from Gjetaas, Inc. at (206) 599-2418. Hi !Finances is also a Windows financial calculator with emphasis on special business calculations such as Investment Analysis, Profitability Index, Markup, Gross Price Margin and Cost-Volume-Profit (Break-even) Analysis with charting. When you get tired of crunching your business numbers, the program will provide college planning, retirement planning or simple amortization planning to keep your personal finances in good shape. Hi! Finance is available from Brightridge Solutions, Inc. (800) 241-7203.

Other applications that may make your life easier and keep a few dollars in your pocket are Scheduling Employees for Windows, Zipper Payroll, Project/Event Planner and Taskman. Scheduling Employees uses sliding bars to schedule up to 100 employees on a daily and weekly basis. The program provides employee information fields and calculates labor costs based on scheduling. For $40.00, its a lot easier than planning schedules on paper. Guia International Corp. (404) 926-6085. Zipper Payroll will take care of payroll necessities using the correct state and federal tax tables, track employees by department, calculate time, deductions, dues and print checks. It interfaces with Quicken, a popular personal finance package, and is a lot cheaper than your accountant. Registration is $62.00 from SoftCraft (206) 728-8427. Project/Event Planner and Taskman are both project schedulers, the first is for Windows the second for DOS. Both will allow the assignment of resources, human and equipment, to particular tasks. Project/Event Planner also allows allocation of income and expense figures to budget projects and Taskman provides step by step assistance. Registration is $29.00 for the Windows planner and $35.00 for Taskman. Contact Sapphire Software (808) 395-5587 for Project/Event Planner and Bill Moore (703) 949-0115 for Taskman.

One final note is in order...

When computerizing your business, do not allow yourself to automatically assume that computerizing the business will make it profitable. While good computer equipment and well-featured software has the potential to increase your productivity, do not forget to utilize all the other tools of your business. Its only when all these tools work together that computers can expand your business opportunities. When shopping for computers or their software, have a clear idea what business needs should be met now and one year from now...then address those needs. If you need to begin marketing and maintaining client contact information, start with that need and don't necessarily invest your time maintaining your payroll, even though the computer can do that. Let your accountant handle those chores for another six months while you establish a firm business foundation and working familiarity with the computer. Then, time permitting, incorporate book-keeping into your business plan over the six month span or thereafter.

Also consider how support staff view the computer. If your staff is not comfortable with computers, discuss their introduction to the computer. This discussion may provide some insight that will save you from purchasing an expensive paperweight. In some instances, people are self-learners. In other instances, you may find the tutorials and on-line help offered by some Windows programs will alleviate your staff's concerns. The input of your staff can also help you identify time-consuming tasks you might not have considered that are well suited to your computer investment. Earlier in this book I even suggested that you involve your staff in evaluating software applications they can use most effectively. This is particularly so in those instances when you depend on autonomous departments for coordinated output. Just as you would look for applications you depend on to work together, your staff expects this same consideration.

SECTION VIII

Chapter 22

Practical Tips and Tricks

This chapter is a compilation of some practical business tips and tricks I've learned in the past few years to improve the efficiency of my computer operations. Some of these tips may be self-evident but I've noticed quite a few people that are surprised when I mention organizing their computer in this way or using the computer in that way. I hope you find at lease one or two "tricks" in this chapter to help you in your business.

TIP #0-KEEP REGULAR BACKUPS OF YOUR HARD DISK

Why is this tip #0? Because it is perhaps the most important instruction and most ignored instruction in safe computing. While everyone is worried about viruses and undeleting erased files, most work is lost to catastrophes that can only be avoided by keeping regular backups. There are companies that make a living recovering data from computer hard disks that have been destroyed in natural disasters or just plain died a natural death. These companies maintain a thriving and expensive business only because people don't back up data that's important enough to pay someone to recover.

If you haven't backed up your data and disaster struck and you're saying "I don't need a lecture now...I need help", trying calling one of these three data recovery services (and good luck!):

Group One Electronics (818-993-4575)
Ontrack Data Recovery (800-752-1333)
Workman and Associates (818-791-7979)

Any number of things can render your data unusable. Computers are stolen, computers are crushed under building toppled by earthquakes, they are flushed under water from hurricanes or floods, they encounter power surges that can do wonders to shorten their hard disk's life and they can just die like any other piece of electronic equipment that's out of warranty.

While some people believe that you will have some warning when a disk is about to die, don't you bet on it. I've seen advice in computer magazines that warned people to run disk utilities on their hard disk and note the number of bad sectors or clusters. This same advice warned that an increase in read or write errors is a sign the disk may soon be dying. That's all very well but let me tell you how I lost my last hard disk.

I walked into the office, turned on the computer and started working. A few minutes into the work day, the mouse stopped moving. Thinking that the computer "froze" for some reason, I re-started it. It wouldn't re-start. Guess what...my hard disk just "crashed". No warning. All my data, including accounting information and time-keeping information was on the computer's disk. All my client files were on the disk...and I couldn't get at them. Guess what I did. I got on the phone, ordered another computer overnight and restored the backup I made the night before the "crash" to the new computer. I and my business had very little downtime. Now guess what would have happened if I didn't have a backup. I would have had to shop for a recovery service, send the hard disk to them and hope the data could be recovered. If it couldn't be recovered, I would have restored my applications to a new computer using the master disks (sans any custom configuring I invested in setting the applications up the way I wanted) and I would have reconstructed my bank records from deposit slips, receipts and bank statements. My billings, assuming I could remember the time I spent, would have to be reconstructed from memory. Any client files would have been irretrievably lost. The downtime and lost productivity would have been enormous, even for a small business like mine. If you lose your hard disk because of a regional disaster such as a flood, hurricane or earthquake, don't expect the recovery service to provide immediate turnaround. Chances are, they will be inundated with work from businesses that didn't backup their data. That means more downtime. The moral of the story is...backups are worth the time and effort.

TIP #1-FAX MACHINES ARE GREAT SCANNERS

I can't believe the number of people that express surprise at this tip. Rather than pay $800.00 to $2,000.00 for a dedicated flatbed scanner, use your office fax machine to fax documents, pictures, logos or other images to your computer's fax/modem. Since the office fax machine is probably has its own dedicated telephone line and your office telephone is on another line or PBX system, you can fax yourself documents and pictures for use in word processors, graphics and drawing applications. The fax machine may even be more efficient than the scanner since most fax machines are capable of holding 10 or more pages at once and automatically feeding them through the machine. Although some dedicated scanners have page feeders, these are options costing $400.00 or more. A few caveats are in order, however.

1. Always use fine mode. If you use standard mode on your fax machine and in your computer's fax software, text and graphics may be transmitted out of proportion, rendering the image useless for your needs. Although super-fine mode is sometimes available on fax machines, most fax software doesn't support any standard beyond fine mode.

2. If you intend to scan text documents into your computer for editing, you will need an Optical Character Recognition (OCR) software application to convert the graphic fax image into editable text. Many capable fax software programs are now including these OCR functions. Winfax Pro 3.0 is probably one of the better fax and OCR programs available today however I have received better conversion results using dedicated OCR applications. To date, I have found Calera's Wordscan to be the best of the new technologies. In testing, I have found Calera's Wordscan to produce significantly better results than other technologies including its direct competitor, Caere Corporation's, new AnyFax OCR technology.

3. If you intend to use a PBX system for sending or receiving faxes check with the installer before connecting your fax/modem. Some such systems utilize non-standard signals to digitally manage such public lines. One system "fried" my modem connector! Other PBX systems can be set-up by knowledgeable installers with separate connections for allowing a fax/modem to activate a PBX line and call out or receive incoming communications. I use the PBX lines in my office system to temporarily connect my portable's fax/modem for incoming or outgoing communications. It's very handy.

TIP #2- ORGANIZE HARD DISK DIRECTORIES BY CLIENT OR PROJECT

My computer already has over four thousand files on its hard disk and I'm sure there are many systems out there with much more. Many such systems have files that are no longer needed and involve past clients or projects. More than once I've heard of companies actually paying computer consultants to visit and clean their hard disks of these extraneous files. This is unnecessary. One reason hard disks become cluttered is the lack of organization. This deficiency is promulgated by many word processor programs that suggest installing subdirector(ies) below the word processor application directory to hold letters, memos and other such documents. As a result, after a while, the letters subdirectory contains a hodgepodge of hundreds of letters written to many different clients and contacts for miscellaneous reasons. Some of these clients may not even be current clients. Wading through this hodgepodge is not only intimidating, its a waste of time.

I suggest providing separate directories for each client and separate subdirectories for each client's project. This accomplishes many objectives. First, letters sent to each client may have the same filename since the files are kept in separate directories. This provides much greater latitude in giving files meaningful names while staying within the filename limitations of DOS and Windows. Second, any other person searching for a document or file can limit their search by client name (a logical name for the directory) or project name (a logical name for the project subdirectory). On a network or computer containing thousands of files, this may not only be appropriate but necessary. Searching even a medium hard disk for a single file can take a long time. Limiting the search to a few directories is far preferable. Third, if a client or project is terminated, the directories can be emptied and deleted with minimal effort. Alternatively, it would be a simple matter to select those directories for backup or archiving and be assured that all files related to that client or project were backed up before deleting the directory. This is simple but effective hard disk organization and, best of all, its free...computer consultants and search software isn't.

Finally, don't forget to also use this method for small applications such as games or utilities. I've seen some game directories holding hundreds of files belonging to twenty or more games. If you grow tired of a particular game, how are you going to find and delete only the files that belong to that application. If you have the game installed in its own directory, that how.

TIP #3-USE SPECIALIZED BACKUP SETS TO REDUCE BACKUP TIME

I touched on this subject in Chapter 14 when discussing backup utilities. Since my backup utility can accommodate multiple backup sets, I separate my files and directories into application files that do not change regularly and client data files and directories that change on a regular basis. Very infrequently, I will backup all my applications and forms using the "Application Files and Forms" setup. This takes approximately 40 disks and 30 minutes but I only perform this type of backup every three months. The "Client Files" set holds all my regularly changing files and can be backed up daily, requiring 4 disks and 3 minutes time. The advantages to this backup system are two-fold. First, I have no investment in a tape backup system. Second, I can perform full backups of directories thereby catching all files added in that workday in addition to those files altered during the day...and it takes only three minutes. Moreover, if I need to restore a single file or all the files I know where to find the file depending upon its nature as an application file or data file and since each day's backup is a full backup of the changed files, I do not have to keep track of differential backups or incremental backups.

If this terminology is confusing to you, refer to Chapter 14, Disk Management Utilities, for an explanation of full, differential and incremental backups, their advantages and disadvantages.

The only disadvantage to this system is that new applications would not be backed up until the next "Application" backup. In most instances, this drawback would be minimal since most businesses do not regularly add applications to their systems and, in any event, the application is available on the original disks and can be easily re-installed. There are a few caveats to keep in mind:

1. If you use Windows, certain files will change regularly although not daily. Template files containing glossary entries and macro commands are one example of Word for Windows files that may change irregularly. Dictionary files are another example. In the Windows directory, program group files may change if you add or re-arrange applications or icons and initialization and configuration files may occasionally change. Most of these files are reasonably sized and do not add much time to a daily backup. As a guide, include files containing the following extensions to your list of daily backups if you follow this routine: ini: cnf, cfg, dat, dic, dot, inf, grp, lex, reg. Always backup your autoexec.bat, config.sys, win.ini and system.ini files on a regular basis.

2. If you are unsure whether a file has been or should be backed up, most backup utilities will provide directory and file windows. Next to each filename, a file date will indicate the last time it was updated and, if an "a" is present in the filename's column, that means its changed since it was last backed up and needs to be backed up again. Over time, these indicators (particularly the "a" indicator") will allow you to determine which files on your computer are regularly changing and need more frequent backups.

TIP #4- KEEP BACKUP SETS AT BOTH HOME AND THE OFFICE

The whole purpose behind backing up your data is to have a copy of the data in case the computer's data is destroyed or stolen. If the computer is destroyed or stolen, your backup tapes or disks may also be destroyed or stolen if kept with the computer. Always keep a relatively current backup set "off-site", at another office or at home. Many businesses utilize rotating backup sets. Having four backup sets marked 1st, 2nd, 3rd and 4th allows backups at weekly intervals resulting in no more than one week's data loss. By keeping alternate backup sets at an off-site location, no more than two weeks data may be lost. Obviously, if your data is critical enough to require daily backups, then this strategy can be adapted accordingly.

TIP #5- WHEN PURCHASING NEW SOFTWARE APPLICATIONS, FIRST MAKE COPIES

This goes hand in hand with keeping backup sets off-site. You should also have two full set of disks for each application you purchase. One set should be stored off-site. I will always recommend first installing applications with the copy rather than using the original disks. My reason for this is simple. Many new applications will require a person to register the software by typing a name and company at the prompts when it is first installed. Many times this information is written onto the floppy disks as registration information as well as the files placed on the computer's hard disk. If the floppy disks are then used to install the application on another computer, you are stuck with the name and company first written to disk. Why might you not want that information written to disk? Perhaps your company has changed its name or you have married or divorced. If the experience was not pleasant (your first business failed, for instance.), then you may not want a reminder every time you launch that application.

> This is also a means of passing illegal copies of software however, since new Federal laws have been introduced increasing the penalties for illegal use and copying, I wouldn't suggest you be tempted.

This method also allows you to transfer the software, in accordance with some licensing agreements, and allow the new owner to register a new name and company.

TIP #6- USE AUTOMATIC BACKUP FEATURES

Almost all newer applications provide some sort of timed or automatic backup feature that saves a copy of the currently open file in the event of a power loss or a system lockup. In the event your computer needs to be re-started (re-booted), the program can provide you with the last saved file copy. Even older applications, such as WordPerfect 5.1 have this feature, but so many people seem not to take advantage of it. Usually, I tell people about this little feature after they've come to me to see if I can recover the file they've been working on for an hour or more before the computer froze or the power went out (during Florida's rainy season, lightning storms kill the power too often for comfort).

While the application will pause for a second or two each time it performs these automatic saves, they are invaluable. Even on my notebook computer, which has automatic battery backup, the computer will occasionally freeze or encounter an error requiring it to be re-started (anyone with Windows can understand this). More than once, I've had the "pleasure" of re-starting the computer, re-loading my word processing application and finding a "recovered" document ready to be re-named and saved. What a relief.

How often do you want the application to automatically save your document. I usually recommend 10 minute intervals. In my opinion, this interval is not too often to frustrate the user but is short enough to recover most work in the interval if something goes wrong. Even if you don't upgrade to newer software, take a look at what you do have, and enable the automatic backup feature if its there. At some time or another, you won't be sorry.

TIP #7- GREAT SOFTWARE NAMES NEVER END IN "0"

Actually I remember reading this comment by a magazine editor at some point but, after years of experience, I have to agree with him. For example, Microsoft Corporation, with its tremendous budgets and teams of talented coders still can't release new versions without needed "patches". Even after releasing five prior versions of MS-DOS, Microsoft still needed to release MS-DOS 6.2 to correct problems with MS-DOS 6. The same holds true for other companies as well.

My point is this...when you are shopping for software, be aware that purchasing version 2.0, 3.0,4.0 or any other "0" may mean taking some risk. I'm an adventurer, although I work with a "net" (data backups), and I don't mind finding minor glitches that I know will be corrected with an interim patch. This is the tradeoff to getting newer, more powerful features with each upgrade of a product. As an example, Word for Windows 6.0's templates do not automatically prompt for variable information as those in version 2.0 did. Consequently, it was my opinion that I was better served by keeping my version 2 templates and using them in lieu of version 6 templates. I still think version 6 was a worthwhile purchase for me. Its background printing, multiple level undo and improved speed and versatility in page layout view are features that were worth paying for. For someone that was counting on a package that would "coach" them through business proposal or letter templates however, I think it was a flop. Being on the "cutting edge" of product upgrades also means that older applications may not integrate as well with updated products. Every time I upgrade my Norton Utilities such as Disk Doctor and Speed Disk, along comes a disk compression scheme, better than the last, that is not compatible with them. As a result, I obsolete my older utilities until they too are upgraded...and the cycle begins all over again. Although I am not advocating avoiding upgrades or new versions due to potential problems, be aware that this is how the computer software industry works, for now and in the foreseeable future, and be prepared.

TIP #8- IF YOU USE DOS, EVEN OCCASIONALLY...

I will occasionally use DOS to check on the status of my disk, my cache or the allocation of memory in the computer to see how some programs affect memory usage. I also use some DOS commands and some DOS command-line programs, like pkzip, in my work. But I can never remember the little variations of each command or the syntax for invoking certain commands...so here's what I remember:

for any DOS command, and many DOS programs that operate from the command line, like pkzip, do this:

1. type the command;

2. type "/"

3. type "?"

The command won't run but you will get, in most instances, a screen printout describing the command, showing how the command should by typed with all its variations and a list of the variable parameters and what they do. If you don't get this, one of three things has happened:

1. the command is not available (either because a file was erased or you are not in the correct directory);

2. the command and "/?" were typed incorrectly; or

3. the command does not support this "help" feature.

As an example, typing "diskcopy/?" at the "C:\>" prompt displays the following screen, explaining the use of the MS-DOS diskcopy command, usually located in your DOS directory:

```
C:\>diskcopy/?

Copies the contents of one floppy disk to another.

DISKCOPY [drive1: [drive2:]] [/1] [/V]

/1  Copies only the first side of the disk.

/V  Verifies that the information is copied correctly.

The two floppy disks must be the same type.

You may specify the same drive for drive1 and drive2.


C:\>
```

When you know the command but don't know how to use it, this simple but effective trick certainly helps. For sophisticated shareware applications like PKZIP, the help screens can help you decipher which of the more than 15 or so parameters you want or need to use. If your interested, you could probably find things you can do with some commands you weren't even aware of.

One other DOS command that gets regular usage on my machine is:

MEM/C|MORE

The straight line between "C" and "MORE" is located on the "\" key usually located below the "Backspace" key. This command can be used either in DOS or in a DOS Window (DOS from within Windows) and highlights the memory usage of your machine, one screen at a time. It will tell you what applications are in memory, how much memory they use and whether they are located in the lower 640K (called conventional memory) or the machine's upper memory (memory area between 640 K and 1024 K). It will also inform on the amount of free conventional memory, free upper memory and used and free extended memory (>1024 K). If an application, particularly a DOS application, refuses to launch, low conventional memory may be why and a quick check using MEM will be a good start.

DOS applications are usually programmed to use only the first 640K of a computer. While this is an oversimplification, it is true that most problems launching DOS applications can be traced to insufficient memory. This is particularly so for newer DOS applications that, in an attempt to keep pace with Windows' graphical interface, use more and more memory. While older DOS applications used 400K or 500K of memory, newer applications may require 600K or more to properly operate. With the TSR programs that occupy that first 640K, and even with new memory managers, many times 600K is not available for the work application.

Two other DOS command line parameters that are repeatedly useful when used with the directory list command DIR are the "/p" and "/w" commands. The first tells DOS to display one screen at a time until prompted for the next. The second parameter tells DOS to display the files in a wide list format. As a result more files are simultaneously displayed. For a complete listing of DIR parameters, of course, type "DIR/?".

Index

Made in the USA
Monee, IL
13 September 2026

62979108R00210